Bilingual Community Education and Multilingualism

BILINGUAL EDUCATION & BILINGUALISM

Series Editors: Nancy H. Hornberger *(University of Pennsylvania, USA)* and Colin Baker *(Bangor University, Wales, UK)*

Bilingual Education and Bilingualism is an international, multidisciplinary series publishing research on the philosophy, politics, policy, provision and practice of language planning, global English, indigenous and minority language education, multilingualism, multiculturalism, biliteracy, bilingualism and bilingual education. The series aims to mirror current debates and discussions.

Full details of all the books in this series and of all our other publications can be found on http://www.multilingual-matters.com, or by writing to Multilingual Matters, St Nicholas House, 31–34 High Street, Bristol BS1 2AW, UK.

Bilingual Community Education and Multilingualism

Beyond Heritage Languages in a Global City

Edited by
**Ofelia García, Zeena Zakharia
and Bahar Otcu**

MULTILINGUAL MATTERS
Bristol • Buffalo • Toronto

For parents and educators, who with their efforts keep US bilingualism alive

And for our own families, whose love in Spanish, Arabic and Turkish, as well as English, have contributed to our own multilingualism

Library of Congress Cataloging in Publication Data
Bilingual Community Education and Multilingualism: Beyond Heritage Languages in a Global City/Edited by Ofelia García, Zeena Zakharia and Bahar Otcu.
Bilingual Education and Bilingualism: 89
Includes bibliographical references and index.
1. Education, Bilingual—New York (State)—New York. 2. Intercultural communication—New York (State)—New York. 3. Non-formal education—New York (State)—New York. 4. Multilingualism—New York (State)—New York. I. García, Ofelia. II. Zakharia, Zeena. III. Otcu, Bahar.
LC3733.N5B53 2012
370.117'5097471–dc23 2012022007

British Library Cataloguing in Publication Data
A catalogue entry for this book is available from the British Library.

ISBN-13: 978-1-84769-800-1 (hbk)
ISBN-13: 978-1-84769-799-8 (pbk)

Multilingual Matters
UK: St Nicholas House, 31-34 High Street, Bristol BS1 2AW, UK.
USA: UTP, 2250 Military Road, Tonawanda, NY 14150, USA.
Canada: UTP, 5201 Dufferin Street, North York, Ontario M3H 5T8, Canada.

The policy of Multilingual Matters/Channel View Publications is to use papers that are natural, renewable and recyclable products, made from wood grown in sustainable forests. In the manufacturing process of our books, and to further support our policy, preference is given to printers that have FSC and PEFC Chain of Custody certification. The FSC and/or PEFC logos will appear on those books where full certification has been granted to the printer concerned.

Typeset by Techset Composition Ltd., Salisbury, UK.
Printed and bound in Great Britain by Short Run Press Ltd.

Contents

Contributors

Laura Ascenzi-Moreno is Assistant Professor of Childhood Education at Brooklyn College. She is a former dual language bilingual teacher and curriculum coach at the Cypress Hills Community School in Brooklyn. Her research interests include bilingual education, multiple literacies, assessment, development of teacher knowledge and school governance. As a Fulbright Scholar in Colombia, she researched the development of pedagogical practices in state-sponsored day care centers. She currently researches how teachers learn from the assessment of bilingual students.

Sharon Avni is Assistant Professor in the Department of Developmental Skills at the Borough of Manhattan Community College of the City University of New York. She received her PhD in education from New York University. Her main research interests include religious education, language socialization and language policy. She has recently published in the *International Journal of the Sociology of Language*. She is currently engaged in a study of the academic socialization of English as a second language postsecondary students.

Isabelle Barrière is Assistant Professor in the Department of Speech Communication Arts and Sciences at Brooklyn College, City University of New York. Her research focuses on the acquisition of different languages and the link between theories, education and the clinic. She is also a research associate at the Research Institute for the Study of Language in Urban Society; and co-director of Yeled V'Yalda Research Institute, located in the largest Head Start program in New York.

Maryam Borjian is Director of the Language Program at the Department of African, Middle Eastern and South Asian Languages and Literatures at

Rutgers University. Her research interest concerns the political sociology of language in society and education. Her works appear in *Encyclopædia Iranica*, *Iranian Studies*, *Oriental Archive* and *Iran and the Caucasus*, and include 'Plights of Persian in the modernization era' (in Fishman & García (eds), 2011, *Handbook of Language and Ethnic Identity*) and 'The rise and fall of a partnership: The British Council and Islamic Republic of Iran' (2011, *Iranian Studies*).

Ruhma Choudhury is Assistant Professor in the Department of Education and Language Acquisition at LaGuardia Community College, City University of New York. Her research interests span language policy, bilingualism, teacher education and critical approaches to language learning.

Jeehyae Chung holds a doctorate and MA from Teachers College, Columbia University, with a concentration in bilingual and bicultural education. Her research interests include bilingual education, language education policies, teaching English as a foreign language in Asian contexts, and immigrant language and culture education in the US context. She is currently teaching at the Hankuk University of Foreign Studies in South Korea.

Nelson Flores is Assistant Professor of Educational Linguistics at the University of Pennsylvania. His work focuses on using poststructural and postcolonial social theory to examine how current US language ideologies marginalize language minoritized students. He has been the Project Director of the CUNY-NYS Initiative on Emergent Bilinguals.

Ofelia García is Professor in the PhD programs of Urban Education and of Hispanic and Luso-Brazilian Literatures and Languages at the Graduate Center of the City University of New York. She has been Professor of Bilingual Education at Columbia University's Teachers College, Dean of the School of Education at the Brooklyn Campus of Long Island University, and Professor of Bilingual Education/TESOL at The City College of New York. Among her most recent books are: *Bilingual Education in the 21st Century: A Global Perspective*; *Handbook of Language and Ethnic Identity*, Vols. I & II (with J.A. Fishman); *Educating Emergent Bilinguals* (with J. Kleifgen); and *Additive Schooling in Subtractive Times* (with L. Bartlett). She is the Associate General Editor of the *International Journal of the Sociology of Language*.

Ameena Ghaffar-Kucher is Senior Lecturer and Associate Director of the International Educational Development program at the University of

Pennsylvania's Graduate School of Education. Her research interests include: immigrants and schooling; citizenship and trans/nationalism; curriculum and pedagogy in international contexts; and literacy and development. She is currently working on an edited volume on migration and education in the global south with Lesley Bartlett.

Maria Hantzopoulos is Assistant Professor of Education at Vassar College, where she coordinates the Adolescent Education Certification Program and is a participating faculty member in the programs in Women's Studies and Urban Studies. Her current research interests and projects involve critical media literacy, peace and human rights education, the education of immigrant youth and urban educational reform. Her work has appeared in a variety of publications, including the *Journal of Peace Education, Schools: Studies in Education* and *Rethinking Schools*, and she is co-editor, with Alia Tyner-Mullings, of *Critical Small Schools: Beyond Privatization in NYC Urban Educational Reform*.

Fabrice Jaumont is Education Attaché at the French Embassy's New York headquarters. He oversees bilateral cooperation and secondary education partnerships. Additionally, he administers the French American Cultural Exchange Council's French Heritage Language and Dual Language initiatives. Trained as a linguist, he was an instructor for the United Nations Language Program, a university lecturer at Trinity College, Dublin and the National College of Ireland, and an assistant principal at the International School of Boston. A PhD candidate at New York University, his research focuses on the role of philanthropy in education and international development.

Naomi Kano holds a doctorate from Teachers College, Columbia University. She holds a BA from Tsuda College in Japan, an MA from the University of Chicago, and an EdM from Teachers College. Her research interests include applied linguistics, language and literacy, bilingual education and second language writing. She currently teaches at Waseda University and Tsuda College in Japan.

Tatyana Kleyn is Associate Professor at the City College of New York in the Bilingual Education and TESOL program. She is co-author (with Sharon Adelman Reyes) of *Teaching in Two Languages: A Guide for K–12 Bilingual Educators* (Corwin Press, 2010). Tatyana is also the author of *Immigration: The Ultimate Teen Guide* (Scarecrow Press, 2011), a book that focuses on current issues in immigration as they relate to youth.

Hannah Kliger is Senior Adviser to the Chancellor, and Professor of Communication and Jewish Studies at The Pennsylvania State University, The Abington College. Dr Kliger's publications focus on the communicative practices and communal organizations of minority groups. In addition to her book on ethnic voluntary associations of Jewish immigrants (Indiana University Press), she has authored numerous articles on communication and culture in immigrant communities. Her current research with the Transcending Trauma Project at the Council for Relationships, where Kliger also maintains a part-time practice, explores resilience and reconstruction in the aftermath of traumatic events.

Wen-Tsui Pat Lo is currently a Senior Curriculum Specialist at the Office of English Language Learners in the New York City Department of Education. In her 24 years of service in the New York City public school system, she has served as an English as a second language and Chinese teacher and as a bilingual/English as a second language supervisor. She is also an adjunct lecturer at Hunter College of the City University of New York.

Anup P. Mahajan is Executive Director of the US Department of Education's Title VI-funded National Capital Language Resource Center in Washington, DC. He is founding Director of DesiLearn, the nation's only government-funded initiative to identify, marshal and strengthen community based K–12 institutions teaching 15 South Asian and Afghani languages. Anup earned a MS in Linguistics from Georgetown University and has over seven years of leadership experience as a management consultant in the Fortune 500 global human resources industry.

Carmina Makar earned her BA in Communication Studies in Guadalajara, Mexico and pursued her Master's degree and doctoral degree as a Fulbright Fellow at Teachers College, Columbia University. Her interest in bringing together cultural studies and education has driven her work in community settings in New York and Mexico. She has served as Lecturer for the Department of Communication and Urban planning at ITESO University and Program Coordinator for Distance Education at University of Guadalajara. Her research interests include language, literacy and transnational approaches to education, as well as emerging methodological approaches to educational research.

Busi Makoni holds a PhD in Applied Linguistics from the University of Edinburgh. She is currently a lecturer in the Department of Applied Linguistics and the Program in African Studies at Pennsylvania State University's College of the Liberal Arts. Her research interests are in second language acquisition, language and gender, language and security of the state, feminist critical discourse analysis, language rights and language policy and planning. Some of her research has been published in the *Journal of Second Language Research, Per Linguam, Current Issues in Language Planning, Journal of Language, Identity and Education* and the *International Journal of Applied Linguistics*.

Maureen T. Matarese, an Assistant Professor in Developmental Skills at Borough of Manhattan Community College at the City University of New York, takes a critical, poststructural approach to institutionally oriented sociolinguistic research, particularly in the areas of literacy, sociology of language and discourse. Her current work uses applied conversation analysis to examine practitioner-client interactions in a wide variety of contexts, including social work, education, and policing institutions in order to describe how policy impacts institutional talk in practice.

Laura Menchaca Bishop holds a Master's degree in International Educational Development from Teachers College, Columbia University, and is presently pursuing her PhD in Sociocultural Anthropology at Cornell University. She has worked in a variety of educational contexts ranging from teaching English to refugees and immigrants at the International Rescue Committee to directing a teacher education program in the Dominican Republic. Her scholarly interests include critical approaches to education for social/political change; migration and schooling; language policy and bilingual education; and human rights.

Kate Menken is Associate Professor of Linguistics at Queens College of the City University of New York (CUNY) and a Research Fellow at the Research Institute for the Study of Language in Urban Society at the CUNY Graduate Center. She is author of *English Learners Left Behind: Standardized Testing as Language Policy* (Multilingual Matters, 2008) and co-editor (with Ofelia García) of *Negotiating Language Policies in Schools: Educators as Policymakers* (Routledge, 2010).

Marie-Michelle Monéreau-Merry is a certified speech-language pathologist and a doctoral student at the Graduate Center, City University of New York. Overall, her primary area of research is in bilingualism throughout the life span. She is examining the psycholinguistic state of mind of native and heritage speakers of Haitian-Creole in the domain of the definite article system.

Bahar Otcu is Assistant Professor at Mercy College, New York. She holds a Doctorate and Master of Education from Teachers College, Columbia University, and Bachelor and Master of Arts degrees from Middle East Technical University, Turkey. Her research interests include bilingual education, applied linguistics, language policies and ideologies, discourse analysis and pragmatics. Her recent publications include a co-authored book chapter titled 'Developmental patterns in internal modification use in requests: A quantitative study on Turkish learners of English' and an individual article titled 'Heritage language maintenance and cultural identity formation: The case of a Turkish Saturday school in NYC'.

Rakhmiel Peltz is Professor of Sociolinguistics in the Department of Culture and Communication and founding Director of the Judaic Studies Program at Drexel University. He has researched and published in both molecular and cell biology and Yiddish and Jewish Studies. He is the author of *From Immigrant to Ethnic Culture: American Yiddish in South Philadelphia* (Stanford University Press), co-editor of *Language Loyalty, Continuity and Change* (Multilingual Matters), and producer and project director of the film, *Toby's Sunshine: The Life and Art of Holocaust Survivor Toby Knobel Fluek*.

Jane Ross is President of the French Heritage Language Program, which works in collaboration with the French American Cultural Exchange. A graduate of Swarthmore College, she has had an extensive career as an educator and educational consultant, and is currently pursuing a PhD in International Education at New York University. Her research focuses on the role of French schools abroad, particularly in the US.

Roozbeh Shirazi is a scholar of education, politics and globalization with a research focus on sociocultural issues of schooling in the Middle East. He is currently a post-doctoral fellow in the College of Education and Human Development at the University of Minnesota, and previously in the Department of Curriculum and Teaching at Teachers College, Columbia University. He holds a PhD in Comparative and International Education with a concentration in Political Science from Columbia University. His current research interests include the intersections of migration, youth citizenship and practices of cultural representation among transnational Iranian youth.

Beth Vayshenker is a doctoral student in Clinical Psychology at John Jay College. She graduated from Binghamton University with a BA in Psychology and a double minor in Business and Russian. Within her Russian minor, she studied the Russian language and focused on relations between the Former Soviet Union and the US during the Cold War.

Zeena Zakharia is Assistant Professor in the Department of Leadership in Education at the University of Massachusetts, Boston. She was the Middle East Education Fellow at Columbia University in New York, where she lectured and conducted research on youth, education and conflict in the Middle East and the Arab diaspora. She was also Tueni Fellow at the Carr Center for Human Rights Policy at Harvard's John F. Kennedy School of Government. Her recent publications consider the interplay of language policy, collective identity and human security in schools, during and after violent political conflict. These interests stem from over a decade of educational leadership in war-affected bilingual contexts.

Introduction

Organization, Content and Purpose of the Book

The chapters in this book are organized to show the different manifestations of bilingual community education. That is, bilingual community education is not a single enterprise, and it does not occur in just one type of space. Bilingual community education includes educational efforts organized by communities in schools, churches, temples, synagogues, community-based organizations, storefronts, playgrounds, homes, hair-braiding salons and many other places. Sometimes these activities take place in an all-day school, whether private or public, but sometimes they occur after school, in the evenings, or on Saturdays and/or Sundays. What all these efforts have in common is that they are organized by parents and communities to ensure that their American children become bilingual and develop the multiple ethnolinguistic identities that will enable them to live in a global world. Rather than viewing these efforts with mistrust, the US public school education system should acknowledge the value added that these programs bring, and collaborate with them to educate bilingual Americans.[1]

All of the chapters included start by exploring sociolinguistic aspects of the language practices of the diasporic communities, including the history of their complex migrations, and of their socioeducational efforts, using the global city of New York as a backdrop. As such, all of the chapters provide multiple perspectives on these bilingual community education efforts. Most chapters, however, offer detailed descriptions of one type of program, and thus, the organization here reflects the focus that the authors have chosen.

We invite you to read these chapters with a broader lens than that which focuses on 'heritage language' education, for these bilingual community education efforts acknowledge the dynamic bilingualism that education in the US must encompass. Rather than focusing on specific languages of inheritance, these bilingual community education programs develop American children's bilingual performances, thus disrupting both the construct of 'heritage language' and that of English-only, by which an American childhood has been defined. The future of American children belongs to those who are bilingual and who can perform the multiple identities that, so far, only these bilingual community education efforts can produce.

This book is our plea to the US public school system – that they take on the serious task of challenging all American children to take up different language practices, and that they offer them options to perform multiple identities and understandings. Alongside academic English and Common Core State Standards, US schools must be able to offer American children a bilingual global future.

Ofelia García
Zeena Zakharia
Bahar Otcu
New York City

Note

(1) Throughout the book we refer to the 'United States', and not simply to 'America', to recognize that the Americas include Latin America and Canada. However, we use the adjective to speak about 'American children' – children in the US whose present and future identities include being US participants and contributors.

Part 1

Conceptualizing Bilingual Community Education

1 Bilingual Community Education: Beyond Heritage Language Education and Bilingual Education in New York

Ofelia García, Zeena Zakharia
and Bahar Otcu

Introduction

This book focuses on educational spaces shaped and organized by American ethnolinguistic communities for their children, what we are calling here *bilingual community education*. Some of these activities include what others might call supplementary or complementary schools – after-school and weekend programs. Others are informal educational spaces. Yet others are private day schools or public school ventures where the community has been the leading force.

We use New York, a global multilingual city, as a case study to explore the structures and meanings of bilingual community education, as well as to better understand American ethnolinguistic communities and their networks in today's globalized world. In doing so, we extend present understandings of 'heritage language education' and 'bilingual education'. We also reconceptualize the notion of an 'ethnolinguistic speech community' for a global world.

In this chapter, we trace the development of educational spaces for US ethnolinguistic communities, as we point to the small amount of attention that these community-driven efforts have received in the scholarly literature until very recently. We discuss the differences in naming these activities ethnic mother-tongue schools, supplementary/complementary schools, heritage language education programs or bilingual education programs. In choosing to name these activities *bilingual community education*, we indicate that the focus of these activities is *bilingual* in nature, and not just the maintenance of an 'ethnic-mother tongue' or the development of a 'heritage language'. In indicating the *community* aspect of these activities, we distance ourselves from bilingual education programs in which the educational agents are other than those within the particular bilingual community, and where the governmental focus is the development of the dominant national language, namely English in the US case.

We divide this foundational chapter into three parts. Section I, Traditions and Context, reviews the tradition and continuities of bilingual community education in the US, and then turns to describing the sociolinguistic situation of New York City to ensure that readers understand how the dynamism and contacts in a global city shape all these efforts.

Sections II and III engage examples from this book to conceptualize *two major theoretical contributions* that we wish to make to the field of language education:

- First, these bilingual community education spaces, because of both their sociolinguistic and their socioeducational characteristics, *go beyond what has been called 'heritage language education', as well as the timid efforts of public US 'bilingual education'* (Section II: Beyond heritage language and bilingual education).
- Second, our cases lead to *new understandings of US ethnolinguistic communities,* beyond those of 'speech communities' of traditional sociolinguistics towards diasporic communities (Section III: Beyond ethnolinguistic communities).

Our chapter closes with a Conclusion that describes some of the challenges that these schools face, and offers recommendations for future directions.

The first part of Section I describes the long tradition of bilingual community education in the US. We pay attention to the role that it has played in different periods of US history. As we do so, we explore the scarce scholarship that has surrounded the existence of these bilingual community education efforts. We also try to disentangle the disparate visions that each name for these activities has conjured.

I: Traditions and Context

Traditions and continuities

The attention paid to the education of American children in public schools has diverted interest from efforts by different US communities to educate their children in ways that reflect their various characteristics, languages, cultures and values. Yet there has been a long US tradition of bilingual community schooling.

Early German language communities established their own bilingual schools with community funds, sometimes aided by public funds. It is well known, for example, that in the late 18th and early 19th centuries there was a sizable network of parochial German-language schools of the Lutheran and the Reformed churches in Pennsylvania and Ohio (Castellanos, 1983; Crawford, 2004; García, 2009a). Although Germans had the largest network of schools that used languages other than English (LOTEs hereafter) in the 19th century, there were other ethnolinguistic groups who also organized their own schools. The Cherokees, for example, established and operated their own educational system in the 1850s, in which their children were taught to read and write Cherokee (García, 2009a).

This tolerance towards the establishment of educational programs by ethnolinguistic communities nearly came to a halt in the xenophobic atmosphere surrounding the early 20th century. Between 1890 and 1930, 16 million immigrants entered the US, increasingly from Eastern and Southern Europe, as well as the Greater Syria region of the Ottoman Empire. Gradually, the great number of Germans in the US, coupled with their enemy status during World War I, fueled suspicion against all ethnolinguistic groups (Crawford, 1992; García, 2009a; Kloss, 1977). The mood of the time was captured by Theodore Roosevelt when he said in 1915: 'There is no room in this country for hyphenated Americanism ... We have room for but one language here, and that is the English language' (as cited in Edwards, 1994: 166).

By 1923, 34 of the 48 US states required that English be the sole language of instruction (García, 2009a). In that same year, in *Meyer vs Nebraska*, the US Supreme Court asserted that Meyer, a parochial school teacher in Nebraska, had not violated the state's 1919 statute that mandated English-only instruction when he taught a Bible story to a 10-year-old child in German (Del Valle, S., 2003). This more tolerant attitude, coupled with the increasing support for 'cultural pluralism', espoused by John Dewey and Horace Kallen, led to additional efforts by some US ethnolinguistic communities to establish educational programs for their own children. Around this time, the Chinese, Japanese, Arabic, Greek, Yiddish and French-speaking communities developed a network of after-school and weekend programs in which their languages and cultures, and in some cases their religions, were taught.

In the 1960s, the ethnic revival that accompanied the era of Civil Rights led to the further development of bilingual education programs, often supported by ethnolinguistic communities, especially Latinos. With funding from the Ford Foundation, a bilingual two-way program was established in the Coral Way Elementary School in Miami-Dade County. The goal of the program was to develop English language proficiency and maintain the Spanish of recently arrived Cuban children, as well as to develop the Spanish language proficiency and the English of Anglo children. This program led the way for the renaissance of bilingual education in the US in the second half of the 20th century. Bilingual programs to teach English, as well as to maintain the Spanish language, were developed by Latino communities in Texas, New Mexico, California and Arizona (García, 2009a). As Castellanos (1983) reminds us, this growth of bilingual education programs in the 20th century started without any federal involvement.

In 1968, the US Congress passed Title VII of the Elementary and Secondary Education Act – the Bilingual Education Act. The Act authorized Congress to put aside money for school districts that had large language minority enrollments and that wanted to start bilingual education programs or create bilingual instructional material.

The ethnic revival of the 1960s (Fishman, 1985a) also fueled scholarly interest in sociolinguistics, bilingualism and ethnic studies. It was at this time that Joshua A. Fishman conducted his *Language Loyalty in the United States* study (Fishman, 1966). 'Ethnic-group schools', or as he later called them, 'ethnic mother-tongue schools', were included in Fishman's study as important community institutions that sustained the life of ethnolinguistic groups in the US (Fishman & Nahirny, 1966). These ethnic-group schools were networks of all-day and supplementary schools organized, maintained and funded (fully or in part) by the ethnolinguistic communities themselves. Fishman noted then three types of such schools that accounted for almost 1885 units:

(1) Day schools that provide instruction in the linguistic, cultural and religious heritages of ethnic groups.
(2) Weekday afternoon schools, or supplementary schools that are in session two or more weekday afternoons throughout the school year.
(3) Weekend schools that normally meet on Saturdays or Sundays.

Fishman noted that these efforts by ethnolinguistic communities to educate their children under community auspices and in languages other than

English were significant for language maintenance purposes. He claimed then:

> Language maintenance in the United States is desirable, in that the non-English language resources of American minority groups have already helped meet our urgent national need for speakers of various non-English languages, and that these resources can be reinforced and developed so as to do so to a very much greater extent in the future. (Fishman, 1966: 370–371)

The activities of these ethnic mother-tongue schools identified by Fishman contrasted sharply with what publicly funded bilingual education programs came to be. In 1974, when the Bilingual Education Act was re-authorized, bilingual education was redefined as:

> [I]nstruction given in, and study of, English and (to the extent necessary to allow a child to progress effectively through the education system) the native language of the children of limited English speaking ability. (As cited in Castellanos, 1983: 120)

Whereas the ethnic mother-tongue schools in the Fishman study, the two-way bilingual education program of Coral Way, and the developmental maintenance bilingual education programs in the American Southwest and elsewhere had as their goal the bilingualism and biliteracy of children, this new definition of public bilingual education restricted it to a transitional goal. That is, the focus of public bilingual education became the development of the academic English (and not the maintenance or development of the language other than English) of those ethnolinguistic minorities who had 'limited proficiency' in English, and often were recent immigrants. Although some bilingual education programs continued to support the development of children's home languages, the federal goal in supporting bilingual education became the improvement of English for immigrants, and not the education of American ethnolinguistic communities in ways that supported their bilingualism and biliteracy.

In the 1980s, Joshua A. Fishman revisited the study of community resources of languages other than English in the US. He again included among these resources the educational institutions that he now called 'ethnic mother-tongue schools' (Fishman, 1980a, 1980b). In the two decades that separated the first study from the second, the number of these ethnic mother-tongue schools had grown from 1885 to 6553. Yet, pointing to the fact that two-thirds of these institutions operated only on afternoons or weekends, Fishman *et al.* (1985: 38) concluded: '[E]thnolinguistic education is supplementary, and therefore it is quite probably too meager to constitute a serious contribution to language maintenance'. Fishman argued then for high-quality bilingual all-day schools, whether community-funded or supported through public funds, oriented toward the task of language maintenance. He said:

> We have been guilty of horrible neglect with respect to our language resources. Language maintenance bilingual education can be one long-overdue step in the direction of reversing this shameful and wasteful policy. (Fishman, 1980c: 170)

By the time that Joshua A. Fishman completed his 1980 study of the community resources of ethnic languages in the US, a new movement was afoot. Spearheaded by Senator Samuel Hayakawa, the Official English movement and US English posed new restrictions on the use of languages other than English, especially in bilingual education. Although efforts to introduce constitutional amendments at the federal level to make English the official language of the US were later abandoned, the movement continued at the state level (Crawford, 2004; García, 2009a; García & Kleifgen, 2010). At the time of this writing, 31 US states have English-only laws.

This more restrictive language ideology and policy has had negative effects on public bilingual education, especially in California, Arizona and Massachusetts, where bilingual education was rendered illegal (see especially, Gándara & Hopkins, 2010). Bilingual education in the US has been progressively silenced, as English-only approaches are favored for the teaching of emergent bilingual students who need to develop English for academic purposes. Despite the recent growth of two-way bilingual education programs (often called 'dual language') and immersion bilingual education programs, as well as the continued existence of developmental maintenance bilingual education programs, the focus of transitional bilingual education programs has become the education, usually in English only, of emergent bilingual students, now called 'English language learners' (see García & Kleifgen, 2010, for a discussion of these discursive changes).

At the same time, however, the number of bilingual and emergent bilingual students who need to develop academic English in US schools has continued to grow, largely because of the global political economy, advances in technology, and the resultant transnational movement of people, information and products. Simultaneously, the US came to understand the importance of languages other than English for national security, especially after the September 11, 2001 attacks and subsequent US-led war on terror.[1] The 2006

National Security Language Initiative seeks to increase the number of US learners, speakers and teachers of 'critical-need foreign languages' from kindergarten to university through funding for flagship programs and other initiatives. Thus, the languages of ethnolinguistic communities have re-emerged as objects of study in the 21st century. With bilingualism restricted in public schools, the emphasis became the 'heritage languages' of American ethnolinguistic communities, especially at the tertiary level.

From the early 1980s, Guadalupe Valdés strongly advocated that secondary and tertiary institutions should develop alternative programs to foreign language education in order to teach Spanish to bilingual students in whose homes Spanish was spoken. She rightly argued that traditional foreign language programs were inadequate for these students (Valdés et al., 1980).

Although the term 'heritage languages' had been widely used in Canada to refer to the languages of ethnolinguistic communities other than English and French since the 1960s (e.g. Cummins, 1983; Cummins & Danesi, 1990), the name was not used extensively in the US until 1999, when the first National Conference on Heritage Languages in America was held at Long Beach, California. As García (2005) has argued, the term heritage language education was adopted as bilingual education faced greater restriction in its efforts to educate bilingual and biliterate Americans. Since then, scholarship on heritage language education has expanded, referring to the teaching of languages other than English to ethnolinguistic minorities for whom the language is 'heritage' (see Brinton et al., 2007). Guadalupe Valdés defines 'heritage speaker' as, 'a student who is raised in a home where a non-English language is spoken, who speaks or merely understands the heritage language, and who is to some degree bilingual in English and the heritage language' (Valdés, 2000: 1, our italics). Brinton et al. (2007) define a heritage speaker as an 'individual exposed to a language spoken at home, but educated primarily in English' (p. 374, our italics).

The differences in conceptualization and ideologies between advocates of bilingual education (of the developmental maintenance or two-way type) and heritage language education are telling. Whereas bilingual education refers to using both the language other than English and English as media of instruction, heritage language education refers to teaching the language other than English, most often as a subject, to bilinguals. Whereas bilingual education efforts are concentrated in the elementary, middle school and secondary school levels, where the use of two languages is seen as a way to holistically educate emergent bilingual Americans, heritage language education efforts are focused in tertiary and secondary education, where language education is departmentalized and language is taught as a subject. Whereas bilingual education offers the possibility of an all-day education through both the language other than English and English, heritage language education is only concerned with the language other than English, and in Brinton *et al.* (2007) seems to define itself as either 'supplementary' or 'remedial', ceding the primary educational space to English. This is in contrast to bilingual education, which defines itself by the use of two languages in education alongside each other.

Yet with the renewed interest in languages other than English occasioned by the passage in 2006 of the National Security Language Initiative, and the waning of true bilingual education efforts, heritage language education professionals argued, rightly, that it would be ethnolinguistic minorities, especially in higher education, who would be most likely to master the 'critical need languages' identified by the federal government – Arabic, Chinese, Hindi, Persian and Russian. As bilingual education yielded to English ideologies and abandoned much of its focus on the development of the language other than English, the heritage language field expanded. The growth was also related to the fact that language minorities other than Spanish-speaking ones were often more comfortable with a focus on heritage language education, rather than a bilingualism that they often associated only with Spanish-speakers and a historic Civil Rights era.

Gradually, community-based programs, such as those that Fishman had called 'ethnic mother-tongue programs' became allied with the heritage language education movement, and not with the dwindling bilingual education movement that distanced itself more and more from the goals of bilingualism and biliteracy. The heritage language education movement, in the form of the Alliance for the Advancement of Heritage Languages, housed at the Center for Applied Linguistics, provided these programs with a much-needed network of support. Furthermore, many of these community-based programs defined their task as simply teaching the 'heritage' language to ethnolinguistic minorities.

What the cases in this book show, however, is that today these programs demonstrate a complexity that is not fully captured by seeing them simply as 'heritage language' programs. These cases also show a commitment to bilingualism that goes beyond the timid US conception of 'bilingual education'. The educational spaces presented here focus not solely on teaching a 'heritage' language, a language of the past, but on living these language practices in the present, and providing students with life experiences and performances that will enable them to practice their bilingualism in a future global world. The goal of these bilingual community education programs in the present is not simply the maintenance of an ethnic-mother tongue, as Fishman would have said, or the development of a heritage language, as heritage language proponents would claim. The goal of these bilingual community education programs is the *bilingual* development of American children living in a global multilingual context. Thus, as the educational aspirations of these ethnolinguistic groups have gradually adapted to an American student body that is now often transnational and transcultural, the reality of these bilingual community education efforts has become bilingual, as students and teachers negotiate the use of the home language practices (which are plural) within the English discourse of the students.

These bilingual community education efforts also differ from what others, for example many Europeans, call 'supplementary schools' or 'complementary schools' (see especially Blackledge & Creese, 2010) in that they also include private day schools, and even some public all-day school efforts where the community has been the catalyst and is fully involved. In including some public school cases, as well as community-based agencies supported by public funds, we argue that bilingual community education does not have to be fully funded by the ethnolinguistic community itself. In cases where those communities have been minoritized, in particular, private resources to organize educational efforts are not available. Including these cases makes the point that US ethnolinguistic communities are able to organize educational efforts for their children that include their bilingualism, while also benefiting from public funds, whether from US sources or foreign government sources, as well as private funds. The funding of these bilingual community education programs is always mixed, and not solely raised by the local community. Thus, these efforts are for American children, funded by a mix of local and global public and private funds, but always in the hands of US ethnolinguistic communities.

The next section discusses the New York City multilingual context in the global present. We do so to contextualize the cases in the book, before we turn to the focus of this chapter in Sections II and III – the reconceptualization of these educational spaces as bilingual community education, and the reimagining of American ethnolinguistic communities as diasporic plural networks.

The global 'Multilingual Apple'

New York City is one of the best-known 'global cities' (Sassen, 1991), because of its important role as a dynamic center for global economics with transnational and cross-border networks. 'The city that never sleeps' is the center of much global economic activity, with its famous stock exchange and corporate headquarters of many businesses. It houses the United Nations and many consulates from all over the world, as well as world-famous museums, operas, educational institutions and media conglomerates. In addition, it is one of the most multilingual cities in the world, a product of its global status that attracts people from all over the world, including powerful elites and immigrants who come for work. As a result, the 'Big Apple', is what García and Fishman (1997/2002) have called a 'Multilingual Apple'. García (1997/2002) has described the city's multilingual development through time. In this section, we limit ourselves to the sociolinguistic situation of the city in 2009, using the US Census data, and comparing it with previous trends.

The problems with language census data are well known. Some of these issues are associated with the fact that data collection is based on self-reporting. Thus, data is likely to reflect ideology or perception, rather than actual language use or proficiency. For example, comparing the 1980 and 2009 US Census language data for New York City, a significant increase in the number of Haitian Creole speakers is noted. However, we cannot tell whether that rise is due to an increase in population or to the greater consciousness among Haitians that they are Creole speakers, rather than French speakers. Another problem is that the categories of data collection and analysis may not reflect local realities. For example, the census counts only French Creole, complicating the issue of whether those identified as French Creole speakers are actually Haitian Creole speakers or speakers of other French Creoles (for more on this, see Barrière and Monéreau-Merry, Chapter 16). Besides Haitian Creole, there are also important New York City (NYC) languages that are not counted separately in the census. This is the case, for example, for Bengali, an important language in the city. The census does tell us that in 2009 there were 111,202 speakers of Indic languages beyond Urdu, Gujarati and Hindi, but it does not specifically tell us which they are. The same problem is faced by African languages, which remain lumped into one category. Yet, Busi Makoni (Chapter 9) argues that claiming one language in multilingual Sub-Saharan Africa, where people speak in many different ways, often having little relationship to 'a language' as named by officials (see Makoni & Pennycook, 2007), may make this task impossible. Many of the chapters included in this volume allude to other problems with solely relying on census data. For example, Ghaffar-Kucher and Mahajan (Chapter 4) refer to the fact that Pakistanis often report speaking Urdu at home, although in reality other languages, such as Punjabi, may be spoken. Finally, because many groups have a high number of undocumented NYC residents, they are under-represented in the census. The majority of the chapters in this book argue that the sociolinguistic diasporic situation of ethnolinguistic groups in New York is much more complex, fluid and interactive than has been traditionally described and than could be understood through looking at the census. However, regardless of the limitations of census data, it does give us an indication of the great ethnolinguistic heterogeneity of New York City.

The multilingualism of New York City is evidenced by the fact that 52% of the population over five years of age (3,712,467 people) speak a language other than English at home (US Census Bureau, 2009). Although Spanish is indeed the largest language in the City, spoken by 24% of the population over five years of age, the language diversity in New York is greater than in most US cities, indicating its global reach. Table 1.1 displays the top 24 languages other than English spoken by New Yorkers over five years of age.

Table 1.1 Languages other than English (LOTEs) spoken by New Yorkers over five years of age, 2009*

	LOTES	Number
1	Spanish	1,869,995
2	Chinese	408,105
3	Russian	202,225
4	French Creole	106,020
5	Italian	101,261
6	French	86,220
7	Yiddish	85,341
8	Korean	74,273
9	African languages	63,890
10	Polish	58,520
11	Tagalog	57,209
12	Greek	56,688
13	Arabic	55,474
14	Hebrew	52,424
15	Urdu	35,408
16	Hindi	34,908
17	German	25,212
18	Japanese	22,210
19	Serbo-Croatian	19,470
20	Portuguese	16,404
21	Persian	11,452
22	Vietnamese	9,849
23	Hungarian	9,409
24	Gujarati	9,336
	Total NYC LOTES speakers	3,712,467

*This data is from the US Census Bureau (2009), *American Community Survey*, Table B16001. The US census does not track numbers for Bengali, which is a big language in New York City, falling somewhere around 50,000

The difference between the reported presence of LOTEs in New York City homes today and that in the past is striking. For example, in 1980 when Joshua A. Fishman conducted his second study of language resources in the US, Italian was the second reported home language in the City. Today, Italian has moved to fifth place. Chinese, which was reported as the fourth language in 1980, has moved to second place, and Russian, which was reported in ninth place in 1980, has moved to third place. Even more striking is the fact that French Creole, which was reported in 19th place in 1980, has now moved up to fourth place.

In 2009 the NYC Latino group, numbering 2,315,041 and making up 28% of New Yorkers, is highly diverse, in terms of national origin, immigration histories and language use. Likewise, the Asian group, numbering 1,004,177, or 12% of the New York City population, comprises peoples from diverse origins and regions in East and South Asia. Table 1.2 displays the composition of the NYC Latino group by national origin, whereas Table 1.3 illustrates the largest Asian group populations.

Whereas New York City in the 1980s was still mostly a Puerto Rican city (see García, 2011a), and Caribbean Spanish (Puerto Rican, Dominican

Table 1.2 Latino groups in NYC with population over 10,000, 2009*

	National origin	Number
1	Puerto Rican	782,222
2	Dominican	582,456
3	Mexican	305,664
4	Ecuadorian	185,022
5	Colombian	111,440
6	Salvadoran	45,291
7	Cuban	43,040
8	Peruvian	39,046
9	Honduran	36,951
10	Panamanian	21,035
11	Spaniard	16,196
12	Argentinean	15,070
13	Venezuelan	12,364
14	Nicaraguan	11,077
15	Chilean	10,866
	Total number of Latinos, NYC	2,315,041

*US Census Bureau (2009), *American Community Survey*, Table B16001

Table 1.3 East and South Asian groups in NYC with population over 5,000, 2009*

	Groups	Number
1	Chinese (except Taiwanese)	464,201
2	Asian Indian	202,408
3	Korean	87,556
4	Filipino	80,890
5	Bangladeshi	43,878
6	Pakistani	34,086
7	Japanese	26,648
8	Vietnamese	14,859
9	Taiwanese	7,154
	Total	1,004,177

*US Census Bureau (2009), *American Community Survey*, Table B02006

Republic and Cuban) was overwhelmingly present, the numbers in Table 1.2 reveal that today Caribbean Spanish-speakers make up only 60% of the Latino population. With Mexicans and Ecuadorians now constituting the third and fourth largest Spanish-speaking groups in the City, other Latin American indigenous languages have also entered the picture. As Makar (Chapter 2) shows, Mixteco has become an important language in the City, although it is not accounted for in the census. More than anywhere in the world, New York City is home to a large number of Latinos who interact in different varieties of Spanish, now all in contact (see Otheguy & Zentella, 2011). The pan-Latino identity that results is fluid and changing, as groups interact with each other and with others, and as individuals with different national origins intermarry (see García, 2009b).

The greater language contact that Spanish-speaking groups experience in New York City is also reflected among many other groups. New York City provides the sociolinguistic context for linguistic and cultural contact among groups that never would have interacted in their countries of origin, or who have been in conflict. For example, the Chinese category includes all who consider themselves Chinese in the US, including those born in the US whose ancestors come from countries such as the People's Republic of China, Taiwan, Singapore, Hong Kong, Malaysia, Indonesia and Vietnam. This category collapses Han Chinese and others who may not be Han Chinese. In counting Asians, the US census separates Taiwanese from Chinese. Yet, linguistically the Taiwanese may have more in common with Mandarin-speaking Chinese than those who categorize themselves as Chinese have in common with each other. In New York, Chinese from the People's Republic of China and Taiwan coexist, blending varieties of Chinese, as well as going beyond political and cultural differences (see Lo, Chapter 18). The same can be said of Indians, Bangladeshis and Pakistanis, who in the US may interact for the first time. Ghaffar-Kucher and Mahajan (Chapter 4) identify, for example, the differences and continuities between Punjabi speakers, bringing Indian Sikhs and Pakistanis from both sides of the national borders into contact in NYC. Japanese, Koreans and Chinese, with histories of occupations and invasions, build a pan-East Asian identity in New York, as they learn to appreciate the continuities between Chinese characters, Japanese kanji, and Korean hanja (see Chung, Chapter 5; Kano, Chapter 6; and Lo, Chapter 18). In addition, Arabic speakers from Lebanon, Egypt, Morocco, Yemen and many other places interact in their different varieties and in so doing shape *'āmiyyas* in New York (see Zakharia and Menchaca Bishop, Chapter 11). However, the complex multilingualism of New York occurs not only because there are many languages other than English spoken in the city, but also because many New Yorkers are bilingual, and even plurilingual, as we have noted above, and their individual practices in LOTEs interact with English, the powerful language of the Big Apple.

Thirty-six percent of New Yorkers were born outside of the US, making it the US city with the seventh-largest foreign-born population. However, although Miami and Los Angeles, cities with larger proportions of foreign-born populations than NYC, have a preponderance of Spanish speakers, only a quarter (24%) of New York City's multilingual population speaks Spanish. Thus, New York, as the city with the largest population, has the greatest language diversity, and the most language resources, in terms of numbers (3,712,467 speakers of LOTEs over the age of five, see Table 1.1).

More than half of New Yorkers over age five who speak languages other than English at home also speak English very well (54% or 2,013,350); yet, 46% claim to speak English less than very well. Thus, New York City's population is not only highly multilingual, but their bilingualism is also highly varied, with almost half still developing English. These emergent bilingual New Yorkers, who are developing their English proficiencies, require services that include the use of additional languages.

In July 2008, Mayor Bloomberg signed Executive Order (EO) 120, mandating all City agencies that provide direct public services to make these services available in the top six languages of New York's emergent bilingual population. This includes the translation of documents, interpretation services and signage. Executive Order 120 also expands other multilingual services, including a 311 Customer Service Center that provides information about city government and non-emergency situations in over 170 languages.

The biggest need for emergent bilinguals who are developing English is, of course, in education. In 2010–2011, 41% of students in New York City public schools spoke a language other than English at home (we think this number is an underestimation, since the census numbers are greater, and parents often do not report their language use to school for fear that their bilingual children will be stigmatized). That same year, one in four students, that is, more than 287,203 students, did not score at a proficient level of academic English (NYCDOE, 2011). Although 50% of New Yorkers who speak LOTEs at home speak Spanish (see Table 1.1), 64.8% of emergent bilingual children in public and charter schools in New York City who are classified as 'English language learners' speak Spanish at home (see Table 1.4). Thus, two-thirds of the current emergent bilingual population developing English in NYC schools is Spanish-speaking. Following Spanish, the Chinese emergent bilingual population makes up 13.6%, whereas speakers of Bengali, Arabic and Haitian Creole follow, making up 3.5, 3.0 and 2.6%, respectively.

The difference between the numbers in Table 1.1 and those in Table 1.4 is telling, for although Spanish and Chinese are still in first and second place, respectively, Bengali, Arabic and Haitian Creole, the other big languages of emergent bilingual New York students, are not as prominent among the language resources of the city. Two main factors influence this statistic. First, groups such as speakers of Russian, Italian and French, big languages in New York, are already highly bilingual and many speak English very well. Second, Yiddish-speakers are mostly Hasidic Orthodox and attend their own religious schools (see Peltz & Kliger, Chapter 13). Students who speak Spanish,

Table 1.4 Top languages of New York City emergent bilinguals

	Language	Number	Percentage
1	Spanish	100,129	64.8%
2	Chinese	21,002	13.6%
3	Bengali	5,396	3.5%
4	Arabic	4,692	3.0%
5	Haitian Creole	3,970	2.6%
6	Russian	3,048	2.0%
7	Urdu	2,898	1.9%
8	French	1,979	1.3%
9	Albanian	987	0.6%
10	Punjabi	896	0.6%
11	Korean	879	0.6%

Chinese, Bengali, Arabic and Haitian Creole not only have high numbers of emergent bilinguals, but they also attend NYC public schools. The chapters in this volume do not strictly represent either the groups that speak the most numerous LOTEs at home or the groups that have the most emergent bilingual students. As Matarese (Chapter 19) indicates, there is little relationship between the number of speakers of LOTEs at home, or the number of speakers of LOTEs who are bilingual or emergent bilingual, and the institutional resources, as well as the bilingual community education programs, that are supported by the efforts of ethnolinguistic groups. For example, because of their use in religious institutions, Hebrew and Arabic are over-represented in community institutional support, whereas Spanish and Chinese are under-represented. At the same time, as Zakharia and Menchaca Bishop's chapter (Chapter 11) indicates, Arabic speakers in New York City are also woefully disadvantaged with regards to bilingual education programs needed.

In Section II of this chapter, we turn to examining the cases in this book as we reconceptualize these community-supported educational spaces as *bilingual community education* rather than heritage language education or bilingual education per se. To do so, we focus first on the sociolinguistic aspects – language teaching and language use in classrooms. We then turn to examining their distinct socioeducational patterns – the role of community and parents, and the forging of educational partnerships.

II: Beyond Heritage Language and Bilingual Education

The sociolinguistic and socioeducational context of bilingual community education programs is certainly different from what the literature describes as either heritage language education or bilingual education. On the one hand, as we will see, the language goals and language use differ from the ways in which heritage language education and some forms of bilingual education describe them. On the other, the ethnolinguistic community itself, especially the parents, are the reason and the motor for the existence of these programs, unlike the way in which these communities are described in the educational literature. Educational partnerships are also prevalent in these educational spaces, unlike the isolation of many public school efforts or the ways in which 'heritage language education' has been often described as being separate and segregated. We start by looking at the sociolinguistic context of these bilingual community education programs, before we turn to the role of the community and parents, and of partnerships.

Sociolinguistic goals and language use

Bilingual community education programs provide a context for American children to live the language other than English, not as heritage, but as life in an American present and a global future. That is, the focus is on the development of a holistic bilingual community in the US, and not just on the learning of an LOTE. Thus, as we will see in this section, their language use is flexible, characterized by what we call *translanguaging* (more on this concept below), and the goal of these efforts goes beyond the simple teaching of language.

As we have said, in heritage language education scholarship, the language other than English is often the sole focus of instruction. Attention is mostly given to the development of the LOTE itself, especially for academic contexts. In so doing, heritage language education programs believe in the sole use of the LOTE in instruction, following direct methods of teaching languages. In contrast, bilingual education programs use the LOTE alongside English. With few exceptions, the educational efforts described here are not just ethnic mother-tongue schools or heritage language programs, but are bilingual in the sense that, besides using the LOTE in instruction, they also use English. The examples that follow in the rest of this chapter are all taken from this volume, and thus reference is made only to the author(s).

Most of the bilingual community education efforts described in this volume use English, as well as the LOTE, to educate. This is the case, for example, for the all-day schools described in this book in Arabic/English, French/English, Greek/English, Haitian Creole/English, Hebrew/English, Spanish/English and Yiddish/English. However, this is also the case for the Saturday program organized by the Russian community (Kleyn & Vayshenker), the community agency program organized by the Mexican community (Makar) and the after-school program run by the Chinese American community (Lo). Implicitly, all the programs here described use both the LOTE and English in instruction. Perhaps it is the Persian-speaking parent in Shirazi and Borjian (Chapter 10: 166) that says it best:

I habitually love and praise my children in Persian, and habitually send them to bed and tell them to brush their teeth in English ... The notion of ethnic language is false; we don't teach Persian to our children as part of their heritage or identity, and tell them that's why they have to learn it, because that ethnicizes Persian. That provincializes Persian ... They will work here, have friends here; they are American, they need to speak English.

Thus, all the community education efforts here described are bilingual in nature, whether they use the two languages explicitly, as a stated goal in their policy, or implicitly in their practices.

Yet, these community efforts go beyond many public bilingual education programs. For example, two-way bilingual education programs and developmental bilingual education programs – the first encompassing two ethnolinguistic groups and the second only one – separate the two languages strictly. In the US these two types of bilingual education programs are increasingly called 'dual language' as a result of the silencing of the word 'bilingual' (for more on this, see Crawford, 2004; García, 2009a; García & Kleifgen, 2010). In fact, these so-called 'dual language' bilingual education programs often pride themselves on the separation of languages, although as García has shown (2011b), there is much flexible language use in the classrooms also (for a critique of the 'dual', see especially García, forthcoming).

Heritage education and 'dual' language education display a monoglossic ideology with regard to bilingualism (for more on monoglossia, see García, 2009a; also see Del Valle, J., 2000). That is, they see bilingualism as linear and additive, as being the sum of two separate languages, instead of acknowledging its heteroglossic character (see Bailey, 2007). Cummins (2007) has referred to this ideology of bilingualism as the 'two solitudes'. Yet, the cases in this book often support a more 'dynamic bilingualism' (see García, 2009a), with multiple language practices in inter-relationship with each other. That is, these bilingual community education efforts show a great deal of flexible language use, as we will see in the next section. This dynamic bilingual use has been called 'translanguaging'. (For more on 'translanguaging', see especially García, 2009a; also see Creese & Blackledge, 2010 and Blackledge & Creese, 2010. Cen Williams, 1996, first used the term to refer to a flexible pedagogy to learn Welsh in Wales.)

Translanguaging

There is a great deal of distance between the monolingual or monoglossic policy stated by some principals and teachers of bilingual community efforts and the heteroglossic practices observed by the authors of these chapters (for more on the distance between language policy and practice, see Menken & García, 2010). For example, the Hebrew day school has a policy of using Hebrew only as the language of instruction and conversation, with English discouraged. Yet, teachers' Hebrew proficiency level and the wide variance in that of students' results in this policy not being observed (Avni & Menken). The teachers in the Yiddish school do not follow the policy of Yiddish-only use in the school, for they claim that the 'mixed form' is the way in which they normally express themselves when they speak with their mothers and others (Peltz & Kliger). The Korean schools also have a policy of using only Korean in instruction (Chung). Chung adds, however, that such 'policy is enforced flexibly by circumstance and at the discretion of teachers' (p. 95). In the Turkish school described by Otcu, teachers often warn students to speak Turkish. Yet, students speak English to each other and often to teachers (Otcu). A sixth-grader in the Greek community school described by Hantzopoulos also reports that, when she does not understand something, the teachers tell her in English and then repeat it again in Greek. Similar phenomena are observed in an Arabic day school, where much translanguaging takes place among teachers and students in the classroom, hallways and playgrounds. While some teachers use translanguaging as an instructional strategy, they struggle to locate their approach within a tradition of a monoglossic bilingual policy (Zakharia & Menchaca Bishop).

The Cypress Hills Community School divides Spanish and English strictly by day and week. Yet, teachers in the upper grades break away from this strict separation to respond to students' communicative needs (Ascenzi-Moreno & Flores). A different trend is seen in the Bengali Udichi School and in Public School (PS) 189, where translanguaging occurs more frequently in the beginning, and less so as students progress. Choudhury describes how, at Udichi, teachers initially use both Bengali and English, but gradually switch to Bengali as students become more proficient in Standard Bengali. In practice, however, as a teacher explains in an interview, students are always permitted to speak in English, which teachers then translate into Bengali, and students repeat (Choudhury). At PS 189, Barrière and Monéreau-Merry describe how students use both English and Haitian Creole orally and in writing during initial stages, but over time, students are encouraged to separate their two languages.

Unlike the programs described above where translanguaging practices violate the monolingual instructional policy, the Japanese school described by Kano has a flexible organizational structure that views bilingualism not as an end product, but as a dynamic process, and clearly rejects the compartmentalization of languages. This is the same practice observed in the after-school program supported by the Chinese American community to help their children excel academically, described by Lo. Because the purpose is to accelerate academic competence, and not just to teach a LOTE, both Chinese and English are used to support learning without any language compartmentalization.

Perhaps it is the case of the educational program supported by the Mexican community agency, Tepeyac, with its use of English, Spanish and indigenous languages, especially Mixteco, that best captures the complexity of the dynamic language practices of these bilingual community education efforts. Makar cites Rivera-Sánchez (2002: 21), who describes what she calls the 'spread community' of the 21st century as 'a recreation of symbolic references and sociospatial transformations in which separated worlds are nowadays in *juxtaposition*' (our emphasis). Makar states: '[R]ather than deterritorializing these languages, members of the community have found a way to reshape their practices'. Like the Chinese American after-school program described by Lo, the educational activities in Tepeyac do not include the teaching of Spanish or English as subjects. Yet, the program facilitators use both languages 'juxtaposed' in tutoring to support the academic needs of Mexican American children. Interestingly, there are classes in Mixteco, but tutoring is not done in Mixteco because the facilitators do not speak it. Yet, the program facilitators encourage Mixteco children to work through Mixteco in order to understand the academic content. For example, a Mixteco-speaking boy is observed drawing a small animal and says and writes '*leko*' next to his drawing, in interaction with a Spanish-speaking girl who then says and writes '*conejo*', and the teacher who says and writes 'rabbit'. Makar makes the important point that these bilingual community education practices, in which the entire repertoire of the children's language practices is activated, would have seldom happened in Mexico, where children with different language backgrounds rarely interact because of the segregation of indigenous and mestizo communities. Bilingual community education in the US goes beyond looking backwards towards the language 'heritage', the language past, and instead focuses on a multilingual future of tolerance and integration that is very much part of American democracy. As the program coordinator says, the emphasis is not on roots, although history is important. The goal of the Tepeyac program is to get the children to understand their place in a multilingual, transnational world and to encourage their plural interactions. In many ways, these bilingual community education programs are as American as apple pie, promoting a sense of tolerance and democratic justice that is sometimes not present in the communities' historical past or even in societal contexts where these languages are widely spoken. The focus of these bilingual community education programs is on encouraging interaction and interdependence among American children with roots that have commonalities as well as differences.

Busi Makoni in her chapter on the educational efforts of Sub-Saharan African communities takes the notion of these bilingual community education efforts even further, offering an alternative language ideology to that of language maintenance and revitalization. African languages, she contends, are not enumerable objects, but are communicative resources. Africans do not simply see their languages as those that are often identified as the big New York African languages – Amharic (Ethiopia), Dinka (Sudan),

Igbo (Nigeria), Kru (southeastern Liberia), Mandinka (Senegal, The Gambia, Mali, Guinea, Côte d'Ivoire), Pulaar (Senegal, Guinea Bissau and Mali), Soninke (Mali, Senegal, Côte d'Ivoire, The Gambia), Swahili (Kenya), Twi (Ghana), Wolof (Senegal) and Yoruba (Nigeria). The 'languaging' of Africans includes complex indigenous communicative resources that go beyond the so-called African languages, and that also include those called English and other colonial languages, such as French. Sub-Saharan African communities in NYC often form associations that use all their complex languaging to offer services to new immigrants, including job-seeking, health matters, immigration, lending and even learning English, but rarely do they establish educational programs to teach what others consider their 'languages'. Rather, their complex languaging is transmitted through socialization in more informal venues, such as braiding salons, churches and households. This, Makoni argues, is in keeping with the African concept of teaching and learning in which everyone is a teacher and any space is an appropriate educational space.

Although, from the outside, these bilingual community education programs may appear language maintenance-oriented and many of the authors herein repeat this idea, in reality the efforts of these programs are much more complex. Their goals are to support the plural lives of ethnolinguistic American communities in interaction with English and a complex and dynamic US society, what García (2011c) refers to as *sustainable languaging*. Rather than isolating, these bilingual community education programs are enriching. Rather than reproducing a past that is often full of pain and inequities, they point to an American future of interactive language and cultural resources.

Beyond language teaching

As we have seen, these bilingual community education projects are not solely teaching language. In fact, to us they are considered bilingual education programs because the language practices of the bilingual community are being used in music, theater, arts, religion, hair braiding, tutoring in academic subjects and many other cultural activities, but also in video, TV and technology. That is, children are precisely performing these language/cultural practices (see Pennycook, 2000; 2010) in situated action, rather than just learning the language, and always doing so in the context of their transnational and transcultural lives. The educational philosophy of the adults in these programs has much to do with Bourdieu's (1991) concept of *habitus*, or the tendency to act in particular ways as inculcated through implicit and explicit socialization. However, as we will see below when we reconceptualize the concept of an ethnolinguistic community, the community of practice (Lave & Wenger, 1991) that results is not homogeneous, as language practices are incorporated into the children's physical selves through different actions, producing a multiplicity of identities.

In describing a series of performances involving songs and skits, and related to Jewish faith and observances in a Hasidic Yiddish yeshiva, Peltz and Kliger express clearly how the focus of these bilingual community education programs is not just the language, but the embodied performance of an identity. The authors comment:

> None of the projects sought a bilingualism that would give the children linguistic proficiency solely. All instructional school programs used Yiddish language instruction as a pathway for transmitting ethnocultural or religious conventions. (p. 215)

The passing on of cultural and religious values is an important reason why parents send their American children to these schools. Yiddish is acquired by Hasidic Jews, Hebrew by Jews, Punjabi by Sikhs, Arabic by Muslims, and Greek by Greek Orthodox, precisely to read holy texts and transmit religious and cultural traditions. In the Hebrew day school, Hebrew is embodied in the embroidery of the Hebrew names in the kippot (skullcaps) of the boys and in the charm necklaces of the girls. Avni and Menken summarize the role of Hebrew in these institutions, saying:

> Unique in its uses and symbolism, Hebrew assumes a pragmatic and ideological function in linking religious, ethnic, nationalistic, and cultural aspects of Judaism, and in uniting Jewish people across time and space. (p. 194)

Ghaffar-Kucher and Mahajan describe how Sikhs send their children to temples, *gurdwaras*, especially to become well versed in the *Mool Mantar*, the most important verses within their holy scriptures, the *Sri Guru Granth Sahib*. It is this text through which American Sikh children learn to read Punjabi and become familiar with the founding principles of Sikhism, including the Five Ks – *kesh* (uncut hair), *kanga* (small comb), *kara* (circular bracelet), *kirpan* (small sword) and *kacha* (shorts) (Ghaffar-Kucher & Mahajan).

The Greek Orthodox Church has also played an important role in the development of supplementary and all-day bilingual community Greek schools. Yet, Hantzopoulos describes how this strict association between the Greek Orthodox Church and the educational programs it runs is limiting; it does not reflect the changing Greek community, in which there is much intermarriage and many who are not members of the Greek Orthodox

Church. Despite all these groups' efforts to transmit a monolithic religious–cultural inheritance, the chapters to come repeatedly assert the disruptions that American children in a US heterogeneous context introduce.

Perhaps one of the examples in the book that most convincingly shows that these bilingual community education efforts are not narrowly focused on the transmission of a 'heritage' language is that of the Saturday school organized by the Russian community (Kleyn & Vayshenker). Not only are there Russian language classes and English language classes, but there is also instruction in maths, physics, chess, theater and art. In an effort to recognize that these are Russian American children, some of these classes are taught through Russian, but others through English. The idea is to transmit to the children the areas of expertise for which the culture associated with Russian has traditionally been known – such as numeracy and mathematical knowledge, chess and physics – and in so doing to develop their bilingualism in English and Russian.

There is great emphasis in bilingual community schools on having children perform their ethnolinguistic identities through music, theater, dance and other relevant practices; thus these classes and activities are an integral part of the curriculum. The Saturday Russian program also offers Russian drama classes, staging performances of modern Russian writers and poets (Kleyn & Vayshenker). The after-school program organized by the Chinese American community includes not only Chinese dance, but also Kung Fu, considered a Chinese martial art (Lo). Tepeyac's after-school program for Mexican American children includes folkloric ballet and soccer (Makar).

Performances of language and cultural practices are at the heart of these community efforts. In the weekend program run by the Turkish community, the children perform their Turkish identity by dressing in red and white for all ceremonies. Every Saturday starts with a ritual in which the children recite 'Andimiz' (Our Pledge). They also sing Turkish songs with patriotic Turkish themes (Otcu). In the Greek schools, children perform during the *yiortes* (holiday) celebrations, and Greek dancing and music are an important part of the performances and the curriculum (Hantzopoulos). The Iranian parents who organize educational programs for their children also often turn to theatrical performances (Shirazi & Borjian). One mother wrote and staged a play that the children performed at an annual *Norooz* (New Year) party. The Fedowsi School, a Saturday Persian program in Westchester County and Long Island, involves children in performances for cultural events, including *Mehregan*, the pre-Islamic Festival of Autumn, *Yalda*, commemorating the winter solstice, and *Norooz,* the Iranian New Year.

The Udichi Performing Arts School is the context for learning Bengali, but always alongside the perfoming arts. Choudhury describes that the day starts with the national anthem of both Bangladesh and the US, followed by Bengali songs, such as Tagore's 'Amra shobai Raja' [We're all Kings]. Lessons in music, art, dance and/or tabla (Indian drum) follow, along with Bengali. The children learn about key events – the Language Movement of 1952, Independence Day, and Victory Day.

Despite the emphasis on the performance of 'Bengalism', the inclusion of the US national anthem alongside the national anthem of Bangladesh points to the children's joint performance of 'Bengalism' juxtaposed with 'Americanism'. It is not just ethnic 'heritage' identities that are being performed in all the bilingual community education programs here described. The performances are of American multiple identities.

Videos, television and technology have become important ways in which these American children live in multiple spaces. For example, Mexican American children in the community program described by Makar watch TV programs directly from Mexico and connect with children in cities such as Puebla. Makar comments:

If the children can simultaneously navigate two distinct spaces, geographical and symbolic, and draw tools from these spaces to make sense of their identity – then their bilingual development becomes an echo of these two spaces, these two languages that interact in the same dynamic way in which they inhabit these two countries. (p. 54)

As in the case of the juxtaposition of 'Bengalism' and 'Americanism' described by Choudhury and referred to above, the simultaneity of spaces, languages and cultures experienced by Mexican-origin children in the activities described by Makar contributes to the construction and recognition of what growing up American means in the complex communities of the present. In performing their complex identities that include features from different contexts always in interaction and motion, the children in all these bilingual community education efforts are reflecting an important way of being American in the global context of the 21st century.

Beyond ethnocultural/linguistic transmission, some of these bilingual community programs offer a possibility for what Zakharia and Menchaca Bishop conceptualize as language education for positive peace. Drawing on concepts from the field of peace studies, the authors suggest that bilingual community education can serve as a foundation for developing positive peace, or promoting the absence of structural violence. It can do so by developing cultural understandings, as well as addressing injustice, discrimination and conflict through language policies and practices that integrate students' ethnolinguistic identities. In contrast, language education for negative peace is framed around a security agenda, or the elimination of direct violence, as in the case of the National Security Language Initiative, in which languages and their speakers are viewed as 'foreign' and, thus, not American. Such language efforts create tensions for bilingual Americans whose languages are not envisioned as part of bilingual American identities, and thus are seen as obstacles to peace. The dynamic forms of bilingual community education that many of these chapters describe may be viewed as language education for positive peace, as exemplified not only by the Arabic case study, which demonstrates how one school attempts to integrate Muslim Americans' linguistic and cultural repertoires, but also in the various other cases offered in this book. For example, Tepeyac, the community agency described by Makar, is part of the National Coalition for Dignity and Amnesty and offers Mexican-origin families protection from labor abuses, advocacy for immigration reform, advice on immigration issues, and consultation on health matters. Such holistic approaches to address forms of structural and cultural violence fall under the purview of education for positive peace.

The bilingual community education efforts in this book provide reciprocal support to the community. Whereas many of these programs support parents and community members in their quest to enable their American children to navigate these multiple worlds, it is the community and the parents that are the backbone of these efforts. The next section describes the extraordinary role that parents, communities and other partnerships play in the lives of these bilingual community education efforts, in the context of understanding how these programs differ from heritage language education, as well as public bilingual education.

Socioeducational context: Collaborations

The US public school is often detached from the community and functions as an island, often responding to the demands of the state and local education departments rather than to those of the community. In New York City, parents who visit schools have to sign in and show identification to school safety agents who are part of the police force. Often this process alienates language minority parents, who feel threatened. Once in the school, there is no guarantee that the staff will be able to assist parents in a language they understand. Realities such as these create much distance between the school and the community.

In contrast, the bilingual community education efforts that we include in this book *are* the community. The linguistic and cultural practices are not considered liabilities, and are not perceived with scorn and fear. Instead, they are precisely the strengths. It is language minority parents and communities that hold the value in these efforts. The educational programs cannot exist without the parents and the community, just as they cannot exist without partnering with others. Thus, the programs themselves constitute a network of collaboration, rather than functioning as separate entities in which only school administrators, teachers and students exist.

The role of parents and community

Parents and communities in bilingual community education efforts are precisely the leaders in establishing, organizing and running these programs. This is in stark contrast with the negative view of minority parents in the mainstream literature on American schooling. Language minority parents are often stigmatized and considered incapable educational partners (Ramirez, 2003). Mainstream schools do not involve parents who speak languages other than English, often ignoring the communities' funds of knowledge as sites of knowledge construction (González et al., 2005). The bilingual community efforts in this book, however, explicitly demonstrate the strength of these parents and communities.

Parents and community members not only organize these efforts, but they are often the unpaid teachers. In Udichi, out of 14 Bengali instructors, six work without pay (Choudhury). In Korean schools, the teachers are mostly parents and are minimally compensated (Chung). Ghaffar-Kucher and Mahajan describe how many of the Hindi programs are run from the basements of homes where parents are the volunteer teachers. In the Princeton Community Japanese Language School described by Kano, 70% of the teachers are parents. The teachers at Atatürk school also teach mostly voluntarily, with only a stipend that covers the cost of commuting (Otcu).

Parents not only contribute as teachers, but are also key in fund-raising. In the Atatürk school parents organize events such as the Turkish Bazaar, where Turkish goods and food are sold to raise funds to support the school (Otcu). In Udichi, Bangladeshi parents organize cultural events, offer help by bringing food and contribute the profits to support the school (Choudhury).

Parents have been the driving force behind the establishment of a 'dual language' bilingual education program at Cypress Hills Community School (Ascenzi-Moreno & Flores), the new French programs (Ross & Jaumont), as well as the Russian, Korean and Chinese programs (Kleyn & Vayshenker, Chung and Lo respectively). In fact, Cypress Hills Community School has a parent co-principal who works alongside the administrative co-principal. It was also an alliance of French-speaking parents who advocated for the establishment of a K–12 bilingual French–English charter school, which opened in 2009. Because parents are so involved, they hold much power in organizing the programs and running them. Ascenzi-Moreno and Flores describe how, when a reading curriculum was imposed on the Cypress Hills Community school by outside agents, the parents, a network of Latino parents from different origins, as well as English-speaking parents, mandated that it be stopped. As the parent-co-director said:

> [T]he school was created by parents who had ownership of the dual language program. They believed in the ideas and found value in the teacher-made curriculum, which they knew addressed the needs of their children and the community, rather than bringing in prescribed curriculum that had no attachment to the community. (p. 225)

Sometimes these bilingual community education efforts are organized by community-based agencies that have been established by the community itself. The after-school programs for Chinese American children described by Lo are managed by not-for-profit community-based organizations, such as the Chinese American Planning Council. In the case of the Atatürk School described in Otcu's chapter, it was the Turkish Women's League of America that founded the school, and continues to donate funds to it. In addition, two other Turkish-American organizations offer indirect support by their presence as umbrella organizations – the Federation of Turkish-American Associations and the Assembly of Turkish-American Associations. French expatriates founded Éducation Française à New York with parents and volunteers offering after-school French classes.

Not only are the parents and communities deeply committed to the educational programs and their continued existence, but they are also linked to other networks and partnerships that have global reach. This shows once again that, rather than isolating, these are efforts that go beyond the ethnolinguistic group itself, beyond the US, and beyond concepts of single identities and unique citizenships. The next section describes some of the partnerships that have made this global reach possible, and that go beyond what traditional monolingual public schools can offer.

Partnerships

Bilingual community efforts are often thwarted by critics who complain that children in these programs are isolated from others in the American 'mainstream'. Yet, an analysis of how these programs operate leads us to understand that these programs have a larger reach across the globe and provide a deeper interactive, international and plural experience than most US public school contexts. Thus, rather than being isolating, these educational efforts provide American children with the global links that the US needs.

Although many of these bilingual community efforts receive books, materials and other resources from foreign governments, this does not represent a 'foreign' orientation, but a global one. First of all, it is the American ethnolinguistic community that often seeks out the partnership with foreign governments (as well as local government), as a means to win support for their own efforts, but not to be controlled by government. Second, the foreign government support is used to ensure that the children are successful in the US by instilling pride in their heritage. The support of foreign governments is used to develop US citizens able to navigate different linguistic and cultural contexts.

A good example of the role and the complexity of these larger complex partnerships is the functioning of the network of schools of the US Korean community. The schools are organized into two networks – the Korean School Association of America founded in 1982, and the National Association for Korean Schools founded in 1985 – and the South Korean government provides textbooks and materials for both (Chung). Yet it is clear that the goal of these educational activities is the academic success of American children of Korean background, and not of Korean children. For example, the Foundation for Korean Language and Culture was established in 1997 not strictly to promote Korean, but rather to establish Korean as an acceptable subject in the SAT subject test in order to advantage Korean American children. The efforts of this Foundation were funded by the Korean conglomerate Samsung and the South Korean government, as well as by the Korean American community. These partnerships have also made it possible to develop dual language bilingual education programs in Korean/English for American children, as well as to increase the teaching of Korean in US public schools (Chung). Through all these partnerships, Korean American children are supported in succeeding in a competitive US global market, in which the Korean language will increasingly be an asset and a resource.

The Japanese government has supported programs to teach Japanese to 'sojourners', temporary residents, since the 1970s. In 1971 Japanese corporations supported the founding of the Japan Overseas Educational Services in order to promote the education of Japanese children abroad. The Japanese government subsidizes rent for school buildings, salaries for teachers and textbooks. In the greater New York area, most Japanese educational programs are under the auspices of the Japanese Educational Institute of New York, founded in 1975 (Kano). However, increasingly, as Kano describes,

Japanese bilingual community efforts focus on the success of Japanese American children in the US (and not 'sojourners'). These Japanese educational programs also support the acquisition of Japanese language and culture by all American children, even those without a Japanese background.

Many other bilingual community education efforts described in this book also receive support from foreign governments for similar purposes to those outlined above. The Greek Ministry of Education provides the Greek textbooks used in many of the church-run Greek schools (Hantzopoulos). The Turkish government provides instructional space in the Turkish Consulate and school textbooks imported from Turkey (Otcu).

The Mexican government supports a Binational Migrant Education Program, which provides funding for teacher exchanges between Mexico and the US and allows students to migrate between the two countries by facilitating a binational transfer document (Makar). The Mexican government also supports a program called Plazas Comunitarias, which supports literacy courses and education in Spanish, implemented through community-based organizations. In all of these cases, it has been the Mexican American community that has advocated for this support, and the programs reflect the transnational nature of the community.

The programs in New York City organized by the Chinese American community also receive support in the form of free textbooks and professional development from the governments of the People's Republic of China and/or Taiwan, through pressure exerted by the Chinese American community (Lo). An example of how the concept of 'foreign' countries and citizenship is disrupted in the complexity of a US global city like New York is the fact that foreign governments often support educational programs that do not correspond to students' national origins. For example, the Taiwanese government and the Chinese government both support programs in Mandarin Chinese regardless of the origins of the students. Thus, one often finds Taiwanese children learning the simplified characters used in Mainland China, and children from Mainland China learning the traditional characters of Taiwan.

The partnerships and collaboration that these bilingual community education programs establish in order to survive should be an important lesson for all educators. Just as the parents and the community stretch to support these programs, the teachers do also. In many cases it is individual teachers who establish unlikely partnerships in order to do their job well. For example, a teacher in a Tamil class has an ongoing relationship with the Canadian Board of Education in Toronto, where they teach Tamil in public schools. They provide her with lesson plans and curricula, which she then adapts for use in the school (Ghaffar-Kucher & Mahajan).

Beyond other governments, some of the bilingual community education efforts included here are supported by New York State, New York City and/or federal funds. That is the case for the public 'dual language' bilingual education programs described in these chapters and some other programs, like many after-school programs. For example, the Chinese American Planning Council, which runs the largest after-school program at PS 20, receives funding from the New York City Department of Youth and Community Development (Lo).

Perhaps the example in the book that shows the most collaboration and the building of partnerships is that of the French American community. The growth of French–English bilingual community programs in New York City is the direct result of collaboration between French/US governmental and non-governmental partners; local, national and international organizations; private foundations; parent groups; and the local NYC Department of Education (Ross & Jaumont). The French Ministry of Education provides help to one-third of the French/English bilingual community programs in New York City in the form of teachers from the French public civil service, scholarship aid for French citizens and program accreditation. The French government also maintains an Agency for French Education Overseas, which offers special grants to support classes in French as a mother tongue. However, it is the collaboration of the New York City Department of Education, together with the French American community, Francophile Americans and French expatriates that has made the French Heritage Language after-school programs possible. The New York City Department of Education provides public school classroom space free-of-charge for these programs.

These partnerships are clearly extensions of parents and communities, as discussed in the previous section. Nevertheless, these collaborative structures clearly show that bilingual community efforts do not isolate or provide a structure for group segregation. Instead, they provide American children with opportunities to understand a global world and to have experiences beyond a local national or ethnic context. Rather than placing them in the disadvantaged position in which American ethnolinguistic minorities are held, which is purported to only be remedied by full linguistic and cultural assimilation to English-only, these bilingual community education efforts place these children in an advantaged position. Their bilingualism and understandings of other cultures and countries set the stage to make them highly competitive in the global market.

These bilingual community education efforts also insert complex language and cultural practices as a definition of what it is to experience an American childhood. This ensures that we go beyond traditional definitions of what it is to be an American 'ethnolinguistic speech community'. This is precisely the topic of Section III of this chapter, which follows.

III: Beyond Ethnolinguistic Communities

The cases in this book enable readers to understand that American ethnolinguistic communities are much more fluid, diverse and complex today than in the past, and that therefore the notion of a static 'speech community' of traditional sociolinguistics may need to be extended to that of *'diasporic plural networks'*. Traditional sociolinguistic analysis of speech communities may need to give way to what Busi Makoni has called 'diasporic sociolinguistics' or what Blommaert (2010) has called the 'sociolinguistics of globalization'. The American ethnolinguistic communities of the present are transnational and fluid, leading us to abandon the traditional notion of a 'speech community'. Fishman (1972b: 22) defined 'speech community' as 'one, all of whose members share at least a single speech variety and the norms for its appropriate use'. Twenty-years later, Romaine (1994) put the emphasis not on the sharing of the same language, but on norms and rules for the use of language. She clarifies: 'The boundaries between speech communities are essentially social rather than linguistic' (Romaine, 1994: 22). Regardless of whether the notion of a 'speech community' uses linguistic or social criteria, it results in the view that there are separate social, cultural or linguistic entities, and that there are nested communities within the nation-state.

In the last 20 years, there has been a shift from understanding speech communities as categories, to recognizing 'communities of practice' (Lave & Wenger, 1991). In the community of practice view, a group may be oriented to the same practice, but not necessarily in the same way. Thus, rather than viewing the community as a homogeneous whole, the focus is on difference and tension as the ordinary condition. Since identity is rooted in action, and not in categories, there can then be a multiplicity of identities.

Postmodern scholarship has problematized the notion of 'community' even further by viewing it merely as a social, political and discursive process. This is the position of language ideology theorists (see Gal & Irvine, 1995; Gal & Woolard, 2001). Thus, an ethnolinguistic community may have little to do with ethnic and linguistic inheritance. Rampton (2006: 17) concludes:

[B]elonging to a group now seems a great deal less clear, less permanent and less omni-relevant than it did twenty-five years ago, and this makes it much harder to produce an account of 'the language of such-and-such a social group', or 'language among the ___' than it used to be.

Language and ethnicity are not simple reflections of 'heritage speech communities', or of 'practice communities'. The social action and networks in which individuals are involved in the here-and-now juxtapose multiple linguistic and cultural identities from which we select features at different times to perform our identities (Rampton, 2006).

As such, in global cities where individuals act and interact closely, there is a proliferation of transnational identities that live 'with and through, not despite, difference; by *hybridity*' (Hall, 1990: 236). American ethnolinguistic communities are fluid and heterogeneous. Although in this book we used the traditional sociolinguistic idea of a 'speech community' to commission the chapters, the chapters themselves reveal the fluid and heterogeneous nature of these groupings. The chapters also reveal the discursive 'inventions' of ethnicity as linguistic and cultural inheritance. Whereas the chapters identify the enormous effort exerted by some of these educational programs in socializing American children to specific language and ethnicity constructions, they also reveal the constant disruptions of these monolithic categories, especially by children, but also by adults.

Busi Makoni is explicit about these language and culture constructions in the context of Africa. She says:

> The concept of African languages as enumerable objects and associated names were products of colonial language ideology reinforced by contemporary, top-down language policy discourses. In pre-colonial and plurilingual urban Africa, languages are best construed not as enumerable entities but as communicative resources. Such resources are plurilingual, heterotrophic, and diversified local practices typical of Africans. (p. 142)

The chapters in this volume show that the concepts of 'heritage languages and ethnicity' in a global city are also inventions. The communicative resources of the children who participate in these bilingual community efforts are likewise plurilingual, heterotrophic and diversified, a product of their constant interactions in plural networks both in the US context and globally.

Diasporic plural networks: Some examples

The communities, as well as the language and cultural practices described in the chapters in this book, are not monolithic or homogeneous. For example, the parents who advocated and built the French 'dual language' bilingual education programs in the City included 'European and Canadian expatriates in Manhattan and West Brooklyn, West Africans in Harlem and the Bronx, Haitians in East Queens and East Brooklyn, and North Africans in West Queens' (Ross & Jaumont: 233). In fact, Haitians constitute 29% of the French 'dual language' bilingual education programs, and 50% of those enrolled in the French Heritage Language Programs in New York City (Barrière & Monéreau-Merry). Although some of the bilingual community education programs that Barrière and Monéreau-Merry describe teach in Haitian Creole and English, others teach in French and English, and yet others use all the language practices of the Haitian community, including English, French and Haitian, and most often in combination. There is clearly a complex diasporic network that is creating a context for different French practices in the city, and so we cannot properly speak of a 'French ethnolinguistic community'. Further, French practices in the City include not only what some might consider English practices, but also practices that include what others might call Haitian Creole, Pulaar, Wolof, Mandinka, Soninke and Bambara practices, among many other West African ones. Diasporic networks in New York City, as all these cases show, are plural with regard to language and cultural practices, national origin and religion.

One such example is the plural Punjabi-speaking community in New York described by Ghaffar-Kucher and Mahajan. Punjabi is written by Indian Sikhs in Gurmukhi script, and is flourishing in New York because of its tie to the Sikh religion. Pakistanis, however, write Punjabi in the Shamukhi script, and because Urdu was chosen as the official language of Pakistan, Pakistani Punjabi-speakers hardly ever write their language. Furthermore, to distinguish themselves from Sikh-Punjabis in New York, Pakistani-Punjabis often claim they are Urdu speakers, even if they are not. Yet, because of their Muslim identity, Pakistanis often prefer to learn to read the Qur'an in Arabic, rather than learning to read Punjabi or Urdu. Thus, Pakistani-Punjabi speakers often interact more closely with different national origin and ethnic groups who are Muslims than with other Punjabi-speakers, or other Pakistanis. Their identity construction in NY is then multiple, complex and different from that which they would have developed if they had stayed in Pakistan. Sikhs also interact in New York more with other Indians, Hindi-speakers or not, as well as with Pakistanis, Punjabi-speaking or not. The ethnolinguistic boundaries are porous and complex, and New Yorkers move in and out of them with ease.

The complexity of the so-called Bengali-speaking community in New York City is described by Choudhury, including not only Bangladeshis, but also Indians from West Bengal. Bengali itself also has many variations. In writing, both Shadhubhasa and Choltibhasha forms are used. In speaking, although the standard in both countries is based on the dialect of Nadia in India's West Bengal, Bangladeshi Bengali has borrowed from Persian and

Arabic, whereas Indian Bengali has borrowed more heavily from Hindi. Bangladeshis are mostly Muslim, whereas Indians from West Bengal are mostly Hindus. Yet, despite these differences, in New York City they often come together and establish networks of communication that would not have been common in their countries of origin.

The Russian-speaking community stretches from Russia to the Baltic Republics of Estonia, Latvia and Lithuania, across the Central Asian nations of Kazakhstan, Kyrgyzstan, Tajikistan, Turkmenistan and Uzbekistan, to the Caucasus states of Azerbaijan, Georgia and Armenia, and the former Soviet republics of Belarus, Moldova and Ukraine, as well as to the diasporas, especially of Israel, Canada and the US. Thus, many of the Russian speakers in New York are multilingual to start with. While the Russian speakers in New York City have historically been Jewish, and many have lived in Israel and also speak Hebrew, the Russian-speaking New York community cannot be reduced to a single ethnicity, national origin or religion, or a single set of cultural or even linguistic practices (Kleyn & Vayshenker). In interacting, the separate constructions of Russianness and the Russian language tied to nation-states in their countries of origin become flexible, plural and complex, as the network is defined by difference and divergence.

Although it is the Greek Orthodox Church that organizes most bilingual community efforts for Greek speakers in the US, many of the children who participate have one parent from a different linguistic, cultural and/or religious background, particularly as the number of inter-ethnic and inter-religious marriages among Greeks and non-Greeks continues to rise (Hantzopoulos). Further, there are children who attend these Greek Orthodox church-run bilingual community efforts who are not ethnically Greek, but instead are Serbian, Syrian or from other national contexts. What brings them to the school is the religious affinity they have with the Greek Orthodox Church. Yet, some ethnic Greeks are not, in fact, Greek Orthodox, but can still attend these church-run Greek schools. Again, it is in the close interactions afforded by NYC that nation-state monolithic identities disappear.

The Chinese community that Lo describes is completely diverse. Some come from Mainland China, others from Taiwan, still others from Singapore, Hong Kong, Vietnam, Laos and Cambodia. Some speak Mandarin, others Shanghainese, Cantonese, Fukienese or Toisanese (Taishanese). Some write the simplified characters used in Mainland China and Singapore, whereas others use the traditional characters common in Taiwan and Hong Kong. In these bilingual community education efforts, all are seen as one. And yet, it is in their interactions within the bilingual community education efforts that the concept of a single Chinese community is simultaneously constructed, and disrupted.

We have already discussed the differences in Spanish-speaking communities, with different national origins, different varieties of Spanish, different languages, different immigration histories, different political relationships with the US, and different racialized identities. Makar's chapter demonstrates that Mexicans in New York are speakers not only of Spanish and English, but also of Mixteco, Zapoteco, Mayan and other indigenous languages. How all of these get re-imagined as one ethnolinguistic group is important to consider. What are the advantages and disadvantages of this discursive 'invention' for Latinos, as well as for the larger US society? Certainly there is a Pan-Latino ethnicity that is constructed in the US, as different national, linguistic and cultural groups interact through language practices that contain features of Spanish. How is this construction used and misused? These are important questions for those of us interested in the education of ethnolinguistic minorities. Makar's chapter also shows that New York Mexicans are quite different in social class as well. New York is home to elite Mexicans, professionals and business people, as well as low-skilled workers. Some have attended only *primarias* (elementary schools), others *secundarias* (junior high schools), yet others *preparatorias* (senior high schools). Although back in Mexico these groups would not have attended the same educational programs, in New York they populate these bilingual community education efforts together. Thus, the interaction of diasporic networks in NYC is more fluid, and democratic, than that of social and ethnic communities in other settings.

Zakharia and Menchaca Bishop suggest that, while the term 'Arab American' is used to represent an Arabic-speaking ethnic collectivity living in the US, its members differ in significant ways. They speak distinct Arabic varieties, participate in various religions, reflect a range of socioeconomic status, have varying degrees of formal education and hail from over 20 countries in western Asia and northern Africa. For some, their migration to the US is another step in a series of displacements and re-settlements, with or without citizenship, making the notion of 'country of origin' incompatible for their description. These immigration histories reflect historical and ongoing instances of political conflict, and some who hail from the region do not identify as Arab or Arab American, regardless of whether they share the language or not. However, in the US, they may begin to identify as such, with or without the Arabic language.

Even the traditionally homogeneous Japanese and Korean 'communities' are fluid in NYC, and have changed in recent history. Whereas before 1965 the Japanese were considered 'sojourners', now more than half of the children in Japanese educational programs are permanent US residents. Many are either English-dominant bilinguals or multilinguals, with parents who speak a language other than Japanese or English (Kano). In the Korean bilingual community education program described by Chung, the Korean 'community' is extremely diverse. Some are professionals who arrived after 1965 with whole families. Others are *kirogi* (goose families), who have come to the US precisely for the opportunity for their children to be better educated and to become bilingual. In the school Chung describes, many of the children are biracial; some are of Korean descent, but have been adopted by English monolingual American families. Most Korean parents now speak English, and parent meetings have to be conducted in English. A Korean language class is available to parents. The school has decided against the offering of Taekwondo in the future, as it is seen, in the US context, as too violent. In balancing an American and Korean way of being, the educators in the school now worry as much about providing a nut-free environment as they do about socializing the children as Koreans.

Although Jewish ethnicity is often presented as monolithic, the chapter by Avni and Menken, as well as the one by Peltz and Kliger, make evident the many differences within what we often call the Jewish ethnolinguistic community. First of all, there are significant differences among Jewish religious movements. Orthodox, Conservative and Reform congregations all run bilingual community education efforts, with great variations, as evidenced when we contrast the efforts on behalf of Hebrew by Avni and Menken, and those on behalf of Yiddish by Peltz and Kliger. Even the term 'Hebrew' itself encompasses Biblical Hebrew, Mishnaic Hebrew, Medieval Hebrew and Modern Hebrew, different not only with regards to the historical period in which they emerged, but also in the functions that they have been assigned. Some Jewish students can only read Hebrew for sacred texts and prayers, sometimes in older varieties of the language. Others read, write, speak and understand Modern Hebrew. In addition, Hebrew has never been the sole language of diasporic Jewish communities or the sole proxy of Jewish identity. Yiddish has always functioned in relationship with the sacred language, Hebrew, but also in inter-relationship with other local languages. Thus, difference itself also defines the diasporic Jewish 'ways of using language'.

Many of the students in the Jewish bilingual community education efforts described are second- and third-generation Americans, and their degree of bilingualism varies greatly. For example, in describing students' proficiency in Hebrew, Avni and Menken say:

> While some students frequently attended weekly synagogue services, and therefore had more opportunities to interact with liturgical Hebrew, others only attended synagogue for bar mitzvah celebrations and/or holidays. This same variability applied to their exposure to native Hebrew speakers

and trips to Israel. While some students had opportunities to speak and listen to Modern Hebrew outside of the classroom, many did not. Likewise, while some students had started day school in kindergarten, other students came to Rothberg after several years in the public schools, and had therefore only recently begun studying Hebrew. (pp. 199–200)

The bilingual continuum in these bilingual community efforts is extremely broad, and today many programs include children for whom these languages are assets, not heritage. That is, many Anglo American children anxious to acquire an additional language have been abandoned by US public schools, and therefore have turned to bilingual community education. Thus, these programs do not reflect static ethnolinguistic communities that speak a 'heritage language', but diasporic networks of communication where individuals are plurilingual, and they share some, and not other, linguistic and cultural features with other members of the network.

The complexity and dynamism of the plurilingualism in the diasporic plural networks in the US is threatening to many who do not understand the potential of a multilingual US, as well as to ethnolinguistic communities who may want to preserve what they imagine to be their static identity. Thus, the tendency is to see language and ethnicity in singular terms, whether in reference to 'English' and being 'American', or to 'Russian' or any other LOTE and being 'Russian' or of any other group. This ideology narrows American children's possibilities to develop plurilingual and translingual practices and multiple identities, which are important for the future of the US. Busi Makoni explains this phenomenon when she says: 'In NYC, the heterogeneity of languages and the complexity of ethnicity are partial consequences of individuals' multiple affiliations, and the tendency in the long run is for each sub-ethnicity to develop its own vernacular' (p. 151). The US sociolinguistic context with its monolingual, monoglossic ideology contrasts sharply with the plural linguistic and ethnic possibilities of these networks. The effect is a narrowing of possibilities, with distinctions and boundaries among groups, and groupings, that may not have made sense in another context. For example Busi Makoni explains that the Dinka in Africa are a heterogeneous group, and they refer to themselves as Moinjaang. However, in New York, at least five different languages fall under the rubric of Dinka. The result is often a categorization along ethnolinguistic lines that is inconsistent with their everyday actions and with the wishes of the people involved.

The effect of considering the examples in this book not as efforts of the ethnolinguistic community, but as assets of diasporic plural networks means that we can leave behind the notion of these languages and communities as being minoritized. In fact, these bilingual community education efforts show that these dynamic plural networks offer assets and resources for a global world that will surpass the narrow need of a monolingual public school system to teach English-only well. Nevertheless, there are many challenges that remain, and much needs to change in order for these bilingual community education efforts and public school efforts to jointly contribute to a meaningful education for American children in the 21st century. The challenges and future directions are considered in the next section, which also serves as the conclusion of this chapter.

Conclusion: Challenges Ahead and Future Directions

All of the examples in this book point to the challenges that remain for bilingual community education efforts. Because these efforts are marginalized and not seen as in the mainstream, the possibilities that these efforts hold for American society are not being realized. A paucity of adequate teaching material, unqualified teachers, poor pedagogy and limited opportunities for professional development are factors that work against these efforts.

As we have said before, most programs use material and books that are sent by foreign governments. However, this material has been elaborated by Ministries of Education to construct their national citizens, and is mostly inappropriate for American children who have language practices that include English, and who may or may not be familiar with the context in which the books were produced. Furthermore, American children who attend these educational programs often are socialized as school children in US public schools with collaborative pedagogical practices. The more traditional pedagogy followed by some of these efforts contrasts sharply with the constructive and transformative pedagogies of American public schools. Many of the educators in these bilingual community education efforts teach today as they themselves were taught, not only in a different era, but also in a very different sociolinguistic and sociopolitical context. Teachers in most of these programs commented on their interest in further professional development to align instruction with the needs of American bilingual children. They are simply overwhelmed by the differences of the children, and do not understand how to individualize instruction to meet their needs. However, there are no structures in any of these programs to help teachers develop appropriate pedagogical techniques to use with American emergent bilingual children who are acquiring languages other than English as a result of these bilingual community efforts. These teachers, for example, know very little about bilingualism in education, about the role of the home language in developing bilingualism, about the potential of translanguaging in classrooms, about scaffolding instruction and about providing multiple entry points to the lesson for individual students.

Despite all the limitations, these bilingual education community efforts have much to teach US public schools, just as public schools would have much to teach these bilingual education community efforts. However, the separation that presently exists between the two systems makes this collaboration impossible. Children get very little recognition for their efforts and hard work. The US public school does not recognize the value of attending these programs, and as a result, children often hide their experiences from teachers and other classmates. In order for children who attend these programs to get maximum benefit, both systems would have to work collaboratively, recognize and value each other's work, and learn from each other.

Because the US public school shuns bilingualism, these ethnolinguistic performances have been pushed into minoritized spaces. That is, the various locales for American children to formally develop Arabic proficiency, for example, have been largely reduced to Islamic centers, schools or mosques. Similarly, learning Greek has been reduced to the institution of the Greek Orthodox Church, and learning Hebrew to the Jewish synagogue. As such, despite the enormous efforts of the communities, parents and children, and their many accomplishments, children who attend these educational spaces continue to be stigmatized and minoritized, instead of being recognized for their enormous assets and resources, as well as their pluralities.

Until US society and US public schools view bilingualism not as a hindrance but as a resource, and welcome the many educational efforts of bilingual community education programs as valuable activities for American children, these efforts will continue to be seen as marginal, and often as suspicious. The loss will be that of US society, and especially of monolingual American children who are going to need bilingual proficiency to work in a global world.

The US has recognized the need to develop bilingual US citizens. The 2006 National Security Language Initiative provides funding for the development of programs, teachers and learning material to expand the teaching of languages other than English, especially those that are critical to national security in K–16. Yet currently, very few American children learn languages other than English in primary schools, and in secondary schools students rarely go beyond the basic level (Rhodes & Pufahl, 2010). Less commonly taught languages such as Arabic, Chinese, Farsi, Japanese, Korean, Latin, Russian and Urdu account for less than 10% of all K–12 language enrollments (*Foreign Language Enrollments*, 2010). Clearly, the US public school today is more concerned with the teaching of English to immigrants than the teaching of languages other than English to all. Public schools simply have not learned the simple lessons on bilingualism offered by Jim Cummins (1979) and Joshua Fishman (1976) over a quarter-century ago – that using the child's home language will result not only in the better use of academic English, but also in the development of a powerful bilingual citizenry, capable of moving the nation into the future.

Whereas the nation uses resources to fund the learning of languages by those whose home languages do not include those practices, it does not recognize the language resources of those who already speak those languages at home. This has often been observed in the literature. What is new in the positioning offered in this book, however, is the idea that ethnolinguistic communities as autonomous and segregated groups do not exist in the US – that what exist are American diasporic plural networks that interact dynamically using many language and cultural practices. New also is the idea that these bilingual community efforts are not just about groups of people maintaining the static language practices of the past, or developing the unchanging language practices of their heritage. These efforts are about educating American children bilingually and transculturally so that these large diasporic networks can build a better US future for all. At present, this is just a dream.

These bilingual community efforts push us further to reconsider the marginal situation in which the US has held its ethnolinguistic communities and their educational efforts. These are not simply 'ethnic' schools, or 'mother-tongue' schools, or 'heritage language' programs. However, at present, that is the way in which we conceptualize them because we have pushed them out of the mainstream educational space. If we really wanted a future in which the US will emerge as leader, we would have to blend and integrate the efforts of these US bilingual community education spaces with those of the public schools and recognize this collaboration for what it could be – the only way of educating *all* American children for the plural networks of the 21st century.

Acknowledgment

The authors are grateful to Sarah Hesson for her careful reading of this manuscript.

Note

(1) This was, of course, not the first time that the learning of languages other than English was encouraged for national security. During the Cold War, the National Defense and Education Act was passed in 1958 to fund the study of 'foreign' languages, especially Russian.

Part 2

Communities Educate their Own Bilingual Children

2 Building Communities through Bilingual Education: The Case of Asociación Tepeyac de New York

Carmina Makar

Introduction

New York City has long been a place of encounters. Immigration legacies comprise the personal stories of those who inhabit the city, and the tissue that binds these stories is one of multiple languages and origins. Recent demographic shifts reveal how the population's changing composition is shaping education policies and practices throughout the city.

According to the New York State Department of Education, in 2009 almost 40% of the student population in New York City (NYC) was of Latin American Origin (NYSED, 2010). This includes students who were born in the US but have foreign-born parents, as well as students who were born outside the US. This grouping is commonly found under the umbrella of the 'Latino' population, which is used interchangeably with Hispanic, or Spanish-speaking population.

Mexican students are the fastest growing group within this Latino population and their presence in NYC classrooms is highly visible. However, these students often face challenges that result from poor connections between pedagogy and classroom demographics (Vasquez, 2004). Further, as graduation and drop-out rates attest, schools are failing to adequately support many of these students.

Families and communities at large are not oblivious to these challenges and are launching efforts to make sense of the schooling environment for their children. The purpose of this chapter is to illustrate how Mexican communities are rounding out their children's language and literacy development through community-led bilingual education efforts. In particular, this chapter showcases the work of Asociación Tepeyac de New York in connecting non-formal education efforts to formal schooling and providing a space for distinct language practices to emerge in a context that goes beyond heritage language education. Tepeyac's program illustrates a bilingual education initiative driven by an active transnational connection to Mexico, integrated language learning strategies and practices, and a holistic philosophy towards diversity and multilingualism. These features are evidenced in the space Mexican students have carved out for themselves, a space in which they recreate their language and identity across both countries, thus shaping their own ethnolinguistic community.

To provide a background to this educational activity, the chapter begins with an overview of Mexican students in NYC and the conditions surrounding their immigration and linguistic experiences. I then describe the work of Asociación Tepeyac in the context of other community organization efforts. Drawing on this case, I argue that non-formal education efforts offer the potential for bridging the gap between home and school culture to provide dynamic bilingualism (García, 2009a). As this chapter will show, this is especially important since it affords students and their families a new perspective on bilingualism that goes beyond heritage language approaches and instead includes other actors such as parents and extended communities in the larger process of bilingual development.

Mexicans in NYC

The Mexican population in New York City is the fastest growing group and third largest after the Puerto Rican and Dominican populations (Smith, 2006). Increasing birth rates for Mexican women, stronger networks within the city and the deepening economic crisis in Mexico are some of the factors that have accounted for this growth spurt in the last decade. Mexicans in New York come mainly from Mexico's south central region, particularly the state of Puebla, and to a lesser extent some regions of Oaxaca, Guerrero and Tlaxcala. Given this growth and diversity, the Mexican population constitutes a useful example through which to explore the language practices shaped and elicited by the Mexican community.

The diversity of the Mexican population is reflected in the linguistic spectrum in both countries (Mexico and the US). While there are more than 500 million Spanish speakers worldwide (Gordon, 2005), different varieties of Spanish exist as a result of its historical and geographical evolution, whose origins begin with the linguistic development of Vulgar Latin and cut across history until the rise of Spanish with the colonization of the Americas at the end of the 15th century. It is an official language in all of the South American countries (except in Brazil, Guyana, French Guiana and Suriname) the six countries of Central America, Mexico, Cuba, the Dominican Republic and Puerto Rico. In addition to Spain, Spanish is also spoken in the Balearic and Canary islands, in parts of Morocco and the west coast of Africa, and also in Equatorial Guinea. In the US, it is widely spoken across many states, particularly Texas, New Mexico, Arizona, California, New York and Florida (Penny, 1991). The US has the world's second-largest Spanish-speaking population after Mexico. In its recent edition of the *Encyclopedia of Spanish in the US*, the Instituto Cervantes of Spain asserts that the US boasts more Spanish speakers than in any country other than Mexico, amounting to an estimated 45 million.

In 2008, the total number of Mexicans in New York City was about 295,000 (New York City Department of City Planning, 2010), a number that does not account for the thousands of undocumented people. Further, since indigenous Mexicans often identify as Mexican, there is no official count for them, but several community leaders have estimated their numbers at around 125,000 and their origins as belonging to the Zapotec, Mixtec and Maya communities (interview, 10 April 2010).

This linguistic identity is conceived under the broader context of the Mexican national identity and the numerous language practices that make up the region. In Mexico, like most Latin American countries, the state has played a fundamental role in the construction and promotion of national identity, a process by which racial and ethnic groups have been excluded from the national narrative (García *et al.*, 2010). This process began with the adoption of Spanish as the national language and the resulting exclusion of the indigenous populations and their languages. Many of today's NYC Mexican immigrants speak indigenous languages other than Spanish.

In their work on bilingual education and the Spanish language in New York, García and Otheguy (1997) describe how Spanish in the city is characterized by the variety of countries of origin among Latinos in New York and thus the absence of a norm that serves as a foundation for the creation of a New York standard. In addition, they posit that the multilingualism of many Spanish speakers, many of whom are proficient in English and other languages, results in the absence of a monolingual standard. These characteristics point to the high degree of diversity in the Spanish spoken in New York City. Zentella (2001: 168) describes how 'the variety of Spanish that each group speaks is an important marker of its individuality, but the Spanish language is also their most powerful unifier thanks to more than 300 years of Spanish colonization'.

The case of the Mexican communities in the US and in NYC in particular illustrates a specific set of unique language practices that result from three main features of this population: (a) their proximity to the Mexican border and thus potential transnational conditions/practices; (b) their rapid and steady growth, which accounts for a larger number of recent newcomers; and (c) the presence of other indigenous languages such as Mixteco, which results in a heterogeneous set of language practices and identities within seemingly homogeneous Mexican communities. The distinctive features of the Mexican population in NYC are reflected in the challenges schools are facing in educating these children.

Immigration Context

Migration from Mexico to the US represents the largest flow of immigrants anywhere in the world (Massey *et al.*, 2002). Since 1970, at least 6.8 million Mexican immigrants have entered the US (Smith, 2006). Throughout the 20th century, migration to the US has flowed consistently except for periods of variation owing to rapid growth and economic development in Mexico. The peaks in migration arose from transformations in the agrarian economy that resulted in a large, mobile supply of wage laborers.

These migration patterns have important implications for the educational system, but not solely as a result of the challenge to attend to culturally and linguistically diverse students. A large part of the studies focusing on language development and language use in immigrant populations is based on the assumption that immigrants settle permanently in the US, whereas for many of these populations, education has been conceived of as a continuum, starting in one country and followed by their arrival in the US. In the case of Mexico, it also includes their possible return to their communities of origin. The nature of the migration flows enacted by the Mexican population points to a transnational group, insofar as the population assimilates and is engaged elsewhere as it maintains connections, builds institutions, conducts transactions and basically nurtures a relationship with its country of origin (Schiller *et al.*, 1995).

Education Initiatives

Mexican immigrant students have educational backgrounds that vary considerably. Some adolescents may have attended *secundaria* [junior high school] and even *preparatoria* [senior high school] in Mexico, while others will have attended only a few years of *primaria* [elementary school], and others may have never enrolled. The Mexican case is unique given the complexity of its immigration patterns. These variations include permanent vs circular migration, legal status, length of stay and region of origin in Mexico, which largely determine language, social class and pre-existing networks in the US among other things. Students from rural areas in Mexico may have been subject to numerous transfers because of their families' agricultural migration patterns, in which case, high mobility in the US is likely.

Mexican students in NYC today are part of what Gándara and Contreras (2009) have called the 'Latino educational crisis'. As a group, they have the least schooling, the lowest per-capita income, the lowest rate of English proficiency and the lowest high school graduation rates among the City's immigrant groups (*La Unión*, 2010).

Because Mexican students have the lowest rate of English proficiency, they are often categorized as 'English Language Learners' (in New York, ELLs). As ELLs, they must enroll in one of three options offered by the New York City Department of Education (NYCDOE): English as a Second Language Programs in which only English is used; Transitional Bilingual Education Programs in which the students' home languages are used only until they are English proficient; or Dual Language Bilingual Programs in which both English and the language other than English is used throughout the child's education. While Mexican students may be eligible to receive academic support in Spanish a current snapshot of bilingual programs in the city reveals that in many cases ELLs are tracked to English as a Second Language classrooms that further segregate them from their peers and hinder their educational development by stripping them of some of the opportunities necessary to go through the educational pipeline in this system.

Problems also arise because as indigenous peoples students of Mexican origin may not speak Spanish and thus they face stronger challenges in developing family and community relationships with school. These relationships are often built by having parents attend school meetings and participate in school-wide activities such as field trips. However, many parents work multiple jobs with several shifts. Given these work demands, parents struggle to find time to be physically present in school activities and this contributes to the perceived notion that Mexican families are not involved in their children's education.

Programs that Target Mexican Students

In addition to formal schooling, efforts to educate Mexican children in New York City come from two different arenas: the Mexican government and community-based organizations. The Mexican government is continuously launching initiatives, two of which are particularly important: (a) the Binational Migrant Education Program, PROBEM (BMEP in English); and (b) Plazas Comunitarias. PROBEM is an example of a Mexican federal policy that has been locally implemented by participating US states, including New York State, to improve the education of migrant children who move between the US and Mexico. Its goal is to reinforce knowledge about the history, culture, values and national traditions of Mexican-origin students who live in the US, thus strengthening their identity and improving their transition from one education context to another. PROBEM provides two main services: teacher exchanges and the Binational Transfer Document. The first is a transnational agreement between US and Mexican governments that provides funding for teacher exchanges in order to share educational experiences that promote continuity of educational practices in both countries. The Binational Transfer Document, on the other hand, allows students who migrate between the two countries to continue their studies by providing information about their academic achievements, including their grades. This helps school authorities on both sides of the border make informed grade-level and subject-area placements. In this case, both governments sign a memorandum of understanding which places emphasis on the interconnection of the two educational systems.

Another relevant effort is the Plazas Comunitarias (Community Town Squares) programs, which is offered throughout the US and is implemented in NYC through a number of designated institutions such as community-based organizations and adult learning centers. Plazas Communitarias provides youth and adults with the opportunity to participate in literacy courses and to start or continue their elementary, middle and high school education in Spanish. Every student who completes his or her education under this program gets a certificate provided by the Mexican Ministry of Education and receives personal tutoring that prepares them to take the examination for the General Education Diploma; that is, a high school equivalency diploma. As of 2010, a binational agreement was announced to expand the Plazas Comunitarias program to provide Spanish language, English as a Second Language and academic content free of charge with the support of state and city educational agencies.

The Role of Communities

There has been a marked increase in formal and informal Mexican organizations in New York City. A recent study of hometown associations identified 20 Mexican hometown associations in various parts of New York City and six others in the larger metropolitan area (Cordero-Guzmán & Quiroz-Becerra, 2005). While there is some level of collaboration between the few formal Mexican community organizations, the relations do not appear to be fully institutionalized, particularly when compared with other immigrant communities such as Colombian or Dominican immigrants. While other large Latino groups have made strong gains by organizing themselves and lobbying, the Mexican community continues to be perceived as disperse, divided and, despite its very large numbers, not as close-knit or as cohesive as other groups.

Those who have studied grassroots organizing for Mexican immigrants in NYC concur that there has been an ever-evolving surge of community-based organizations and initiatives that are born and die within a short time. This lack of sustainability is often due to difficulty with funding, especially in recent years. In addition, the heterogeneity of the communities that have been clustered under the Mexican flag allows for organizations to target groups with varying characteristics, making collaboration between these institutions often difficult or unnecessary.

Of the many efforts that have been launched to target the Mexican community, there are a few that have been running for a substantial amount of time (five years or more). Examples of well-established community organizations are the Mixteca Organization, MEXED, MASA and Asociación Tepeyac, which among a few others, are organizations that have gained leadership by strongly advocating for the community. This chapter features the case of Asociación Tepeyac because its structure, educational programs and community practices are representative of the work Mexican organizations are doing. Further, it reflects how a school–community continuum may be implemented to provide bilingual education rooted in students' backgrounds and cultures.

The Case of Asociación Tepeyac

Asociación Tepeyac has been widely studied as a result of its size, its long-term presence in the city, and most importantly because its programs are highly regarded by the community. While many of the other Mexican community-based organizations run college-bound preparedness programs targeting high school students, Tepeyac continues to be one of the few organizations that provide educational programs for children as well as youth.

Tepeyac was founded in 1997 as a non-profit, community-based organization to promote social welfare and human rights for undocumented Mexican immigrants in New York City. As of 2010 it serves approximately 10,000 members through a network of 'Guadalupano Committees', or base groups that are located around the city and in upstate New York. Many of these committees existed prior to the 'formal' foundation of Tepeyac; some go back to the 1980s, when they worked in local religious groups in Catholic parishes run by priests, nuns and lay people trained and commissioned by the Church. The Asociación Tepeyac brings these committees together and through the central office provides outreach and educational programming targeting the Mexican population citywide. The services it provides deal with labor abuses, insufficient wages, accidents suffered on the job, immigration problems, raids, deportations, deaths crossing the border and health problems, among other issues. In the educational realm, Tepeyac provides high school equivalency preparation (General Education Diploma), computer workshops and its largest educational endeavor, the Finding Our Roots program, which is described in the next section. In addition to its work in NYC, Tepeyac is part of the National Coalition for Dignity and Amnesty, together with more than 160 organizations, unions and churches across the US.

Finding Our Roots after-school education program

Tepeyac's after-school and summer program is designed to address the academic, social and cultural needs of the children in their community by providing different strategies to enhance the schooling experience of the students and their families. Tutoring is conducted in English and Spanish. There is also content area support in reading, writing and maths. The program has a special English as a Second Language component for youth and adults, but the rest of the units and pedagogical strategies operate under a philosophy of having no language separation and working with the students in both languages to target their specific needs. The program integrates a cultural–artistic component to activate students' identity through the study of history and arts, and incorporates a physical education element that is put into practice through soccer and folkloric ballet. Activities are held five days a week and provide focused academic and language support, particularly through literacy engagement strategies.

In addition to Spanish and English, Tepeyac offers classes in Mixteco and tries to integrate these children into their educational programs, even when they lack program facilitators that speak Mixteco. One program coordinator stated: 'By providing support in their own terms, and especially an awareness that we value the language, we believe the children themselves can produce the necessary scaffolding for the development of their language' (interview, 3 May 2010). Working with speakers of English, Spanish and Mixteco, in addition to other indigenous languages that arrive in lower numbers (i.e. Zapoteco), poses a challenge for the implementation of pedagogical strategies. When asked about the philosophy underpinning their language policies and practices, the program director asserted:

> Nuestro tratamiento del idioma no tiene una filosofía distinta al resto de los programas. Estamos procurando que los niños sean bilingües, que el español no sea una segunda lengua ni la lengua de su casa, ni que el inglés sea sólo para la escuela. Partimos de lo que Tepeyac siempre ha representado, estamos aquí como mexicanos y tenemos derecho a mantener ese vínculo, con nuestra lengua, con nuestra cultura.
> [Our language policy is no different than the policies that guide the rest of the programs. We are trying to shape bilingual students. We don't want Spanish to be a second language, the language spoken at home, or have English be only for school. This is what Tepeyac stands for. We are here, as Mexicans, and we have a right to keep that connection with our language, our culture, alive.] (Interview, 23 April 2010)

Thus, three main features characterize the program's pedagogy and philosophical foundations: (a) an active transnational connection to Mexico; (b) integrated language learning strategies and practices; and (c) diversity and multilingualism. The following sections elaborate on each of these characteristics.

Active transnational connections to Mexico

Transnational practices are featured in the teaching strategies of Tepayac's facilitators, the language practices of the students and the nature of the activities organized by the program and by the larger organization. In the development of the curriculum, teachers draw from context that is relevant to the children and rooted in current happenings in Mexico. Themes such as the latest decisions in the transfer of soccer players from one team to another, the latest *telenovela* (soap opera) and even the dire situation of violence between drug lords constitute spheres that naturally emerge as domains for language development. Further, by using technology to recreate maps, to watch TV programs directly from Mexico instead of the US version of Univisión and even to connect with other children in cities such as Puebla, teachers create connections that enable these symbolic spaces of interaction to act as arenas for bilingual development. If the children can simultaneously navigate two distinct spaces, geographical and symbolic, and draw tools from these spaces to make sense of their identity, then their bilingual development becomes an echo of these two spaces, these two languages that interact in the same dynamic way in which they inhabit these two countries. These practices mirror what García (2009a: 45) has termed translanguaging, that is, 'multiple discursive practices in which bilinguals engage in order to make sense of their bilingual worlds'. Mexican students' translanguaging practices are embedded in the larger community structure that does not sanction the use of these two spaces and these two languages. In particular, their sense of belonging to *their* two countries is not restricted to the borders of Mexico and the US, much as dynamic bilingualism is not bounded by one language plus another (García, 2009a). Liliana Rivera-Sánchez (2002: 21) asserts that immigration in today's global society 'cannot be understood by reference to spatially demarcated national or local cultures in strict terms [...] the image of spread community implies, a recreation of symbolic references and socio-spatial transformations in which separated worlds are nowadays in juxtaposition'.

From the link of these two geographically separated worlds, Mexico and the US, we can see a third space emerge, an arena that draws from this juxtaposition to recreate a unique social and linguistic space. This third space is both symbolic and tangible insofar as it hosts the culture and imagination of these communities as well as material products of this juxtaposition. The translanguaging practices of these children can be seen as a material manifestation of this third space. Thus, rather than deterritorializing these languages, members of the community have found a way to reshape their practices; these students inhabit their own space, a third space that is rooted in the lived practices of the City, many of which are elicited by the community of Tepeyac (for third space, see K. Gutierrez, 2008).

A significant example of this is the yearly marathon called 'Antorcha Guadalupana' (Guadalupe Torch, which alludes to the Virgin of Guadalupe, Patron of Mexico). This marathon starts in Mexico City with a single person running with the torch. Then, the torch is passed from hand to hand along a route that crosses the whole of Mexico, then crosses the border and continues, never extinguishing the torch, all the way through California and across the US, to finally reach its final destination, Saint Patrick's Cathedral in New York, on 12 December, the day of the Virgen de Guadalupe. By this last stretch and after many months of running, Fifth Avenue in NYC is filled with thousands of people running and celebrating a profound icon of Mexican identity and religiosity. When prompted to talk about events like this, students assume them to be natural events in their community, their discourse clearly reflecting that they acknowledge two levels of interaction and identity: New York City and their Mexican community as an active entity embedded in the larger context of US culture and language.

Integrated language building strategies and practices

Much of what children are prompted to do in Tepeyac's educational program is an act of storytelling. As Engel (1997: 3) notes: 'Storytelling is perhaps the most powerful way human beings organize experience'. Every choice students make is a narrative succession, meaningful, linked to the orality of their cultures and, as Bruner (1996) suggested, this narrative allows for cognitively powerful experiences to be reconstructed. Students are encouraged to use real-time, real-space scenarios to make sense of their language and literacy practices. These language-building patterns allow for students to acquire meta-linguistic awareness of their learning processes and let the languages 'seep in'. In the words of one of the facilitators: 'así dejamos que se les filtre' [that's how we let it filter/seep in] (interview, 23 April 2010). This filtering is activated by having no language separation and integrating language and literacy development strategies into a single unit of intervention in which personal narratives, storytelling, read-alouds and grammatical review are bundled into a holistic strategy for language development. Integrating these domains into their personal experience allows for a direct engagement with each of the students. Facilitators strive to create meaningful links between these community spaces and their schooling practices, but they are well aware that children are pushed to become school learners much more than they are encouraged to be players, artists, talkers and friends (Genishi & Dyson, 2009).

Diversity and multilingualism

An important characteristic of the community and the programs at Tepeyac at large is the remarkable diversity they embody. During the literacy hour, the program puts all students of the same age range together, regardless of the language they speak (Spanish, English, Mixteco, etc.). During that time, students interact with each other and build upon each others' work. For example:

Juan, a 10-year-old Mixteco boy is drawing an elaborate picture of what a farm looks like. Nayeli, who is sitting next to him, grabs a brown crayon and draws a round animal. She then tells him, 'conejo' [rabbit]. He repeats, 'conejo' and then writes down 'leko' [rabbit in Mixteco] on his paper. When the activity is done, the teacher comes down to pick up one of the drawings and prompts a follow up activity on the board. She then takes both their drawings and writes: *'Perro*/Dog' on the blackboard. Nayeli reacts and says: *'No es perro; conejo!'* [It's not a dog; it is a rabbit!] To this, Juan draws a dog on his piece of paper, and writes *'tìnà/perro'*. By the end of the activity everyone was using *'tìnà/*dog/*perro'* and *'leko/* rabbit/*conejo'*. (Classroom observation, 22 April 2010)

While the exposure to these three languages was not planned or scripted by the teacher, it became a central element of the activity as a result of the children's interaction, and more specifically, their burgeoning ways of grasping what surrounds them and trying to communicate it to others.

This exchange would have seldom happened in Mexico, given the segregation of indigenous communities from most Spanish-speaking communities and the general disdain of white *mestizos* for indigenous languages. The efforts of bilingual–intercultural education in Mexico have evolved, but they often meet with resistance by communities on the ground. Indigenous groups argue that, for education to be truly intercultural, white mestizos should also be learning indigenous languages. This is the paradox of the immigration experience: it is in exile where these Indigenous languages and Spanish begin to learn how to interact with one another, for they share the transformative challenges of living and speaking in a new land. In this NYC community, many students embrace their unity of being Mexican while acknowledging their linguistic and cultural differences. It is in this context where new ethnolinguistic communities emerge.

Not all Mixteco speakers feel the same way, however. Many parents of students in the program enrolled their Mixteco children under the assumption that they would learn English. Some would rather not have them speak Spanish at all. There were cases in which Mixteco families preferred to avoid all communication with their children than speak Mixteco to them: 'porque aquí no les sirve de nada y no más los discriminan' ['because they can't make any use of it here and they are discriminated against'; interview, 12 May 2010]. This Mixteco mother's perception of discrimination reveals that members of the Mexican community are aware of their language hierarchies. Some families think it best not to speak Mixteco, only Spanish, which they perceive to have higher status. Others decide to bury both Mixteco and Spanish completely in favor of English, which they see as key for educational success in their children.

Despite the different approaches families have to their children's language development, their active participation in the community and in the rest of Tepeyac's activities does make a difference in the way these children relate to their culture and their countries of origin. Facilitators working to support the language and literacy practices of these children all evidenced a complex understanding of their language development, allowing them to freely use their languages while still providing a rigorous structure from which to work. While bilingual activities were held at specific times and with scripted methods, it was evident that the language practices to which children were exposed were being shaped by the larger context of Tepeyac's activities, and more importantly by the sense of belonging they felt by participating in these community efforts.

The Roots program reports positive outcomes in terms of academic achievement, and while striving to provide a space in which these children can have a current and active connection to their country, the program coordinator asserts that the name is an unfortunate choice for their philosophy: 'We are not only about the roots; we are not talking about the pyramids and the folk culture, although history is an important part of our program. We want these children to recognize themselves today, in the many ways Mexico is part of them and they are part of the country, whether they were born there or not' (interview, 3 May 2010). This echoes García's (2005, 2009b) assertion that, while heritage languages may be a noble effort in the framing of language revitalization, it is a step towards the past, and away from bilingualism and the dynamics of the present: 'By leaving the languages in the past, the term heritage languages connotes something that one holds onto vaguely as one's remembrances, but certainly not something that is used in the present or that can be projected into the future' (García, 2005: 601). Further, García asserts that Spanish in the US is not simply a heritage language, but one that is spoken, alongside English, by millions of people. This philosophy reflects a balance between 'roots' and 'wings'; roots keep these communities grounded to their culture through different languages and voices, and wings allow them to freely travel in the present, from one country to another, from one language to the other in a dialectic exercise of their identity and their dreams.

Conclusion

Much attention has been paid to the role of schools in providing supportive learning environments for diverse populations such as Mexican students in NYC. However, inquiry into the potential of community efforts in bilingual education has lagged. Bilingual programs in schools can learn from the strategies employed in these communities. In particular, this chapter has described how Asociación Tepeyac draws from students' transnational backgrounds to develop integrated language strategies in the context of multilingualism. Bilingual education in the context of the organization is designed with the goal of supporting students through their educational trajectories. Thus, these community efforts are not isolated from formal schooling goals, and represent a useful construct from which to envision stronger collaboration between schools and communities.

In today's global scenario, the case of the Mexican community and the efforts of organizations such as Tepeyac mirror the situations of multiple communities in countries throughout the world. In the course of its life, Tepeyac has been part of exchanges with organizations in France, Spain and Morroco which work under very similar conditions. The case of the community described in these pages is certainly not unique to New York City, although there are particularities to the Mexican case and the nature of the immigration flows.

The lessons that can be drawn from exploring this case point to the increasing need to connect community education efforts to formal schooling processes. Demographic shifts occurring today are evidencing a strong disconnect between classroom curricula and the students they serve. The role of many of these community organizations has been to pick up where the schools have left off, often trying to complement with limited resources the work of schools. Teachers and community facilitators have much to learn from each other. Community settings such as Tepeyac privilege the culture and background of the populations they serve. Their language development strategies are often driven more by intuition than by academic rigor, and many of them could benefit from effective teaching strategies from seasoned teachers in school settings.

Students today, embodied by the faces of the Mexican children who diligently attend Tepeyac's after-school program, are able to produce their own bilingual development strategies if they are given the freedom to think, speak, grasp, dream and dynamically construct their own language and their own space. Their language development is fostered by the community at large and the different variables that are meaningful for them, whether it is art, sports or a simple nostalgic souvenir of their life in the countryside. The complexity of this process further points to the need to go beyond heritage language programs and acknowledge the role of communities in shaping their own goals for bilingual development, which are rooted in the present and their nuanced identities.

The case of Tepeyac shows how community efforts reshape the status of Spanish in a city that has long battled with Spanish as the language of the poor, the undocumented, the Other. While the number of Mexicans in NYC is increasing rapidly, as is the Latino population in general, these numbers do not accurately reflect the nuances in their language practices and their culture and identity (García, 2009b). The transnational condition of both the programs and the students evidenced in this case constitutes a call to go beyond the nation-state to understand these language processes, and to draw from their linguistic and cultural resources to design effective educational strategies.

3 Raising Bilingual and Bicultural Bangladeshi-American Children in New York City: Perspectives from Educators and Parents in a Bengali Community Program

Ruhma Choudhury

Introduction

Upon reaching their destination, Bangladeshis in the US, like other ethnic communities, are inevitably faced with the demands of assimilating and acculturating to the dominant culture of their new environment. While the desire to succeed is high, severing ties with the home culture and language for many is inconceivable. In the adaptation and acculturation process, Bangladeshis (ethnically Bengalis) continue to maintain ties with their communities in the hope of preserving their cultural distinctiveness. In this respect, community-based Bengali schools play a major role in keeping the language and culture alive and well. This paper examines how one such school educates American children of Bengali descent so that they grow up to be bilingual and biliterate.

In providing a portrait of the Udichi Performing Arts School, I demonstrate the ways in which a community whose particular history is vitally tied to its language seeks to teach its language and distinct cultural traditions. In doing so, the school promotes a philosophy that binds them to a larger humanity. It is through this distinctiveness and universal quality that this school articulates the aspirations of this immigrant community as new/bilingual Americans.

Bengali Language and Cultural Identity

Bengali[1] is an Indo-Aryan language that evolved around 1000–1200 AD from the Magadhi Prakrit, a vernacular form of the ancient Sanskrit language. Three eras mark the history of Bengali: Old Bengali (100–1400 AD), Middle Bengali (1400–1800 AD) and Modern Bengali (since 1800 AD). Old Bengali survives through *Caryagiti*, Buddhist devotional songs. These mystic verses are considered to be the oldest records of the written Bengali language. The Middle Bengali period witnessed the rise of the narrative poetry genre, and religious themes mostly dominated the content. On the other hand, Modern Bengali – the Bengali that is spoken and written today – emerged during the literary renaissance of Bengali in the 19th century, initiated through the works of Michael Madhusudan Datta and Bankim Chandra Chatterjee, who were considered the founders of modern Bengali literature. The language developed further through the works of novelists such as Rabindranath Tagore, Buddhdeb Basu and Sunil Gangopadhyay.

Bengali has two literary styles. Until the 1930s, *Shadhubhasa*, the literary style based on Middle Bengali of the 16th century, was used in formal situations and in writing, while *Choltibhasha*, modeled on the dialect spoken in Nadia, an Indian district on the border with Bangladesh, was the medium of more informal discourse. Today, both *Shadhubhasa* and *Choltibhasha* are used as the standard written forms. The main differences between the two involve forms of pronouns and verb conjugations.

Spoken Bengali has wider variations. The accepted spoken standard form of Bengali in both Bangladesh and West Bengal of India is based on the dialect of Nadia, but there are a few noticeable differences between the Standard Bengali of Bangladesh and that of West Bengal. The main differences are of a lexical nature, and these lexical alternations are mainly due to distinct religious and cultural traditions of the predominantly Muslim Bangladesh and largely Hindu West Bengal. The standard used in Bangladesh, for instance, has a high proportion of words derived from Persian and Arabic. A case in point is the greeting that the Muslim Bengalis/Bangladeshis use. They greet with the Arabic expression *assalamualaikum* instead of *nômoshkar*, its Sanskrit counterpart.

Various regional dialects exist, but most dialects bear a close resemblance to the spoken Standard Bengali and are generally understood by speakers of other dialects. However, there are some dialects, particularly those from the Chittagong and Sylhet regions, that only superficially resemble the Standard. Both Sylheti and Chittagonian differ from the Standard in their pronunciation and vocabulary, making the Standard and these dialects mutually unintelligible.[2]

Herder (1986/1772) argued that languages create nations. His thesis rings true for the Bengali language and Bangladesh. After the independence of India and Pakistan (comprising East and West Pakistan) in 1947, the Government of Pakistan declared Urdu to be the state language, a decision that Bengalis in East Pakistan (present day Bangladesh) opposed, demanding that Bengali be awarded official status alongside Urdu. When this was denied, a series of protests broke out in support of Bengali, the most notable of which was the Language Movement of 1952. On 21 February of that year, several students were killed in a protest rally, which then led to prolonged civil unrest. The Pakistani government was forced to relent and award Bengali official status in 1956 (Imam, 2005). However, by then Bengalis were geared for full independence and went to war to gain it in 1971. Later, in 2000, UNESCO declared 21 February International Mother Language Day (Imam, 2005). Over the years, the Bengali language has become a symbol of pride for Bangladeshis, living both at home and abroad.

With nearly 230 million speakers, Bengali now ranks sixth among the world languages. It is primarily spoken in Bangladesh and the Indian states of West Bengal and Tripura. It is also spoken where Bangladeshi and Indian Bengali diasporas are located in the UK, the US, Malaysia, Canada, Australia and the Arab Gulf states, where several million expatriate workers reside.

Bangladeshis in the US

Bangladeshis comprise one of the recent waves of immigration to the US, but they belong to one of the fastest growing ethnic groups, based on the percentage growth from 1990 to 2000 (US Census Bureau, 2000). This is largely due to the Immigration and Naturalization Act of 1965, which abolished the national origins quota system. According to the US Census Bureau (2007a), there are 76,048 Bangladeshis residing in the US. Many of these are visa recipients from the Diversity Visa Lottery Program. The vast majority of them are concentrated in large metropolitan cities such as New York City, Los Angeles, Chicago, Atlanta, Washington, DC, Miami, Houston and Dallas (Jones, 2010). The majority of these immigrants maintain strong ties to

Bangladesh (Jones, 2010). Unlike the British-Bangladeshis, who are mostly Sylhetis from the Sylhet district, Bangladeshi-Americans represent Bengalis from various districts of Bangladesh.

Bangladeshis in New York City

New York City (NYC) houses the largest Bangladeshi population in the US. According to the US Census Bureau (2000), New York City's Bangladeshi population increased by 471% from 1990 to 2000 (from 4955 to 28,269). About 85% of Bangladeshi New Yorkers were foreign-born in 2000, and more than 77% of these immigrants came to the US between 1990 and 2000. Census data also show that more than 4% of the City's Asian population is Bangladeshi. Compared with other Asian New Yorkers, the Bangladeshi population has slightly higher educational levels, but is considerably less fluent in English, experiences higher poverty, earns lower incomes and lives in larger households (US Census Bureau, 2000). More recent data indicate that 64,874 Bangladeshis live in NYC (American Community Survey, 2007a). The majority live in Queens, with 35,990 residents, Brooklyn, with 13,551, the Bronx with 10,928, Manhattan, with 3253, and finally, Staten Island, with 1152 (American Community Survey, 2007a).

Bangladeshi Students in NYC Public Schools

Valdés (2001: 38) defines a heritage language speaker as 'someone who is raised in a home where a non-English language is spoken and who speaks or at least understands the language and is to some degree bilingual in the home language and in English'. Most Bangladeshi students in NYC schools fit this description. Bengali ranks third among the most common home languages of students who are learning English in NYC public schools (City of New York Department of Education, 2011). Of the 154,466 students designated as English Language Learners (ELLs) in NYC, 3.5% (5396 ELLs) speak Bengali at home (City of New York Department of Education, 2011). In the current NYC educational system, Bangladeshi-American children have limited opportunities to develop their Bengali proficiency, however.

Community-based private Bengali language schools offer Bangladeshi-American children language and culture instruction for a few hours during weekends. While the primary focus is to teach Bengali language and culture, these schools provide more than what has been termed 'heritage language education' (i.e. the maintenance of home language). In fact, the goal, as the description of Udichi Performing Arts School in the next section demonstrates, is to promote children's development of bilingualism and biliteracy.

There are several Bengali community language schools, of which the most notable are the Bangladesh Institute of Performing Arts, established in 1993, and the Udichi Performing Arts School. These schools are usually run privately and are staffed by volunteers from the community. Even though they serve an important function for the Bangladeshi community by providing Bengali education to the children, their work is often seen as unrelated to mainstream public education. For instance, NYC public schools rarely recognize the Bengali education that the children receive in these community-based schools. As such, the children do not get any credit for taking lessons there. The situation of these Bengali schools parallels the predicament of other community bilingual schools in that their efforts receive little attention. Thus they remain largely invisible to the larger community (Tse, 2001a, 2001b).

Udichi Performing Arts School

Language is the means through which cultural heritage is obtained, reconstructed and passed on (Skutnabb-Kangas, 1981; Sung, 1985). This section draws on observations and interviews at the Udichi Performing Arts School in Jackson Heights, Queens, to understand one school's efforts to provide education in Bengali as a means of conveying and reconstructing heritage. The purpose of the study was to understand how the Bangladeshi community educates its children and the potential impact of community-based educational programs on children's bilingual and bicultural development. Extensive observations of school and classroom practices were undertaken in the summer of 2010. Interviews with three teachers, four parents and a school administrator provide further insight into the school's philosophy, policies and practices as they relate to educating Bangladeshi-American children.

The Udichi Performing Arts School is a non-profit organization that is privately run and funded. It began in a garage in Queens as a performing arts school but has expanded over the years to become one of the few Bengali schools to offer both Bengali language and performing arts classes. The school moved to its current location in a public school in Jackson Heights in 2003 to accommodate its growing population (129 students are registered, but only 62 of them attend classes regularly). Each year, it obtains a permit from the NYC Board of Education to use the school premises. Students who come to Udichi are aged six years and over, with the majority falling within the 6–11 age group and attending public NYC elementary schools. Around 20 students go to middle school and 10 go to high school. The children may enroll any time throughout the year. There are 14 instructors, six of whom work without pay. When asked about their voluntary service, one of the teachers explained, 'We do volunteer work because we want to contribute. We are doing something for our community' (interview, 15 August 2010). The teachers who get paid receive a token amount for their services.

Udichi is a weekend program in which classes are held every Sunday from 12 noon until 6 p.m. The day commences with the assembly, at which the national anthems of both Bangladesh and the US are sung. Inclusion of both anthems suggests that the school authorities are attentive to the children's multiple allegiances. Immediately following the assembly, students are led to their Bengali and performing arts classes. They are required to take lessons in Bengali along with music, art, dance and/or tabla (Indian drum) classes. The Bengali classes are held in the cafeteria, where four to five students congregate around a table for their lesson. Each table is considered a class, and there are six to seven such classes that run concurrently. Teachers reported that they use both Bengali and English initially to communicate with the children, but they gradually switch to Standard Bengali as students become more proficient in the language.

The dance classes are held in the auditorium while music and tabla classes are held in classrooms. Each class runs for one hour. At the end of the hour, students rotate so that those who were in Bengali classes take one of the performing arts classes (e.g. music, dance or tabla), while those who were in performing arts classes come to the cafeteria for their Bengali lessons. The classes for children are over by 3:30 pm. The late afternoon classes are scheduled for more advanced students and adult artists in Udichi Shilpi Ghosti NY, a performing arts group of professional singers and dancers,[3] who use this time to practice or rehearse for cultural shows. The children also partake in these functions, which showcase their achievements. In fact, these events serve as a means to recruit prospective students whose parents, charmed by the performances, enroll their children in Udichi to learn Bengali language and culture.

Policies, practices and beliefs

The school is open to all who are interested in learning Bengali language and culture; at present, the students enrolled are Americans of Bangladeshi descent.[4] While the Bangladeshi-American children generally receive a strong English education in the US public school system, Roni,[5] the lead administrator, has observed that their Bengali education is mostly neglected in schools. He asserts that programs such as Udichi represent an option for children who want to develop proficiency in Bengali (interview, 15 August 2010). Likewise, the teachers see the language as a bridge, connecting the children and their relatives in the US and Bangladesh. For example, one of the teachers, Sumi, told me that, if children know Bengali, they 'can talk to their grandparents'. She further added, 'If they love their parents then they should learn their language' (interview, 8 August 2010).

The program promotes a Bengali-only policy on the school premises to increase opportunities for students to use their Bengali. To this end, the teachers try to encourage children to use Bengali by pretending not to understand English, especially with children who have been at Udichi more than a few months. For example, Sraboni, one of the teachers, insists that students communicate with her in Bengali at all times: 'sometimes when children ask us something in English, we say we don't understand English, so explain to us in Bengali' (interview, 15 August 2010). However, when children struggle to express themselves in Bengali, she allows them to speak in English, which she then interprets into Bengali and gets the children to repeat after her. Through mimicking Sraboni, the children get to practice the language.

The school also serves as a meeting place for parents, who often decide to stay for a chat with other guardians while classes are in session. Roni considers this to be beneficial to children's language development because these adult interactions provide concrete examples of language use.

The program aims to develop learners' sense of Bengali pride and identity by familiarizing the children with a 1000-year-old Bengali tradition, which Roni refers to as 'Bengalism'. He maintains that this foundational school philosophy is not defined by 'religion, gender, or political affiliation, but by our humanity' (interview, 8 August 2010). When asked to expand, he explains that 'Bengalism' focuses on commonalities to which Bengalis can relate (e.g. common language, literature, food) rather than issues that can be divisive (e.g. religious and political affiliations). As such, 'Bengalism' is promoted through activities that unite Bengalis, such as the celebrations of the Language Movement and the Bengali New Year in which all Bengalis can participate.

An ancillary goal of the program is to help develop children's social consciousness by raising awareness about social responsibilities towards family and society. In discussing this concern, Roni maintains, 'While the US society stresses upon individual rights and freedom, we teach children about social responsibilities through stories of sacrifices made to free Bangladesh' (interview, 8 August 2010). He feels that these stories of sacrifice teach children to be good citizens who are committed to serving their families, community and the larger society.

Curriculum

The curriculum aims to develop in students an appreciation for Bengali culture and knowledge of Bangladeshi history, while concurrently developing their Bengali language. Considerable effort has been made to create a curriculum that adopts the philosophy underpinning 'Bengalism'. In line with this philosophy, children are introduced to key events leading to Bangladesh's inception. Among these, the most notable are the Language Movement of 1952, and Independence Day and Victory Day, celebrating Bangladesh's independence from Pakistan. Bengali New Year is also presented as an important cultural landmark. Each year, Udichi organizes cultural functions commemorating these special days in which the children participate through activities such as the recitation of poetry, traditional songs, and dance. Their parents volunteer to organize these events, offering help by bringing food and decorating the stage.

The curriculum is designed to teach and reinforce the acquisition of all four language skills: listening, speaking, reading and writing. Four levels of Bengali classes are offered and children are placed in each based on their proficiency. Each level takes approximately one year to complete. At the first level, students identify the letters of the Bengali alphabet and recognize sound–letter associations while simultaneously learning the spelling rules. At the next level, they form words by combining letters. They also memorize nursery rhymes and songs, such as Tagore's 'Amra Shobai Raja' [We are All Kings], which they perform during cultural events.[6] Once they are in the third level, the students are taught to make sentences. In addition, they read stories, such as fairy tales, poetry and nursery rhymes. These stories are often taken from textbooks used in third and fourth grades in Bangladesh. Some instructors supplement these by using stories that they themselves write. At the last level, the teachers prepare children for public speaking. The children are also required to read long passages and write paragraphs on given topics.

The children are assessed throughout the year to measure their progress, which in Roni's view has to be 'flexible and cannot be too rigid' (personal communication, 16 August 2010). The children are given three exams at different times of the year and their cumulative score is used as the major criterion for passing the level. In addition to that, the teachers constantly monitor children's performance through such means as class participation and quizzes to determine student progress.

The school follows a 'no social promotion' policy, whereby children are retained if they perform below level expectations. Even though the policy is the main reason behind student attrition (every year the school loses about 10 students), Roni defends this policy because he believes children with comparable language competencies should be put in the same level. When a child falls behind, he instructs teachers 'to give extra time to help students move to the next level but that is all we can do' (interview, 8 August 2010). He argues that it does not benefit the student to promote him or her to the next level without sufficient preparation to meet the challenges that await him or her. In general, it takes four years for a student to graduate, and after the completion of the program, the children get certificates. Roni reports that he has provided 25–30 certificates over the last few years.

While adhering to the goals outlined in the curriculum, the teachers exercise freedom in pursuing their distinctive teaching styles, which are influenced by their personalities and their teaching philosophies. Sumi, for example, follows a bottom-up approach to pronunciation because she considers it to be very important in language acquisition:[7]

> I put a lot of emphasis on pronunciation. I get them to repeat words and to get the right pronunciation. For many this [Bengali] is a new language. Many children come who cannot speak [Standard Bengali]. They don't speak Bengali at home. These children speak dialects at home so that we have to work on their pronunciation. (Interview, 15 August 2010)

Thus, Sumi encourages her students to pay close attention to letter and sound associations because she thinks a full phonetic and phonological explanation of the sounds is necessary. In her classes, students can use English when needed. She gets them to translate materials such as nursery rhymes and short poems from English to Bengali and vice versa. To keep students motivated, she brings authentic materials such as newspapers to class; the students use them to identify letters, words, etc. For advanced groups, she gets them to read the paper out loud and monitors their pronunciation.

Unlike Sumi, Sraboni's focus is more macro, and she believes that the purpose of education is to produce socially responsible citizens. She is also a strong supporter of authentic materials in the classroom and advocates using technology to teach students Bengali. For instance, not all children get the chance to visit Bangladesh annually, so she suggests using video clips of famous sites to familiarize students with various tourist attractions in Bangladesh. She further adds that video clips such as documentaries on poverty or homelessness can also be used to develop students' social conscience. By watching them, she believes students may grow motivated to help.

Selim, on the other hand, focuses more on fluency. He argues that lessons need to be made interesting and fun; otherwise the students will lose interest in Bengali 'if we begin by teaching them academic Bengali from the beginning or give difficult words' (interview, 15 August 2010). According to Selim, 'We have to start by teaching simple vocabulary'. He thus proposes teaching high-frequency words, because 'they will encounter these words in reading and on TV [Bengali channel] or when they hear spoken Bengali'. He maintains that, if too much emphasis is placed on language accuracy, the children lose interest in the lessons, resulting in withdrawal from the school.

Although each instructor has his or her own distinctive style of teaching, they all agree that the children acquire more than language at Udichi. The children's Bengali identity is constructed through linguistic and cultural references to which they are exposed at the school.

Parents' and children's views

According to parents of students at Udichi, they enroll their children in Bengali schools in the hope that their children will grow up to be bilingual and biliterate. It is important for them that their children learn to speak, read and write Bengali for a number of reasons. First, they believe children can stay connected with immediate and extended families through Bengali. For example, Lina reports that her daughter uses Bengali to talk to her grandmother in Bangladesh. Since Lina's daughter is a fluent speaker of Bengali, she is able to act as an interpreter for Bengali parents at her public school. In other words, bilingual Bengali children can extend help to the community through their knowledge of Bengali. Lina also encourages her daughter to continue polishing her Bengali in the hope that her additional language will open doors to better educational and employment opportunities.

Parents also believe that knowing Bengali will help their children embrace their cultural heritage. For them, Bengali serves as a vehicle for cultural identity. For this reason, many encourage their children not just to learn the language, but also to develop an appreciation for Bengali songs and dance. Rima articulates the connection between language and cultural identity in saying:

> We are Bengalis. If we do not teach our children Bengali, our son will slowly move away from our culture; a distance will be created and he will forget our culture. If he forgets the language, he will forget – maybe not the parents – everything else about the culture. Through language, a link is created. I will continue sending him to this school as long as he is not fluent or cannot read and write in Bangla well. (Interview, 8 August 2010)

Other parents mirror Rima's concern that, if they fail to teach their children Bengali, there will be language barriers between American-born Bangladeshi children and their relatives in Bangladesh. If Bengali is not taught from an early age, they will become more reluctant to communicate in it afterwards. With time, these children will be emotionally alienated from their parents.

In the opinion of parents and teachers, the benefits of learning Bengali are not as obvious to children, however, at least not at first. The teachers and parents I spoke with maintained that 95% of children attend Bengali classes because of parental insistence; they come because their parents bring them. The second reason is friends. For example, Rima says the her son comes to school because, 'he has some [public] school friends here' (interview, 15 August 2010). Similarly, Parvin maintains that her daughter is a regular attendee because she has made many friends here who are from different public schools. In fact, Udichi offers children from different NYC public schools the opportunity to forge friendships. As Roni points out, 'one child might live in Ditmars, another from [sic] Woodside, and they can meet and have fun' (interview, 8 August 2010). Others, Lina observed, 'come to relax and to take a break from their other life' (interview, 15 August 2010).

Once they enroll, children begin to develop interest in Bengali language and performing arts subjects. Rima's son, for instance, 'enjoys painting. He is slowly getting interested in Bengali songs and now wants to practice singing' (interview, 8 August 2010). She believes that children, even those who are reluctant to attend school at first, gradually begin to enjoy what Udichi has to offer.

Challenges Faced by Udichi

Udichi has numerous internal challenges. First, funding is an issue. The current tuition fee is US$35 per month, but the majority of the students who have been attending school for more than a year still pay US$25. This money is used primarily to pay the teachers and the security personnel's salaries. The rest of the expenses are paid with the money earned from events organized by Udichi Shilpi Ghosti or from the personal funds of the administrators.

The second issue is the number of instructional hours. On average, a student gets 25 hours of instruction a year, which Roni considers insufficient to develop language fluency and accuracy. Given the situation with instructional hours, he maintains that the progress a child makes in a year is marginal, so he tries to give parents a realistic expectation about their children's achievement by explaining that developing literacy skills in Bengali takes a long time. Given this situation, he argues that children need to be immersed in Bengali both at the community school and at home if they are to become fluent in Bengali. To this end, he insists that the instruction at school has to be reinforced and supplemented by learning at home.

While parents are committed to bringing their children to these schools, Roni complains that there is often no follow-up support at home:

We need parents' support to make the children's education a success. We request them to go over with their children whatever we teach here three to four times a week at home. Some parents cooperate, while others are not able to give children time with their assignments and homework. That is the case with not many parents. As a result, students' proficiency in Bengali varies. (Interview, 14 August 2010)

Thus, Roni wishes that parents' commitment extended beyond simply bringing children to Udichi. Assisting with their assignments would hasten student progress in the language. When asked about this issue, Rima, one of the parents, defended the parents' seeming indifference, which she attributed to their lack of knowledge of performing arts subjects, such as music or dance, and to their busy life schedule. Despite good intentions, many parents are unable to help their children with their home assignments simply because they work double shifts and are left too exhausted by the end of the day to assist them with their homework. The parents' work commitments also affect children's attendance; for instance, some children either come to school late or leave early because of their parents' work schedules. Missing too many instructional hours can negatively affect learning outcomes.

Lack of motivation on the students' part is another issue that Roni and some teachers report. In their opinion, some of the children resent coming to school on weekends. Roni explained that this is more common with adolescents, but student attrition can begin as early as eight years of age as the children become more involved with their public school education. Sraboni attributes the attrition to the children's failure to see the value in learning Bengali. In her view, the children's main focus is English language acquisition, which explains to her why they are reluctant to invest in the maintenance of the mother language. Hence, some ask her, 'What will I get from learning Bangla?' or 'What is going to happen with Bangla?' In response, she encourages them by saying, 'When you go to Bangladesh, you can talk to your grandparents' (interview, 15 August 2010). By emphasizing this 'language as a bridge' aspect, she hopes to retain as many students as possible.

Another reason for student attrition is the mismatch between the parents' and the institution's philosophies of teaching and learning. For instance, many want their children to learn Bengali the way they were taught in Bangladesh and often complain to Roni, 'My child learns only two words today. That is not enough' (interview, 8 August 2010). They put pressure on teachers and when their demands are not met they often remove their children from the school. Despite these challenges, Udichi strives to provide the best educational environment it can to foster students' language development and pride in their heritage.

Conclusion

Community-based schools such as Udichi serve as rich linguistic and cultural resources where an American child of Bangladeshi descent can become bilingual and biliterate. By promoting bilingual proficiency, these schools provide students with the necessary skills and predisposition to work in an increasingly globalized world. In spite of these benefits, the community-based language schools' efforts to educate students remain largely unappreciated in mainstream society. Labeled as 'heritage schools', their work is often seen as unrelated to the education students receive in public schools. In their case, the term 'heritage schools' is a misnomer, because as mentioned earlier, these community-based schools aim to support students' development of *both* English and ethnic languages.

Currently, the responsibility for maintenance and development of children's bilingualism lies with the families and the ethnic community. Families and community-based schools alone cannot preserve the children's home culture and language. The proverb 'It takes a village to raise a child' is certainly appropriate in this context. Public school teachers and administrators need to be made aware of the benefits of community language education (Compton, 2001). Community-based schools can work in conjunction with public schools to provide children with a rich and diverse educational experience. Shin (2006), for instance, suggests that ethnic communities and public schools could collaborate to offer classes on language and culture for teachers as part of their professional development. Children could also take classes in their own languages to fulfill the second language requirement of the public school system. These efforts would ensure the survival of languages other than English in the US.

Notes

(1) Bengali is the English word for Bangla, the national language of Bangladesh and an official language of India.
(2) While most speakers of Sylheti and Chittagonian would understand Standard Bengali (from exposure via media, education, etc.), the reverse is not always true. Speakers of Standard Bengali who do not identify themselves as natives of these regions would hardly understand these dialects.
(3) Many parents of the children also participate in Udichi Shilpi Ghosti.

(4) Currently all students enrolled are of Bangladeshi descent. However, the school welcomes anyone interested in learning Bengali language and culture.
(5) Each participant is assigned a pseudonym to protect his or her identity.
(6) Rabindranath Tagore is the poet laureate of India and Bangladesh.
(7) A bottom-up approach engages language learning from the most basic building blocks, such as words, and then proceeds to more complex structures.

4 *Salaam! Namaste!*: Indian and Pakistani Community-based Efforts Towards Mother Tongue Language Maintenance

Ameena Ghaffar-Kucher
and Anup P. Mahajan

Introduction

With the accelerated interconnectedness of the global economy, there is an unprecedented need for American citizens to develop competencies in languages beyond English. Yet opportunities to learn languages other than English in the US are limited for many students to a handful of languages such as French, Spanish, Chinese and, more recently, Arabic. Moreover, for immigrants who do not speak these languages, the prospects of developing literacy in their native languages are particularly limited. Research shows that, without active intervention, these languages are lost over time on both an individual and a community level, and typically die out within three generations (Wiley, 1996). Thus, efforts to maintain community languages often rest on the shoulders of the particular immigrant communities.

Over 40 years ago, Fishman *et al.* (1966) noted the influence of various community-based institutions, such as language schools and religious congregations, in preserving languages within ethnolinguistic communities. This is exemplified in some South Asian communities in the US. Despite a steady influx of immigration from Bangladesh, India, Nepal, Pakistan and Sri Lanka over four decades, the US K–12 education system has made minimal progress in developing resources for South Asian language learning (Gambhir, 2001; Shinge, 2008). As with other ethnic groups in the US, many South Asian communities have responded to this landscape by marshaling existing local resources to meet the needs of language maintenance with varying success. In this chapter, we focus on the particular issues and challenges that face Indian and Pakistani communities in Queens and Brooklyn for the teaching of Punjabi, Hindi and Urdu to school-age children. Although funding, teacher training, appropriate instructional materials and administrative infrastructure remain problematic, many South Asian adults are actively involved in the maintenance and development of their various languages through a variety of language schools and programs. This involvement stems from a concern for passing on to future generations the essence of South Asian cultural and religious heritage. South Asian immigrant parents often have a strong desire for their children to retain these traits while simultaneously adapting to American culture (Warsi, 2003). As such, culture and religion are intricately woven into community-based efforts to maintain one's language, or in some cases, to learn new ones.

In this chapter, we explore essential issues related to South Asian community language education and provide two thumbnail case studies of programs administered by Indian communities in the New York metropolitan area, specifically in the borough of Queens: a weekend Hindi program in Flushing, and a Punjabi program administered through a local Sikh temple in Richmond Hill. The permanence of these programs provides a noteworthy contrast to the absence of Urdu language programs in the New York-based Pakistani communities, an issue we also address in this chapter.

While members of the Punjabi, Hindi and Urdu language communities share a general purpose and broad ethnic commonalities, the case studies presented here show that significant differences exist between these groups regarding their approach to language education and the role ascribed to language in shaping cultural, religious and second-generation identity. We engage in an analysis of emerging trends and themes, highlighting the role of community-based institutions in immigrant language maintenance. Key to understanding this role is the recognition that Indian and Pakistani community-based efforts are not solely focused on teaching language and culture, but also offer spaces to use them, through interaction with peers and adults. These community-based schools are the places to nurture ethnic identity.

We begin with an overview of the sociolinguistic context of Hindi, Punjabi, and Urdu. Following this discussion, we provide a synopsis of the immigration history of Indians and Pakistanis to the US. We then describe, broadly, the status of Hindi, Urdu and Punjabi within these communities, and conclude the chapter with a presentation of two successful programs for community-based language maintenance.

From One Diverse Land to Another

The symphony of languages heard in New York City can be a daunting experience for newcomers, but this diversity is familiar to Indian and Pakistani immigrants. The Indian subcontinent is home to over 200 distinct languages and thousands of dialectical variants. Thus while the linguistic symphony in New York City sounds different from that of Lahore or Delhi, there are many familiar melodies in the presence of several South Asian languages in the City. This chapter focuses primarily on three of the major languages spoken in the region and among the South Asian diaspora in the boroughs of New York City: Hindi, Punjabi and Urdu. Within the Indian subcontinent, Hindi is the most widely spoken language and has over 400 million speakers; it is also one of India's official languages. Urdu is the official language of Pakistan, and although it is widely spoken and understood, it is the mother tongue of only 6–8% of the 170 million-strong population. Punjabi is the primary language spoken in the Punjab region, which straddles the border between Pakistan and India and constitutes a province in the former and a state in the latter. The region known as the Punjab is the largest distinct regional area in the subcontinent.[1]

The relationship between Hindi, Punjabi and Urdu requires some explanation, as there is much misinformation about these languages, which has implications for education policy. Urdu and Hindi are mutually understandable. Both are Indo-European languages that were formerly known collectively as 'Hindustani'. In fact, many would argue that they were essentially the same language until their scripts were modified during the early 18th century for political reasons (King, 1994). During this time, the ruling British colonizers politicized the Urdu/Hindi languages to deepen the growing rift between the Muslims and Hindus by encouraging the idea of Urdu as a language for the Muslims and Hindi as a language for Hindus (Das, 1991). They did this by *Sanscritizing* Hindi and *Persianizing* Urdu (Das, 1991: 142). Subsequently, through efforts at Fort Williams College, Hindi adopted the Devanagari script (which is also the modern day Sanskrit script), while Urdu adopted the Shahmukhi script, which is a Punjabi script derived from the Nasta'liq font of modified Arabic. Urdu is also heavily influenced by Persian. Thus today Hindi has a growing Sanskrit lexicon and Urdu a more

Persian-oriented one. As a result, language has become a strong signifier of identity, with Hindi being associated with Hindus and Urdu with Muslims.

The case of Punjabi is as complicated. There are in fact two distinct Punjabi scripts. In Indian Punjab, where Punjabi is primarily spoken by the Sikh population, it is written in Gurmukhi script, created in the late 17th century by Guru Nanak, the founder of the Sikh religion. Thus, the language is strongly entwined with religion. In Pakistan, however, Punjabi is written in the Shahmukhi script. Thus, while Urdu and Punjabi in Pakistan are written in the same script, they sound quite different. However, most Urdu speakers can understand Punjabi speakers and vice versa, although they are not mutually intelligible like Hindi and Urdu. While Indian Punjabi is a thriving written and spoken language, Pakistani Punjabi is fast becoming an oral language and is rarely written anymore. This may be partially attributed to the push for Urdu as the official language and medium of formal instruction in schools in Pakistan's Punjab.

In the US, most people's understanding of Punjabi is that of Gurmukhi Punjabi, in great part because of the vibrant Sikh community and their efforts to maintain their language in both written and oral forms. Thus, in order to distinguish themselves from Sikh-Punjabis, Pakistani-Punjabis in the US often claim that they are Urdu speakers. As a result, demographic information regarding Punjabi in the US usually refers to Gurmukhi Punjabi, while Urdu tends to conflate Urdu and Shahmukhi Punjabi. For the sake of simplicity, in this chapter, when we refer to Punjabi, we are referring to the language and script of Indian-Sikh Punjabis. Before continuing on to explain the different approaches between these groups in terms of language maintenance, we provide a brief overview of the migration history of immigrants from the South Asian subcontinent (specifically India and Pakistan).

South Asian Community Immigration History

South Asians have had a long immigration history in the US. The first South Asian, known simply as 'the man from Madras', is documented as early as 1790 – a visit to Salem, Massachusetts by an Indian from Madras who was accompanying a sea captain (Gibson, 1988; Najam, 2007). Prior to the early 1900s, visits by Indians to American soil were sporadic and the first significant South Asian immigration to North America began in 1903. Between 1903 and 1908, about 6000 Punjabis entered North America through Canada, and nearly 3000 crossed into the US (Kang, n.d.). The majority of these immigrants were illiterate and semi-literate laborers from agricultural and/or military backgrounds. For decades in the early 20th century, Punjabi farming families had sent their sons out of Punjab to earn money. These laborers were primarily peasant Sikhs and some Muslims from the Doaba and Malwa regions of Punjab province in Northwest India, as well as small numbers of Hindus, Sikhs and Muslims from areas in upper India.

Between 1903 and 1908, Punjabis came to the Pacific Northwest from Canada to work in lumber mills and logging camps. As they moved down into California, they began working in mills, farms and railroad construction. By 1908, a small community of Punjabi laborers had established itself in the Pacific Coast states. There were over 6000 Punjabis in California by the end of 1910.

In the decades following, legal controversy ensued regarding the racial classification of Indians. This confusion of classification had implications for naturalization rights. Overall numbers fell drastically after 1923, and consisted of a few students pursuing higher education and some 3000 undocumented men (Gibson, 1988).

It was not until the passage of the landmark Immigration and Nationality Act of 1965 (the Hart–Celler Act) that unprecedented numbers of immigrants from India, Pakistan, Bangladesh and Sri Lanka arrived in the US. With the end of immigration quotas based on race, religion and nationality, South Asian immigrants from a wide spectrum of ethnicities, education levels and professional backgrounds entered the country. Moreover, while the initial waves of immigration were dominated by men, the Family Reunification clause encouraged the arrival of women and children. During the 1980s, 85% of Indian immigrants were admitted to the US on the Family Reunification visa, whereas only 1% came on occupation-based visas (Maira, 2002). There is little data for Pakistanis; however, one can assume that a similar pattern of immigration took place for this population.

Another landmark immigration policy that led to increasing numbers of South Asian immigrants was the Diversity Lottery Program. Initiated in 1995, the Diversity Lottery Program, popularly known as the 'green card lottery', stipulates that the US government must award 55,000 green cards to persons from countries that have been less represented in employment and family-based preference categories in the country. Currently, this program serves as the primary driver behind present trends of South Asian immigration, resulting in recent influxes of Pakistanis and Bangladeshis. While Indians were ineligible to participate from the outset, owing to the size of their population in the US, thousands of Pakistanis won the lottery until 2002, after which they also became ineligible. Bangladeshis, however, are still eligible for the lottery and the recent influx of Bangladeshi immigrants is largely a result of this form of immigration (see Choudhury, Chapter 3).

Obtaining accurate demographic data about South Asians in the US is difficult owing to a lack of comprehensive and consistent statistical reporting across the various subgroups. For example, the US Census did not introduce the category 'Asian Indian' until 1980 (Koshy, n.d.). Other South Asian groups, such as Pakistanis, employ the category of 'Other Asian' and must report their race in conjunction with this option. Despite the lack of widely available disaggregated data, conservative estimates suggest that there are approximately 3 million South Asians in the US, with Indians comprising the vast majority (2.6 million), followed by Pakistanis (333,000). South Asians live primarily in metropolitan areas on the East and West coasts, and major hubs include, in descending order: New York, New Jersey, the San Francisco Bay Area, Chicago, Los Angeles and the Washington, DC metro area. However, there are sizable emerging populations in various parts of the US, including Houston, Atlanta and Seattle (South Asian Americans Leading Together, n.d.).

According to the 2009 American Community Survey, out of the 202,000 Indians and 34,000 Pakistanis living in New York City, 148,000 Indians and 13,000 Pakistanis reside in Queens, representing the largest concentration of these groups in any major urban region of the country. Furthermore, Queens has the second largest Sikh population in the nation after California. Thus South Asia's ethnic, linguistic and religious diversity is densely represented in many religious, cultural, community and professional organizations in several enclaves in Queens, including Jackson Heights, Flushing, Richmond Hill, East Elmhurst, Queens Village, Briarwood, Astoria, Forest Hills and Corona.

South Asian Language Education in New York City

The two case studies in this chapter are reasonably prototypical in a number of respects, particularly in terms of settings and challenges. Most South Asian community language programs are located in homes, community centers and religious institutions. The first case study considers Punjabi language learning in a Sikh temple in Richmond Hill, Queens, while the second looks at a weekend Hindi language program in Flushing, Queens.

No formal or non-formal community-based education efforts exist to support Urdu in New York. There are, however, for-profit organizations that teach Urdu, as well as courses in institutions of higher education. Although Urdu, as the national language of Pakistan, is a high-prestige language for speakers, the home language of many Pakistani-Americans is Punjabi. Another factor decreasing the prioritization of Urdu is the population's affiliation to Muslim identity, rather than Pakistani nationality. Thus, for many Pakistani immigrants, learning how to read the Qur'an in Arabic is considered to be more important than learning to read Urdu. As a result, many Pakistani children will go to mosques to learn how to read the Qur'an, the initial stages of which are mostly conducted through rote memorization, rather than through learning the Arabic language for everyday use. However, the home language is often Urdu or Punjabi and not English, especially in homes where the parents speak limited or no English (as is often the case for mothers).

At one time, however, a bilingual Urdu/English middle school existed, and currently there is a public high school that offers Urdu as part of its foreign language department. However, the school has never been able to secure a certified Urdu teacher, and therefore, Urdu is taught by non-Urdu speakers, if at all. The program has been in existence for over a decade with minimal programmatic and administrative investment in Urdu learning. Interestingly, Pakistani-American parents have never voiced any real concerns or complaints about this issue.

In stark contrast to this situation, perhaps the most organized of all South Asian community-based initiatives are those found among the Punjabi-speaking Sikhs. Muslims and Hindus by and large show relatively little interest in Punjabi once they move out of the Punjab. On the other hand, when Sikhs, the smallest group within the Punjabi-speaking community, take up the role of guarding the interests of Punjabi, it understandably turns into a potent symbol of their religious heritage (Mann, 2008). Their close-knit community has been well documented in many studies, including Greta Gibson's 1988 ethnography of a Sikh community in California, which argued that, rather than assimilate to the host community, Sikhs have been able to partake in what Gibson termed 'accommodation without assimilation'. Essentially, this means that Sikhs have been able to maintain their culture, language and mores, while also becoming vibrant members of the larger American public. Part of this success is attributed to the Sikh's strong sense of community and religion-based identity. Further, because the Gurmukhi script is intrinsically tied to the Sikh religion, in order to practice religion Sikhs must learn Gurmukhi. Thus, going to temple both to pray and learn one's language is almost a given in the Sikh community.

The picture of Hindi is quite different. Owing in part to the influence of India as a rising economic power in the 21st century, Hindi is experiencing a limited resurgence in university enrollments around the country (Shinge, 2008). US citizens are increasingly confronted with the realities of global competition in commerce and trade, and Hindi language learning has

assumed new implications and motivations for students in US higher education and private organizations.

In comparison to efforts for the teaching of Urdu and Punjabi, however,
it is important to note that these geopolitical realities do not offer any distinct advantages to the advancement of Hindi instruction within immigrant communities, including those of New York. Interaction in Hindi is
largely confined to the domains of the home, for relationships with relatives
and friends, and for specific intra-ethnic community-related uses. Hindi,
like Urdu, is not a liturgical language, and with English dominating as the
lingua franca for Indian communities across the world, Hindi language preservation has become intricately tied to community motivations, resources
and capabilities, which differ radically between Indian American communities across the US.

In New York, there are many community-based organizations that
follow a 'Sunday school' model to teach Hindi. Classes are typically held on
weekends in which students learn not only literacy in Hindi but also about
Indian history and culture. Often, these classes are administered through
community resources and funding, and parents are highly involved in the
activities, planning of curricula and teaching. These programs often take
place in temples and other community centers, although they are not all
religiously motivated.

A high degree of intra-group interaction typifies community life in South
Asian communities, and ethnic identity formation is a crucial, if not central,
factor for these organizations' efforts to teach their respective languages to
children. As important loci for students to socialize with each other and
nurture their South Asian identities, community-based schools involved in
the teaching of Hindi (as well as religious ones in the case of Punjabi) provide
opportunities for children to cultivate language development through interaction with adults in cultural and religious events.

Religion through Language, or Language through Religion? The Case of Punjabi

As already mentioned, Queens is home to the second largest population
of Sikhs in the US (Chhaya Community Development Corporation, n.d.).
When the first Sikh temple, referred to as *gurdwara* in Punjabi, was founded
in Richmond Hill in 1972, fewer than 100 Sikh families lived in New York
City. Since then, the community has grown. There are presently approximately 300,000 Sikhs in the New York metropolitan area and 20 gurdwaras.
These numbers continue to grow steadily.

Owing to the centrality of Punjabi literacy and proficiency to Sikh culture and religion, language learning is of the utmost importance for children within the community. From a very young age, children begin to attend the gurdwara to learn the verses of the *Sri Guru Granth Sahib*, the holy scriptures of the Sikhs. They immediately begin learning the individual sounds of the Punjabi alphabet. During classes, students speak in Punjabi and focus on becoming well-versed in the *Mool Mantar*, the most important composition contained within the *Sri Guru Granth Sahib*. This opening verse must be memorized and repeated until it becomes a habitual practice for the student to recite it without visual aid. After learning its full meaning, children are taught the sounds and meaning of each and every word in the verse.

Gradually, as they progress, students learn to construct simple sentences. They are introduced to founding principles of Sikhism, including the Five Ks. These Five Ks, or *panj kakaar/kakke*, are five items of faith that display and show the wearer's respect for the tenth Sikh Guru who lived at the end of the 17th century, Guru Gobind Singh. The five items are: *Kesh* (uncut hair), *Kanga* (small comb), *Kara* (circular bracelet), *Kirpan* (small sword) and *Kacha* (shorts).

Once students have demonstrated their initial competency in the sounds and simple constructions of Punjabi, they advance towards developing their Punjabi language use and cultural knowledge. The children read and recite larger passages of the holy scriptures, in addition to learning about the community from which they come. It is at this stage that Sikh Punjabi language efforts converge with programs like those of the The Hindu Temple Society in North America, the largest and oldest Hindu religious organization in the country, which we describe below.

At advanced stages of learning, the Sikh children are taught primarily to develop their communicative proficiency. They are encouraged to speak with each other as well as their elders in the gurdwara and in the community. In the final years of learning, the students often regularly attend religious services at the gurdwara and actively participate in recitations and singing of *Gurbaani*, or sections of the holy scriptures and books.

Because the language is tied to the Sikh religion, the learning of Punjabi for Sikhs is essential and the holy scriptures are the basis of teaching the language in the gurdwaras. Thus, Sikh communities do not need to seek or adapt instructional materials nor develop language-learning texts, as do programs for other South Asian languages. This is different from the Hindi case: Hindi is not the language of Hinduism, and therefore Hindi language programs must develop culturally and linguistically relevant materials. The same is true for the teaching of Urdu – thus explaining why there is a greater push for Arabic learning than Urdu, since Arabic is the language of the

Qur'an. In other words, the teaching of the Punjabi language and culture in Sikh communities is *through* religion, whereas in a Hindi language classroom, religion is a thematic unit. Despite different approaches, in both cases, practices and beliefs are not inherent but are learned. Hindi community teachers must develop a broad set of lesson plans that highlight diverse aspects of Indian life, including religion (Urdu teachers could ostensibly do the same). Thus, while both Punjabi and Hindi teachers invest their own time, effort and money in developing activities and lessons, Punjabi teachers are at a slight advantage since they do not need to create instructional materials and texts for their students to practice Punjabi, whereas Hindi teachers do, as illustrated by the case that follows.

Communal Identities and Language: The Case of Hindi

During the 1970s, several enclaves in Queens witnessed a large influx of Indian immigrants. As the numbers grew, so did the need to establish religious, cultural and professional organizations to support this fledgling group. Flushing, New York was chosen as the site of the Hindu Temple Society in North America (HTS), the largest and oldest Hindu religious organization in the country. Like many founders of American-based Hindu associations, the founders of the HTS believed that their children would need a temple to ground their religious and cultural identity. Surviving completely on financial support from the community since its inception, approximately 20,000 members gather annually to participate in a variety of religious and cultural activities.

In 1998, a community outreach center was built adjacent to the temple, including facilities to house and administer an educational youth program to teach Hindi, Kannada, Malayalam, Tamil and Telugu. According to the current outreach director, parents within the HTS asked for the establishment of the language programs, so that their children would preserve their Indian identity.

The Hindi program takes place every weekend throughout the year (along with classes in Kannada, Tamil and Telugu) for a student body exceeding 100 children on any given Saturday morning. Registration fees help sustain administrative costs and are used to develop materials for the classes. The students range in age from 5 to 27 years old and are to some degree bilingual, as most of them come from homes where both English and Hindi are spoken. However, few are equally competent in Hindi and English. The classes are divided into several sections based on language proficiency and last for one hour. The proficiency of the students ranges from English-dominant students without any Hindi literacy to those who are familiar with Hindi writing.

Community-based language schools around the country, like the one at the HTS, face substantial obstacles because the teachers and administrators are volunteers and not trained language teachers with pedagogical expertise. In interviews with community leaders and staff, lack of funding, problems in administrative infrastructure and lack of instructional materials emerged as common concerns. A major problem reported was that planning was too often short-term. Many programs are not overseen by national organizations and are run from the basements of homes and in the halls of temples, and their leaders do not have access to institutional resources and national networks. As a result of these realities, family involvement is quite extensive; parents are volunteer teachers and are actively involved in the homework and assignments of children. Parental demand also often dictates what languages are taught in the school.

Because the majority of the students are English-speaking second-generation children of immigrants, the children have limited contact with speakers of Hindi in everyday life. These children often shrug off identification with a culture they know little about, contact with which is limited to elements of popular Indian culture, such as the Bollywood film industry of India. Afraid of being labeled stereotypical first-generation immigrants, most young adults are embarrassed by parental efforts to promote their families' cultural and linguistic roots.

These issues have, in totality, increased the burden of innovation and creativity for the teachers and administrators of the HTS to develop a sound and culturally relevant curriculum for students. Teachers are constantly challenged to develop their own lesson plans that will appeal to South Asian-American students. The lack of commercially published instructional materials is often cited as a major challenge to the effectiveness of the teachers' efforts. As one teacher said, 'since most materials come from India and my students are from here, I always have a challenge' (interview, 26 August 2010).

Certainly, there are possibilities for reducing or at least sharing this burden. For example, in one Tamil class, the teacher developed an ongoing relationship with the Canadian Board of Education in Toronto, where they teach Tamil in public schools. This is critical for the teachers' success in the classroom, since the Canadian curriculum has been developed for students of all ethnic backgrounds. The Canadian Board and this teacher share lesson plans and curricula, which the teacher adapts for her own use in the school. This not only saves her time, which is unpaid and voluntary, but also allows her to continuously tailor her curriculum to the needs of the students, despite her limited expertise in pedagogy. These kinds of relationships reduce the burden on teachers of such minority languages, but opportunities to establish them are not commonly available for South Asian language teachers. Thus, teachers of Hindi and other languages such as Telugu and Kannada do not have such opportunities, and therefore must invest their own time, money and resources in the preparation of teaching materials. For example, authentic materials from India are used to teach children various aspects of language and culture. While these practices assist the teachers in developing lessons, a focus group of four teachers cited challenges in teaching stories and literature from the motherland because they are difficult for the students to follow, since the majority were born and raised in the US. Thus teachers regularly create their own worksheets and activities, which may or may not be effective because of their lack of preparation in language teaching.

The teachers and staff unanimously agree that opportunities for professional development and training would strengthen their confidence in the classroom while broadening their skill sets and networking with other language teachers. The case of the HTS program highlights the challenges parents face as teachers of their own languages, without adequate training and financial resources to support their goal.

Conclusion

We have shown that strategies toward intergenerational language transmission vary from one South Asian language group to another. Within the South Asian communities examined in this chapter, religion and culture are driving forces behind community-based language approaches, albeit with different thrusts: the Sikh community possesses a straightforward approach to mother tongue maintenance, as religious practice is intrinsically tied to Punjabi language learning. This is augmented by the Sikh Punjabis' long immigrant history in the US, which gives them a great deal of social, cultural and linguistic capital to draw on to create a biliterate and bicultural community. This is vastly different from the cases of Urdu and Hindi. In the case of Urdu, Pakistani-Americans are keen that their children learn to read the Qur'an, an activity that is conducted in Arabic and at the expense of Urdu literacy. Hindi-speaking Indians, on the other hand, are adamant that their youth retain aspects of their native culture (including religion), and look for ways and means to develop fluency in Hindi while balancing assimilation in a widely English-speaking community as bilingual Americans.

Much can be learned from these community-based efforts (or lack thereof). Clearly, these cases are indicative of the importance of having a shared vision and the will to execute it. The cases of Hindi and Punjabi especially demonstrate the creativity, resourcefulness and perseverance of a community committed to the emergence of a bilingual generation of young Americans, despite challenging circumstances. The vast array of Hindi and Punjabi ethnic and cultural organizations provides numerous possibilities for educating the younger generation in their respective languages. Reflective of the growing dynamism of diasporic plural networks, organizations like the HTS are fundamentally community-oriented, and their intent to preserve and promote community interests is often explicit in their statements of purpose. This community orientation, by and large, leads these organizations to work in expansive ways that encompass a broad range of cultural and educational activities, often sponsoring language. While the Pakistani community has not risen to this challenge, there are certainly possibilities. Local government policies and initiatives that support community-based teaching of mother tongues in these communities, but also in the schools that serve them, would certainly be welcomed by all. Such policies and initiatives would help create programs where they do not exist and further support existing initiatives, such as those in the Hindi and Punjabi communities. This is particularly important given the growing significance of the region to the US in terms of either economics (India) or politics (Pakistan). While the cases of Hindi and Punjabi give us an indication of the possibilities of community-based efforts for language maintenance, more research is needed to understand ways in which greater community and institutional support could further the vision and goals of these bicultural communities.

Note

(1) British India comprised present-day Bangladesh, India and Pakistan. In 1947, the region gained independence from Britain and was divided into two countries. All contiguous Muslim-majority states formed Pakistan. Pakistan was thus divided into two land masses, West and East Pakistan, with the huge land mass of independent India separating the two. The united but physically divided Pakistan was short-lived. In 1971, after a bloody civil war, East Pakistan gained independence from West Pakistan to become Bangladesh.

5 Hidden Efforts, Visible Challenges: Promoting Bilingualism in Korean-America

Jeehyae Chung

Introduction

Korean-Americans have made various efforts to preserve their language and culture. This chapter attempts to illuminate those efforts and the issues and challenges related to them. After a brief description of the Korean-American community, I focus on Korean language teaching in the US, the accomplishments that have been made and the issues that have arisen. Turning the spotlight onto the New York and New Jersey area, this chapter considers the case of one community-based Korean language program in New York City. Through an analysis of this program, I argue that its current evolutions suggest the future portrait of the Korean-American community as being continuously painted and repainted by the Korean-Americans themselves. I also call for more diversified and hybridized reconceptualizations of what being Korean-American means and how bilingualism and biculturalism are defined, as well as careful reconsiderations of how these fluid and ever-changing definitions might be reflected in Korean language instruction.

Korea and its Language

South and North Korea are located on the Korean peninsula, which borders China to the north and west, and shares seas with Japan to the east.

The written history of Korea goes back to 2333 BC, when the first kingdom was established on the peninsula. After many royal dynasties and Japanese occupation (1910–1945), the two Koreas separated with independent governments following the Korean War (1950–1953). Throughout its history, Korea's location between Japan and China has led Koreans to have continuous contact and relations with the Japanese and Chinese. Such close contact has had a strong impact on Korea's culture, including a constant competitive tension with Japan and the influence of Confucianism. Chinese influence was a contributing factor in the birth of the Korean writing system, called Hangul. Until the mid-15th century, the Korean language only existed in oral form. Writing could only be carried out in Chinese characters, which was a prestigious asset, exclusive to the aristocrats in the highly stratified society of those times. King Sejong (1418–1450) of the Chosun dynasty wished all Koreans, regardless of class, to be able to express themselves in writing, and developed a new writing system. Hangul, which was developed by King Sejong and his scholars, and which was officially promulgated in 1446, is a unique script that is not similar to any other writing system in the world. At present it comprises 14 consonants and 10 vowels that are combined together to build syllables (Figure 5.1). Hangul is phonetic, meaning that, as long as one knows the sound properties of each consonant and vowel, the Hangul script can be easily decoded. There are various dialects in both South and North Korea, but they are mutually intelligible and the script is the same.

Even with an independent writing system, Chinese continues to have a strong presence in the Korean language. Chinese (Sino-Korean) words

Consonants	ㄱ ㄴ ㄷ ㄹ ㅁ ㅂ ㅅ ㅇ ㅈ ㅊ ㅋ ㅌ ㅍ ㅎ
	*some consonants can be combined to make compound consonants
Vowels	ㅏ ㅑ ㅓ ㅕ ㅗ ㅛ ㅜ ㅠ ㅡ ㅣ
	*some vowels can be combined to make compound vowels

Example of combing consonants and vowels to construct syllables:

ㄴ + ㅏ = 나   ㅁ + ㅜ = 무   ㅇ + ㅗ + ㅣ + ㄴ = 왼   ㅅ + ㅗ + ㄴ = 손

나 + 무 = 나무 (tree)   왼 + 손 = 왼손 (left hand)

Figure 5.1 Hangul

- 뉴욕에는 많은 한국인이 살고 있다. =
New York에는 많은 韓國人이 살고 있다.
[There are many Koreans living in New York.]

Figure 5.2 Sino-Korean words in Hangul and Chinese characters

comprise approximately 60% of the contemporary Korean lexicon, while the remaining 40% of the lexicon is occupied by pure Korean words and loan words from other languages, including English (Sohn, 2001). Sino-Korean words can be written out in both Chinese characters and in Hangul, just as English loan words can be written out in English and in Hangul. Figure 5.2 shows this comparison.

Sino-Korean words generally account for substantial and meaningful vocabulary, and therefore, while knowledge of Sino-Korean words may not be necessary for simple colloquial interactions, it is required for one to fully participate and function in work settings, carry out academic work, understand the news and fully engage in highly contextualized conversations.

Another signature feature of the Korean language is the highly complicated honorific system. Ihm *et al.* (2001: 199) state that the Korean honorific system is 'more highly developed than in any other language'. The Korean culture of age-based hierarchy is based not only in Confucian culture but also in this characteristic of the language. Therefore, it is not unusual for unacquainted Koreans to exchange information on their ages in order to figure out how to address each other when they meet for the first time. Research has shown that learning the honorific system and the accompanying cultural traits is extremely challenging for English-speaking Korean-Americans learning Korean (Jo, 2001; Park, 2006), especially as knowing how to properly use honorifics is essential in order to be regarded as a native-speaker and to be accepted by native-speaking Koreans.

Koreans in the US: Past, Present and Future

Despite the distance, South Korea has maintained strong political and economic ties with the US since the Korean War. In fact, the US has the second largest population of people of Korean descent after China. According to the 2008 American Community Survey, approximately 1.6 million people living in the US self-identified as Korean (US Census Bureau, 2008a). Most Koreans living in the US originate from South Korea.

Korean immigration to the US has occurred across several periods (Kim, 1988; Min, 2000; Shin, 2005), with the first being in the early 1900s, when groups of Korean men went to Hawaii to work on sugar cane plantations. This migration coincided with a period of turmoil on the Korean peninsula in which Korea lost its autonomy to Japan in 1910. The laborers who went to Hawaii had left their home country with the hope of returning, but most could not. With Japan's occupation of Korea and the exclusion of Asians from immigrating to the US (1921–1965), Koreans who went to the US before the mid-1960s were mostly wives of American soldiers who fought in the Korean War, Korean adoptees or a small number of Korean students.

After the US Immigration and Naturalization Act was amended in 1965, the number of South Koreans immigrating to the US soared. The majority of those who are now regarded as first-generation Korean-Americans arrived from the late 1960s to the early 1980s. After the end of the Korean War, South Korean society continued to experience social and political unrest. The US was sought as a land of opportunity. The post-1965 Korean immigrants differed from their predecessors in that they had attained high levels of education, came as whole families and came determined to pursue a new and better life for their families in the US (Min, 2000; Shin, 2005). Partly owing to their lack of English proficiency and credentials, most first-generation Korean-Americans willingly experienced downward mobility in terms of their socioeconomic status (Min, 2000) and pursued highly labor-intensive jobs. Hard work and tenacity led many Korean-Americans to later on establish their own businesses, while very few entered the general job market. Perhaps owing to such patterns of settlement, Koreans are known to work and socialize within the Korean community (Hurh & Kim, 1984; Min, 2000) and prefer to live in enclaves (Logan et al., 2002). Los Angeles, New York City, Chicago and their vicinities are representative locations with dense Korean populations.

More recently, South Korea has developed a strong and thriving economy. As a result, Korean immigration to the US has slowed down, but US Census data show that the number of Koreans in the US has nonetheless continued to increase. Georgia, New Jersey and Virginia have recently emerged as popular destinations for recently arriving Koreans. Circumstances that may have caused these Koreans to leave their homeland might include the impact of the Asian economic crisis in the late 1990s, or the intense competitiveness of South Korean education that brought about the rise of a new social phenomenon called 'kirogi' [goose] families, who flock to foreign countries to secure better educational opportunities for their children at the price of family separation (Ly, 2005). There is also an increasingly high influx of non-immigrant status Koreans entering the US, many with prospects of pursuing post-secondary studies (Monger & Barr, 2010). A large majority of the kirogi families and non-immigrant students may be temporary sojourners who will eventually return to Korea.

At any rate, the profiles of Korean-Americans are changing and diversifying. On the one hand, new generations of bilingual and bicultural US-born Korean-Americans are growing up and advancing in society. On the other, newer Korean immigrants have picked the US as a place of settlement, but have had first-hand experience of South Korea as a developed country. Thus the images and meanings relating to Korea that earlier immigrants might hold potentially diverge from those of their children, and from those of the more recent immigrants who have seen and lived in modern South Korea.

Korean Language Teaching in the US: Efforts in and out of the Community

Differences aside, all Korean-Americans painstakingly struggle to establish a good life in the US for their families, while at the same time trying to maintain their language and culture (Hurh & Kim, 1984; Lee, 2002; Lee & Kim, 2007). Korean schools are the main vehicles through which Koreans attempt to transmit their language and culture. The majority of Korean schools are run by religious organizations, but there are also independent schools that are run under the auspices of various community organizations. Classes are typically held on weekends, and the schools mainly teach the Korean language, with the addition of history and culture. In general the schools are run under difficult conditions; the teachers, most of them parents, are not well compensated compared with the effort and time they invest, and classes are often held in borrowed facilities. These schools are run wholly by the dedication and devotion of parents, which is reflected in the schools' histories.

Korean schools have existed from the very early stages of Korean immigration to the US, but the number significantly increased in the 1980s, especially around the time Seoul hosted the 1988 summer Olympic Games (Sung, 2003). The Seoul Olympics marked a milestone in South Korea's economic development and heightened a sense of patriotism among Korean-Americans. So many Korean schools were sprouting in the US that a movement arose to systematize a support network. Educators and parents from southern California, Arizona, New Mexico and Nevada established the Korean School Association of America in 1982, and educators and parents from the remaining states came together to establish the National Association for Korean Schools (NAKS) in 1985. At present, there are approximately 1200 member schools in NAKS alone. These organizations serve Korean schools and their teachers by holding national and regional conferences, workshops and publishing periodical literature. The South Korean government maintains tight connections with these organizations and supports them by providing textbooks and material developed and produced in Korea, and in a loose sense, monitors the schools through local consulate offices.

Expanding the reach of the Korean language within American education has also been an aspiration of Korean-Americans. In 1997, Korean-Americans spearheaded by Korean school leaders embarked on a grassroots movement to have Korean accepted as a foreign language subject in the SAT subject test, a test students can take to enhance college admission credentials. After petitioning and fundraising within the community, the goal was finally realized when the Korean conglomerate Samsung fully provided the funds to achieve the goal. The Foundation for Korean Language and Culture, which was launched for the purpose of coordinating efforts to establish Korean as an SAT subject, now promotes Korean language teaching in American public schools with funds from the South Korean government. According to the Foundation, there are 64 K–12 public schools that teach the Korean language, including 10 two-way immersion bilingual education programs in the Los Angeles area, and one in New York City.

Despite such investment, it is questionable whether or not there are fruitful returns. Students appear to view attending Korean school as a forced experience to fulfill parents' expectations, and do not feel that Korean school teachers take their needs and interests into account (Lee, 2002). Young Korean-Americans often perceive the Korean language as having low prestige and utility in American society (Lee & Kim, 2007), and do not value Korean schools. In other words, while Korean-Americans have shown a strong desire to teach and maintain Korean and have established schools to do so, research suggests that the complex needs and identities of young Korean-Americans are not fully acknowledged.

Issues and Challenges

The accomplishments in having Korean taught to a wider population do suggest a promising future. However, several studies have shown that Koreans are experiencing rapid language loss (López, 1996; Min, 2000; Portes & Hao, 1998) and census data confirm these findings. Census data reveal that while, in 2005, 26.5% of Koreans had reported speaking English only, in 2008 the number had increased to 30.4% (US Census Bureau, 2005, 2008a). At the same time, the number of Koreans reporting speaking a language other than English decreased from 73.5% in 2005 to 69.6% in 2008 (US Census Bureau, 2005, 2008a). Researchers have identified various factors to explain why the Korean language, and possibly culture, has failed to be inter-generationally transmitted, despite seemingly favorable conditions (Jeon, 2008; Jo, 2001; Lee, 2002; Lee & Kim, 2007; Min, 2000; Min & Kim, 2005; Shin, 2005). The most important factors may lie within the Korean community itself. In general, a theme that cuts across all factors is the discrepancies between and lack of understanding among Korean immigrants, in particular between the young and old.

The first issue concerns a discrepancy among Korean immigrants on how Korean-American identity may be defined. Koreans seem to share a belief that knowledge of one's language and culture has a strong correlation with forming a firm and sound identity (Cho, 2000; Jeon, 2008). However, with the rapid rate of diversification within the Korean-American community, definitions of what Korean-American identity is may vary. Past efforts by older, dominantly Korean-speaking Korean-Americans, seem to reflect an imposition of arbitrary solutions to accomplishing sound identity development – Korean 'heritage' and tradition, and 'perfect' bilingualism. For English-speaking young Korean-Americans, college seems to be a good time and place to connect with their Korean identity outside of their families by taking Korean language courses. In fact, enrollment in Korean courses has seen a significant increase in recent years (Furman et al., 2007). However once the students attend these courses, they find themselves needing to reconstruct what they know and unlearn the Korean to which they are accustomed (Jeon, 2008; Jo, 2001). The standard textbook Korean that they learn in these courses is quite distant from the Korean that they have used in the private domain, and they struggle with the authentic Korean they learn in these courses, which includes honorifics and Sino-Korean words. For these Korean-Americans, the Korean language holds a symbolic value linked to their identity, but they find that the Korean language that they call their own is ousted and degraded as 'non-standard' and 'incorrect'.

Another challenge lies in the perceived value of English versus Korean, particularly in academic achievement. Shin (2005) found that, while Korean parents have high expectations for their children in maintaining strong Korean proficiency, they do not necessarily take action to make it possible. She explains that Koreans do want their children to retain Korean; however, because the Korean language has little or no immediate bearing on school performance, once school grades come into the picture, Korean falls back in priority. In order for children to excel in school, flawless English is imperative, and therefore the desire for their children's academic success overrides the desire for their children to maintain their Korean language and culture. Shin (2005) also mentions the imbalance in perceived prestige between English and Korean. Koreans generally perceive the English language to embody prestige and American-ness (Jeon, 2008). Since the societal value of

Korean in American society is low, and since there is an understanding that the outcome of all academic work lies in the premise of impeccable proficiency in English, English takes a leading role.

Koreans and the Korean Language in New York and New Jersey

The state of New York has the second largest concentration of Koreans after California. Koreans account for 2.6% of the entire population in the borough of Queens (US Census Bureau, American Factfinder, 2006–2008). New York City has been a traditional destination for new Korean immigrants, but in recent decades New Jersey has risen in popularity as a place to settle. The number of Koreans in New Jersey increased by 69.6% between the 1990 and 2000 Censuses. Unlike California, where the Korean-American community is three times the size of that in New York and Korean language programs in public schools are quite well established, the Korean language is not served well within public schools in New York and New Jersey. Currently in New York City there are 14 public schools that offer Korean language classes: five in Queens, including one bilingual education program at the elementary level; seven in the Bronx; and two in Manhattan. Most of the programs were started by efforts within the Korean-American community to serve the dense populations of Korean students in the schools. For example, one of the schools in Queens had initiated its Korean class with the temporary purpose of providing support for recent arrivals from Korea. In New Jersey there is only one high school that offers Korean, which started just recently in September 2010, entirely with support from the Korean-American community in New York and New Jersey. On the other hand, there is an abundance of Korean schools in the area – 86 in New York and 46 in New Jersey. In the section below, I describe the case of one community-based Korean school in Manhattan. I rely on observations and interviews conducted with the teachers, principal and students in 2007.

The Case of a Community-based Korean School in Manhattan

Presently in its 26th year of establishment, the Manhattan Korean School (pseudonym) is one of the oldest Korean schools in the NY/NJ area. The independent school was established by, and continues to be partly run under, the sponsorship of a Korean-American professional organization. In the beginning, the school was established with the aims of not only teaching the Korean language and culture to the organization members' children, but also providing the families with a safe place to leave their children while the parents worked on Saturday mornings.

Classes are held every Saturday morning in the facilities of a public school in Manhattan, where most of the students' families reside. The students' ages range roughly from 4 to 13. There are 11 classes, organized by level and age. Class organization may change every semester, depending on student enrollment. Korean language is the main subject, while Korean history and culture are also taught. The majority of teachers are native Koreans who came to the US to pursue studies in New York; teachers with teaching experience or educational training are favored by the school.

The ultimate goal of the school and its parents is not necessarily to establish the children's Korean identity, but simply to expose the children to the language and culture so that they can develop sustainable interest. The school's policy is to use only Korean in instruction, but this policy is enforced flexibly by circumstance and at the discretion of teachers. Every year, as the profile of the student body changes, students' needs also change. Within the past few years the school has been experiencing quite substantial changes owing to the evolving student composition, requiring it to make adjustments in programming and curriculum.

Until a few years ago, dominantly Korean-speaking parents were the majority, while the number of dominantly English-speaking parents was low. By 2007, while all of the families still had Korean backgrounds, most spoke English as a home language, and there were also a number of biracial families. Children from these newly emerging families do not have the same exposure to the Korean language and culture that students from Korean-speaking families have. Most of the parents are affluent and work in professional occupations. The principal of the school explained that the interest of English-speaking Korean-background parents grew when she changed the way the school was promoted. Instead of listing the school only in Korean language media, as in the past, she started to advertise the school in English-language magazines with high circulation in Manhattan. Through these advertisements, and then by word of mouth, the school found its current population.

As the student body evolved, the school went through some adjustments. For example, based on strong requests from parents, the school had to adopt practices not familiar to other Korean schools, such as strictly promoting a nut-free environment for children with nut allergies, and cutting the Taekwondo program as some parents considered the sport to be too violent. In another shift, all communications with parents are now carried out in English, rather than Korean. If homework was given in Korean, the parents would sometimes complain that they could not help out and would demand homework to be given in English, or bilingually. Meetings, either among parents or together with teachers, started to be wholly conducted in English. In addition, an adult Korean language class for parents began just a few years ago.

Such demands from the parents reflect their will to make the school their own. For the English-speaking Korean-American parents of the school, the school serves not only as an educational space for their children, but also as a place to build their own community. These parents were attracted to the school because they did not feel comfortable at other Korean schools where Korean-speaking parents were the norm; they felt left out. They have now formed a robust network, and the parents' association has a strong presence, supporting the school by holding fundraising events and family mixers to facilitate networking between parents.

Students have been going through changes as well. They expressed mixed feelings of frustration about their Korean proficiency and having to attend school on Saturdays, but they generally shared an understanding that they are Korean-American, not just American. Twin brothers who had been attending the school since they were four and who were 11 at the time of the research, well embodied the Korean school experience. Their mother is a native-speaker of Korean, born in Korea, while their father is a dominantly English-speaking second-generation Korean-American. When asked if they felt anything had changed because of going to Korean school, they responded negatively. In class, the two would insist on speaking in English, saying that speaking Korean is 'not our thing. We don't like speaking in Korean any-more' (interview, 17 March 2007). A tension could be sensed between the two and the teacher who insisted on using Korean.

Class observations revealed this tug-of-war between students, who preferred to be able to use the language they feel most comfortable with, English, and the teachers, who were adamant about having the students adhere to speaking only Korean in class. The following excerpt from observational notes illustrates this tension: 'S(tudent) asks something to T(eacher) in English, and the T says that she can't understand him and then he asks in Korean' (classroom observation, 17 March 2007). As such, the teachers seemed to be adamant about using only Korean in class, while the students felt the need to use English in order to effectively express themselves.

Later, when the twins were interviewed in the private setting of their home, they surprisingly expressed excitement about how their Korean had been improving: 'We just speak in Korean to our mom now. The main questions are like, what are we eating for dinner, when is Daddy coming, and for jokes … Now we're starting to speak with our dad, and we also speak with our cousins, 'cause they live in Korea' (interview, 14 April 2007). Despite the resistance they displayed at the Korean school, they seemed to be proud to have the ability to speak in Korean with their family members. They seemed to desire Korean school instruction that reflected and gave credit to their bilingual identities. The following interview excerpt demonstrates their idea of language use in Korean school:

Chung: What if the class was taught in English? How would you feel about that?
S: Awkward.
Chung: What do you think is the best combination?
S: Teach us in Korean, and give us homework in English. Give us directions/questions in English.
Chung: But you feel fine about speaking in Korean in class?
S: Yeah, we understand it. (Interview, 14 April 2007)

The principal, who is an active member of NAKS, explains that the school is so unique within the Korean school network that other educators and teachers simply do not understand, and often conflict arises when discussing how the school can participate in existing NAKS activities. Notwithstanding, the principal foresees her school to be the future of Korean schools and therefore believes Korean schools need change, in practices and philosophy, so that they can better cater to up-and-coming Korean-Americans.

Looking Ahead: Making Way for the New

The present chapter has attempted to underscore the hard work Koreans have invested in promoting bilingualism and biculturalism for their children, and to identify what the obstacles are in pushing that effort further. Korean schools have been and still are a vehicle for Koreans to transmit their language and culture to the next generations and fill a hole in public school provision. While research shows that students do desire to learn their language and culture, they prefer to do so in their regular schools (Lee, 2002), rather than in such community-based institutions. Moreover, the status of Korean language teaching in public schools has improved, but the value of Korean seems to pale compared with parents' zeal for their children's academic performance, where only English is valued. As such, the Koreans seem to have been at a crossroads between holding on to their roots and establishing themselves in American society. However the case of the Korean school in New York reveals an entirely different dimension. The adaptations that this school has been facing and that other Korean schools will eventually face are changes that are inevitable as the Korean-American community becomes more heterogeneous than homogeneous, and less Korean and more American. The changes in the Manhattan Korean school are that much more meaningful because they were driven by the English-speaking second-generation parents. Explicitly the school may appear to be aiming at transferring the Korean language and culture to their offspring, but a deeper look inside shows their desire and hopes to help their children embrace and enhance the resources that are readily available to them, both linguistic and cultural.

The Koreans are a relatively recent immigrant group in the US, and it seems that they are going through a period of transition. In order for this transition to occur smoothly and meaningfully for all, Koreans need to make space for more voices, especially those of the younger generations of bilingual and bicultural Korean-Americans. There needs to be a rethinking of what being a Korean-American is, and how bilingualism and biculturalism are conceptualized. It may or may not matter whether younger generation Koreans can speak Korean fluently, or have an in-depth understanding of 'Korean culture', as long as they can call it their own.

In order to reap valuable results for students, both the Korean-American community and American society as a whole need to feel a sense of responsibility and get involved. A viable plan that involves both Korean schools and public schools would be collaboration between the two, either in the form of offering credits for Korean school attendance, or as school partnerships so that both sides can contribute and also benefit. It is vital that both public school teachers with students of Korean background and members of the Korean-American community, including parents and educators, embrace and understand the needs of the next generations of Korean-Americans. As the case of the Manhattan Korean school shows, opening opportunities for all youth to explore their identities in the present and feel confident as bilingual and bicultural Americans will help establish new conceptualizations of what an ethnolinguistic community is in the US. These ethnolinguistic communities and the assets they possess are and should be the backbone of helping the US survive and furthermore thrive as a truly multicultural nation.

6 Japanese Community Schools: New Pedagogy for a Changing Population

Naomi Kano

Introduction

Most Japanese families outside Japan, both in New York and around the world, send their children to Japanese weekend community schools. The Japanese government has been involved with these schools since the 1970s. At that time, the learners were assumed to be sojourners, or students who would re-enter the domestic Japanese education system after a few years, and the pedagogy reflected their need for reintegration upon repatriation. However, since that time the Japanese population in New York and the US has changed. Now, more than half of the learners at Japanese weekend schools in the US are the children of permanent residents (Calder, 2008). Such a demographic trend calls for a change in pedagogy underpinned by theoretical understanding and educational philosophy, because the learner population has different educational needs.

The Princeton Community Japanese Language School (PCJLS) provides a 'dynamic bilingual community model of schooling' (Bartlett & García, 2011) that recognizes the complexity of the population it seeks to serve. Rather than separating Japanese expatriate students from American students of Japanese descent, as in more traditional program models that follow the Japanese national curriculum, PCJLS distinguishes itself by providing an integrated learning environment for the Japanese language community. The school's dynamic learning model questions the static idea of ethnolinguistic communities, and challenges the conventional practices at Japanese weekend community schools. Thus the language programs and educational efforts that PCJLS provides go beyond what has been called 'heritage language education', as well as public US 'bilingual education'. As stated in Introduction of this volume, 'heritage' and 'US public bilingual education' display a monoglossic ideology where bilingualism is seen as linear and additive. In contrast, PCJLS, acknowledging the increasingly fluid and heterogeneous nature of Japanese language community, views bilingualism not as an end product, but as a dynamic process.

This chapter draws on observations and interviews at PCJLS to consider various pedagogical practices that characterize the school's dynamic learning model. In order to situate the school and its educational issues, the chapter opens with a brief description of relevant features of the Japanese language and the population in the US who speak it. I then discuss the pedagogical practices of Japanese weekend schools more generally, and their underlying political discourse. Finally, I compare the prevailing model with practices at PCJLS, with a view to exploring a new pedagogical approach for Japanese bilingual community education.

The Language and the Script

The Japanese language has certain characteristics that have important implications for language learners. First, the spoken language closely reflects social relationships that are in some respects very different from those of most Americans. These need to be taught to enable learners to socialize in a Japanese language environment. Positioning oneself through the language is considered an essential skill to avoid giving offense and potentially rupturing relationships.

Before the 4th century, the Japanese people had no formal writing system. Literacy was introduced to Japan in the form of the Chinese writing system. The 'ideographic' Chinese writing system is very rich, but has its own features and limitations. In particular, its use in non-cognate languages, such as Japanese, entails the use of 'fixes' and various adaptations, which result in a very complex system. As a result of this complexity, learning this system has become the core emphasis of the Japanese educational curriculum, and like the spoken language, this needs to be learned at great effort from an early age. Thus, in addition to the role of instilling national identity, the particular characteristics of the language make weekend schools even more important for overseas Japanese children, especially for sojourners.

The Population that Speaks Japanese

The number of speakers of the Japanese language exceeds 130 million people, who are largely concentrated in Japan. In addition, there are a number of immigrant communities, chiefly in Brazil and the US. The Japanese population in the US was estimated to be 766,875 in 2009, according to the American Community Survey (US Census Bureau, 2009). California has the largest population (278,515), followed by Hawaii (172,400; US Census Bureau, 2009). Small communities of Japanese residents and sojourners are also found in most major urban centers and many manufacturing communities throughout the world.

In the US, Japanese descendants rarely speak Japanese fluently after the second generation, owing to a strong tendency to assimilate (Consulate-General of Japan in Los Angeles, n.d.). This tendency is partly due to the unhappy history of Japanese immigration to the US in the first half of the 20th century. At present, there are two distinct groups among ethnic Japanese living in the US. One is Japanese-Americans, the descendants of Japanese who have migrated to the US since the late 19th century, and the other is expatriate Japanese who sojourn in the US for several years and eventually return to Japan.

The Immigration of Japanese People to the US

Migration from Japan to the US began in significant numbers during the Meiji era (1868–1912). The number of Japanese immigrants grew steadily until 1907 when the governments of Japan and the US reached a 'Gentlemen's Agreement' that put an end to the immigration of Japanese workers (i.e. men), but permitted the immigration of spouses of Japanese immigrants already in the US. The Immigration Act of 1924, however, banned migration from Japan almost completely. Having survived the processes of internment during World War II, coupled with incessant and institutionalized racial discrimination in the postwar period, the younger generations in Hawaii and California responded by gradually becoming assimilated into mainstream culture.

During the Meiji era, Japan-towns were created as a result of widespread Japanese immigration to the US. These communities usually had Japanese language schools for the immigrants' children, Japanese language newspapers, Buddhist temples and churches. The largest Japan-town was that in downtown Los Angeles, which at its peak had approximately 30,000 Japanese-Americans living in the area. The World War II internment of the Japanese led to the decline or disappearance of most of those communities.

The Immigration Act of 1924 stopped immigration from Japan almost entirely. Because of this, all Japanese-Americans born between 1924 and 1965 were born in the US. Besides the usual generational differences, the citizenship and English language ability possessed by this second generation served to draw a clear distinction between them and the preceding generation. Owing to persistent institutional and interpersonal racism, however, many of the second-generation Japanese married within their racial community, which gave rise to a third distinct cohort of Japanese-Americans. Japanese immigration resumed after the 1965 amendment of the Immigration Act, which abolished the national origin quota system and ended 40 years of restrictions on immigration from Japan and other countries.

Owing to growth in the Japanese economy after WWII, economic migration from Japan to the US largely ceased. After the 1970s, however, rapid and sustained Japanese economic growth led to a dramatic increase in the number of Japanese employees and their families living outside Japan. Today, the communities in the greater New York region include mostly expatriates and newly arrived first-generation Japanese immigrants, and this population is the driving force behind a movement to establish new ways of educating their children. This chapter describes their efforts.

Educational Programs in the US[1]

Japanese language education in the US comprises various types of programs that serve three general groups of learners: (1) 'heritage language' programs, which mainly target Japanese-American children; (2) Japanese as a 'foreign language' programs geared toward non-Japanese learners; and (3) programs that employ Japanese as a medium of instruction to teach native speakers. Japanese community language programs originally began in Hawaii in the late 19th century for the children of the Japanese community, and soon expanded to the mainland, especially to California. However, during World War II, the suspension of community language teaching resulted in a shrinking number of Japanese speakers within the immigrant community.

Japanese foreign language instruction in the US developed much later. During the 1980s and 1990s, high school student enrollment in Japanese language classes rose. In the 1990s, the College Board began to offer Japanese language as one of the possible SAT subject tests for US college admissions. The Japanese Advanced Placement Exam became available in May 2007. Most four-year colleges and universities recognize Advanced Placement exams as qualifying exams for college credit and/or placement into advanced coursework at US institutions.[2]

Since the 1970s, Japan's rapid and sustained economic growth has led to a dramatic increase in the numbers of Japanese employees and their families living outside Japan. This has resulted in the development of Japanese-language education programs aimed at 'overseas' speakers of Japanese. As of 2010, the government of Japan has recognized 88 full-time Japanese schools and 201 weekend supplementary schools throughout the world. These overseas schools are not just teaching language per se, but they are also educating students through the Japanese medium as an extension of the Japanese education system.

The issue of Japanese overseas education is of primary concern to those who work abroad, and the overseas Japanese families expect the Japanese government to support their children's Japanese education. The Japanese government has been subsidising rent for school buildings and salaries for teachers to improve and standardize the education in overseas Japanese schools. As of 2006, the Japanese Ministry of Education, or MEXT,[3] officially recognized three Japanese day schools in the US mainland. In addition, there were 87 supplementary or weekend schools, which were supplied with at least one teacher by the Japanese government. Enrollments determine the number of teachers sent and paid for by the government. A school whose enrollment is more than 100 is entitled to receive one teacher, two teachers for 200, three teachers for 800, four teachers for 1200 and five teachers for 1600 students.

The Japan Overseas Educational Service was officially founded on 29 January 1971 through the initiative of Japanese corporations engaged in overseas business activities. It is a non-profit, private organization aimed at promoting the education of Japanese children abroad in accordance with the government's policy of overseas education. With the approval of MEXT and the Japanese Ministry of Foreign Affairs, the Service has made significant contributions to promoting the education of Japanese children overseas, such as teacher recruitment, funding for school facilities and provision of textbooks.

Present Educational Issues in the Japanese Community

As of 2007, approximately 20,000 Japanese children were reported to Japanese Consulates[4] as residing in the US. Among these, approximately 12,500 were simultaneously enrolled in local schools and Japanese weekend schools. Thus more than 60% of the population was undergoing what Nagaoka (1998) calls 'bi-schooling'.

Bi-schooling is the norm among Japanese communities, especially in big cities, such as the New York metropolitan area. Undergoing bi-schooling, however, poses a challenge to the children of both sojourner and permanent resident families, because the practice emphasizes academic learning in two languages. The students have to fulfill both the academic requirements of local schools and achieve their age-norm as stipulated by MEXT.

The MEXT website shows that Japan's educational discourse and practice continues to reflect an attempt to mold students at US weekend schools into the Japanese monolingual model, to allow returnees an easy and smooth re-entry into the Japanese education system. Such an idea is ambitious for US permanent residents, whose aims for Japanese schooling are restricted to learning language and culture. They do not require the rest of the Japanese school curriculum, and they feel it unrealistic to replicate the five-day Japanese study week in four or five hours on the weekend. Even for the sojourners who will probably return to Japan, aiming for age-norm achievement within the Japanese curriculum is not necessarily an effective approach. Although the Japanese student population in the US comprises entirely bilinguals to various degrees, the pedagogical practices at weekend schools are based on an inapplicable monolingual norm.

MEXT policy documents, such as the website, project a deficit discourse about overseas Japanese students who are compared with their monolingual peers in Japan, through such expressions as 'they need to catch up with their peer students in Japan'. Furthermore, the children of US permanent resident families are seen to be generally 'weaker in Japanese compared to sojourner children', and therefore 'display more difficulty in catching up the set syllabus'. This is very unfair both to sojourner and permanent resident children. The sojourner children are compared with their monolingual peers in Japan and projected as deficient. The permanent resident children are compared with sojourners within this same deficit model based on a monolingual standard, which ignores the diverse linguistic and social backgrounds and strengths of these bilingual students.

Japan's educational discourse does not address the differences in linguistic practices among students, but favors the terms that associate their educational attainment with physical distance from Japan. Such frequently used expressions as *overseas Japanese children* (海外子女) and *returnees* (帰国生) may be rooted in Japanese cultural values that emphasize attachment to one's group, as Nakane (1972) suggests. However, this discursive practice hides rather than reveals the complexity and flexibility of bilingual's language usage, and appears to reject the idea of bilingualism by reflecting a model of what Heller (2006) calls 'double monolingualism'. In contrast, the Princeton

Community Japanese Language School advocates a more nuanced approach, and implements an alternative pedagogical model, which I discuss further in this chapter.

The Japanese Language in New York

Demographics and New York communities

The New York tri-state region has the largest Japanese population on the East Coast of the US. In 2007, the Consulate-General of Japan in New York reported 54,301 Japanese residents in the state of New York, the majority of whom were concentrated in New York City and its adjacent areas. There were 51,705 Japanese in the New York tri-state area, of whom 23,020 were residents in Bergen County, New Jersey, an area particularly favored by Japanese residents. There the Japanese population spreads along the Hudson River, from where residents commute to New York City. Westchester, New York is another favorite area, where many communities of Japanese residents and sojourners reside.

Educational programs in New York City

Most Japanese educational institutions in the New York area are organized under the auspices of the semi-official entity, the Japanese Educational Institute of New York. The Institute was founded in 1975 as a non-profit, private organization aimed at supporting the education of Japanese children in the greater New York area. The Japanese Educational Institute is funded by subsidies from the Japanese government as well as donations by companies that engage in business activities in the area. As of 2011, it operated five officially recognized schools that are supported by MEXT: two day-schools and three weekend-schools. In addition, there are also two additional private day schools, five weekend schools, as well as seven nursery schools in the metropolitan New York area under the management of the Japanese Educational Institute.

The economy has been a driving force in determining the number and composition of the student population in Japanese weekend schools, and in shaping Japan's educational policy for overseas students. Recently, a radical decline in the enrollment of sojourner students has been observed owing to Japan's economic downturn, which has resulted in fewer Japanese corporate overseas postings. When combined with a growing number of children of permanent/long-term resident families, these trends have resulted in changes to the size and composition of the student population in weekend schools.

These are common issues affecting Japanese weekend schools, irrespective of geographical area. For example, the San Francisco Japanese School, which had 1115 students in 2006, and is the second largest Japanese weekend school in the world, reports that it is confronting the same demographic shifts that create issues for educational programming. In weekend schools, language separation has been taken for granted. This is rooted in a linguistic ideology that shapes and is shaped by political, social as well as cultural discourse on language. The decline in enrollment inevitably results in less financial support, including manpower provided by MEXT. However, the existing pedagogical practices that generally offer a *diluted* version of the national curriculum to the children of permanent residence families are failing to attract as many students as they once did.

Japanese weekend schools, where a monoglossic ideology of protecting the Japanese language from English still dominates, say they are searching for a new direction. They are seeking more dynamic, flexible views toward educating the increasingly diverse student body. The Princeton Community Japanese Language School offers an alternative model, educational philosophy and pedagogical practices.

Princeton Community Japanese Language School: A Symbol of Unification of Diversity in the Japanese Community

Princeton Community Japanese Language School (PCJLS) is a weekend school that offers a variety of classes in Japanese on Sunday afternoon, serving children and adults in Princeton, New Jersey and beyond. It is the leading Japanese school in the greater New York region in teaching children and youth and employing the philosophy, pedagogy and content of Japanese education.

Originally, PCJLS was founded in 1980 by five Japanese researchers from Princeton University to serve children coming from both Japanese and American communities. Formerly, PCJLS operated on the campus of Princeton University. It relocated to Rider University in 1996, where it presently operates. The town and its adjacent area embrace a growing population of permanent Japanese residents, and the campus is accessible from New York City and other areas in New Jersey where the larger Japanese population is concentrated. As such, the attendance of the school has grown over time, and it has increasingly enriched the quality and variety of the programs to accommodate learners with diverse backgrounds and different needs and purposes. The growth of PCJLS as a Japanese school reflects the demographic changes of the Japanese population in the New York metropolitan area, as the school attempts to fulfill a role appropriate to the needs of the times.

PCJLS sees its pedagogical function as resting on three pillars. The programs at PCJLS aim to teach (1) academic subjects to Japanese students through the Japanese medium; (2) Japanese as a heritage language; and (3) Japanese as a foreign language. The school includes English-dominant learners with both Japanese and non-Japanese backgrounds. What makes PCJLS distinct from other weekend Japanese schools is its appreciation of the diversity among its learners, and its application of a set of eclectic teaching practices that aim to serve the variety of multilingual populations in their student population.

School organization and the rationale behind it

One of the marked strengths of PCJLS is the consistency in the administrative and legal status of organizational units that meet different social and educational needs of learners. PCJLS comprises two organizational components, which the school calls *divisions*. Division 1 is a *hoshu-ko*, an officially recognized supplementary school formally supported by MEXT. Division 2 is called the Princeton Course, which offers Japanese classes for English-dominant bilingual children and adults who have had no exposure to Japanese. While Division 1 is in compliance with the MEXT regulations, including a principal sent and paid for by MEXT, Division 2, the Princeton Course, is entitled to exercise autonomy, which allows PCJLS to implement flexible and varied programs to serve learners with diverse needs. While Division 1 uses the same textbooks that are used in Japan, Division 2 draws on the original syllabi, and uses original teaching materials. In this way, Division 1 prepares students to return smoothly to a school or college in Japan. Division 2 prepares students to sit for US-based exams, such as the Japanese Advanced Placement test and the Japanese SAT II subject test. As such, the systematized lesson units aim to address both short-term and long-term goals for learners.

The flexibility in structure and educational practice of PCJLS supports the bilingualism or multilingualism of individual learners. Ms Toshiko Calder, the Chair of the Board of Trustees, says:

> Through the language, the students feel the sense of connection to peers with different backgrounds and goals, which provides a unity to the whole student body, some of whom will eventually return to Japan and others will remain here for the rest of their life. The sense of legitimacy of being a part of an officially recognized school helps nurture the pride

of learning Japanese. I believe such shared experiences through language learning are essential to foster mutual respect among students, and we can see this actually growing among those who have learned and spent time together in this school. Furthermore, having two divisions in one single school system allows more appropriate placement of students, which in turn allows them to move across programs and divisions when necessary. (Interview, 28 February 2010)

The variety of programs coupled with the flexible organizational structure enhances the sustainable learning of students with diverse learning needs and objectives. According to Calder (2008),[5] as a result of opening Division 2 for students whose dominant academic language is English, the dropout rate has declined. This is because, in addition to the appropriate placement, small-sized multiage classes in Division Two are designed to accommodate the gaps between age-norm expectations and proficiency in the language. Such an arrangement is, however, an unlikely option under the usual MEXT provision, where age-norm programming is rigid and non-negotiable, owing to the national curriculum guidelines.

The students

PCJLS accepts any student above the second grade who wishes to learn Japanese. Many PCJLS students of permanent resident Japanese families are either English-dominant bilinguals or multilinguals with a parent who speaks a language other than Japanese or English. The placement is primarily based on a consultation with the student, the parent(s) and a teacher. The children of permanent resident families of Japanese origin are enrolled either for Japanese as a foreign language, or for the heritage language course in Division 2.

Pedagogy and instructional strategy

Despite the time constraints that bi-schooling students commonly face, PCJLS makes every effort to provide learning opportunities that are meaningful to students. Overseas Japanese schools often confront the discrepancy between conventional pedagogy that assumes the monolingual model and the actual proficiency in their learners' Japanese. Under those circumstances, schools normally end up providing a diluted version of the national curriculum by lowering the requirement and simply lessening the workload. Such changes tend to result in a negative downward spiral in which the students lose interest and motivation for learning, because such arrangements do not intellectually stimulate the students. Bilingual students learning at Japanese weekend schools are more cognitively developed than their command of Japanese might indicate. Tapping into the cognitive skills and knowledge that the bilingual students have gained through their dominant language, e.g. English, PCJLS offers a variety of programs that are academically challenging and stimulating. A series of lessons at PCJLS often covers interdisciplinary subjects, such as language, science, social studies, history and current affairs. Through this approach, PCJLS rejects a compartmentalization of language use, especially with regard to the learners' thinking process. Such a process may be characterized as translanguaging; that is, the use of complex discursive practices to develop bilingualism and biliteracy, and further conceptual and cultural understandings.[6]

Chinese characters are generally considered a challenge for English-dominant learners, and character learning may hinder their learning of Japanese. Accordingly, the PCJLS teachers have designed a series of original *kanji* workbooks. Each page contains a group of 10 words that are semantically related. As explained earlier, *kanji* are normally considered to be ideographs and are used to write content words, so this is an effective approach to building vocabulary. Official Japanese language textbooks specify a particular set of *kanji* to be learned in each grade, and age-norm expectations are rigid, so many bi-schooling Japanese children find it difficult to learn *kanji* at a pace determined by the national curriculum guidelines. At PCJLS, the students work on *kanji* learning as homework through the original materials, and take a quiz in class. There are six levels in the *kanji* classes, and the top two tiers prepare the students for the Japanese Advanced Placement test. Using these original materials, the students also learn how to use a Japanese dictionary of Chinese characters. This is an indispensable skill for the independent learner as it is otherwise extremely difficult for an English-dominant bilingual learner to read texts written in Japanese. During my observations of PCJLS classes, I found that students as young as grade 2 could recognize the major components of each Chinese character and knew how to count the strokes in the right order, all of which is not easy, especially for young students. At PCJLS, the students learn *kanji* systematically, so the skills necessary to develop their knowledge of *kanji* further become second nature to them.

The teachers

At PCJLS, nearly 70% of the teachers are also parents, the majority being mothers of students enrolled in the school. Reflecting the diversity of the student body, the teachers' backgrounds also vary; they may be the wife in a mixed-race couple, or a parent in a permanent residence family. Some teachers have themselves experienced bi-schooling when they were young. Therefore, the teachers share not only dedication and commitment, but also knowledge about the students' backgrounds and specific needs. According to one of the high school teachers, grade 7 is a difficult age for English-dominant bilingual learners, the majority of whom are children of mixed-race married couples. Many of them begin to display negative attitudes toward learning Japanese, as their other interests and social lives develop. My teacher-informant told me that she and a colleague have consequently decided to wait until their students become more conscious of their own ethnic identity and more eager to learn Japanese. In the meantime, this grade 7 teacher attempts to sustain her students' motivation by teaching *practical* skills and knowledge that the students can easily apply in authentic situations, such as talking with their grandparents living in Japan, shopping or dining in Japanese, and so on. Then, when the right time comes, the students are encouraged to learn more academically sophisticated language and develop their biliteracy skills. An arrangement such as this would be an unlikely option within the rigid age-norm national curriculum stipulated by MEXT.

The families at PCJLS

Parents serve as an invaluable resource and actively support students' learning at PCJLS. The teachers often give homework that involves the parents. Through this, the students have more opportunities to learn the language, and the parents become a part of their learning. They become involved in school activities such as fundraising, book management in the library and organizing school events. They also take turns to perform duties such as assisting teachers setting up the classrooms and watching the children during recess to ensure their safety and that of the environment. Such cooperative activities help strengthen parents' connection with the school and with the wider Japanese community.

A community model of schooling

Princeton Community Japanese Language School is firmly rooted in the community, and has successfully developed an alternative model of how to serve the educational needs of the Japanese communities. As a dynamic bilingual community model of schooling, PCJLS views bilingualism not as an end product, but as a process, and thus clearly rejects the compartmentalization of languages. Its flexible organizational structure accepts each bilingual student as a whole being, and accommodates the multiplicity and fluidity of bilingualism of each student. Strong leadership and a vision that is not afraid of taking the school in a new direction are central to this achievement.

Certainly, in other weekend schools, there are individual teachers who question and challenge the monolingual model. However, what distinguishes PCJLS is an educational philosophy that is upheld by the entire school and dynamic pedagogical practices that embody the rationale. The community members, namely the teachers, the students and their families, share an educational philosophy that embraces diversity and bilingualism. Thus PCJLS provides an arena where children of Japanese descent from diverse backgrounds and learners of Japanese as a foreign language can share their learning experiences under the same roof, respecting each other's aspirations and efforts to learn the Japanese language and culture. The finely tuned teaching methods and the elaborate programs are devoted towards developing bilingualism in general, and biliteracy in particular.

Conclusion: An Alternative Pedagogy for a Changing Student Population

The populations of Japanese weekend schools in New York and around the world are changing. This highlights the tension between the unrealistic expectations of the Japanese government and the needs of the students, emphasizing a need for a new pedagogy. Bilingual and other innovative approaches that are more sensitive to the needs of a varied student body offer promise.

Princeton Community Japanese Language School shows what one such approach looks like, and suggests what it might achieve. The strength of PCJLS as a community school comes from its consistency in policy, pedagogy and practice. The legitimacy and freedom that each Division of PCJLS possesses accommodates a wide variety of bilingual experiences in the student body, which has never received sufficient attention in the overseas supplementary Japanese school administration documents. Despite the large number of bi-schooling Japanese students in the US, who by definition are plurilingual, the policy documents address them simply as *overseas Japanese children*. The expression is used to contrast them with their counterparts in Japan. Consequently, overseas bilingual Japanese students are apparently categorized as second-class speakers of Japanese who do not meet the age-norm that MEXT stipulates. By showcasing the heterogeneity of learner population through the varied programs, PCJLS has successfully captured the changing reality and created a safe space for Japanese bilingual students and all American learners of Japanese language and culture. Clearly, PCJLS is another example of diasporic networks of communication where individuals are plurilingual.

The historical development of the Japanese community in the US indicates that assimilation towards the mainstream culture and language maintenance are often mutually exclusive. PCJLS has thus been attempting to challenge the Japanese educational, as well as political, discourse and the myth of monolingualism in the emerging multilingual global society. Multilingual and multicultural populations are an asset for all humankind in the 21st century, because they can act as agents to bridge potentially destructive gaps in communication and culture. Bilingual community education programs have a key role to play in fostering a global perspective in the coming generation.

Notes

(1) The figures in this section come from the Japanese Ministry of Education website, which is an excellent resource for readers who want more information (http://www.mext.go.jp/a_menu/shotou/clarinet/002.htm).
(2) See the College Board website at http://professionals.collegeboard.com/testing/ap
(3) The complete name of the Ministry is: Ministry of Education, Culture, Sports, Science and Technology, commonly known as MEXT (from MECSST).
(4) Such reporting entitles children to free Japanese school textbooks.
(5) See Calder (2008) Power Point Presentation 補習校における母語支援 −プリンストン日本語学校の実践から (in Japanese) at http://www.slidefinder.net/2/2008calder/23357071
(6) See Williams, as cited in Baker (2006) and García (2009a) for a definition and discussion of translanguaging.

7 Turkishness in New York: Languages, Ideologies and Identities in a Community-based School

Bahar Otcu

Introduction

There are more than 130 languages spoken in New York City (NYSED, 2004). Unfortunately, many of these languages are not taught in its public schools. Interestingly however, most English-speaking immigrant communities have found ways of preserving their original languages and cultures, key among them being community-based complementary schools. Three decades ago, Fishman (1980b) underlined the identity-shaping function, frequency and popularity of these schools for their ethnic communities, and called for more research on them.

This chapter focuses on the case of the Turkish community in New York City (NYC) – a growing but understudied US ethnic group. Drawing from a larger linguistic ethnography (Otcu, 2009, 2010a, 2010b), this chapter examines the role and function of a Saturday school in helping to maintain and develop Turkish and form a Turkish cultural identity particular to the US. The chapter points to the function of the school in the lives of Turkish immigrant adults and their American-born children, making evident the differences between the two generations' views of Turkishness. We will see that, despite the best efforts of Turkish immigrant parents to develop the Turkish–English bilingual capacities of their children, and the efforts of Turkish educators, a true bilingual future for these children cannot be assured without the understanding and support of mainstream educational programs.

Sociolinguistics of Turkish

Turkish belongs to Turkic languages through the Altaic language family. It has the largest number of speakers of all Turkic languages, amounting to 40% of the total (Kornfilt, 1997). Although the roots of Turkic languages are controversial, it is widely accepted that Turkish is related to Mongolian and Tungusic languages, constituting the Altaic family. Other hypotheses state that Turkic languages also include Japanese and Korean in the east, as well as Hungarian and Finnish in the north, to include the Uralic family, hence comprising a Uralic–Altaic language family (Kornfilt, 1997). Turkic languages, including Turkish, are spoken in locations ranging from Eastern Europe to northwestern China.

Following the fall of the Ottoman Empire and establishment of the modern Republic of Turkey, Turkish was made the official language of the state in the 1924 Constitution (Çolak, 2004). Since then, it has been the official and dominant language of Turkey, spoken by nearly 70 million people. It has co-official language status in Cyprus together with Greek, and is spoken by nearly 19% of the population there (Kornfilt, 1997).

Turkish uses the Latin script containing 29 letters with a few adapted to the language. Since it is a phonetic language, each letter corresponds to one discrete sound:

A B C Ç D E F G Ğ H I İ J K L M N O Ö P R S Ş T U Ü V Y Z
a b c ç d e f g ğ h ı i j k l m n o ö p r s ş t u ü v y z

The first grammar of the Turkish spoken in Anatolia, the larger part of Turkey located in Asia, dates back to the 16th century, and the first Turkish grammar written by a European to the 17th century (Dilaçar, as cited in Taylan, 2002). Some distinct characteristics of Turkish grammar can be listed as follows:

(1) morphophonemic alternations governed by vowel or consonant harmony rules, for example, the suffix -lar/-ler, which makes a word plural, changes according to the preceding sound in a word:

çan	[bell]	çan**lar**	[bells]
kedi	[cat]	kedi**ler**	[cats]

(2) agglutinative morphology, for example,

Biz	New York'a	gidiyoruz [We are going to New York]
1st p. pl.	Obj + to	V + aux + 1st p. pl.

(3) verb final word order, that is, 'subject, object, verb' (SOV) main word
     order, which permits variation, for example,

Biz New York'a gidiyoruz	[We are going to New York]
New York'a gidiyoruz biz	[We are going to New York]
New York'a biz gidiyoruz	[We are going to New York]
Gidiyoruz New York'a biz	[We are going to New York]
Gidiyoruz biz New York'a	[We are going to New York]

(4) nominalized subordinate clause structures and pro-drop properties
     (Taylan, 2002), for example, New York'a gidiyoruz (subject pronoun
     'Biz' [We] is dropped as the verb is already inflected with it).

Standing out as an integral part of the Turkish linguistic and cultural history is Turkey's most important language planning effort, i.e. the Turkish
Language Reform. It took place between 1928 and 1980 (Doğançay-Aktuna,
1998), and has been studied by many sociolinguists to date (e.g. Fishman,
1971; Hayhoe, 1979, 1998; Nahir, 1977; Lewis, 2002). The Turkish Language
Reform was the most important step in accelerating Atatürk's goal of forming a modern nation-state out of the remains of the Ottoman Empire. In
1928, Kemal Atatürk's decision to abandon the Arabic script that had been
used for centuries and adopt the Latin alphabet with minor modifications
(Bereday, 1964 as cited in Hayhoe, 1998) gave a start to the Turkish
Language Reform. There were two essential undertakings in the whole
movement: (1) the script reform – the adoption of the Latin alphabet; and
(2) the language reform – the purification of the lexicon and grammar rules
from the influence of other languages, especially Arabic and Persian
(Doğançay-Aktuna, 1993), which were considered as languages of the back-
ward past.
    After Atatürk personally introduced the new Turkish letters on 9
August 1928, classes were held to teach them to higher officials, deputies,
university professors and intellectuals (Çolak, 2004). A nationwide education campaign started the following semester, establishing education in the
new alphabet and forms for schoolchildren and setting up *Millet Mektepleri*
(Nation Schools) for compulsory adult education (Çolak, 2004). A commission called *Dil Encümeni* (The Language Commission) was in charge of producing the 'new Turkish Standard Dictionary' by replacing foreign-origin
words with pure Turkish words until the establishment of the *Türk Dil
Kurumu* (Turkish Language Association, TDK) in 1932 (Çolak, 2004: 75).
The TDK became the major language planning agency, aided by politicians,
teachers and other interested people from all walks of life until the 1980s.

In the 1980s, however, the work of TDK was limited by newly elected governments. Since the mid-1980s, both state-planned and unplanned language policies (e.g. the rapid spread of English) have been observed in the country.

History of Turkish Immigration to the US

There have been three waves of immigration from Turkey to the US – at the beginning of the 19th century, after World War II and in the late 1980s (Kaya, 2004). Between 1820 and 1920, during the first wave, 291,435 people came to the US, representing the largest immigration from the Ottoman Empire. Only 50,000 of them were Muslim Turks (Ahmed, 1986). For these first-generation Turkish immigrants, religion (being Muslim or Ottoman) rather than ethnicity was the primary marker of identity.

Between the 1950s and early 1980s, the second wave brought to the US highly educated professionals, such as engineers, doctors, academics and graduate students, for training purposes. These immigrants were nationalistic and secular in their views. A number of Turkish-American organizations were established during this second wave, and one of them was the Turkish Women's League of America (TWLA), established in 1958. Atatürk School, the focus site of this chapter, was established by this non-profit organization in 1971.

The third and last immigration wave between the mid 1980s and the 1990s was stimulated by globalization. The most diverse group of Turkish immigrants, including businessmen and blue-collar workers, arrived. Since the 1990s, the Diversity Immigration Visa Program (also known as the US Lottery System) has brought an increasing number of Turkish immigrants to the US every year.

US demographics and present settlements

The largest Turkish community in the US today is concentrated in and around metropolitan areas such as New York, New Jersey, Washington, DC, California, Florida, Texas and Illinois. There has been an increase in the size of the Turkish-American population in recent years. According to the 2005 American Community Survey, there were 164,945 people with Turkish ancestry in the US, although this number is listed as 189,640 in the 2008 American Community Survey (US Census Bureau, 2005, 2008b).

Most Turkish-Americans usually have much higher educational levels than Turkish populations who have immigrated to European countries

(Akinci, 2002 and Karpat, 1995, as cited in Kaya, 2003). They have situated themselves in the middle class and are highly integrated into the larger American culture (Kaya, 2003). They also have increasingly established Turkish-American organizations and institutions throughout the US, which reach out to the community, mainly through internet websites and electronic newsletters, which are mostly bilingual. These organizations are gathered under two bigger umbrella organizations, namely the Federation of Turkish-American Associations and the Assembly of Turkish-American Associations. Every year in May, the Federation organizes a Turkish Day parade in NYC, and thousands of Turks come from all around the US to march about 15 blocks from Madison Avenue to Second Avenue. At the end of the parade, Turkish people gather at Dag Hammarskjold Park on 47th Street and Second Avenue to spend the rest of the day. A small fair, where Turkish food, groceries and gift items are sold, and a free music concert by two famous Turkish singers take place here. Turks also have their own newspapers, radio and TV programs, clubs and restaurants, and social clubs all around the US and NYC[1]

K–12 Programs

There are presently two types of educational programs for K–12 students of Turkish families in and around New York. One of these programs is the Atatürk School, a community-based Saturday school, which is the focus of this chapter. Having been established in 1971, it holds special importance since it is the oldest continuously operating school among those that serve the Turkish community in the US. There are also two private Turkish all-day schools. These are Amity School in Brooklyn and Pioneer Academy of Science in New Jersey.

Private schools

Brooklyn Amity School (BAS) and Pioneer Academy of Science (PAS) (in Clifton and Cherry Hill Township in New Jersey) are private schools founded in 1999 by Turkish-American businessmen. Both BAS and PAS operate in accordance with the New York State Department of Education regulations. An average of 200 students from all ethnic backgrounds are enrolled, but the majority are Turkish-Americans. They follow a college preparatory curriculum that emphasizes maths and science. The medium of instruction in both BAS and PAS is English, but a few hours of Turkish are offered as an elective course. Students are required to be involved in school activities and competitions, one of which is the annual Turkish Olympiads organized in the US and Turkey every year.

BAS and PAS are similar because of their ideological orientations. Among the NYC Turkish community, these schools are known for their closeness to 'Gülen cemaat', a religiously oriented controversial Turkish movement that includes followers of Fethullah Gülen. Gülen is a former 'imam' who considers himself a prophet (Sharon-Krespin, 2009) and is associated with the concept of 'moderate Islam' recently introduced to Turkey as opposed to 'secular' Turkey. Gülen has been under close inspection by the Turkish military since the 1970s because of his illegal Islamic summer youth camps in Turkey (Sharon-Krespin, 2009). Since 1998, he has been living in the US. In recent years, he has been praised in the West and the US as a reformist of Islam and advocate for tolerance because he emphasizes the commonalities between Abrahamic religions (Sharon-Krespin, 2009).

Gülen owns many schools and universities in Turkey and tens of 'Turkish schools' abroad, which aim to bolster his movement. On the other hand, his private schools in the US, mostly charter schools, have recently come under scrutiny and their purposes have been investigated. Sharon-Krespin (2009: 55) claims that schools such as BAS and PAS are known to indoctrinate students as Muslims 'not so much "in school", but through direct proselytism "outside school"' (Sharon-Krespin, 2009). It is the community they create and their extracurricular activities that are said to achieve their goal. The Turkish Olympiads that have taken place since 2003 both in the US and in Turkey are organized by sponsors of the Gülen movement. Other ways in which these schools promote Turkishness is by organizing activities in Brooklyn and New Jersey on Turkey's 23 April Children's Day every year. They also frequently invite Turkish diplomats to give speeches in their schools or visit them in Washington, DC or New York with a group of Turkish-American students (Brooklyn Amity School, 2011; Pioneer Academy of Science, 2011). There is no connection between these schools and Atatürk School, the focus of this chapter, which is described below in detail.

Community-based Complementary Schools

The focus of this chapter is the other program type for the Turkish-American community in NYC region, complementary schools. Even though there have been several weekend schools established for the Turkish-American community over the years, only Atatürk School has been operating for 40 years.

There are no previous studies that have taken place in a Turkish school in the US, and the exact number of Turkish heritage schools in the nation is not known. However, Atatürk School shares comparable characteristics with the Turkish complementary school researched along with three different ethnic schools in England (Creese *et al.*, 2008). The websites of certain Turkish-American organizations also point to the existence of their own weekend schools, mainly located in Chicago, Orange County, Rochester, Michigan, North Carolina, San Diego, Philadelphia and Washington, DC. These schools have been established since the 1990s. Student enrollment in these schools is between 15 and 70, and the age range of students is from 3 to 15. The schools operate on Saturdays or Sundays for 1.5–2 hours in the mornings. They also follow a secular education system like Atatürk School, and focus on teaching students how to write, read and speak in Turkish, and expand their knowledge of Turkish history, geography, music, folk dances, culture and, in rare cases, mathematics.

Atatürk School

Atatürk School operates on the second floor of the 10-floor Turkish Consulate opposite the United Nations in Manhattan. The second floor is a large hall that carries no trace of a school during the week. On Saturdays, it is turned into a make-shift school, divided into six by room dividers. Each section creates a classroom space with a portable whiteboard and seats. Since there are no concrete walls between classes, teachers' voices and activity sounds are easily heard from one classroom to another.

The school takes place only on Saturdays from 10 am to 4 pm from October to June. It does not observe any official holidays, and therefore, there are no breaks throughout the year. Pre-school and elementary school-aged children (4- to 14-year-olds) of Turkish families are placed in classrooms based on their proficiency in Turkish. Because of this proficiency-based place-ment policy, older students such as 11-year-olds can sometimes be placed in the first-grade class, which is composed mainly of 7-year-olds.

The graduates from the fifth grade receive a certificate equivalent to a Turkish elementary school diploma. With this diploma, they can satisfy the foreign language requirement in their regular schools, receiving 3.5 credit points upon graduation from their school. If they happen to move back to Turkey, they can continue their education without losing a year.

Atatürk School is not funded by the Turkish Government. The only sup-port from the government is providing instructional space in the Turkish Consulate and grade-level elementary school textbooks imported from Turkey. Only the founder organization, the TWLA, sponsors the school. It operates entirely on a voluntary basis through donations from the TWLA, as well as from parents and philanthropists. For instance, the TWLA organizes events such as the 'Turkish bazaar', where Turkish goods and food are sold. These bazaars are open to the public, and their earnings contribute to school expenses such as stationery, books and small gifts given to students on special days.

School community and leadership

There is a clear effort on the part of the Turkish community in NYC to maintain Atatürk School. Because the continuation of successful leadership is seen as the most important aspect, it has been given priority in the by-laws and the general assemblies of the board members of the TWLA every two years.

The present principal, who is a role model and a dedicated leader, has been in charge for the last 15 years. She is a middle-aged, kind and energetic woman, whose smart clothing style and tactful way of talking, acting and treating people clearly show that she is the school's leader. Having obtained her teaching credentials in Turkey, the principal has been living in the US since 1982. She selects the teachers to be hired, creates the academic calendar, registers students, keeps student records, handles the school budget, coordinates activities and maintains close contact with all the students' parents. While it is mainly the principal's responsibility to select the teachers, the TWLA also participates in the teacher selection process since the principal asks their opinion.

All administrators indicate that teachers at Atatürk School should have been educated in Turkey, and have had experience teaching elementary school. In addition, teachers should be able to communicate and establish dialogue with students easily, love children and be able to be both a friend and a teacher role model simultaneously. Administrators highlight that teachers should value old Turkish values, and be tolerant and patient to students' reactions when they assert their American identities:

There are our values that belong to us, that especially belong to Turks. For example when a teacher comes, standing up, being silent, being respectful, when the teacher speaks or when asking for the floor, raising your hand. At first these are hard for them ... The biggest thing I face here is that sometimes our students show their reactions to some incidences *extremely*, I mean in a way that we can't expect in Turkey, that can't be given to a teacher ... For instance s/he can say I'll call the police because of the smallest reason. ... They can express their reactions

I mean *in a very harsh way*. This is why we have to be very patient. (Principal, interview, 8 March 2008, original in Turkish)

Atatürk School now has 10 teachers – the grade level teachers who teach Pre-K and grades 1–5 grades, and teachers who teach arts, drama, music and folk dancing. With the exception of music and folk dancing, all teachers are female. Many parents or relatives of students work as teachers. They have regular jobs during the week, and teach almost voluntarily. The small amount of annual tuition pay, about US$325, allows the TWLA to offer teachers a salary that roughly meets their transportation expenses. The main qualities of teachers are their love and respect for Atatürk, the founder of modern Turkey, and their willingness to commute long distances to Manhattan to teach every Saturday.

Students' parents are willing to come from NYC's different boroughs, upstate New York, and New Jersey. Mothers are mainly in charge of bringing their children to school, rather than fathers. A majority of the parents are first-generation immigrants, mostly recent arrivals. There are also children of transnational families who are in the US for a short time. Parents' ages range between 32 and 49, with a mean age of arrival to the US of 26. The majority of the school parents are married to Turkish-born spouses (77%), with the remainder married to either non-Turkish or Turkish born outside of Turkey (Otcu, 2009, 2010a, 2010b). Most parents (73%) have higher education, and the top reason for coming to the US is to pursue a graduate degree.

The majority of children in Atatürk School (73%) were born in the US. The rest of the students (27%) were born in Turkey, but have been living in the US for more than five years (Otcu, 2009, 2010a, b). Hence, following Portes and Rumbaut (2001), the students are mostly second-generation immigrants.

School Practices and Policies

Three main kinds of activities reflect teaching of Turkishness in Atatürk School – educational practices, routines and rituals. All of the Turkish national and religious holidays, as well as important days, are celebrated with a ceremony, which establishes a collective Turkish identity among the school community. Students perform their Turkish language and cultural skills in all ceremonies. They are required to be dressed in red and white in all these ceremonies, to reflect the colors of the Turkish flag.

Every Saturday starts with a ritual, in which the children recite 'Andımız' [Our Pledge], a piece of verse similar to the Pledge of Allegiance. Afterwards, students disperse to their classrooms until lunchtime. While they are in class, a parent is on duty and waits outside the hall. Other parents wait in the school and socialize by talking or drinking tea. Other parents sing Turkish songs in a choir they have organized. Yet others go shopping and sightseeing. They come back with food for their children at lunchtime – a period of socialization for the parents. On the first and second floors, home-made Turkish food, pizza and drinks are available. All food is sold for low prices and the proceeds go to the school budget.

Lunchtime is the only break throughout the entire day. Students unwind with activities like playing and running on the second floor, which gets over-crowded during this time. At around 2 pm, music education starts. Here, room dividers are opened and five grade levels come together to sing Turkish songs accompanied by the music teacher's piano. They sing marches, patri-otic songs and folk songs from Turkey, which stands out as students' favorite activity. The titles of some of the songs are as follows: *Onuncu Yıl Marşı* [10th Year Anthem], *Hoşgelişler Ola* [Welcome Mustafa Kemal Pasha], *Gençlik Marşı* [Youth Anthem], *Atam Sen Rahat Uyu* [Sleep in Peace My Atatürk] and *Bir Köy Var Uzakta* [There's a Village Far Away]. All of these songs have similar themes – restoration of Turkey after the War of Independence in the early 1920s, the speedy success of modern Turkish Republic in its early years, the role of the Turkish youth in preserving the modern state, and being united as a nation despite living in the remotest regions of Turkey.

School ends at 4 pm, and the parents or relatives of children pick them up from school. If the students are members of the folk dance group or if they need to attend rehearsals for an upcoming show, they stay and practice until 6 p.m. Teachers hold their weekly meeting after school, staying until 6 p.m. or later.

Because the school implements the Turkish elementary school curricu-lum, teaching of language and culture overlaps. All lessons include language skills such as detailed analyses of texts via reading and answering questions, and students are constantly exposed to Turkish. Cultural information is imparted in social studies or life studies and Turkish lessons, rather than in separate culture-focused ones. Both curricular and extracurricular activities are secular. Religious education sessions are kept at a minimum. Pedagogical techniques follow traditional methods, namely rote memorization and reci-tation, writing, dictation, read-alouds, summarizing and language tests. In terms of classroom interaction, teacher-oriented initiation–response–follow-up (Sinclair & Coulthard, 1975) structure is observed most of the time.

Students are mainly English-dominant, and there is a Turkish-only policy. Adult clientele frequently warn students, 'Speak Turkish!' Students know they should speak Turkish to adults, but they contest this rule by speaking English to each other. Pennycook (2003) refers to such language choice as *performativity*, which questions pre-given identities and indicates performing identities via the use of language. Students frequently assert their American identities via the use of English. Rarely do they speak Turkish to each other when talking about their Turkish homework. Adults accommodate students' varying needs too. Especially in elementary levels, where students' Turkish proficiency is low, teachers translanguage (García, 2009a) in giving instructions and calling numbers. For example, during one observation, a teacher said:

Evet e sesini artık öğrendik. Şimdi sayfa yirmiüç. *Page twenty-three*. Ne diyoruz biz ona Türkçe? Yirmiüç
[Alright we learned the /e/ sound. Now page twenty three. *Page twenty-three*. What do we call it in Turkish? Twenty three]. (Field notes, 20 October 2007)

Reflected through the Turkish-only policy and school practices, adults frequently 'other' the non-Turkish elements in their lives, while they collectively embrace Turkishness via 'we-code'. In an interview, a parent verbalized the importance of this school as follows:

Because it's a school *abroad* in a way, it's introducing Turkey, like a center somehow. Because I mean, the schools in Turkey don't introduce Turkey. Because all of them are already the same. But here in the consulate's building, I mean already in a building representing Turkey in a *foreign* country established under the roof of a building representing Turkey. In a way it represents Turkey. (A mother, interview, 9 February 2008, original in Turkish)

In this comment, the parent has referred to the US as 'abroad', a frequent term used by the first-generation parents. The central position of the school indicated in this comment emphasizes its ability to bring together both generations of Turkish immigrants collectively.

Challenges

The administrators deal with many challenges that the school faces. While it is advantageous to be in a central and special building such as the Consulate, there are logistic difficulties that this position brings. For example, professional development for teachers is difficult because there are limited time and resources. The teachers, most of whom have experience teaching in Turkey in the past, continue teaching through traditional methodology. One teacher explains:

> If there were more [i.e. materials and resources in the school], I believe we would be more successful. *We are successful* now as well. We still go on with old methods. (Laughs) But with the old methods too *I believe we are successful*. (Third-grade teacher, interview, 23 February 2008, original in Turkish)

The teachers also express dissatisfaction with child-unfriendly physical settings, noisy classroom environments, lack of up-to-date educational materials, and limited school time. They accept these challenges as a reality and try to do their best. Parents likewise point to the same issues as challenges, adding lack of recess times and inability to improve the teaching to this list.

Another challenge the school faces is its disconnection from the mainstream public schools that the children attend, other than facilitating an additional 3.5 foreign language credits. Administrators and teachers almost never refer to American mainstream education in terms of practices and policies. Parents indicate their childrens' complaints on Saturday mornings, as it is an extra school day for them. One student's parent says:

> Sometimes they complain because Saturdays are extra. I tell them, I mean, we are not the only ones that do this … I say Greeks, Hispanics, and Arabs, your other friends also go to other schools, and you need to do this. I tell her 'it will help you in the future, and you will thank me'. Then she understands. (A mother, interview, 26 January 2008, original in Turkish)

Students know Atatürk School's limitations in comparison to their regular schools, but they do not criticize or complain about these – at least verbally. Students indicate that they like the school once they come and they accept it as it is. Following is an excerpt from an interview I conducted with Damla, a first grader:

Bahar: Is there anything that you want to be better in this school? Like there's something but you'd be happier if it is in some other way?

Damla: No, I like it just how it is. (Interview, 26 January 2008, original in English)

The principal of Atatürk School has a positive outlook regardless of challenges, and believes that the school will continue for many years, improving each year: 'Our biggest wish is to be able to prepare that foundation, present our students with better things' (interview, 8 March 2008, original in Turkish).

Benefits for the Community

Atatürk School connects the Turkish-American children to their heritage, especially via a focus on Atatürk, and to the social and academic life in Turkey. This connection is a dynamic one, letting the children perform Turkishness as a living identity of the present. This dynamic connection, which students can carry back and forth whenever they travel between both countries, is significant as it pertains to the intergenerational transmission of the language and cultural values from first generation to second generation. As Fishman (1991) argues, language maintenance depends on transmission across generations, and schools alone cannot reverse language shift without further steps that take the community language beyond the classroom. The parents are aware of this fact and try their best to achieve this at home and through school.

Through creating a connection to Turkishness, the school also builds a collective Turkish-American identity. Both this connection and collectivity yield contentment mainly for adults. The administrators and teachers express their pleasure at the expectations met by students, the general quality of the education and the commitment of the teachers. Parents also feel pleased with their children's progress in Turkish, but especially with the children's development of a bilingual and bicultural identity. The former TWLA president expressed this sentiment:

It seems to me that in a very dominant culture, we raise young people, who know the original culture that they come from, who can also be integrated into this culture, and who can manage to live in both countries by learning about these two countries, instead of becoming a person with problems in the future because of not learning about the culture that their family come from. (Interview, 14 March 2008, original in Turkish)

Conclusion

Turkishness and Americanness go hand in hand, and at the same time sometimes challenge each other in this school. The adults – as first-generation immigrants holding on to their essential values and ideas – see the US as a foreign country and refer to English as a foreign language. Their overall beliefs and ideologies meet in the desire that their children know and be attached to their Turkish background. The children, on the other hand, exhibit fluid and hybrid identities. They reject the adults' Discourses[2] by speaking English to their peers in the school, but they also speak Turkish to adults and accept their Discourses. These observations parallel Fishman's (1980b: 243) argument that an ethnic mother tongue school moderates and modulates 'ethnic uniqueness at the same time that it channels Americanness via the community's own institutions'.

In an era when bilingual education has been silenced (García, 2005, 2009a), this overall function of ethnic mother tongue schools is worth highlighting. These complementary schools fill gaps in the current educational system by promoting the home languages of young bilingual students, and thus going beyond traditional heritage language education. They also transcend bilingual education, because as Wang and Green (2001) suggest, instead of the mainstream K–12 school system trying to identify students as belonging to a certain heritage, the community-based schools provide natural environments with their ethnolinguistic communities and their cultures.

Constant repetition of Discourses (e.g. a Turkish-only policy, respect, silence, Turkish national history, Atatürk) points to the production and reproduction of ideologies in the Turkish school. It is through these ideologies that the Turkish school is created as an institutionalized language ideological site (Kroskrity, 2000). It is again through these ideologies that the Turkish school ensures 'the repetition and ritualization of the situations that sustain' it (Gee, 1999/2005: 83). Within these ideologies, students are situated at different points, mainly because of the limited time of exposure to education in the home language. Schools like Atatürk School cannot continue to serve their students after elementary school when it is essential to not only maintain but also develop home languages (Otheguy & Otto, 1980), along with English. Unless the opportunities afforded by these community complementary schools are expanded and linked to the efforts of mainstream public schools, precious language resources and cultural knowledge will be wasted and children of immigrants will not become bilingual. True bilingual education is the most meaningful way of teaching and developing languages other than English in the US. If mainstream public education were reorganized to meet the language, cultural and academic needs of children of immigrants, and students of different language origins, there would be considerable benefits not only for learners but also for their communities and the US society at large.

With the present assimilationist language policies of the US, including educational policies that mandate 'students' annual progress reports that are based on written standard English assessments' (Menken as cited in García, 2009a: 86), English is being emphasized in mainstream education at the expense of students' home languages and their bilingual development. In such an environment, it is only a dream to wish for true bilingual education for second-generation Americans. Thus, the community-based schools like Atatürk School are an important means to develop the bilingual capacities and cross-cultural understandings of American children that will serve us well in an increasingly global world.

Notes

(1) For detailed information on Turkish media, visit: http://www.turkishconnection.com/media.htm
(2) According to Gee's discourse analysis model employed in the larger study, all discourses are ideological. Gee (1999/2005) makes a distinction between 'Discourse' with a 'capital D' and 'discourse' with a 'little d'. 'Discourse' with a 'little d' is language in use, or the way language is used on site to enact activities and identities. Gee argues, however, that 'activities and identities are rarely ever enacted through language alone' (1999: 6–7). It is when 'little d' discourse (language-in-use) integrates with non-language components to enact specific identities and activities that 'big D' Discourses are involved. Gee's Discourse with a big 'D' brings together both language and non-language elements (e.g. sign systems, beliefs, attitudes etc.) to explain how language is situated in and influenced by the context in which it is used.

8 Going to Greek School: The Politics of Religion, Identity and Culture in Community-based Greek Language Schools

Maria Hantzopoulos

Introduction

The Greek-speaking diaspora in the US, the majority of whom have roots from the nation-states of Greece and Cyprus, has had a long history of establishing community-based Greek language programs in the places where they live. These programs, often affiliated with the Greek Orthodox Church, have ostensibly provided space for some to maintain the Greek language, to prevent language loss and to preserve some aspects of Greek culture and identity. While there is certainly no singular definition of Greek culture and identity, particularly as Greek populations have resided across most continents and throughout Europe, the significance of maintaining some sort of 'Greek-ness' has had historical significance for many who identify themselves as Greek. Particularly during times of foreign domination and minority status in non-Greek-speaking nation-states or empires, the preservation of Greek language has been one of the essential binding forces for their identity (Constantakos & Spiradakis, 1997). As a result, this historical link between language, culture and ethnic survival is inherently connected to the many reasons why Greek speakers have continually established language schools in their diaspora communities.

In the US, Greek-speaking populations immigrated in large numbers throughout various waves in the 20th century, establishing themselves as part of more long-standing immigrant groups at the turn of the century and more recent ones in the latter half. Throughout these periods, community-led organizations and language schools, mostly connected with the Greek Orthodox Church, have played central roles in preserving a sense of 'Greek' identity in the new homeland. Since the mid-1970s however, Greek immigration to the US has steadily waned, plausibly creating less fertile conditions for language maintenance, as the numbers of people from Greece and Cyprus have decreased. According to many scholars of Greek America, this decline in immigration, coupled with an increase in inter-faith and interethnic marriages, poses an existential threat to both Greek language maintenance and cultural survival in the US (Constantakos & Spiradakis, 1997; Georgakas, 2004–2005). Yet, community-led language organizations, mostly affiliated with the Greek Orthodox Church, still exist and thrive nationwide, particularly in communities where there remain high concentrations of those who identify as Greek.

Nonetheless, these shifts in immigration and demographic patterns present a new challenge for Greek-speaking populations in the US. As the immigration of these populations declines in the 21st century, what role does community-led bilingual education play in how this particular speech community educates its children to speak Greek? What are the possibilities and what are the limitations of these religious institutions as sites for developing dynamic bilingualism and biculturalism for the Greek community? The purpose of this chapter is to consider how shifting demographics may complicate existing ways in which these schools have operated in Greek-speaking communities.

Moreover, I raise questions about how these schools might mediate cultural plurality, identity politics and religious affiliation. Both historically and contemporarily, there have been, and are, ethnically identified Greeks who are not Greek Orthodox (e.g. Catholics, Jews & Muslims), as well as Greek Orthodox communities that are not ethnically Greek (e.g. Arabs, Serbians), thus disturbing the idea that religious affiliation with the Greek Orthodox Church automatically identifies someone as ethnically Greek. Additionally, many of the children who attend these schools are from inter-ethnic unions among Greeks and non-Greeks from various religious backgrounds. These points are specifically salient not only because they trouble singular notions of ethnic identity, but also because they muddy the ways in which religion has often been a (mis)signifier for 'Greek-ness'. This does not diminish the laudable commitment of the Greek Orthodox Church in providing community bilingual education. However, by interviewing school administrators and parents of children who attend an after-school program at a local church in New York City, I shed light on the possibilities and limitations of these institutions as sites for dynamic Greek biculturalism and bilingualism, providing new understandings of this US ethnolinguistic community that is often (mistakenly) viewed monolithically.

The Languages of Greeks: Historical and Contemporary Overview

Spoken by approximately 12–15 million people worldwide,[1] Modern Greek is the official language of Greece and is one of the official languages of Cyprus and the European Union. Greek, an Indo-European language in origin, has metamorphosed and changed throughout time (see Table 8.1). When Greece broke from Ottoman rule with a series of uprisings between 1821 and 1830, and became recognized as an independent nation-state in 1831, the new government laid the foundation for what is known as Modern Greek. Over time, however, the Greek language came in contact with and was influenced by other languages, including Latin, Aramaic, Hebrew, Slavic, Italian and Ottoman Turkish (see Constantakos & Spiradakis, 1997; Dragoumis, 2006).

Modern Greek has two main varieties that have been in use since the end of Ottoman rule: Dimotiki, the popular and vernacular form of the language; and Katharevousa, literally the 'Pure' form, which imitates classical Greek. Until fairly recently, Katharevousa was the official language, written and spoken in formal contexts, including schools, the armed forces, newspapers, law, medicine and broadcast media. Its use elevated the variety to more elite status, while Dimotiki served as language of the masses, spoken colloquially by most Greeks and generally only written in creative contexts. While there were always linguistic, political, and ideological

Table 8.1 Languages of the Greeks

Language	Period
Mycenaean Greek	14th to 8th centuries BC
Classical or Ancient Greek	8th to 4th centuries BC
Hellenistic Greek	4th century BC to 4th century AD
Byzantine Greek	*ca* 330 to 15th century AD
Ottoman Greek	15th to mid-19th centuries AD
Modern Greek	Mid-19th century AD to today

polemics surrounding the usage of 'pure' vs 'popular' Greek (and for some, this continues), the Greek government finally adopted Dimotiki as the official language of the nation in 1976 (Dragoumis, 2006). Six years later, in 1982, they moved further in simplifying Greek orthography from polytonic to monotonic, resulting in more widespread accessibility of the language in its written form.[2] This shift has more or less become fully implemented in all of Greece (Constantakos & Spiradakis, 1997; Demakopoulos, 1989/2000). Although Dimotiki is now the official form of Greek, spoken regional varieties of Modern Greek continue to exist in Greece, Cyprus and other diaspora communities, many of which are unique and quite distinct from each other (Horrocks, 1997).

Greek comes into regular contact with a number of other languages in Greece and Cyprus, including those of the long-standing communities that speak Turkish (the other official language of Cyprus), Albanian, Bulgarian, Macedonian and Romany. Additionally, recent immigration to Greece and Cyprus from around the world have introduced other languages in both countries, including Russian, Urdu, Hindi and Arabic (Constantakos & Spiradakis, 1997; Greek Census, 2001). The extent to which the more recent populations in these countries speak Modern Greek varies, depending on several factors related to their immigration, work and educational status.

Finally, forms of Greek have not only been spoken in Greece and Cyprus, but have also been used historically in long-standing communities in Albania, Turkey, Egypt, Ukraine, Palestine, Corsica and southern Italy, as well as by Greek-speaking immigrants that have settled in various parts of the world, in particular in the US, Canada and Australia. While these latter populations and their children often speak Greek in their new homelands, the form of Greek they use has influences from and interacts with English. Many Greek-Americans and some scholars (Van Dyck, 2006) refer to this phenomenon as 'Gringlish'; however, others argue that this concept, much like 'Spanglish', can be reductive (García, 2009b; Otheguy, 2003). Rather, these scholars suggest that communicative practices used by bilingual communities draw on complex linguistic and cultural knowledges, and that bilinguals in fact 'translanguage' by engaging in multiple discursive practices to make sense of their multilingual worlds (see García, 2009a).

Greek immigration to the US and New York City[3]

Populations of Greeks have resided in the US since before the inception of the nation-state, including communities in both St Augustine, Florida and New Orleans, Louisiana in the 18th and 19th centuries. Greeks immigrated to the US in several waves, including large-scale immigration in four general periods: 1890–1922, 1923–1939, 1940–1950 and 1960 to the present (Constantakos & Spiradakis, 1997). That said, the actual figures of how many Greeks have immigrated to the US over time are nearly impossible to ascertain since immigrants are counted from the country from which they arrived. According to Constantinou (2002: 94),

> A Greek from Alexandria is classified as an Egyptian, and a Greek from Constantinople (Istanbul) as a Turk. This fails to count the number of Greeks that emigrated from the Hellenic diaspora (Turkey, Balkan countries, Egypt, and Cyprus). As a result, many immigrants of Greek ancestry were not counted as Greek.

Nonetheless, immigration records still document an approximate, although not wholly accurate, record of Greek influx into the US.

During the initial period of Greek immigration, most of the migrants were illiterate and under-educated young men who had no English language skills and came for economic reasons, with the intent of returning 'home'. They generally settled in three major areas: the Western states, to work on railroad construction; the New England states, to work in textile and shoe factories; and the urban centers of New York and Chicago, to work as peddlers or in factories. By the 1920s, many US Greeks were leaving the factories to establish businesses like restaurants and hotels, revealing their more permanent status. Furthermore, female Greek immigration and the establishment of Greek families with American-born children also increased in this period, augmenting the permanent status of the Greek-American community. However, soon after this first phase, quotas were established that restricted immigration from Greece to the US. The Johnson–Reed Act of 1924, for example, limited immigration to 100 Greeks per year. This quota was raised to 307 in 1929, where it remained until the 1960s (Constantakos & Spiradakis, 1997). This restriction had two significant consequences for the community: (1) American-born Greeks began to outnumber foreign-born Greeks (except in New York City); and (2) there was a massive scramble to acquire American citizenship by those who were already in the US. These changes helped define the 'Greek-ness' of the Greek-American community and led to a decreased usage of the Greek language in the US.

Post World War II immigration, nonetheless, contributed to a revival of Greek life and identity in the US. While the quota remained in effect through 1965, laws were changed that enabled the entry number of Greek immigrants to be 'borrowed' from future years, so that the actual number of immigrants from a particular year could exceed quota limitations. Under these new provisions, approximately 70,000 Greeks immigrated to the US between 1945 and 1965 (Constantakos & Spiradakis, 1997). Most of these immigrants settled in large urban centers, including New York City and around Boston, Massachusetts. Further, the Immigration and Nationality Act of 1965 also increased the number of Greeks coming to the US, as the previous quotas were lifted and family reunification visas became unlimited. It was during this time that Astoria, Queens became the largest destination for Greek immigration, establishing it as the 'Greek-town' of today. While Greeks also settled in other parts of New York City (NYC), including Washington Heights and Bay Ridge, their large and predominant presence in Astoria contributes to the perception that the neighborhood is the largest Greek 'city' outside of Athens.[4]

The 2009 Census American Community Survey revealed that there were 1,390,439 Greeks in the US. The US State Department states that an estimated 3 million American residents claim Greek descent, suggesting that the Census figures may underestimate the total numbers. According to the 2009 American Community Survey, 163,337 who claimed Greek ancestry were born outside of the US. Of those, 85.4% entered the US before 1990, 7.9% between 1990 and 1999, and 6.8% after 2000. Despite the decline in rapid immigration, 26.1% of Greeks still speak Greek at home, and 6.2% of Greeks speak English 'less than very well'.

New York State claims the highest number of those identifying as Greek (185,024) followed by California, Illinois and Massachusetts (US Census Bureau, 2009). The 2009 American Community Survey Estimates also put the figure of people who claim Greek ancestry in New York City at 91,289, making up 1.08% of the whole NYC population. Of those who claimed Greek ancestry in NYC in 2009, 31,707 (35%) are foreign born and 56,688 (62%) speak Greek at home (US Census Bureau, 2009). Additionally, of those who do speak Greek at home in NYC, 38,536 (42%) claim to speak English very well and 18,152 (20%) claim to speak English less than very well. The percentages of those who speak Greek and do not speak English well are much higher in NYC than in other parts of the country, suggesting that the high concentration of Greek speakers in one area contributes to a more robust bilingual community.

Church-run Greek Language Education Programs in the US

In spite of declining immigration to the US, there are many ways in which ethnic Greeks create formal spaces for Greek language development. According to the 2011 Greek Orthodox Archdiocese Yearbook, there are 340 parish afternoon and Saturday schools and 30 parochial day schools in the nation. There are also 41 Modern Greek studies programs at colleges and universities in the US and Canada (Modern Greek Studies Association, 2011), and continued active membership in community and professional associations. Most of the schools that emphasize Greek language and culture are operated by the Greek Orthodox Church, although there are some institutions outside of the academic sphere that offer Modern Greek instruction in more secular spaces. These include institutes, community centers and programs in public schools (Hellenic Education Network Abroad, 2011). Further, many of these formal educational spaces sit side by side with informal spaces in which the use of Greek language is encouraged. These include places such as music shops, cafes, churches, restaurants, the workplace and people's homes. This paper focuses on the institutionalized educational spaces that exist for Greeks to educate their children.

There are 11 Greek Orthodox parochial day schools that operate under the auspices of the Direct Archdiocesan District, with an enrollment of 2244 students for the 2010–2011 school year, which is up from 1923 for the 2009–2010 school year (Greek Orthodox Archdiocese of America, 2011). The day schools employ 39 teachers of the Modern Greek language and culture. According to the Archdiocese, the St Demetrios Cathedral in Astoria is the only community in New York City and the US that sustains a high school. While the school adheres to the New York State mandates regarding curricula and student assessment, and follows the regulations of the New York City Department of Education, the school also offers 'an academic program of high standards that incorporates the teaching of the Greek Orthodox faith and the universal Hellenic ideals, customs, and traditions' (St Demetrios Astoria School, 2010).

The majority of Greek children in New York (and in the US), however, formally learn about Greek language and culture at afternoon and Saturday schools that are also sponsored by the Church. In the New York City Direct Archdiocesan district, there were 46 Greek afternoon/Saturday schools in operation during the 2009–2010 school year with an enrollment of 3503 students (up from 3475 students from the previous year) and with 235 teachers of Greek language and culture (Greek Orthodox Diocese of America, 2011). These numbers demonstrate that a significant number of Greek children in NYC attend these after-school programs, since 16.3% (about 14,880) of the NYC Greek population is aged 5–17.

The role of language in Church-run schools

In 2010, I visited and met with the director of one such school in Astoria, Queens. The school is housed adjacent to a well-established Greek Orthodox

Church and is also one of the longest operating afternoon Greek schools in the US. In fact, the Greek afternoon school actually pre-dates the establishment of the Church. In addition to the afternoon school, the Church has been operating a K–8 day school since 1957, as well as the only Greek Orthodox day high school in the country since 1982. At present, there are over 700 students that attend the day school.

According to the school website, the purpose of the afternoon and Saturday school is to 'provide an opportunity for Greek American students attending public school to learn the Greek language and history', although it also runs classes (beginning, intermediate and advanced) for adults. Given the various needs of the community, the school offers classes for K–6 students twice a week for two and a half hours or on Saturdays for four hours. The curriculum not only covers Greek language (reading, writing and speaking), but also emphasizes Greek history, Greek Orthodox religion, Modern Greek culture and instruction in Greek dancing and music (although according to the principal, the latter is optional or mostly relegated to special events). For older students who want to take the Comprehensive Exam in Modern Greek, which NY State accepts for Regents credit in foreign languages, the school offers a preparatory course (and boasts a 100% pass rate). There is also free bus transportation provided from neighborhood public schools for students attending the Greek afternoon program during weekdays.

The school had a lively, communal feel to it when I visited on the first Saturday session in 2010. Families had just returned from summer vacation, so classes started a half-hour later than scheduled, as parents, children and teachers milled about the hallways reconnecting after not seeing each other for months. While official Greek language instruction takes place in the classroom, I also heard mostly Greek spoken among people in the hallway, with English phrases and words sometimes peppered in the conversation. Since the afternoon school is housed in the day school, most of the posters and artwork on the walls reflected the work that students in the day school had produced. The visual images that filled the hallways seemed to reinforce a commitment to Greek language and an exploration of Greek 'culture' that benefited the afternoon and Saturday students.

The principal of the afternoon and Saturday school is a seasoned educator who has been at the school for over 36 years. Before becoming principal, he worked in the day school and was head of the Greek language department. Overall, he has taught Greek language for over 50 years, four of the years in Greece before he immigrated to the US. He is deeply invested in the education of the children. He made a point of circulating from to room to room to greet the children and help them get settled. Throughout our interview, which was conducted in both Greek and English, he reiterated that there is an emphasis on both Greek language and culture. While the afternoon and Saturday school serves only grades 1–6, kindergarteners are often admitted into the program; for those beyond the sixth grade, the school also has a small alternative program. In this sense, the school is trying to meet the varied needs of the community.

When I asked him to elaborate on what was meant by 'culture', he explained that the cultural program focuses on the history of ancient and Modern Greece, religious education and the geography of Greece. While dance is optional, there ends up being a strong music, theater and dance component when students prepare for the *yiortes* [holidays] at which they have performances for the school and greater community. These *yiortes* include *25th tis Martiou* [Greek Independence Day], Christmas, *Yiorti tou grammaton* [Greek Letters Day], *28th tis Octobrio* [national holiday celebrating resisting Italy at the start of World War II] and June graduation. Nonetheless, he noted that language learning is the central aspect of the curriculum. Emphasis is placed on building vocabulary, understanding grammar and spelling, and the usage of oral language. The textbooks used for language learning are from a series that are sent from Greece and endorsed by the Greek Ministry of Education called *Matheno Ellinika* [*I am Learning Greek*]. According to the principal, these are the best available texts for Greek language instruction of diaspora children, because Greek educators who once taught in the US are the authors. He noted that there are other books used for religion and history. The principal affirmed that all activities in the classroom are conducted in Greek.

According to the principal, the majority of students, around 80%, speak Greek at home or with some other family. For the children who come in with little or no Greek (approximately 20%), the teachers translate, if necessary, but really try and focus on practicing oral dialogue in Greek. This is usually around themes that are important and often used in daily experiences (like going to the store or meeting someone for the first time). However, one grade 6 student suggested that fluctuation between Greek and English may happen more frequently. She did not speak much Greek at home, although she had some exposure through the community in which she lived, visiting her Greek-speaking grandparents and occasional visits to Greece. She commented, 'When I really do not understand something, they let me know in English too. But they do also try and stick to Greek ... but they do use English a lot too' (personal communication, September, 2010). Two other parents I interviewed also acknowledged the occasional use of both languages. In fact, one parent stated:

Personally, the fact that the kids are exposed to the Greek language is why I sent them there. I know they try, the teachers ... I've seen and heard and spoken to them ... they try even though some of the kids really don't understand. Like my little one, when it comes to instruction ... she kind of gets lost. But they try. They keep repeating the Greek. When the kids don't understand they say it in English and repeat it in Greek again. Again, it's that organization ... that structure. There's a plan on how they do things. (Interview, 8 September 2010)

Here, this parent indicates that fluctuation between Greek and English helped her child understand more clearly, and later in the interview suggests that these methods helped her child learn more Greek. In this sense, this process to support language acquisition adopts a 'translanguaging' pedagogical approach, one that involves using both languages when speaking, listening, reading and writing throughout the lesson (Bartlett & García, 2011; García, 2009a). Throughout this process, the role of Greek is not diminished, despite the occasionally necessary usage of English.

The role of religion in Church-run schools

Since Greek language schools are operated and funded by the Greek Orthodox Church, there is clearly a component of religious education embedded within the program. Parents have differing perspectives on the role that religion played in sending their children to a particular language school. One of these parents I interviewed stated a religion contributed to a holistic approach that helped her child re-connect with her Greek 'identity'. She stated:

Well because first of all ... it has a good reputation as far as the afternoon school was concerned. I felt it was important because you know they do the language, the writing, the reading, the mythology, geography, which is great because we don't get that in public schools, unfortunately. Then they also put a little bit of religion in there too, so they are exposed to that. I just felt that was really important because they are definitely not going to get that at home as much as they are in a classroom setting. You know honestly, because I don't speak it at home, that was an extra thing for me ... Because when you're not in Greece, it's harder to keep that connection, they try to foster that connection. Even if you're here, some of these kids might now have been to Greece but they get exposed to that culture through the school. Even my kids did go, it kind of all connects together ... when you put what they're exposed to here and when they're actually there. (Interview, 8 September 2010)

While she conflates religion, ethnicity, culture and language, this parent expresses that all of these are interlinked and suggests that these religious contexts are important for language education.

Another parent, however, did not care for the religious aspect of the curriculum, but sent his children to the school so that they could get exposure to the language. In this sense, he did not equate religion with language, but felt that this was the only space in which he could obtain formal Greek instruction for his children. One other parent, who did not mind the religious education at the school, also appreciated that it was not the central aspect of the curriculum. Her older daughter originally attended another Greek school that was run as an afterschool program in her public day school (they rented space there). Despite the convenient location, she was not as satisfied with the level of language instruction, feeling that the school

> was just a little more focused on religion then anything else. And it just wasn't very organized. There was no lesson plans ... no structure [sic]. It was just the nuns pretty much doing what they could. So really, I was not happy. Then she got to the point where this was where she was going to be. There was nothing extra coming her way. (Interview, 12 September 2010)

Thus, the emphasis on religion over language instruction became a deterrent for her. While she identified as religious, and did not mind the religious component, she did not want that to supersede the instruction of Greek language.

Discussion: Re-thinking Greek-ness

As the native-born Greek population diminishes both in NYC and the US, it is clear that family will no longer be the primary source of language acquisition, especially as more Greeks assimilate into the English-speaking fabric, fewer native-born Greeks immigrate to the US, and others continue to intermarry with non-Greek-speaking people. This chapter, therefore, sheds light on ways in which Greek-Americans are attempting to maintain their language and culture apart from the historical vehicle of the Greek family. Like other chapters in this volume, it illuminates how community-led educational efforts take up where conventional heritage language education and US public bilingual programs leave off, particularly when entire communities are left out of these initiatives altogether.

While many disagree about the effectiveness of such after-school educational initiatives as sole vehicles of language acquisition, the data reveals that these schools serve as important spaces to facilitate the development of the Greek language, curb language loss and preserve some specific aspects of Greek culture. This does not suggest that these schools can operate without the support of parents. Nonetheless, the relationship between religious beliefs and ethnic identity remains underexplored. In the case of the parents I interviewed, religion was either not a major reason for sending their children to church-run Greek language schools, or its presence did not trump the cultural or language education of the school (and in fact, for some, enhanced the reasons). Nonetheless, they all identified on some level as Greek Orthodox, even if they came from inter-faith and inter-ethnic families. While there are countless examples of non-Catholics sending their children to Catholic school, the principal of the day school indicated that the school only admits children that either have at least one parent who is Greek (and ostensibly Orthodox) or non-Greek but of Orthodox faith.[5] As a result, religion can be a determining factor in who attends church-run language schools. Either way, language education is often coupled with religious instruction, regardless of the main reasons parents have for sending their children to these schools.

This raises questions about the linkages among Greek language learning, cultural education and religious (Greek Orthodox) instruction; in particular, it posits whether or not this relationship promotes a singular notion of Greek identity. By conflating the idea that religious affiliation with the Greek Orthodox Church automatically identifies someone as ethnically Greek, these schools present a singular notion of Greek-ness that in effect marginalizes some of the population that is in fact Greek. As the more traditional Church-controlled contexts for language-learning come against shifts in Greek American ethnic identification, other alternatives need to be explored. Singular and static notions of Greek ethnic identity need to be troubled, and the ways that religion has been used to define it need to be disrupted.

Moreover, at a time when both immigration from Greece and Cyprus have declined and inter-faith and inter-ethnic unions have risen, Georgakas (2004–2005) suggests that the future of Greek America rests on the creation of a true binational identity. Georgakas (2004–2005, p. 5) continues: 'central to the emotional and psychological comfort of the binational personality is genuine bilingualism. Greatly easing the practice of this bilingualism are the new communication technologies ... thus, being located in one area where there is only a minuscule Greek community is no longer a barrier to accessing contemporary Greek culture'. In many ways, this de-centers schools as the primary formalized spaces by which to cultivate bilingualism, suggesting that new, globalized information technologies may also facilitate this passage that recognizes the dynamic interchange between the motherland and the diaspora. Yet, attention must also be paid to the way that (bi)national identity is constructed, considering whether religion (or other singular signifiers) holds primacy, as well as taking into account the ways in which the demographics of Greece and Cyprus are rapidly changing. Given that these countries are now viable destinations for immigrants from around the world, Greek identity and nationality are further complicated, particularly as some of these groups remain permanently over time. While Greeks in the US may not be directly affected by such shifts in the demographic landscape, the continued emphasis on linguistic and cultural preservation remains constant. If binationality and bilingualism is to be further nurtured and embraced, the very future of the community might benefit from reconsidering what in fact constitutes Greek-ness.

Notes

(1) See BBC Languages Portal; http://www.bbc.co.uk/languages/european_languages/languages/greek.shtml
(2) Greek polytonic orthography notates Ancient Greek phonology, so that each symbol indicates a different type of pitch accent or presence of a certain sound when speaking. Monotonic orthography is simplified; it notates Modern Greek phonology and requires only two diacritics.
(3) An earlier version of this section appeared in Hantzopoulos (2005).
(4) In recent years, there have been many other ethnic and speech communities that have settled in Astoria, also partly a result of the 1965 Act that increased entry eligibility for immigrants to the US from all parts of the world. While there was always a large presence of working-class Italian, Croatian and Colombian immigrants in the neighborhood, there is now an increasing presence of Brazilian, Bangladeshi, Bosnian, Mexican and Arab (mostly Egyptian and Moroccan) immigrants, such that a part of 36th Avenue is known as 'Little Banglesdesh' and a good portion of Steinway is considered 'Little Egypt'. There also has been a large influx of white English-speaking urban professionals who view the neighborhood as safe, trendy and close enough to Manhattan, and have recently settled in increasing numbers. Moreover, many children of the post-war Greek immigrants have moved out of the Astoria neighborhood and have settled in other areas of Queens like Bayside and Whitestone.
(5) The principal did convey a story in which two Latino siblings (aged 9 and 11) came to the school to see if they could study Greek. While there are many Latino students in the school, they always have at least one Greek parent. In this case, they did not and were also not Greek Orthodox. He explained that, to accommodate their situation, he set up private lessons for the children, at which, he noted, they were thriving.

9 Community-based Initiatives and Sub-Saharan African Languages in the 'Big Apple'

Busi Makoni

Introduction

This chapter draws on research conducted in New York City (NYC) during the summer of 2010. The research investigated community-based initiatives that focus on teaching African languages to children of African immigrants. The goal of this chapter is to establish whether any formal or informal community-based educational spaces exist where African languages are taught and how these structures operate. The chapter argues that African languages are learned in many different informal educational spaces, dovetailing with the African concept of teaching and learning: everyone is a teacher, and any space is an appropriate educational space. The underlying assumption, nonetheless, is that the movement of educated as well as unskilled migrants to America has created contemporary worldwide networks of communication that connect the nations of the world, and which facilitate the rapid movement of ideas and languages across the planet. As expected, the American ethnolinguistic speech communities have been affected by the effects of the interconnectedness of the world through globalization, thus creating contexts that go beyond the notion of heritage language learning. Put differently, the current American 'ethnolinguistic speech community' reflects this global interconnectedness, which cannot be explained in terms of our current understanding of the concept of heritage language.

While the literature on structural descriptions of African languages is substantial, very little, if any, has focused on African languages spoken by

Africans in the US, let alone in NYC. In this chapter, I seek to fill this gap. Attempts to do so are difficult because of the complex backgrounds from which Africans originate and the changes that might have occurred in the use of African languages as a result of the contacts between speakers of different African languages and between speakers of African languages and speakers of non-African languages (e.g. Spanish, Chinese) that are widespread in NYC.

While a majority of scholars would maintain that numerous languages are found in Africa, they do not agree about the exact number. In addition, the relationship between a linguistic referent and its object is not stable (Harris, 2009; Hutton, 2010), a point forcefully articulated by integrationist linguistics when describing Western contexts. In this regard, any study of community-based initiatives focusing on the teaching of African languages reveals multiple contradictions and contestations. First, it assumes a clear conceptual understanding of the referent for the term 'Africa'. Yet there is no consensus in African studies on what constitutes Africa. Therefore, writing about African languages in NYC raises the issue of geographical and epistemological boundaries. As Zeleza (2003) points out, the concrete and symbolic borders of the continent are variable. For instance, one common assumption is that the continent lies between the Sahara and the Limpopo River (the northern boundary of South Africa). From this viewpoint, North Africa is not part of Africa but is seen as closer to Europe, both racially and historically. Furthermore, Egypt is seen as part of the Middle East rather than Africa. Sub-Saharan Africa, sometimes termed 'black Africa', is viewed as 'the real Africa'. In writing about African languages, we therefore find ourselves engaging important matters of history and politics, as well as geography.

This chapter focuses on Africans from Sub-Saharan Africa, rather than the largely Arab-speaking North Africa. However, inasmuch as we draw this distinction, it is fraught with theoretical problems. For example, in the Sudan, the distinction is based on a number of different descriptors, such as language, religion and politics, raising the question of whether all these descriptors have to be fulfilled for one to be legitimately categorized as an Arab or African, or whether only one descriptor is enough and, if so, which one. Because of the multiplicity of what it means to be an Arab or African, the distinction is not incontrovertible, rendering our identification of African languages somewhat arbitrary and subjective, even though we present it as objective.

Second, controversy surrounds the idea of what constitutes African languages. The concept of African languages as enumerable objects and associated names were products of colonial language ideology reinforced by contemporary, top-down language policy discourses. In pre-colonial and plurilingual urban Africa, languages are best construed not as enumerable entities but as communicative resources (Makoni, 2011). Such resources are plurilingual, heterotrophic and diversified local practices typical of Africans (Pennycook, 2010). In order to capture such diversity, it is necessary to compose individual life histories and biographies and the role of language therein. Because so much variation exists within each label and among speakers, it may be more difficult to identify the speakers of the same language, leading to a situation that can be described as exhibiting 'a plurality in singularity'. In spite of the practical and theoretical problems of determining languages in such plurality, we still use categories that imply homogeneity for purposes of clarity.

Finally, in Africa it is widely believed that English and all other former colonial languages are inextricably tied to success. Indigenous African languages, on the other hand, are viewed as limiting opportunities. One would therefore expect African immigrants in America to shift completely to English; however, African immigrant communities are engaged in activities that facilitate learning indigenous African languages *and* former colonial languages, albeit with very limited resources. Another contradiction is that, although American-born African immigrant children consider themselves to be native speakers of English, most of them take English as a Second Language classes based on the recommendations of their teachers.

Drawing on interview data from Africans from different Sub-Saharan countries living in NYC, this study sought to address the following interrelated questions: (1) are there any community-based African language teaching initiatives in NYC, and if so, what is their operational structure? If not, how are African languages maintained? (2) What are the attitudes of African immigrant groups (young and old) toward learning African languages in NYC? Research has shown that interest in maintaining an ethnic language among children of immigrants is largely influenced by parents' and peers' attitudes toward these languages (Luo & Wiseman, 2000). Therefore, asking this second question was necessary because the success of community-based initiatives depends on the commitment and positive attitudes of community members.

Community-based language initiatives place the tools for teaching and learning in the hands of communities (Corson, 1999; Kenner, 2004). Communities provide a time, a location and volunteers from their home countries who offer classes on weekends or after school. Communities also provide support materials that they develop themselves or purchase at their own expense. In this regard, communities set their own provision for language teaching. Such an endeavor is achievable only if the community is invested in maintaining its languages.

Indirectly, a study of such initiatives touches on the degree of loss of linguistic and cultural identity among African immigrants. Insisting that

African immigrant children are taught African languages suggests a strong sense of African identity and nationalism that develops as a result of loneliness and dislocation. Most of the projects and activities related to the teaching of African languages are driven by a desire to 'preserve' African languages and cultures. This idea is founded not on whether the languages are endangered, but on the fact that they are *imagined* as endangered. The issue, therefore, is a discursive one.

The Context: NYC in the African Imagination

Africans in NYC are a minority among immigrant groups, overshadowed by groups from the Caribbean, Asia and Latin America (Perry, 1997). African immigrant populations generally hold college degrees and are better educated than Asians and African-Americans. Most African immigrants came to America after 1960, when the quota system was lifted. Since then, the African immigrant population has increased exponentially. Approximately 55% of the African immigrant population is male (Collier, 2006), and African male immigrants tend to have two families: one in America and another in Africa (Stoller, 2002). These 'transnational husbands' shuttle between their homes on a regular basis in order to keep in touch with their 'roots'. African immigrants, both male and female, view marriage as a quick and easy route to citizenship. Most African immigrants do not consider their residence in NYC as permanent, regardless of whether they have Green Cards or have been granted citizenship. The word *home* refers to Africa, and NYC is viewed as a place where they work.

Even though talk of returning home is widespread, rarely have Africans voluntarily returned *en masse* to Africa because of fears of being regarded as failures if they return empty-handed. NYC has a mythical status in the African imagination as a symbol of prosperity and opportunity. These images are shaped by international news networks and popular sitcoms that portray well-integrated, affluent black families. However, this incomplete portrayal leads to unrealistic expectations of success in NYC. The extreme hardships faced by most Africans as they struggle to navigate complex immigration laws are erased, and the necessity of English literacy for navigating the complex fabric of NYC life is underestimated.

A small but increasing number of Africans born in America are children of African immigrants. These children often speak English as a first language and have varying degrees of proficiency in the languages spoken by their parents. Because African immigrants tend to settle in the same urban and suburban areas as other immigrants from the same country, their children attend the same schools. From the American perspective, African immigrant children born in America are regarded as African-American. However, these children prefer to be called American-Africans because being referred to as African-Americans provides a misleading characterization of their histories, suggesting that they are descendants of slaves. At the same time, in an effort to adjust to life in NYC, African immigrant youth try to speak and act like African-American youth so that they can 'pass' as African-American, efforts that African-Americans do not necessarily validate (Rampton, 1995). Relationships between the two groups are often strained, leading to cohesive groups among African school children that might not have existed prior to starting school.

Sociolinguistics of Africa in NYC

The wide range of countries represented in NYC means a wide range of African languages, including Swahili (Kenya); Twi (Ghana); Wolof, Pulaar and Mandingo (Senegal); Igbo and Yoruba (Nigeria); Dinka (Sudan); Amharic (Ethiopia); and Kru (southeastern Liberia). Mandingo is also spoken in a large part of West Africa in countries like Mali and Guinea and is the main language of Gambia, whereas Soninke is spoken in Niger, Gambia, Mali and other regions in West Africa. Pulaar, although associated with Senegal, is also spoken in countries such as Guinea Bissau and Mali. Multiple Southern African languages are found in NYC as well. Although this chapter focuses on immigrants from Sub-Saharan Africa living in NYC, a large immigrant population from North Africa speaks Arabic and French, yielding a complex sociolinguistic map.

Africans from the same country or ethnic group tend to congregate in certain areas of NYC. It is estimated that the Bronx has the highest concentration of African immigrants in America (Stoller, 2002) and the highest number of Ghanaians, mainly those who speak Twi (Obeng, 2008). Harlem, on the other hand, is referred to as 'Little Senegal' because of the concentration of Senegalese in this area. Since most Africans live in specific residential areas where there is intense interpersonal interaction with members of their ethnicity, pressures to learn other African languages are limited. Most African immigrants believe that improving their proficiency in English is more important than learning other languages used in NYC, such as Chinese or Spanish, since they believe English facilitates and enhances their commercial activities (Collier, 2006; Stoller, 2002). Children, on the other hand, learn languages such as Spanish or Chinese as part of school requirements.

In NYC, African immigrants have formed associations that are organized in terms of ethnicity, country of origin or city where they are based (e.g. the Association of Speakers of Yoruba or the Sudanese Association of NYC). These associations offer advice to new immigrants on how to navigate and settle in America. They also serve as lending institutions and provide dispute resolution centers, assistance on health matters (Owusu, 1998) and assistance in job seeking and setting up informal businesses. Overall, the associations provide 'social insurance against poverty' (Deumert *et al.*, 2005: 303) and facilities for learning English; however, they do not typically offer the explicit teaching and learning of African languages. Because of the deliberate ways community identities are formed, these associations can best be described as 'intentional communities', reflecting the Africans' underlying sense of agency in constructing these associations.

Data and Methodology

This study sought to establish whether community-based initiatives in NYC focused on teaching African languages to children of African immigrants and the form these initiatives took, such as whether they were formal or informal and what their operational and organizational structures were. In addition, the study sought to identify the attitudes and feelings of immigrant parents and children born in America toward learning African languages in a context in which English is the dominant language.

The informants were drawn from three African immigrant populations. Forty adult immigrants (i.e. individuals who were born in Africa and had taken up residence in NYC as adults) participated, 25 of whom were male and 15 of whom were female. Of the 25 males, five had a college-level education, and of the 15 females, eight had a college-level education. The remaining seven females, all from Senegal, had been in America for 11 years, but their spoken English could be characterized as telegraphic speech. They did not work, and most of their activities were restricted to the home environment. The adult informants were drawn from different African regions, religious affiliations and professions, including hair braiders, traditional dress-makers, clergy, college professors, vendors, restaurant owners, researchers, attorneys and physicians. The second group of participants consisted of children of African immigrants who were born in NYC and were either being taught or had been taught African languages. Fifteen children (five females and 10 males ages 10–20) participated. All had visited Africa at some point in their lives. The final group of participants consisted of young African immigrants who came to America as children and currently attend either middle school or high school in NYC. This group consisted of five males from different countries in West Africa. Informal interviews were conducted on Manhattan streets, in restaurants and at the African market located on Harlem's 125th Street. The interviews focused on community-based initiatives for teaching African languages and on the attitudes of the different groups toward the teaching and learning of African languages in the diaspora.

Findings: Effective Education from an African Perspective

African language teaching takes place at a community level, but unlike other immigrant communities, these efforts do not occur in formal schools or programs. Rather, African immigrants are actively engaged in language teaching and other forms of language transmission in community venues, such as braiding salons, churches and households. This informal education is generally conducted within the family by mothers and grandmothers. 'Resource materials' often include old newspaper clippings written in African languages and videos and recordings of TV programs from their home countries. Southern African informants indicated that they used videos of popular African language-based programs, such as *Isgud snayisi* and *Hlala Kwabafileyo* (Zulu), *Mukadota* and *Parafina* (Shona) and *Emzini Wezinsizwa* (Zulu, Xhosa, Sotho and Tswana). Children are encouraged to watch these recordings in order to learn about cultural practices central to their identities. Parents explain the meanings behind the different stories and the ways they relate to cultural practices (e.g. the meaning behind colloquial expressions such as *'dadewethu ngimfunge'* [my sister I swear] in *Emzini Wezinsizwa*).While culture is dynamic, it is often presented in these lessons as if it were static.

Participants' attitudes toward the teaching of African languages differed significantly in terms of gender, socioeconomic background, level of education and age. Overwhelmingly, adult females, regardless of socioeconomic background or level of education, felt it necessary for their children to learn and be able to speak African languages because they considered these languages to be part of one's cultural identity. English, they pointed out, is essential for life in NYC, but African languages are also essential because they are, first and foremost, Africans. African women's active role in using and promoting literacy in indigenous African languages is consistent with their roles in Africa. In most African cultures, women are considered the 'keepers of culture' and 'guardians of familial heritage' (Kouritzin, 2000: 15). It is therefore not surprising that women feel strongly about 'the preservation and transmission of a culture and a language' (Estable, 1986: 11) in a foreign country.

The relationship of African women, particularly Senegalese women, with English is ambivalent and somewhat contradictory. On the one hand, they feel pressured to learn and use English, particularly in their commercial activities (Collier, 2006); on the other hand, they resist using English and resort to the use of interpreters to interact directly with clients. For instance, Maimouna, a Senegalese woman who had been in NYC for 11 years, said, 'I do not speak English. When I angry with the system, I use a bit English. I speak Pular, and Nancy interpret for me' (interview, 14 June 2010). It seems Maimouna resists using English because she associates it with 'the system', which is, according to her, oppressive in that it has not provided her with the success she had dreamed of when she was back home. Interestingly enough, Kadija (from Senegal) pointed out that a Senegalese woman in NYC started *Afrikanspot*, a bilingual newspaper written in French and English. It seems that women resist learning English but insist on teaching their children African languages in order to help them cope with the challenges of being in a foreign country (Morrow, 1997). This linguistic resistance may suggest fear of 'anomie' (Spolsky, 2000), or surrendering to American identity. Yet the bilingual newspaper shows a desire for integration. It is evident that this ambivalence reflects the dynamic nature of bilingual identities. Because bilingual identities are performed and co-constructed through bilinguals' language practices (including their language choices) and through their discursive reconstitution of these practices, the Senegalese women appear to resist English but embrace it through the bilingual newspaper.

This study also uncovered a sharp contrast in attitudes between old and young females. Among the female children of immigrants, three out of five did not see the benefit of learning African languages because English is the language used in NYC. Although it might appear that these young female immigrants are focused on the integrative purpose of learning English, the focus is actually on the instrumental dimension for learning English. As Rita, one of the young females, pointed out, 'To get a job here you need English. To get directions to get to places, you need English. So why waste time learning something you won't use, something you don't need every day?' (interview, 15 June 2010).

Interestingly, this view was shared by 20 of the 25 adult male informants, who thought that learning African languages was not beneficial to their children and that the only language important for their children's success was English. Yet they also stated that they teach their children the traditions, culture and histories of their home countries and impart life lessons that they were taught by their own fathers about their family histories. To these males, it seems that cultural identity is still central but can be maintained through means other than language. While the remaining five adult males all pointed to issues related to culture and identity as reasons their children needed to learn African languages, they disagreed on the role that language plays vis-à-vis culture. While some clearly felt that it is inconceivable for culture to exist without language because 'the history and culture of a people is carried through language' (interview, 15 June 2010), others felt a need to 'disarticulate' the association between language and culture. In their view, humans create culture; therefore, humans can change culture so that it is not tied to language. Nonetheless, those who argued that culture finds representation through language lamented the lack of formal facilities where their children could learn their 'real' languages.

One of the parents described immigrant children who only speak English as 'amakhebece' (Ndebele for shelled peanuts that have no nuts inside) or 'Oreos' and 'coconuts' (black on the outside but white inside). These terms refer to something akin to Frantz Fanon's 'Black skin white mask', the divided self-perception of the Black Subject who has lost his native cultural originality and embraced the culture of another 'white country' associated with colonization and oppression. Because of the inferiority complex engendered in the mind of the Black Subject, he appropriates and imitates the cultural code of the colonizer – the American language and culture in this case.

While informants held strong views about the need to learn African languages, they also saw the roles of English and African languages in the lives of immigrant children. For instance, two female immigrant children thought that, although English was essential for everyday life in NYC, knowledge and proficiency in African languages were equally important for fitting in with relatives back home: 'They kinda don't understand us when we speak English, so it's like, if we speak the languages they speak, that'll be cool' (interview, 14 June 2010). They also pointed out that it would be ideal to use African languages if they met other immigrant children whose parents came from the same country as theirs, creating a community of sorts away from home. As Rita stated, 'It's silly to speak English to Kenyan friends – if we speak Swahili, it will make us bond . . . as people from Kenya' (interview, 14 June 2010).

All of the younger males felt that learning African languages was essential, and most had rudimentary knowledge learned from their mothers at home or through family networks in church or visits to hair salons. The reasons for learning African languages ranged from being able to impart this vital aspect of identity to their own children to more mundane motives such as 'hooking up hot babes' (interview, 14 June 2010) back home. The younger males also listened to African radio stations and watched videos from their respective countries. The fact that their proficiency in African languages was, in their view, limited concerned them. Ugochuku, one of the informants, underscored the fact that, inasmuch as learning African languages is important for cultural maintenance, it also promotes bicultural competence, which is badly needed in America, where there is much talk about diversity. In Ugochuku's terms, 'You know if you bicultural, you good at solving and managing conflicts across different people, and that is what diversity is about, but it must start with you, knowing who you are, your roots first' (interview, 14 June 2010). In Ugochuku's terms, to be able to embrace a foreign culture without compromising one's own cultural identity, one needs to be socially grounded in one's own culture.

Another young male participant pointed out that his future business plan was to open a school where African languages, arts and culture would be taught in order to enable people from the same ethnic group or country to construct and maintain a strong sense of identity. For the children of immigrants who are rejected by African-Americans, having such community-based initiatives, the informant thought, would create a sense of belonging to a community. They would be able to socialize with peers who shared their cultural background and maintain links with their family and 'home' community. Such schools, the informant maintained, were 'a missing link' in their life in NYC (interview, 14 June 2010).

Lastly, the five males who had come to NYC in their early teens had experienced hardship in school owing to their inability to speak English in a way that their teachers and peer groups could understand. Abeeku recounted that, whenever he tried to answer a question in class, his classmates would shout, 'Go back to Africa', and he was 'snubbed' by his teachers because they did not understand what he was saying. These informants also could not understand most of what their teachers were saying. As Imeka stated, 'The English we learned back home is different from the one everyone speaks here' (interview, 14 June 2010). Nonetheless, these students benefited from English lessons organized through the associations. The setting was not threatening, as they were taught by individuals who understood their culture *and* the American education system. Interestingly, the five males felt that community initiatives should offer African languages as well because 'we from Africa can teach the African kids born here Igbo, and they can teach us English' (interview, 14 June 2010).

Clearly, the learning of African languages in NYC contains a gendered dimension. Older females are the most committed teachers, although the rather informal teaching methods inadvertently lead to high attrition rates, as most children find excuses to avoid reading the newspaper articles or watching the videos, especially the girls. The younger male children of immigrants are the most willing and committed learners. For them, learning African languages is part of the acquisition of cultural 'identity, self-assertiveness, an ethnic/ national pride' (Obeng, 2008: 179).

Discussion and Conclusion: Community Teaching of African Languages

With the complex nexus of issues that African immigrants face in NYC, it is not surprising that formal supplementary schools or community-language education initiatives have not been formed. In spite of reduced pressures to teach and learn African languages, some teaching and learning occur at a community level. In community-based associations, there is greater focus on those who need assistance settling in NYC, hence the teaching of English to young immigrants. In this regard, associations reflect the key parameters of education as understood in African contexts: developing a sense of belonging and participating actively in family and community affairs as well as understanding, appreciating and promoting the cultural practices of the community at large (Reagan, 1996).

In NYC, community-based associations, families and churches attempt to sustain the collective and social nature of education and retain its material and spiritual senses. Community education is, therefore, organized via associations, burial societies and clans. The same individual may belong to multiple associations at the same time or shift from one association to another. In NYC, the heterogeneity of languages and the complexity of ethnicity are partial consequences of individuals' multiple affiliations, and the tendency in the long run is for each sub-ethnicity to develop its own vernacular.

However, determining which language to encourage a child to learn is complicated because parents may view learning African languages differently. Most families find themselves having to choose the languages their children will learn, particularly in situations in which the parents speak different languages or one is an American citizen and the other an African. In such situations, most parents opt to have their children learn English. However, many children desire to learn African languages for various reasons, including cultural identity. They feel a certain level of disconnect with NYC, which is often captured in discourses about 'home', suggesting that America is not imagined as one's place of origin, even for the American-born children. However, the practices and attitudes of immigrants reflect a contradiction: adopting English will, in all probability, facilitate their employability, yet they feel that American cultural practices are inconsistent with cultural traditions back home, which ought to be taught to children born in the diaspora. The contradiction is based on the perception that 'the immigrant culture is incompatible with the emigrant culture' (Kouritzin, 2000: 28).

The relationship between the diaspora and 'home' contexts is extremely complex. Ironically, even though some of the diasporic communities are challenging the status of particular nations, such as the Sudan, the teaching of these languages and the forming of associations along ethnic lines reinforce the epistemological status of notions about national origin that they are politically challenging in their home countries. In the associations, languages are framed in positivistic terms, as monolithic, homogeneous categories, creating distinctions that may not exist in the home country or, alternatively, perpetuating a categorization that is inconsistent with what the speakers themselves might have preferred to use.

Furthermore, diaspora sociolinguistics is not a mirror image of sociolinguistics of home environments. For example, the Dinka are a heterogeneous group spread across many different countries in East Africa, Uganda, Congo and the Sudan, and rarely refer to themselves as Dinka but as Moinjaang (People of the People). The teaching of African languages in NYC, therefore, is a highly sophisticated form of language standardization because at least five different languages fall under the rubric called Dinka. The selection of one of these languages excludes others from 'official' recognition and deprives them of the same social status.

Notably, not all African immigrants regard themselves as part of a diaspora, which to some extent explains the continued reference to Africa as 'home' and NYC as a place of work. Individuals who feel they are not in a diaspora may not feel the need to invest time and energy in community establishments since they have to use their time in America to their maximum benefit, and learning African languages may not necessarily be one of the key aspects on their agenda. Conversely, Africans who feel that they are part of a diaspora may regard retaining and passing on African languages as important because they fear their cultures and languages will be lost. The idea of language loss or endangerment is not a reality because most Africans seem to live within the same neighborhoods or attend the same social events, making it difficult to envisage how the languages might be endangered.

The discourses of endangerment might be a political expression of the social anguish of minoritization. When transposed to the US, all African languages are minoritized, irrespective of their status in Africa. An analysis of African linguistic practices in NYC, therefore, must address the complicated processes by which dominant languages are minoritized and the psychological impact of such processes. Whether members of the same community and different socioeconomic classes react to the processes of minoritization in identical ways or to the same degree is unclear. Individuals in lower socioeconomic classes may not feel pressured to maintain so-called indigenous languages because they take their continued use for granted and have higher priorities related to daily life concerns, such as alleviating poverty or mitigating the adverse effects of economic deprivation.

Finally, it is important to stress the availability and significance of choice. Africans are not dominated by English; instead, learning to use or to promote the use of African languages is an exercise in agency (Irvine, 2009). In severely restricted circumstances, some choices are meaningless in that they do not necessarily change life circumstances; this may include the learning and teaching of African languages in NYC. However, learning African languages in NYC has symbolic value and is driven by a desire to create and consolidate one's identity. One of the consequences of the diasporic proclivity of identity is that, when used in a 'soft' sense, it may be ambiguous and complex. Therefore, the argument that Africans may vary their identities between different settings should mark the beginning of an enquiry rather than serve as an explanation itself.

10 Persian Bilingual and Community Education among Iranian-Americans in New York City

Roozbeh Shirazi and Maryam Borjian

Introduction

The sociolinguistic practices of the Iranian-American community remain understudied. While certainly present as part of the linguistic landscape of New York City, Persian speakers, in particular Iranian-Americans, are not as visible as other ethnic groups in the city.[1] The under-reporting of the number of Iranians in New York and the US in general exacerbates this low profile. Owing to anti-Iranian sentiment engendered by the 1979 hostage crisis, hostile media representations of Iranian society and culture, and their opposition to the government policies and practices of the Islamic Republic of Iran, many Iranian-Americans have historically opted for a strategy of ethnic non-disclosure, or passing as 'Persian' rather than Iranian (Bozorgmehr, 2007; Shirazi & Nazemian, 2005). Furthermore, the majority of Iranian-Americans do not live in ethnic enclaves in New York City, barring a small concentration of Jewish Iranians in Rego Park, Queens. Thus there is no 'Little Iran' or 'Irantown' counterpart to Chinatown or Little Italy in New York City. The absence of a central cultural institution serving Iranians in New York also contributes to low visibility of the Iranian-American community. While there is a permanent Iranian mission to the United Nations in New York, this institution does not function as an umbrella cultural center for Iranian-Americans living in New York. Furthermore, there is no cultural house or language institute (comparable to Alliance Française or the Cervantes Institute) that serves as a center of cultural or language education activities for the community. Zohreh, a Persian language instructor at NYU, notes that this absence of a central cultural center has contributed to a decentralized Iranian cultural landscape in New York City. As a result, cultural activities occur on a small scale and usually originate in, and cater to, specific social networks and communities, as opposed to all Iranians in New York.

Similarly, while there are small weekend and after-school language programs, there are no public schools that offer Persian language instruction in the City. For these reasons, there has been very little information available on the Iranian community in New York and its sociolinguistic spaces and practices.

Drawing on data from the 2009 US American Community Survey as well as data collected from conversations and interviews with parents and educators, this chapter explores how and why the Iranian community in New York engages in bilingual community education, which includes both informal efforts by communities and parents as well as school programs, and examines efforts being made to teach Iranian culture and Persian language to children. In order to situate these issues within their socio-historic context, the chapter briefly reviews the history of Iranian migration to the US and presents case study data with Iranian-American parents and educators in New York City. The emerging themes from these interviews show Iranian parents view bilingualism not only as a source of preserving family ties and cultural heritage, but also as a resource for developing new transcultural identities and academic competencies. In doing so, this case study contributes to new understandings of ethnolinguistic communities that transcend the view that they exist primarily as 'speech communities' or spaces of 'cultural reproduction'.

Overview of the Persian Language

Persian is a member of the Indo-Iranian branch of the larger Indo-European language family. It originated *ca* 6th century BC in Persis, a region on the southern Iranian Plateau, and the home of the Achaemenian dynasty (550–330 BCE), founders of the first Persian Empire.[2] At its zenith, the Achaemenian Empire held territories from Central Asia to Egypt and from the Indus River to Anatolia. Old Persian served as one of the literary and administrative languages of the Persian Empire and appeared primarily on royal inscriptions, clay tablets and seals.

Old Persian evolved into Middle Persian, which became the administrative and religious language of the Sassanian Persian Empire (224–651 CE). Under the Sassanians, Middle Persian literature flourished, including Zoroastrian religious texts and translations from Syriac, Greek and Indian sources on science, medicine and astronomy.

The Islamic conquest of Iran and the collapse of the Persian Empire (633–656 CE) was a turning point in the history of the Persian language. Adherence to Zoroastrianism declined as Islam spread across the Iranian plateau during the 8th to 10th centuries, and Arabic became the administrative and academic language of the growing Islamic Caliphate. The Persian language remained widely used despite the Islamic conquest, but not without going through major adaptation. The script of Middle Persian was abandoned, as it was closely associated with the Zoroastrian religion. A modified variant of the Arabic alphabet, known as the Perso-Arabic script, with different pronunciation and additional letters, was adopted to write the language. Furthermore, words with Zoroastrian connotations were abandoned and a considerable number of Arabic words were incorporated into Persian as a result of the spread of Islam. Persian literature in this new form proliferated during the 9th to 11th centuries, leading to a distinct Iranian cultural identity during the medieval Islamic era (Borjian & Borjian, 2011).

Today Persian is spoken in Iran, where it is known as *Farsi*; in Afghanistan, where it is known as *Dari*; and in Tajikistan and Uzbekistan, where it it is known as *Tajiki*. The language is also widely spoken by members of the Iranian diaspora dispersed throughout Europe, the Middle East, Americas, and Oceania.

Iranian Immigration to the US

Prior to 1950, few Iranians immigrated to the US. From the mid-19th century until the mid-20th century the Iranian population in the US did not exceed 2000 individuals (Bozorgmehr, 2007; Lorenz & Wertime, 1980). After 1950, there was a change in both volume and pattern of Iranian migration to the US, which can be classified into two broad chronological phases: the first phase or pre-revolutionary era (1950–1979), and the second phase or the post-revolutionary era (1979 to present).

First phase (1950–1979)

The first phase of Iranian immigration to the US began in 1950, during the reign of Mohammad Reza Shah Pahlavi, and ended with the Islamic Revolution of 1979. During this phase, there was a gradual increase in the number of Iranians in the US, reaching the highest peak in 1975–1978. Yet, the available statistical data indicates that the majority of Iranians who entered the US during this phase were classified as non-immigrants (e.g. visitors or students), and only a minority of them were classified as immigrants. Bozorgmehr and Sabagh (1988) note that the number of Iranian immigrants to the US averaged only 273 per year during the 1950s, 890 during the 1960s and 3700 in the 1970s. Yet, the number of nonimmigrant Iranians climbed sharply from an annual average of about 1400 in the 1950s, to 6000 in the 1960s and 51,000 in the 1970s (Bozorgmehr & Sabagh, 1988).

The causes of low migration to the US prior to 1979 were in part economic. Iranian oil revenues steadily increased from $34 million in 1954–1955 to $17.1 billion in 1974–1975 (Katouzian, 1981). The economic opportunities engendered by this growth deterred Iranians from immigrating to other countries. Yet, as Iran was undergoing intensive economic growth, its educational system could not meet the economy's demand for skilled labor. This led to an increased demand for study-abroad programs and a rise in demand for such opportunities, preferably in advanced industrial countries. As such, during this phase, the presence of Iranians in the US was mostly temporary (Bozorgmehr & Sabagh, 1988).

Second phase (1979 to present)

The Iranian Revolution of 1979 abolished the monarchy and led to the creation of the Islamic Republic of Iran. Since the Revolution, there has been a steady and noticeable increase in the number of Iranian immigrants to the US. Available statistical data from the US Census indicate that the number of Iranian immigrants in the US has increased from 5861 in 1978 to 128,000 in 1980, 235,521 in 1990, 338,266 in 2000, and 469,569 in 2009 (US Decennial Census 1980, 1990, 2000; US Census Bureau, 2009).

In post-revolutionary Iran, economic hardship as well as social, religious and political persecution were widespread and often targeted the professional and middle classes of Iranian society. Universities and schools were closed or restuctured to ensure a sufficiently 'Islamic' education and to purge Western cultural references and influences from the curriculum. As a result of these measures, large numbers of Iranians, often highly educated, migrated from Iran to Western countries as immigrants or as political or religious refugees.

Based on the 2009 American Community Survey and 2006–2008 American Community Survey 3-Year Estimate, the geographical distribution of Iranians in the US can be summarized as follows.[3] The state of California ranks highest in residents of Iranian descent in the US, with an estimate of 232,427, the majority of whom reside in the Los Angeles metropolitan area. The states of Texas and New York rank second and third with a total Iranian population of 29,782 and 28,668 respectively. The metropolitan Washington, DC area has an Iranian population of 25,424.

Language Use in US Households: Persian vs English

Among the 20 languages most frequently spoken in US households, Persian ranked 17 in the US 2000 Census. Out of 338,266 Iranians in the US, 312,085 of them, or 92%, reported using Persian at home. Only 26,181 (0.07%) reported using English in their households. While the high use of Persian in Iranian-American households may imply a low English proficiency on the part of this immigrant group, the opposite is true, with 86% of Iranians stating that they knew English very well or well (US Census, 2000). This reflects the diasporic and transnational nature of the US Iranian community, and suggests 'the simultaneous coexistence of different languages in communication' or a dynamic bilingualism on the part of Iranian-Americans (García, 2009a: 119). Given the high percentage of Iranians who report speaking Persian at home and the dearth of research on this immigrant community and its sociolinguistic practices, we explore here how and why Iranian-Americans use and learn Persian. In the following section, we present findings from an exploratory case study of the Iranian-American community in New York City.

Case Study Methods and Participants

During 2010, this study engaged nine Iranian-American residents of New York City in in-depth semi-structured interviews and informal conversation to understand their sociolinguistic practices and views regarding language and culture. Three participants were selected via purposive sampling, as they were known to the authors as parents or Persian language educators. These participants then referred six additional Iranian-Americans for participation in the study. In some cases, the participants had collaborated on, or participated in, Persian educational programs. Six of the participants resided in Manhattan, two in Queens and one in Brooklyn.[4] All but one of the participants are 'first-generation' Americans, having moved to the US as adults. The remaining participant was born in Queens to Iranian immigrants, and is considered 'second-generation'. The interviews were conducted in English and Persian over the phone and in person. Oral consent was obtained prior to the interviews and all participant names have been changed to protect the confidentiality of their responses. While the participants were not randomly selected, their professions and high levels of educational attainment are consistent with characterizations of Iranian-Americans as an 'affluent' and 'highly educated' ethnic community, as reported by other studies of the Iranian-American community (Bozorgmehr, 2007; Mossayeb & Shirazi, 2006; Motashari, 2003). Iranians are a highly educated immigrant group in the US. According to the 2006–2008 American Community Survey 3-Year Estimates, 29.9% of Iranian-Americans over the age of 25 have a bachelor's degree and 28.6% have a graduate or professional degree.

Schools

The Iranian community in New York is served by a combination of several small-scale Persian educational programs, often started by parents or a solitary educator, as well as larger schools supported by charitable foundations and civic organizations. This section provides a brief description of existing schools and small-scale Persian language educational programs started by individuals and parents. It also presents interview data relevant to parent perceptions of such institutions and programs.

Institutionally affiliated schools

The Ferdowsi Persian Language School was established in 1986 by the Iranian-American Society of New York (IASNY) to promote the Persian language and culture. IASNY describes itself as 'a non-profit, non-political and non-religious organization whose charter includes promotion of Persian language, heritage and culture'.[5] The school, which meets on Saturday from 10 a.m. to 1 p.m., is held in Westchester County and Long Island, and has students enrolled in Kindergarten through grade 4. The Ferdowsi School also holds several extracurricular activities and events throughout the year, including events for *Mehregan*, the pre-Islamic Festival of Autumn, *Yalda*, commemorating the winter solstice, and *Norooz*, the Iranian New Year. The purpose of these events is to familiarize students, some of whom have never traveled to Iran, with Iranian culture, art, history and civilization.

The Razi School is a private Islamic school located in Queens that provides Persian language classes as part of its curriculum. Razi is part of the Islamic Institute of New York–Imam Ali Mosque and provides K–12 instruction in an Islamic setting, as well as Persian and Arabic as second languages starting at the elementary level.[6] Razi School has come under increased scrutiny since US federal prosecutors accused its parent organization, the

Alavi Foundation, of being a front for the Iranian government in 2008.[7] The Alavi Foundation describes its mission as 'promoting charitable and philanthropic causes through educational, religious and cultural programs ... by making contributions to not-for-profit organizations within the US that support interfaith harmony and promote Islamic culture and Persian language, literature and civilization'.[8] Owing to its explicitly religious character and alleged affiliation with the Iranian government, Razi School is not considered a 'typical' setting in which Persian is learned and taught by the Iranian diaspora. For example, none of the participants in this study were affiliated with the school, and in some cases, did not know about its existence. One parent, Tara, explicitly stated that she would not consider sending her daughter to Razi because of the school's Islamic dress code and values. Another parent, Mojgan, said she did not see a place for religion in teaching and learning Persian.

Community-based programs

Several of the parents we spoke with had participated in or helped organize educational programs for their children to learn Persian. These included playgroups for young children, theatrical performances staged in Persian with elementary and middle school-aged children, or language classes that were sometimes housed in private homes, as well as in community and religious institutions. One of the reasons commonly cited for participation in these programs was convenience. At the time of the study, there were no large-scale Persian programs in Manhattan, and several respondents spoke about the difficulty of having to commute to Westchester, Queens or Long Island for Persian classes. Similarly, parents often organized classes or Persian cultural activities with other parents who had children of the same age. While these initiatives helped to engender a sense of community, they were often *ad hoc* and tended to subside once families became busy, or the children lost interest as they grew older. Some parents in the study elected to have their children study with private tutors, who were often referred through word of mouth. These parents again cited convenience as the main reason that they sought tutoring for their children, rather than more formal school settings.

Children's theater

Ladan, who has a 15-year-old daughter named Minoo, used her background in theater to organize a play for her daughter's Persian class when she was seven years old. Ladan saw the play as a way to galvanize the children's waning interest in Persian, and provide them with a creative outlet for expression in the language. The students in Minoo's class made up the cast, and the play was first performed in 2002 at an annual *Norooz* (New Year) party and was well received. Ladan continued staging the play during *Norooz* celebrations for five additional years, attracting the attention and enthusiasm of more children and families each year. Attendance and participation peaked at 25 children and an audience of approximately 400 students. While short-lived, Ladan believes her efforts left longer-lasting effects:

> The play became this annual event where being and speaking Persian was cool and made you special, it was a point of pride for Minoo and the kids. The audience would go berserk for the kids and the play, and the kids realized that Persian is not a dead language – it's something that people love and understand around them. For Minoo, that was a huge and important experience. (Interview with Ladan, 21 June 2010)

The plays also held special meanings for Ladan and many of the parents involved in staging it. Ladan wrote the plays based on children's stories featured on television and radio programs she listened to growing up in Iran. 'We took bits and pieces that were remembered from the radio when we were growing up in the 1960s ... the kind of silly things that all the parents knew, and when it got put in the play, it was an incredibly funny thing for the audience to hear the kids speaking Persian like when they were kids' (interview with Ladan, 21 June 2010). She stopped participating in the play when her schedule changed and some of the parents wanted to change the format of the play to that of a talent show to showcase individual performers. According to Ladan,

> That was in principle the opposite of what I was trying to do – I was trying to build community, not this showing off talents individually. I was interested in building community. Also, Minoo and the other kids were getting older, and I didn't think they were interested in doing it anymore. I was interested in it not only being in Persian; I wanted it to be real theater – not just kids getting up and dancing or lip-syncing, I wanted it to be a creative event. (Interview with Ladan, 21 June 2010)

By aspiring to build a linguistic and cultural community through the creative arts, Ladan's theater program draws attention to the multimodal ways in which parents and bilingual education programs support the education of children to use language for functional linguistic interrelationships (García,

2009a). Learning Persian is not simply about signaling 'Iranianness' or acquiring literacy; rather, Ladan made her teaching of Persian a site for new experiences and part of these students' daily lives.

Weekend classes for community-building

Mojgan first started her Persian class in Greenwich Village in 1997 after returning from a trip to Iran with her seven-year-old son Kourosh. Kourosh, whose father is American, did not grow up hearing or speaking Persian in the home on a regular basis. As a young boy, Kourosh had difficulty communicating with his grandmother when she visited from Iran and would become frustrated when spoken to in Persian. Several years later, when he went to Iran with his mother for the first time, Kourosh enjoyed his experiences and meeting his family, and expressed an interest and desire to learn Persian. According to Mojgan,

> The trip to Iran was a 180-degree change for him. After two months in Iran, he was adamant about speaking Farsi [Persian], and asked me to only speak to him in Farsi. When we came back, he went around showing off his Farsi to non-Iranian people ... He was so proud of knowing Farsi. (Interview with Mojgan, 2 July 2010)

Mojgan started her class in part to support Kourosh in his efforts to learn Persian. She created fliers and advertised her school as one for young children on a Persian language radio program, but received many phone calls from Iranian young adults and parents of Iranian teenagers who had similar struggles communicating with their relatives and other Iranians in Persian and wished to learn it. The school opened with 12 students who came from all five boroughs of the city, and some from Connecticut, to meet once a week on Saturday. Because of the small enrollment, the students were not separated by age. While the class met for four years, it was limited in terms of curriculum and did not extend beyond an introductory level. The younger students expressed frustration in having to come to a two-hour class on the weekends in addition to their regular schoolwork. The demographics of the class gradually changed as well, as more teenaged and adult students registered and younger students left the course. Still, Mojgan sees the class as a success because of its community-building impact:

> Going back to 1997, there weren't many Iranian kids in New York, or perhaps they were babies or too young for school. Our students didn't

really have Iranian friends, that isolation wasn't good either, so the school was good for creating relationships and friendships ... which is exactly what happened. The goal was for them to come to this relaxed happy environment, to learn how to read write, and speak ... and then we would give them certificates, but I didn't want it to be too formal. That was my method. The class I had didn't have religion or politics; that is why I was proud of my class. (Interview with Mojgan, 2 July 2010)

In this case, like that of the theater program, the emphasis of the school was on cultivating a dynamic bilingualism and sustaining linguistic inter-relationships among the students and their families. Mojgan is considering whether to offer the class again, this time making it part of a larger effort to open an Iranian cultural center in New York. She believes learning Persian will help Iranian children in the US to maintain their family relationships, and will allow them to feel close to their culture and history by allowing them to read Persian literature. Mojgan has recruited a teacher who used to teach Persian in Iran and is currently applying for non-profit status, identifying possible donors within the New York Iranian community, and looking for a site to start her new center.

Towards an early childhood model

Forough, a novelist and professor, is in the process of creating a Pre-Kindergarten to fifth-grade school in Manhattan. A mother of four, Forough has taken her elementary school-aged children to Ferdowsi School in Westchester County. She sees an absence of age-differentiated Persian language curriculum and pedagogy, and wants to create a curriculum that is appropriate for young learners, with a child-centered curriculum and reinforcement through learning activities. Citing a desire to collaborate and avoid 'reinventing the wheel', she wants to collaborate with the Ferdowsi School to open her school in Manhattan:

We are such a small community; it makes sense to build on what's out there, rather than to strike out on our own. We really don't have a lot of resources to facilitate this type of work. It really falls upon parents to bring it all together to make something happen. So this approach can be good and bad, because while it's community-based, there hasn't been a systemic way of bringing things together. It makes sense for me to collaborate with them, rather to go out on my own. We have to pool our resources when we can. (Interview with Forough, 22 June 2010)

Forough states that ideally she wants to have the school accredited and would partner with the New York City Department of Education to open her school, but she does not see that as feasible for the time being. This is in part because of the politicization of Middle Eastern and South Asian languages such as Persian, Arabic and Urdu, among others. Citing the negative publicity and suspicion that was created around the establishment of the Khalil Gibran International Academy in Brooklyn (an English–Arabic 'dual language' bilingual public school), Forough believes that the school has to be privately organized and funded for the time being to avoid the kind of criticism that 'obviates the teaching of Persian' (interview with Forough, 22 June 2010). Despite the growth of interest and grants made available by the federal government for schools to teach languages deemed 'critical' to national security (such as Persian), Forough does not see such grants as a viable source of funding for her school:

> For me, State Department money is not viable. That (funding a school that teaches Persian) might be an ancillary benefit for the State Department, but my intent is not to create a youth group for that purpose ... I would avoid all politically motivated funding sources. That includes people who have a particular political vision for Iran. (Interview with Forough, 22 June 2010)

Forough believes there are many benefits to teaching children Persian, and fostering their bilingualism and multilingualism. First, she sees language study as the best way to learn about other cultures and embrace cultural diversity. For Forough, the study of languages in general has cognitive benefits as well, engendering a 'certain quickness in your thinking and verbal skills' that is useful for all endeavors. For Iranian-American youth, she thinks fostering a Persian learning community will help make their cultural connections more tangible and reduce feelings of isolation or disconnectedness from Iran:

> It is a way of connecting with people in Iran, a culture and country that children growing up here may not know yet, but that is very important to their parents. It's part of what makes them understand who they are. In general, although our citizenships may be 'whatever', our identities are more complex. Identities are not like hats; we have more than one at a time, and identity is a composite of many different things. It's a composite of Iranian and American, and the Iranian needs to be nurtured as well. That can happen through learning language, culture, history, and music. (Interview with Forough, 22 June 2010)

Similar to the views of other respondents in this study, Forough sees bilingualism as a valuable resource for children to sustain and create connections across cultures, as well as with the cultures and peoples of Iran. Given that she sees identities as multiple and contemporaneous, students' bilingualism helps to inform and enrich their hybrid identities.

Home Learning

Many parents also make efforts to reinforce Persian language and Iranian culture at home. While some see the preservation of a heritage language as a means by which to safeguard a sense of identity and culture, several parents in this study maintain alternative views. Tara, a film producer who was born in the US, is married to a German man and has two pre-school-aged children. Her husband speaks to the children in German, and Tara, who does not read and write Persian, says that although her Persian 'isn't great', she speaks to her children in Persian most of the time (interview with Tara, 2 June 2010). Her children also encounter Persian at Tara's mother's home and her sister's home. Tara recently discovered and joined a Persian language playgroup in Brooklyn that has been organized by some Iranian parents or parents with Iranian spouses. For Tara, learning Persian is more about maintaining a sense of connectedness with family, rather than preserving culture:

> I grew up in Queens, around kids whose families basically said, 'you are born here, you don't need Farsi, so we are throwing that out'. So at family gatherings, we'd sit around, and they would have no idea what was going on. For me, it's not about maintaining culture, it's more about communicating with family, and really having this language in their back pocket, as another form of intelligence, something else they can hold onto. What's Iranian culture to me? It's the interactions that I have with my family. The language and the food, and things like that – that's what it is to me … not so much heritage, or religion, and things like that. It's about her experience, not me passing anything else along; that's why I do it. (Interview with Tara, 2 June 2010)

In emphasizing the importance of bilingualism in facilitating family relationships and new experiences, as well as fostering cognitive abilities, Tara shares the views of the other respondents; bilingualism is less about the reproduction of a putative 'Iranian' identity than it is about developing a new hybridized one. For Tara, 'Iranian culture' is a socially situated practice, constituted by interaction, rather than a standard transcript to be memorized. Moreover, Tara's experiences with the playgroup illustrate the importance of parents not only as teachers, but also as active facilitators and organizers in creating bilingual spaces of learning, play and interaction for their children.

Said and Azadeh, both professors, echoed some of Tara's views as well. They speak Persian and English at home with their preschool-aged children, and occasionally Swedish. Azadeh was born in Iran but grew up in Sweden. She sought a Swedish childcare provider in New York in part because she wanted her children to have affinity for multiple cultural realms. While Said and Azadeh speak to each other in Persian and both think it is important for their children to have knowledge of Persian, they do not wish to speak it solely to preserve a heritage or identity because they challenge the notion of language promoting a 'cultural authenticity'. Rather, they use Persian with their children when it feels natural to do so, citing terms of endearment as an example. According to Said,

> Language is very emotional. I don't have any ulterior motives with language. I habitually love and praise my children in Persian, and habitually send them to bed and tell them to brush their teeth in English ... The other part of it is that, the notion of ethnic language, is false; we don't teach Persian to our children as part of their heritage or identity, and tell them that's why they have to learn it, because that ethnicizes Persian. That provincializes Persian ... We cannot impose identity – our kids don't need an ethnic identity, they need to feel loved and happy, they need protection and stability, in whatever language. (Interview with Said, 9 June 2010)

By underscoring the fact that he speaks with his children in multiple languages, Said's comments are indicative of a dynamic conception of bilingualism, or plurilingualism, where the simultaneous coexistence of different languages is not only possible, but also preferable (García, 2009a). Said does not wish to ethnicize the Persian language by making it the primary marker of his children's 'Iranian' heritage. His wife Azadeh similarly believes that knowledge of Persian is not as important as having a shared sense of values with her children:

> What is more important to me than language is culture, and a sense of humanity. Everyday, I strive to teach those values, and to have them care about the world. With language, they will work here, have friends here, they are American, they need to speak English. I would love for them to

learn Persian well someday, to read the *Shahnameh*, but Persian is easy to pick up, and if they want to learn it, they will have an advantage in doing so. (Interview with Azadeh, June 9, 2010)

While expressing a desire for her children to learn Persian well someday, Azadeh does not see it as the sole imperative for their development as humane and successful individuals. Similar to other parents in this study, she is interested in facilitating the cultural and educational experiences needed for her children to care about the world and relate well with others.

Concluding Thoughts: Lessons for Educators

The Iranian-American community of New York City is diffuse and diverse, and as a result, approaches to Persian bilingual community education have developed accordingly. In addition to identifying programs and sites of Persian language education in New York City, this case study highlights a range of views regarding the relationship between language and culture among Iranians. In particular, the study contributes to an understanding of community-based educational programs in a sizable Iranian community in the US. It demonstrates that parents play central roles in creating and participating in Persian language educational programs as teachers and organizers, for reasons that transcend preservation of heritage or culture.

The emerging themes from this chapter invite discussion and reflection from educators and policy-makers. Critics of bilingual education often decry bilingualism as a zero-sum game, or a disservice to students by obstructing the learning of English or 'becoming American'. Yet such claims are not supported by the voices and experiences presented here. The desire of parents in this study to teach Persian can be understood as a wish to provide *additional* avenues of expression to their children, *additional* connections to their families, *additional* exposure to cultural diversity and *additional* resources to further their intellectual development and academic proficiency. Bilingualism is not, as Said notes, a means to 'ethnicize' or 'ghettoize' Iranian-American youth (interview with Said, 9 June 2010). Moreover, various parents note that their decision to encourage their children to learn Persian is often associated with cognitive and cultural benefits that transcend ethnic membership. As Tara, Said and Azadeh indicate, being Iranian in America is not created nor circumscribed by language. Rather, the multimodal teaching of Persian highlighted in this chapter reflects the formations of dynamic bilingual identities and a process of *transculturation*, in which knowledge of Persian contributes to a hybridized and transcultural identity for Iranian-American children.

As Forough and many other educators have stated, knowledge of another language is the best way to learn about other cultures and embrace cultural diversity. The programs and approaches these parent educators have developed demonstrate how Persian bilingual community education transcends language learning, and serves as a complex site of identity negotiation and performance that reflects the diversity of voices and views within the Iranian-American community in New York City.

Notes

(1) The term 'Iranian' is used to refer to people with historical origins in Iran. Since Iran is a multicultural and multilingual society, Iranians may be Kurdish, Arab, Azeri, Baluchi, Turkoman, etc. The term 'Persian' is used in two ways: first, to refer to the official language of Iran; second, some individuals use the term as a national designation, i.e. 'Persian' rather than 'Iranian'.

(2) 'Iran' and 'Persia 'usually refer to the same geopolitical entity. Persia is also commonly used to refer to Iran in a historical context, including the Persian Empires of antiquity. In 1935, however, the nationalist administration under Reza Shah Pahlavi successfully replaced 'Persia' with 'Iran'.

(3) Data was not available on the 2009 American Community Survey in which the population of Iranians was below 65,000 statewide. In all states other than California, the population estimates were drawn from the 2006–2008 American Community Survey 3-Year Estimates.

(4) The participants in this study were secular and well educated. None of the participants referred to their religion or professed any religious beliefs during the course of the interviews. Tara grew up in a household with Jewish and Muslim parents, but stated that religion was not a major component of her home life. Three of the participants are faculty members at regional universities, three were self-employed or worked part time, two were not working, and one worked for a film organization.

(5) See the Iranian American Society of New York Mission statement at http://www.iasnewyork.org/about.php

(6) See Razi School Curriculum at http://www.razischool.org/pub/curriculum.asp

(7) See MSNBC, 'Federal case threatens mosques, charity work' at http://www.msnbc.msn.com/id/33918736/

(8) See the Alavi Foundation Mission Statement at http://www.alavifoundation.org/page01.shtml

11 Towards Positive Peace through Bilingual Community Education: Language Efforts of Arabic-speaking Communities in New York

Zeena Zakharia and Laura Menchaca Bishop

Introduction

Arabic bilingual community education has a long history in New York that reflects over a century of diverse Arab migrations to the US. Because immigration and its related educational and linguistic processes cannot be divorced from their sociopolitical contexts, this chapter engages a political economy approach to look at the immigration history of Arabic-speaking peoples since the late 1800s, in order to understand the historical, sociopolitical and transnational dimensions of contemporary Arabic language education in a global city.

In order to understand language in context, we begin with an overview of the sociolinguistics of the Arabic language, its speakers and their immigration histories. The term 'Arab-American' is often used rather homogenously to represent an Arabic-speaking ethnic collectivity living in the US. The term is also often conflated with 'Muslim-American'. While the term does connote the shared language of Arabic, its members differ in many ways, and some who originate from the region do not share the language, or do not self-identify as Arab or Arab-American. Arab-Americans speak distinct dialects, participate in various religions, reflect a range of socio-economic statuses, have varying degrees of formal education and hail from diverse countries in western Asia and northern Africa. Arab-Americans also differ from each other according to the wave of immigration, or generation, from which they come, and according to the climate of reception they experienced upon their arrival. For some, their immigration to the US is a reflection of multiple displacements and re-settlements, rendering the notion of 'country of origin' incongruous.

In considering the growing interest in learning and teaching the Arabic language in the US, this chapter draws on concepts from the field of peace studies to introduce the notion of language education for negative or positive peace. It frames contemporary Arabic language programs within the security agenda of negative peace, while bilingual community efforts reflect the marginalized interests of education for positive peace. After reviewing historical developments that pushed early bilingual education efforts of Arab-Americans to the periphery, we focus on the challenges posed to contemporary forms of Arab-American bilingual community education.

Focusing on 'the eye of today's storms' (Bayoumi, 2008: 7), the chapter considers the efforts of one Islamic bilingual community school to teach the Arabic language in New York City. We argue that attention to the sociopolitical context is central to understanding the challenges to teaching and learning the Arabic language. The case demonstrates that bilingual community education falters in a climate that emphasizes language education for negative peace, in which the language that is viewed as 'foreign' is also viewed as the object of security. It is through language education for positive peace that bilingual Americans flourish, with their languages and cultures acknowledged and celebrated as one of the mainstays of American identity in the 21st century.[1]

Sociolinguistics of the Arabic Language and its Speakers

Arabic is one of the oldest recorded languages and has enjoyed continuous use and spread, bearing symbolic and functional significance in religious and secular domains across a diversified geography. The sections that follow provide a brief overview of the language, its salient features and the immigration histories and present US settlements of its speakers.

The language and the script

The multiple spoken varieties of Arabic are together referred to as *'āmiyya* and constitute generally mutually intelligible home languages, which are neither written nor formally taught at school. *'Āmiyya* varies within and across countries, with increasing divergence between varieties across greater geographic distances. *'Āmiyya* has also diverged over time from *fuṣḥā*, the literary, mostly written forms of Arabic, which include Classical Arabic, deriving from the Qur'an, and Modern Standard Arabic, its contemporary form.

Classical Arabic and Modern Standard Arabic are considered 'high status' varieties and are nobody's home languages. They are more conservative than *'āmiyya*, exhibiting little change over time and space. Modern Standard Arabic is taught in schools and used in contemporary written texts across the Arabic-speaking world. It also constitutes the shared spoken variety in all formal and official contexts, such as government and media communications. Thus all education in Arabic is at least multi-dialectical, drawing on *fuṣḥā* for formal curricular teaching, *'āmiyya* for classroom and non-formal communication, and where practiced, Classical Arabic to read the Qur'an and other classical or religious texts.

Grouped together, these varieties of Arabic may be considered one macro-language; linguistic criteria would designate them as multiple languages, but social and political considerations render them one single language with an unfixed number of spoken varieties and fluid boundaries between them. As such, Arabic is spoken by over 280 million people, by some estimates, and serves as one of the six official languages of the United Nations.

While the origins of the language pre-date Islam, its pre-colonial expansion is associated with the spread of Islamic teaching, including religious and scientific scholarship across the urban centers of the Middle East and North Africa. Later, the development of print capitalism in the first half of the 19th century, with its related technological advances, further promoted the Arabic language across a dialectically and religiously diverse region under Ottoman rule. During this period, Christian minorities, in particular, contributed to the advancement of the Arabic language as the vehicle for a modern national identity that affiliated diverse peoples in a mounting resistance against Ottoman imperialism and Turkification. In turn, a vibrant Arabic press would accompany early, largely Christian, immigrants to New York and other US settlements in the mid to late 19th century.

Arabic is a Semitic language whose script is commonly dated back to the fourth century AD, when it evolved from the Aramaic script. The long-recorded history of the Arabic language is generally a source of pride for Arabic-speaking peoples and peoples of Arab descent. Written Arabic employs an abjad writing system, or an alphabet comprising mainly of consonants, as well as three long vowel sounds, /ā/, /ī/ and /ū/. Because the Arabic language contains more consonants than its predecessor Aramaic, new letters were introduced during the seventh century by adding dots to existing letters. In addition, diacritics were added to designate short vowel sounds for full vocalization. These marks appear in the Qur'an, and in other complex religious and literary texts, as well as in books for children and other learners, to ensure accuracy in the reading of the text or to avoid ambiguity of meaning. The resulting alphabet includes 28 letters, which like most abjads, are written horizontally from right to left. Most letters of the Arabic alphabet are joined, and the form of the letter changes depending on whether it is placed at the beginning, middle or end of the word, or stands alone. The complexities of the language, its grammar and other features can be daunting for learners, regardless of whether they are speakers or not. Still, the Arabic language continues to enlist new learners.

Growing interest and spread

Arabic is widely spoken throughout western Asia and northern Africa and is an official language of 25 countries and territories.[2] Although many of these countries are traditionally thought of as Arabic-speaking or members of the Arab League, there are other countries not typically associated with Arabic in which there resides a large Arabic-speaking population. For example, the UK, France and the US are currently experiencing a significant influx of Arabic-speaking immigrants.

The fact that many countries around the world are experiencing an unprecedented rate of migration, alongside previous historical waves of migration, signals that Arabic has been, and continues to be, in contact with numerous other languages. In northern Africa, for example, Arabic shares a linguistic landscape with languages such as Berber, Beja, Bedawi, Dinka, English, French, Somali and other languages indigenous to the region. Because many countries in western Asia have experienced immigration from India, Iran and Pakistan, speakers of Hindi, Farsi and Urdu are often also in communication with Arabic speakers. Likewise, owing to the spread of Islam, Arabic is increasingly found in countries such as Bangladesh, Indonesia and the Philippines. As the locations in which Arabic is found diversify, the number of languages with which it comes into contact undoubtedly also continues to swell, creating new lexical and translanguaging phenomena.

According to some sources, Arabic is currently among the fastest growing languages in the world. It was the fastest growing language studied at US universities, with a 46.3% growth in enrollments between 2006 and 2009, and ranking eighth on the most studied language list in 2009 (Furman *et al.*, 2010). It stands among the top 10 languages used on the Internet and has also shown the largest percentage growth on the Internet over the past 10 years (Internet World Stats, 2011).

While its popularity is certainly attributable to cultural, religious and economic influences, it is also attributable to political concerns. Since the mid 2000s, the increased study of Arabic in the US has coincided with the US government's naming of Arabic as a 'critical-need' language. In 2006, President George W. Bush introduced the National Security Language Initiative, an 'inter-agency effort coordinated by the White House to increase dramatically the number of US residents learning, speaking, and teaching critical-need foreign languages' (US Department of Education, 2008). The Secretaries of State, Education and Defense as well as the Director of National Intelligence are primarily responsible for directing the initiative, which strives to increase programming in critical-need languages from the kindergarten level to the university level (US Department of Education, 2008).

Despite recent national interest in the Arabic language, however, support for Arabic instruction in schools has lagged. It has been faced with suspicion, controversy or staunch opposition, particularly where it has been developed by or for the Arabic-speaking community. As a result, the locus of Arabic–English bilingual education in New York has shifted from the center of Arab-American community life to the periphery, where its contemporary vitality lies largely in Islamic education.

History of immigration to the US

Arab immigration to the US is thought to date back to the 15th century, when Arabs accompanied Spanish explorers to the Americas (Kayyali, 2006). However, the first significant wave of Arab immigration to the US began in the 1870s and consisted largely of Christians from the Ottoman provinces and administrative districts of Syria, Mount Lebanon and Palestine (Naber, 2008).[3] The early immigrants were classified as coming from 'Turkey in Asia', along with other Ottoman subjects of the period (Samhan, 1999, as cited in Naber, 2008); however, they culturally identified as 'Syrian' (Naff, 2002) and their immigration is largely attributed to acute political violence and economic hardship in the region (Naber, 2008).[4]

Immigration reforms led to the classification of Arabic-speaking immigrants as 'Syrians' after 1899, and further distinguished the 'Lebanese' in the 1920s, following the emergence of Lebanese national identity under French rule. According to historical records, 60,000 immigrants of Arab descent, mostly males, entered the US between 1899 and 1910 (Rouchdy, 1992), settling in or near cities. New York City (NYC) served as the gateway and the 'mother colony' for Arab immigration to the US (Naff, 2002).

In New York, the immigrants quickly established merchant settlements, beginning with the pioneering enclave on Washington Street in Lower Manhattan, and then moving across the East River to the vibrant manufacturing economy of Brooklyn in the 1880s.[5] Many were pack-peddlers and sojourners, seeking to bring their fortunes back to their families in their homelands. Throughout this period, the Arabic language served to sustain the ethnic and religious vitality of the early Arab Christian settlers through Arabic-speaking parishes and a vibrant press (Cristillo & Minnite, 2002), which circulated news of the growing community through Arabic and bilingual newspapers (DiNapoli, 2002; Sawaie & Fishman, 1985). At the same time, a number of educational efforts were underway to maintain and develop the Arabic language, and by 1911, 114 professional Arabic teachers had entered the US (Houghton, 1911, as cited in Sawaie & Fishman, 1985). In time, however, with the assimilation of these early pioneers, the centrality of Arabic to religious and secular community life began to shift, with lasting consequences.

Coupled with the Great Depression, the quota system established in 1924 by the Johnson–Reed Act slowed immigration between World Wars I and II.[6] At the same time, the emergence of Arab nation-states, following Ottoman and European colonization, generated new categories of immigrants. Arab-American national identity emerged during this period and was evident in early transnational Arab organizations (Bawardi, 2006, as cited in Naber, 2008).

The second wave of immigration remained relatively small, but was marked by the 1948 Arab–Israeli war, or Palestinian Nakba, which created a mass migration of dispossessed Palestinians to the US, along with a second group comprising Egyptians and other Arabs (Orfalea, 2006). This wave differed demographically from the first in significant ways: first, they were better educated, with the majority of males holding college degrees; second, over half were Muslim; third, they were financially established; and finally, they did not come to the US directly from their homelands, but rather via other destinations (Orfalea, 2006).

The 1965 US immigration reforms resulted in a third wave of immigration. Regional instability, including the ongoing Arab–Israeli conflict and civil wars, propelled this wave of immigration. Demographically, these immigrants resembled their predecessors. However, numerically, nearly 11 times as many immigrants arrived between 1967 and 2003 than during the second wave, constituting almost 800,000 immigrants, a quarter of whom were Palestinians (Orfalea, 2006). They came through other states as a consequence of the 1967 war. The second largest group of immigrants during this period were Lebanese, who fled at various points during the 15-year civil war (1975–1990). In addition, Egyptians came in large numbers during this period, almost half comprising minority Coptic Christians. The fourth largest group were Iraqis following the Iran–Iraq war (1980–1988), UN sanctions on Iraq (after 1990), and the US-led war on Iraq (starting 2003). This third wave of immigration is also characterized by Yemeni immigration in the context of the protracted Yemeni civil war.

Thus Americans of Arabic-speaking origins have a long history of immigration and settlement in the US, but their demographics changed after World War II, becoming more diverse (Naber, 2008). While early immigration was primarily Christian and from the Ottoman region of Greater Syria, later migration included larger numbers of Muslims, some as a result of multiple displacements. With the current upheavals across the Arab world, this migration is likely to continue.

US demographics and settlements

According to the US Census Bureau's 2006–2008 American Community Survey (US Census Bureau (2006–2008), at least 1.5 million Americans trace their heritage to the Arab world.[7] Of these, 42% are foreign born and roughly 55% speak a language 'other than English' at home, presumably Arabic, but not necessarily. Arab-Americans come from diverse faith traditions, including various sects of Islam, Christianity, Judaism and the Unitarian Druze faith, with at least half of US Arabs believed to come from Christian traditions.[8] Over 80% of Arabs in the US are US citizens and they tend to work in the private sector (88%), with a majority (73%) employed in managerial, professional, technical, sales or administrative domains (Arab American Institute, ca 2010a). Two-thirds of Arab-Americans are concentrated in 10 states, with one-third of all Arab-Americans living in California (243,343), Michigan (151,149) and New York (145,609; US Census Bureau, 2006–2008).[9] Like their predecessors, 94% of Arab-Americans live in metropolitan areas (Arab American Institute, ca 2010b).

While at least 22 Arab countries are represented throughout the US, the largest groups originate from seven countries: Lebanon (32%), Egypt (11%), Syria (10%), Palestine (5%), Morocco (5%), Iraq (4%) and Jordan (4%), with the category of 'Arab/other Arab' representing 29%.[10] In fact, Arab-Americans who identify as being of Lebanese descent comprise the largest group in every state, except for New Jersey, where Egyptian-Americans have the greatest representation (Arab American Institute, ca 2010b). Similar to other immigrants, peoples of Arab descent have historically migrated to where fellow nationals have settled. Thus, in California, the majority of the Arab-American population is of Egyptian, Iraqi, Lebanese, Palestinian or Syrian descent, while in New York, it is of Lebanese and Egyptian descent, and in Michigan it is of Iraqi and Lebanese descent (US Census Bureau, 2006–2008).

Educational achievement

Arab-Americans have a strong commitment to the education of their children and as a group have attained higher educational levels on average than the US population as a whole. For example, more than 46% of Arab-Americans have a bachelor's degree or higher, compared with 28% of US citizens, and 19% of Arab-Americans have a masters or doctoral degree, compared with a national average of 10% (US Census Bureau, 2006–2008). Overall, 89% of Arab-Americans hold at least a high school diploma.

The New York City metropolitan population with Arab ancestry has fared equally well in terms of their educational attainment, with approximately 85% of those aged 25 or older holding at least a high school diploma or its equivalent (compared with 79% of New Yorkers) and 42% holding at least a bachelor's degree (compared with 34% of New Yorkers). These figures are nearly equal for males and females in each category (US Census Bureau, 2007–2009).

Arabic-speaking students designated as English language learners (ELLs) by the NYC Department of Education have seen steady increases since 2002 (NYCDOE, 2007, 2009a, 2011). According to the New York City Bilingual Education Student Information Survey,[11] during the 2010–2011 academic year, students from Arabic-speaking backgrounds comprised the fourth largest language group among ELLs (after Spanish, Chinese and Bengali), with 4692 students, or 3% of the ELL population in New York public schools (NYCDOE, 2011). Of this group of Arabic-speaking ELLs, 44.6% were identified as originating from Yemen (NYCDOE, 2011).[12] Both Yemen and Egypt ranked among the top 15 countries with more than 500 students entering NYC public schools as new immigrants in 2010–2011 (ATS Immigrant Survey 2010–2011, as cited in NYCDOE, 2011). During that same year, Arabic ranked among the top five languages spoken by ELLs in 26 of 34 districts surveyed in New York.

Arabic in New York and its Educational Programs

The New York population that self-identifies as having Arabic-speaking ancestry increased by almost 23% from 2000 to 2008, according to US

Census estimates (Arab American Institute, *ca* 2010b). This section provides a demographic snapshot of these bilingual New York communities, their increased visibility and contemporary educational efforts.

Arab New Yorkers

Approximately 181,270 people living in the New York metropolitan area identify as having Arab ancestry, with 90,000 of these individuals residing in New York City proper (US Census Bureau, 2006–2008). Of those 181,270 individuals, approximately 58% report that they speak Arabic in the home and approximately 58,105 were born outside of the US (US Census Bureau, 2006–2008). The majority of these foreign-born, Arabic-speaking individuals live in Brooklyn (mainly in Bay Ridge–Bensonhurst, Gravesend–Homecrest, Sunset Park–Industry City and Borough Park), Queens (Astoria) or Manhattan (US Census Bureau, 2006–2008). It is thought that these figures are severely under-reported and that the statewide population of Arab New Yorkers is closer to 405,000 (Arab American Institute, *ca* 2010b). Although the median household income of Arab ancestry New Yorkers is $61,597 and the per capita income is roughly measured at $31,624, roughly 15% of all Arab ancestry New Yorker families currently live in poverty (US Census Bureau, 2006–2008).

Brooklyn, the borough with the largest representation of foreign-born Arabic-speaking communities, has primarily been home to Egyptians, Lebanese and Syrians. Queens, which boasts the second largest community of foreign-born Arabic-speaking individuals has hosted mostly Egyptians, Moroccans and Lebanese. Finally, Manhattan has most recently been home to Lebanese and Egyptian immigrants (US Census Bureau, 2006–2008).

In/visible students before and after 11 September 2001

Educational studies and personal narratives from the late 1980s and early 1990s suggest that children of Arab descent were largely invisible in NYC schools, despite their influx as a consequence of political strife in Palestine, Lebanon and Iraq. Early immigrants assimilated into urban life, socially and linguistically (Benson & Kayal, 2002) and newer Arab-Americans were generally not on people's radars prior to 11 September 2001 (Bayoumi, 2008).[13]

However, the terrorist attacks of 11 September 2001 (hereafter 9/11) and the US-led wars in Iraq and Afghanistan catapulted Arab-Americans, and Arab-Muslim-Americans in particular, from 'invisible citizens' to 'visible subjects' (Jamal & Naber, 2008), framing them as the new 'problem' of American society (Bayoumi, 2008: 2). During the first six months after 9/11, bias crimes against Arabs, Muslims and those assumed to be either surged by 1700% (Bayoumi, 2008). In a 2006 *USA Today*/Gallup Poll, 39% of Americans admitted to harboring prejudice against Muslims, and 54% said they could not vote for a Muslim president in a 2006 Bloomberg/*Los Angeles Times* poll.

For students, this visibility meant increased scrutiny and overt displays of bigotry, including micro-aggressions from fellow students, teachers and the larger public (Cristillo, 2008; personal communication, Principal, 19 May 2011).[14] For Islamic schools and educational programs that teach the Arabic language, it meant surveillance and increased visitation from government agents (interview, Principal, 20 May 2011). In general, there was a sense from parents that their lives had changed (Zakharia, 2006). It is in this climate that the first dual-language bilingual Arabic–English public school in the US attempted to open its doors in New York in 2007, under tremendous opposition, which we discuss further below.

Bilingual community efforts in New York

By and large, the majority of Arabic language instruction programs currently available in New York City to students in grades K–12 are offered through mosques or Islamic centers. According to the Muslim Consultative Network, a community strengthening organization in New York City, there are 35 to 40 sites at which Arabic language instruction is offered in some capacity. The impetus for their founding has most commonly been a response to community demand. Several school officials have indicated that, because the Arabic language plays a central role in Islam, Muslim parents are especially concerned about their children learning the language. Thus the schools enroll Arab-American students, as well as sizable populations of African, European, Pakistani, Bengali, Indian and Guyanese Americans, which speaks to the growing diversity of Arabic learners in New York.

Social service organizations focusing on Arab-American affairs in New York City also contribute significantly to Arabic language instruction. The Arab American Family Support Center (AAFSCNY), one of the largest Arab-American social service organizations in the country, offers Arabic classes as part of its middle school programming and also provides English and Arabic literacy classes as part of its adult programming. The adult women's Arabic literacy class emerged in September 2003 in response to demand from a Yemeni-American mother who voiced her wish to learn how to read and write in Arabic, when she was approached by the AAFSCNY teacher, as part of the Center's outreach activities, about enrolling her children in Arabic classes (Zakharia, 2006). After consulting with the AAFSCNY director and assistant director, the teacher told the woman that, if she brought enough women to form a literacy class, she would teach them. By February 2004 the class had grown to 12 Yemeni-American women.[15]

Other community-based organizations, such as Alwan for the Arts, an arts and cultural organization, also offer several levels of Arabic instruction, and the Arab American Community Center for Economic and Social Services offers English and Arabic literacy classes to adults. Although other organizations, such as the Arab American Association of New York and the American Mideast Leadership Network, do not offer Arabic language programs directly, part of their mission to support underserved communities of Arab-Americans in New York City includes referring families to language services in the City.

In 2010, the New York City Department of Education (NYCDOE) Office of English Language Learners listed one middle school and one high school as having transitional bilingual education programs that support Arabic speakers. Both schools were located in Brooklyn. Further, in 2007, the NYCDOE opened its first community-led Arabic–English dual language bilingual school in Brooklyn. It was the first of its kind in the country. Supported by the Bill and Melinda Gates Foundation, the Khalil Gibran International Academy (KGIA) was developed in partnership with New Visions for Public Schools, the AAFSCNY and other community partners, under the leadership of Debbie Almontaser and a design team from diverse linguistic, ethnic and religious backgrounds. Almontaser is a Yemeni-American public servant and a community activist and educator, with an established record of community organizing for interfaith dialogue and understanding among New York's diverse religious faiths. As the Project Director for the development of KGIA and later KGIA's Interim School Principal, Almontaser hoped that the school would foster increased understanding and better relations between Arab-Americans and their peers (Elliott, 2008). A central theme of the school was therefore to 'build bridges of understanding', and to develop Arabic language learners as 21st century global ambassadors and 'brokers of peace' (personal communication, Almontaser, 20 May 2011).

However, just weeks before KGIA was scheduled to open, critics of the school mounted a campaign to derail her efforts, alleging that the school had a 'militant Islamic agenda' and arguing that Almontaser was a 'jihadist', 'radical' and '9/11 denier' (Elliott, 2008; US Equal Employment Opportunity Commission, 2010). A heated public debate ensued, led by a small but vociferous group of objectors who identified themselves as the 'Stop the Madrassa Coalition'. The controversy eventually resulted in the forced resignation of Almontaser, a move that was later ruled as being discriminatory. This resignation, coupled with the NYCDOE's poor stewardship of the school in its first three years of operation, led to the 2011 decision to close KGIA, severely jeopardizing Arabic bilingual programming.[16]

The controversy over the school revealed a fundamental lack of understanding about Arab-Americans as diverse, multi-faith and multiracial peoples, and the conflation of the Arabic language and its speakers, whether US citizens or not, with militant Islam, and thus the limited ways in which language, religion and citizenship are imagined in bilingual education. The objectors viewed the bilingual school as promoting a form of 'soft jihad' (Teague, 2009). The case also demonstrates the narrow 'space' within which Arabic language education has been permitted to operate in the post-9/11 climate of New York, highlighting the extent to which the sociopolitical climate impacts bilingual community education in the public domain.

The effect is to limit the ways in which Arabic language education is envisioned, reducing it to 'foreign' language education and narrowing the impetus for funding to a security agenda. In this sense, Arabic language education in the public domain is not envisioned as part of developing American bilingual identities for global facility in the 21st century. This distinction sets bilingual community education, which in its dynamic form serves as education for positive peace, apart from the Arabic language programming supported by the National Security Language initiative, which frames language teaching in terms of a security imperative, or education for negative peace. Like the adult Arabic and English literacy classes of the AAFSCNY, which Yemeni women students viewed as a means to develop Arab understanding, the goals of the interfaith community-led program at KGIA offered an example of bilingual education for positive peace. This form of education addresses conflict by establishing equitable structures, addressing various forms of institutionalized discrimination and injustice, and developing cultural understanding, as the fundamental building blocks of a comprehensive peace.[17]

The next section focuses on the efforts at one Islamic bilingual community school in New York City to teach the Arabic language. We argue that attention to the sociopolitical context is a critical component of understanding the challenges to teaching and learning the Arabic language in a climate that emphasizes language education for negative peace, and frames Arabic as the 'ethnic-mother tongue' or 'heritage language' of a 'foreign' Other.

The Case of an Islamic School in Brooklyn

The Brooklyn Islamic School (pseudonym) began teaching Arabic in 1995. It is a community-founded and community-governed pre-K–12, private, non-denominational Islamic school that teaches both the New York State curriculum in English and the Arabic language, starting in the pre-kindergarten. Students study in gender-segregated classes, taking 10 periods per week of

Arabic language and literacy instruction in the early years, and five periods per week from grade 1. In addition, they engage in Islamic studies, which includes history, as well as the reading of Islamic literary and religious texts.

According to the Principal, all of the teachers and staff are Arabic–English bilinguals, except for himself and one other teacher. Students and teachers come from diverse Arabic-speaking Muslim backgrounds. In addition, in recent years, owing to the changing demographics of the school community, in tandem with an improved reputation for quality education, the school has been attracting larger numbers of non-Arabic-speaking Muslim students, including Pakistani-Americans, Bangladeshi-Americans and Albanian-Americans. Thus, in addition to Arabic and English, Bengali, Urdu, Turkish, Bosnian and Albanian can be heard around the school. However, the entering kindergarten class remains largely composed of children of Arab descent; 20 of the 25 students in this class are described by the Principal and class teachers as either 'Arabic dominant' bilinguals or 'non-English speakers' at the time of enrollment. Other entering students are 'English dominant' or Urdu- or Bengali-speaking students. In recognition of this diversification, the governing board has also modified its composition to include two members who do not hail from Arabic-speaking backgrounds.

Tuition comprises the primary source of school funding, with additional financial support from community members through donations and student fundraising drives. Parent volunteers provide additional community supports for the running of the school and its special events.

Both Arabic and English are taught and used to communicate in the formal and non-formal spaces of the school, although students are more likely to be heard speaking English and parents Arabic. In these bilingual spaces, a variety of dialects, including Egyptian, Palestinian, Yemeni and Sudanese varieties, intermingle with English, as exemplified by the following observation:

> When I enter the school, I am greeted by 'assalāmū'alaikum [peace be with you], by the receptionist. In the waiting room for the Principal, two teachers speak to each other in Arabic ... It is a bilingual space; the office staff, teachers and parents enter and exit the space, speaking in both languages [Arabic and English] and in multiple dialects [of Arabic 'āmiyya]. A boy is brought in by a teacher; he is sick and an adult speaks to him in Arabic, telling him that he will be taken home. He responds in English. (Fieldnotes, 19 May 2011)

The observations described here reflect the larger school space in which Arabic and English live in tandem. The languages are also visually displayed through student work throughout the classrooms and hallways.

According to the Principal, the school seeks to develop student ability in spoken and written *fuṣḥā*, in part in order to access the Qur'an and other Islamic literatures. However, 'to what extent it serves that end is a question' (interview, Principal, 19 May 2011). Arabic teachers in the upper grades echoed this concern in interviews and a focus group discussion, in which they identified what they perceived to be the challenges to Arabic language development among their largely Arab-American students. The following excerpt from observations of a girls' kindergarten Arabic lesson provides a starting point for looking at what the Principal, in describing the learning of Arabic, refers to as a 'loss of momentum over time' (interview, 19 May 2011).

> Nineteeen girls sit on the carpet in rows in their green and blue uniforms in front of their teacher who is seated on a low chair beside a white board . . . The teacher draws an elephant on the white board. She asks in English: 'Who can tell me something about *al fīl* [the elephant] in Arabic? A sentence? Yes – a *jumla* [sentence]?' (Fieldnotes, 19 May 2011)

In this Arabic literacy lesson, the teacher solicits sentences in Arabic *fuṣḥā* about an elephant. She uses both Arabic and English in the process, to ensure understanding among bilingual students of non-Arabic speaking backgrounds, and to ensure comfort among Arab-Americans (personal communication, 19 May 2011).

Students' hands shoot up in excitement to offer different sentences about the elephant, and they offer, in Arabic *fuṣḥā*, phrases such as: 'God created the elephant'; 'The big elephant cleans the small elephant'; 'The elephant eats a peanut'. The teacher then draws a rabbit onto the back of the elephant, and a story progresses, frame by frame, with new sentences being created in *fuṣḥā* about the rabbit and the elephant. In the process, students ask in English for vocabulary ('How do you say peanut?') and the teacher asks for definitions, translanguaging throughout ('What does *barmīl al mā'* [bucket of water] mean?'). They sound out the words and the teacher adds them to the growing storyboard. The lesson is interspersed with movement, as the students stand up to imitate the elephant and the rabbit. The teacher then asks them to recall the story. They switch roles and now the students are together retelling the story of the elephant and the rabbit in *fuṣḥā*, using the new vocabulary that was developed during the lesson. As each vocabulary word is used, the teacher invites them to write it on the white board. The teacher continues to translanguage. They sing a song in Arabic about a rabbit with associated movements, using two fingers at each temple to make ears. Then they jump like rabbits to their seats at colorful tables. They are instructed to write a paragraph in *fuṣḥā* about the elephant and the rabbit. Keywords from the storyline are written on the board in Arabic (walk, fall, drink, etc.). They use these words to retell the story in their notebooks, accompanied by an illustration.

According to the kindergarten Arabic teacher, they have not seen the text of the story, but they have been working all year to build a strong foundation in *fushā* through two hours of Arabic instruction per day. The lesson is fun and engages different modes of learning. The students appear to enjoy retelling and writing the story.

In the boys' kindergarten class, two students present to the researcher the work in their Arabic notebooks with what appears to be great pride. The notebooks are filled with their own texts and illustrations. The Arabic teacher explains that she creates her own resources to make learning fun, including flashcards for phonics, story books and coloring books. They begin with phonics and finish the year being able to read and write paragraphs in Arabic.

However, the Principal and Arabic teachers at the Brooklyn Islamic School note that, by grade 7 or 8, students begin to lose momentum or interest in learning the Arabic language. Indeed, observations of high school Arabic classes suggested that lessons do not fully engage advanced learners. According to one teacher, the reason why Arabic teaching is more problematic in the higher grades is because of the pressure of other subjects required for passing high school and going to college. This situation frames Arabic as a burden to students. Students respond by not wanting to move up in Arabic levels in the high school years. They try to negotiate increased course credit for advanced Arabic classes in order to make the effort worthwhile. The language is also increasingly narrowed by this tension to becoming 'only a language. It loses relevance because it is no longer central to their intellectual life' (interview, teacher, 19 May 2011). With a lack of clear incentives, student motivation to learn the language begins to lag. According to teachers, this loss of motivation manifests itself in student misbehavior (focus group, Arabic teachers, 27 May 2011).

In addition, the Saudi curriculum employed for 'non-native' Arabic learners does not reflect the demographic reality or experience of Muslim-American learners. Teachers identified this gap and cited several examples. One teacher noted: 'The books have nothing in them about being Arabs in America or being Muslims in America' (interview, teacher, 26 May 2011). While teachers are able to cope with this diversity in the pre-K and kindergarten classes, the disconnect widens in the upper grades, where teachers expressed feeling less equipped to deal with the complexities of teaching diverse bilinguals. One teacher expressed her dissatisfaction with her own pedagogical understanding, saying: 'Sometimes I feel like I don't have enough skills as a teacher to supplement my teaching materials. So I try to benefit from the English teacher. I look at the English books to get an idea about topics and skills and how the materials are designed. I peek in on English classes to get ideas about what to do in Arabic' (interview, 26 May 2011).

The Principal is concerned about developing the professional qualifications of the teachers and their Arabic language abilities as well. According to the Principal, the teachers do not amply engage critical thinking in the Arabic classroom. He has shifted the teaching of Islamic Studies from Arabic to English because of the challenges of finding teachers who excel in both the Arabic language and Islamic Studies.

Observations and interviews revealed that much translanguaging takes place between 'āmiyya and fuṣḥā among both students and teachers in the classroom, as well as in the hallways and playground. Teachers face difficulties in maintaining a policy of fuṣḥā-only in the classroom and view this as a form of failure. Furthermore, Arabic teachers in the upper grades struggle to maintain what they expect of an Arabic-only classroom, because students translanguage between Arabic fuṣḥā, 'āmiyya and English, and in the process, 'some [English] words slip out' for teachers as well: 'You slip, and then you try to fix it, but they [students] ask in English and this makes you slip [into English]' (interview, teacher, 26 May 2011). Thus a tension emerges between the flexible heteroglossic practices exhibited in the teaching and learning process, and the inflexible monoglossic policies and deeply engrained beliefs about the development of separate languages, a phenomenon that has been amply described by Blackledge and Creese (2010) in a study of multilingualism in complementary schools.

What is interesting about the monoglossic policies and beliefs is that, at the same time that they are promoted by teachers, they are simultaneously undermined, not only through their classroom practices, but through a nagging counter-belief that translanguaging, as an instructional strategy, is good for language learning. In interviews, teachers articulated this counter-belief in describing how students learn. One teacher explained:

I believe that it's important for me to draw on both languages [Arabic and English] to help students draw connections, to understand, even if they are new to Arabic. They can use more intellectual resources that way, by drawing on both [languages]. (Interview, teacher, 19 May 2011)

The Principal notes that one of the strengths of the school is the familiarity that teachers have with their students, which allows them to address students in Arabic or English depending on the student's strengths and capacities and the context of communication.

According to an Arabic teacher, however, the Arabic language carries low status within the larger social context and garners poor respect within the Arabic-speaking community: 'If we respected our language, we'd have an impact on students' (interview, 26 May 2011). This comment points to deeper issues regarding challenges to teaching the Arabic language in a post-9/11 environment. The same teacher continues: 'We just don't have respect for our *ḥadāra* [civilization/history]. We need to feel good about ourselves to be able to build on this'. In addition, the Principal describes the disbelief expressed by parents in the school community when he announced that the school had achieved a 100% graduation rate: 'The parents just did not believe it. They came up to me after to check if it was true ... They essentially raised doubts about the ability of an Islamic school to achieve academic excellence' (interview, 19 May 2011).

Such comments point to the ways in which the sociopolitical context has impacted the self-esteem of bilingual communities and this Arab and Muslim educational community in particular. Since 9/11, the Brooklyn Islamic School has contended with increased surveillance and student and teacher experiences of bigotry in wider society. According to the Principal, debris from the Twin Tower attacks landed in the schoolyard, and with it came a profound change in experience for Arab- and Muslim-Americans. In the immediate aftermath, this was felt as an 'attack on all things Muslim', which made the school's Muslim-American students feel 'unwanted'. However, although 'matters died down a bit ... still today the prejudice is there', and while this is not always tangible, it is felt by the community in various spaces and in the profiling of Arab- and Muslim-Americans (interview, Principal, 19 May 2011).

Frequent school visits from members of the police department, the State Department and journalists have contributed to the sense that the school is being watched. The Principal adds: 'They always want to see how we teach Islamic Studies and social studies, which includes global studies and Islamic history. They don't realize that we have a problem teaching it well! They just want to know: do you teach against the US Constitution?' Such pressures have prevented the school from engaging students fully with current events in the Arab world that could help them to see their positive role as global ambassadors, or to address tensions among Arab-American students in the school. According to the Principal, there is concern that innocent comments could be used to 'provocate against the school' (interview, Principal, 19 May 2011).

Within this context, students openly question their teachers about why they are learning the Arabic language, according to a focus group conducted with eight Arabic teachers (27 May 2011). They show resistance to learning through misbehavior, stating that they are never going to use the language. Teachers attempt to respond by drawing on the importance of the unity of the religious community and the centrality of the language to understanding the miracle of the Qur'an and community wisdom. They articulate the significance of the Arabic language for broader communication. One teacher explains:

> They learn culture through language, so if they have more languages to choose from, it's like having different colors. They can say, 'I like this from orange and this from blue'. It gives them more choices to see things in different ways. (Interview, 19 May 2011)

This notion of choices and language as a vehicle for 'seeing' things in different ways is central to the positive development of bilingual American identities, in which integrating knowledge in two languages goes beyond 'heritage language learning' and emerges as the cornerstone of bilingual community education. However, such education comes up against a sociopolitical climate that emphasizes language education for negative peace, wherein the Arabic language is viewed as 'foreign' within a security framework. Developing content and pedagogy that recognize students' complex identities, language practices and experiences as Arab- and Muslim-Americans and that addresses the injustices wrought by the political economy can lay the foundation for a positive peace framework through which bilingual Americans may flourish.

Conclusion

The relationships between language, conflict and peace-building is complex. From a peace studies perspective, bilingual education can be conceptualized as having a negative or positive peace orientation. This chapter demonstrates how the Arabic language has been pushed to the periphery of bilingual community education, where it has been largely limited to private Islamic schools and centers. At the same time, the Arabic language has been propelled nationally as an object of 'foreign' language study, as part of a security agenda. Within this sociopolitical context, Arabic community education programs, such as those established at K–12 Islamic private schools in New York, struggle to engage students in productive Arabic education, especially in the later years.

Historical and contemporary global, regional and local conflicts generate a sociopolitical climate that simultaneously promotes and opposes bilingual education for particular target groups. As this chapter illustrates, Arabic language education in particular has been promoted for security purposes, or negative peace; and in seeming contradiction, it has been staunchly opposed for programs that are perceived to serve the Arabic-speaking community. It follows that bilingual education during conflict is supported for those who are perceived to be 'American' and opposed for those who are perceived to be 'outsiders', namely in this case Arab-Americans. This happens even when bilingual education serves to address conflict by providing greater cultural understanding and equality for minoritized groups, or an education for positive peace.

Bilingual education from a positive peace perspective mitigates the negative impact of the sociopolitical context by respecting the complex relationships between language, culture and identity for bilingual Americans, going beyond 'ethnic-mother tongue' maintenance or 'heritage language' development. By integrating the social and linguistic experiences and practices of bilingual Arab and Muslim-Americans, bilingual education for positive peace carries the potential to promote peace in the lives of individual students and broader society by addressing discrimination and the narrow definitions of what it means to be American. As this chapter illustrates, understanding the broader historical and sociopolitical trajectories in which bilingual community education is framed is central to developing effective instructional content and strategies for bilingual Americans in the 21st century.

Notes

(1)   This chapter is largely based on a study of Arabic–English bilingual community education conducted in 2010 and 2011. The study engaged a survey of Arabic community language programs; participant observation at two Islamic schools in Brooklyn and Queens; analysis of program documents and media reports; a focus group of eight Arabic teachers at one Islamic school; and interviews of community leaders, teachers and principals at schools, mosques and community centers in New York. The study is part of a longer-term inquiry into Arabic language education in New York that began in early 2004 with a study (conducted by the first author and Hala Al Kayyali) of a Yemeni-American women's Arabic literacy class in Brooklyn. It then developed in several stages, with an identification effort (2004–2005, 2010), and documentary analysis and key informant interviews by the first author related to the controversy around the first Arabic-English dual language public school in New York (2007–2011).

(2)   Arabic is an official language of Algeria, Bahrain, Chad (with French), the Comoros (with French), Djibouti (with French), Egypt, Iraq (with Kurdish), Israel (with Hebrew), Jordan, Kuwait, Lebanon, Libya, Mauritania, Morocco, Oman, the Palestinian National Authority, Qatar, Saudi Arabia, Somalia (with Somali), Sudan (with English), Syria, Tunisia, the United Arab Emirates, Yemen and Western Sahara. In addition, although not an official language, Arabic is widely used in Eritrea.

(3)   The religious composition of Arab immigrants during this period is commonly cited as 90–95% Christian and 5–10% Muslim and other.

(4) According to Naber (2008), historical accounts suggest a number of political and economic reasons for the immigration of early Arabic-speaking pioneers to the US. The general consensus is that early immigration from Mount Lebanon followed from economic setbacks in the mid 1800s resulting from the opening of the Suez Canal, which diverted world trade from Syria to Egypt, allowing Japanese silk to become a major competitor to the Lebanese silk industry. In addition, Lebanese vineyards were nearly destroyed during this period by a pest. Growing dissatisfaction with Ottoman rule, impending conscription of Christians into the Ottoman army, and other pressures wrought by population growth also served to inspire immigration. By some accounts, American Presbyterian missionaries, who established schools and dispensaries in the Ottoman region during this period, also encouraged immigration to the US.

(5) See Benson and Kayal (2002) for a collection of essays on the Arab Americans of New York prior to 9/11, including their immigration histories, settlement, diversity and assimilation into a New York tradition of commerce, entrepreneurship and the arts.

(6) The Johnson–Reed Act limited the annual immigration of a country to 2% of the number already living in the US in 1890.

(7) The Arab American Institute estimates that over 3.5 million Americans are of Arab descent, noting that the US Census Bureau identifies only a portion of this population through the question on ancestry. For an explanation of the undercount see http://aai.3cdn.net/63c6ecf052bdccc48f_afm6ii3a7.pdf

(8) By some estimates, only one quarter of Americans of Arab descent are Muslim (Orfalea, 2006). However, this figure has been disputed and others have approximated the Muslim population of Arab-Americans to be closer to half the total. The historical 'invisibility' of US Arab Christians in American society and the sudden 'visibility' of Arab Muslims after 9/11 may contribute to the false perception that US Arabs are Muslim (see Jamal & Naber, 2008 for an excellent discussion of the in/visibility of Arab Americans and the related historical and contemporary racialization processes before and after 9/11).

(9) Arab Americans live in all 50 states. The seven other states that enjoy sizable Arab-American populations include Florida (99,872), Texas (85,680), New Jersey (82,257), Illinois (66,808), Ohio (65,965), Massachusetts (61,827) and Virginia (50,916) (Arab American Institute, ca 2010b).

(10) The category of 'Arab/Other Arab' represents those individuals who chose to describe themselves as having 'Arab' ancestry in general as opposed to associating with a country of origin in particular. Their migration histories may predate the creation of nation-states in the region.

(11) The Bilingual Education Student Information Survey is an annual survey of all public school students who are designated as English Language Learners by the NYC Department of Education, and who are eligible for English as a Second Language or bilingual education programming.

(12) The other significant groups of Arabic-speaking ELLs in 2010–2011 were identified as originating from NYC (31.2%), Egypt (12.1%) and Morocco (2.2%) (NYCDOE, 2011).

(13) While Arab Americans were not in focus prior to 9/11, 'race prejudice' was cited in the New York Arabic press as a problem facing Syrian American youth as early as 1927 (DiNapoli, 2002). Arabs more generally have had a long history of negative stereotyping in American popular culture. See Jack Shaheen's extensive scholarship

on Arab stereotyping in American film, TV and other media, including children's programs. Arabs are one of the few groups that continue to be negatively depicted in American popular media without sanctions (Benson & Kayal, 2002).

(14) The extensive Muslim Youth in NYC Public Schools Study, which drew on the experiences of 633 students, found that Muslim Arab students were twice as likely to be teased or taunted about being Muslim or 'terrorists' than other Muslim students (Cristillo, 2008). Participants cited a number of incidents of bigotry experienced by themselves or a family member.

(15) In 2004, a study of the women's Arabic literacy class conducted by the first author and Hala Al Kayyali found that the Yemen-born American women engaged in the class had had little or no schooling in Yemen owing to a complex context of educational underdevelopment in their home villages. Perhaps as a result of this deprivation, they placed high priority on their children's public schooling and viewed their own learning of Arabic as a 'gift', to fulfill a childhood dream of attending school, and as an opportunity to reverse injustice, to read the Qur'an for themselves, and to improve communications with other Arabs.

(16) An AAFSCNY press release on 30 June 2011 announced that the school would be moved, and after transitioning out its middle school students, would re-open in due course as an International Baccalaureate public high school. This effort is supported by the AAFSCNY and other community partners.

(17) The concepts of positive and negative peace are used extensively in the peace studies and peace education literature and are commonly attributed to the scholarship of Johan Galtung.

12 Educating for Jewishness: The Teaching and Learning of Hebrew in Day School Education

Sharon Avni and Kate Menken

Introduction

There is an irrefutable theological and cultural tenet within Judaism that teaching and learning are necessary conditions for safeguarding tradition and guaranteeing continuity. Given the multiplicity of ways of practicing or identifying oneself as Jewish in the US, it is perhaps unsurprising that American-Jewish education involves a wide range of religious and communal institutions, each defining the contours of Jewishness in its own way. These experiences include day schools, supplementary schools, synagogue-based programs, community centers, college and university programs, youth movements, summer camps, educational trips to Israel, early childhood programs, adult and family programs, retreat centers, museums, online sites and broadcast media.

Yet one constant thread that weaves its way through the tapestry of American-Jewish educational practices is that of the Hebrew language. As a link between the three distinct pillars of Judaism – religion, nationalism and peoplehood – Hebrew plays a central role in the construction and maintenance of Jewish faith, culture and identity. However, Hebrew language education is extremely complex. Not only do reasons for learning Hebrew vary widely according to how each educational institution defines Jewishness within the communal context it serves, but the language itself comprises multiple varieties that have evolved over thousands of years.

The New York metropolitan area is home to the world's largest Jewish population outside of Israel, and Jews currently comprise about 12% of the 8 million residents of New York City. Despite a recent dip in demographic trends, the perception of New York City as a city with a strong Jewish presence remains undisputed. This 'New York effect' (Horowitz, 1999) provides a distinctive context for Jewish religious and ethnic life, and has enabled Jewishness in New York to become a social category of consequence, one that both Jews and non-Jews living in the city recognize and accept. For this reason, the New York metropolitan area has the highest concentration of Jewish educational institutions in the US. Approximately 132,000 students attend 350 Jewish day schools in New York with another 29,000 students in New Jersey (Schick, 2009). The largest share of statewide enrollment is in the City itself, where approximately 93,000 students study across the five boroughs. While the highest concentration of students is in Orthodox (i.e. Hasidic) schools, non-Orthodox schools continue to attract families.

This chapter examines the language use, beliefs and policy of Hebrew teaching in Jewish day school education – a common educational model across the US, wherein students are provided with a Jewish and secular education in one school that they attend for the entire school day. We focus specifically on the role of Hebrew in the construction of religious and cultural identity. We begin the chapter by offering an overview of Jewish day schools in the US, as well as the sociohistorical and linguistic dimensions of the Hebrew language. Then, through ethnographic and linguistic data, we examine educational practices and language ideologies in a private, non-Orthodox Jewish day school in New York City.

Supporting the central threads of this book, the case of Hebrew bilingual community education in the US requires pushing the boundaries of traditional conceptualizations of 'bilingual education' rooted in monoglossic ideology and territorial nationalism (García, 2009a) as well as 'heritage language education', with its focus on languages of the past (García et al., Chapter 1). Whereas on the one hand the efforts of Hebrew day schools are far more bold in their support for bilingualism than typically occurs in US bilingual education programs, they also foster a living bilingualism among Jewish children and home language practices far more complex than is captured by the term 'heritage language'. As we discuss below, Hebrew is not the spoken home language of US Jews, nor is it expected that through Jewish educational programs it will become so. Yet Hebrew holds special status within the Jewish community because of its use as a language that indexes and evokes Jewish religiosity and culture (Schiff, 1997/2002).

Jewish Day Schools in Sociohistorical Context

Jews have a long-standing history in the US, as the first Jewish settlers arrived in New Amsterdam in 1654 from Brazil. Large-scale immigration began with a wave of Jews from Germany in the mid 19th century, seeking to escape discrimination and economic hardship. This was followed by a mass immigration of Eastern European Jews fleeing persecution and poverty, with over 2 million Jews arriving between 1880 and 1924 (Diner, 2006). Once in the US, these new Americans made efforts to integrate themselves into American society. For instance, by 1906 Jews comprised the majority of students learning English in New York night schools (Wenger, 2007). This sociological shift eventually resulted in the loss of the many different languages spoken by Jewish immigrants, and today, the majority of US Jews are native English speakers (Fishman, 1985b).

Whereas Jews in the US prior to World War II believed that 'Jewishness was something almost innate', with little need for formal education (Wertheimer, 1999: 17), throughout the 1900s, as the Jewish population dispersed across American society and the community became less residentially segregated, it became more difficult for families to pass on religious beliefs and practices. In one historian's words, Jewish identity ceased to be 'a matter of course' and became a matter of 'choice – a conscious preference' (Wertheimer, 1999: 17). In response, Jewish communities in the US actively sought out ways to guarantee cultural and religious transmission. As was the case for other immigrant groups facing assimilatory pressures, Jewish communities created formal educational institutions to provide cultural and religious reinforcement.

In the early 1900s, public school education was favored by Jewish leaders who believed it would enable Jewish youth to attain the social and economic integration that had previously been denied to them in Europe (Goren, 1970). Religious education, including the teaching of Hebrew, was almost exclusively seen as an enrichment activity for Jewish children, taking place in supplementary after-school or Sunday programs.[1] However, growing concerns throughout the early and mid 1900s for safeguarding Jewish continuity and preventing the complete 'Americanization' of second-generation, US-born Jewish children resulted in a new-found commitment to intensive Jewish education, not only among the Orthodox, but also among other denominations of American Judaism (Schick, 2000; Wertheimer, 1999).

Throughout the 1970s and 1980s, demographic changes within the Jewish community contributed to a collective consciousness of urgency in the American-Jewish community. Decreasing birthrates among Jewish families, changes in residential patterns drawing more Jews away from large centers of Jewish populations and growing acceptance of intermarriage propelled a perceived 'crisis of continuity' that came to a peak in the 1990s (Commission on Jewish Education in North America, 1991).[2] As a result, organized American Jewry in the early 1990s sought to curtail any further disintegration and set out to influence how individuals felt about being Jewish, believing that stronger identification would result in a greater commitment to carry on Jewish customs and rituals. Hence, non-Orthodox Jewish day schools, which had originally been created between the two World Wars to balance the religious priorities of committed Jews with demands for a high-quality secular education devoted to citizenship, became the focus of attention.

In the past decade, Jewish day schools have become the centerpiece of communal efforts to safeguard Jewish continuity and strengthen Jewish identity in the US (Elkin, 2002; Partnership for Excellence in Jewish Education, 2007). Policy-makers, philanthropists and educators have evinced a strong commitment to day school education, focusing their attention on building, financially supporting and strengthening the teaching practices of these educational institutions in which youth can be immersed in an educational experience whereby the main identity lies in being Jewish.

During the 2008–2009 academic year, there were 228,174 students in 800 Jewish elementary and secondary day schools located in towns and cities across the US (Schick, 2009). While the term 'day school education' may imply a monolithic pattern of education, the reality is otherwise. These enrollment figures represent students attending a wide variety of schools that reflect the denominational differences across the American-Jewish religious spectrum. In the US, there are presently three main Jewish religious movements or denominations – Orthodox, Conservative and Reform Judaism – for which four categories of day schools exist. Three align to the specific denominations and one is explicitly transdenominational. Orthodox schools (i.e. Chabad, Haredi, Modern Orthodox and Centrist Orthodox) comprise by far the largest sector of Jewish day schools and the fastest growing. They range from Orthodox boys-only schools (called yeshivas) to co-educational schools. The second category of day schools includes schools affiliated with the Conservative movement, including the well-known Solomon Schechter Jewish day schools. The third category encompasses day schools affiliated with the Reform movement. The final category, the transdenominational community day school, emphasizes high-quality, pluralistic programs and is currently the fastest growing sector of non-Orthodox day school education in North America (Schick, 2009).[3] What is important to underscore in discussing the broad range of Jewish day schools is their inherent reflection of the internal differentiation within American Jewry. Put differently, despite the encompassing label 'Jewish day school' that is used as an identifying marker, at the operational level (and often at the religious or spiritual one), an Orthodox yeshiva and a pluralistic community day school are rather different entities.

Despite their differences, across the wide variety of day school programs available for Jewish youth in New York City and elsewhere, the learning of Hebrew is an essential tenet. Written and/or spoken Hebrew is taught at almost all day schools, although how and why the language is taught varies widely. For instance, while in many non-Orthodox day schools, and in some Modern Orthodox ones, the language of instruction for certain content subjects might be Hebrew, in other schools Hebrew will be strictly reserved for liturgical purposes and sacred textual study, with English (and/or Yiddish, in the case of some Orthodox schools) used as the medium of instruction.

While Hebrew is used for liturgical and religious rituals, the language is typically not used for everyday purposes among non-Orthodox US Jews. In this regard, Hebrew education is very different from other programs for language minority children in the US, such as bilingual education programs found in US public and private schools and some of the community programs discussed in other chapters of this volume. Unique in its uses and symbolism, Hebrew assumes a pragmatic and ideological function in linking religious, ethnic, nationalistic and cultural aspects of Judaism, and in uniting Jewish people across time and space.

The Case of Hebrew

To understand the complexities surrounding the teaching and learning of Hebrew as a central component of communal maintenance, it is necessary to briefly review how the language has evolved over time. Hebrew is an umbrella term that subsumes numerous varieties – Biblical, Mishnaic, Medieval and Modern – each linked to a distinct sociohistorical period (Chomsky, 1957; Mintz, 1993; Myhill, 2004). Biblical Hebrew (also referred to as Classical Hebrew), the oldest, is the language of the Bible and includes various dialects. This variety evolved into Mishnaic Hebrew, used by the rabbis in the second and third centuries for scholarly texts and liturgy. This, in turn, evolved into Medieval Hebrew, starting in the seventh century and continuing throughout the 10th century. Modern Hebrew (also referred to as Israeli Hebrew) is the product of the Zionist agenda in the second half of the 19th century to revitalize Hebrew as a language of everyday use (Glinert, 1991). Out of the 13 million Jews in the world, Modern Hebrew is spoken as a native language by some 5.4 million people in Israel, and approximately

2–3 million people speak the language to various degrees in Argentina, Australia, Brazil, Canada, France, Germany, the Palestinian West Bank and Gaza, Russia, the UK and the US.

Understanding how Jews have used Hebrew over time is another important consideration in the teaching and learning of Hebrew. One of the characteristic features of Jewish culture in the Diaspora has always been its polyphonic nature (Harshav, 2007). Historically, Jews living in the Diaspora have always been multilingual, speaking the language of the dominant culture, a Jewish language for everyday communication with other Jews (i.e. Judezmo in Spain and Yiddish in Europe), and Hebrew as *lashon hakodesh* [sacred language]. In contemporary American society, American-born Jews generally speak English as their primary language, with the exception of some Orthodox communities who maintain Yiddish as a language of daily communication (Myhill, 2004).[4] Most American Jews have limited exposure to Hebrew outside of the classroom and/or synagogue, and do not speak Modern Hebrew, but typically do learn to read and write Biblical Hebrew to varying degrees of proficiency.

Given this situation, it is clear why the teaching and learning of Hebrew is a complex pedagogical task (Shohamy, 1999). Hebrew language educators must confront its polysemous nature as a sacred language used in scripture and liturgy, its modern revitalized form as a language of communication in the State of Israel and its iconic function as a marker of Jewish ethnic and cultural identity. While some Hebrew educational contexts, particularly those based on immersion models, strive for bilingualism with students attaining proficiency in speaking, listening, reading and writing Modern Hebrew, others look to develop proficiency in activities surrounding the reading of sacred texts and prayers written in older varieties of the language. In the section that follows, we examine how this complexity is negotiated within a day school, wherein Hebrew language study plays a central role in the school's overarching mission to instill in students a strong sense of Jewish identity in the face of secular, assimilatory pressures.

The Research: Hebrew in Use

To get a better sense of the role of Hebrew in Jewish education, we present data from an 18-month study of the teaching and learning of Hebrew at Rothberg,[5] a non-Orthodox private day school located in New York City. The data presented here are drawn from a larger multisited ethnography conducted by Sharon Avni (first author) examining how the language practices at the school framed and structured the production of religious identification (Avni, 2008). The study involved observing, audio-taping and interviewing one cohort of students in seventh and eighth grades in their Judaic and secular classroom activities, and during a two-week trip to Israel. Rothberg intentionally integrated Jewish and secular studies throughout the day so that religious studies would be perceived as 'on par with everything else that kids are studying' (Principal interview, 12 April 2005). Hebrew language and Judaic studies, although treated as autonomous subjects, made up the Jewish component of the classroom schedule. Students studied at least 45 minutes of Modern Hebrew every day, and these classes were conducted in Hebrew. Additionally, students were exposed to other varieties of Hebrew during daily prayer services, and Bible and sacred textual studying. Hence, Hebrew learning at Rothberg included:

(1) reading liturgy (Biblical, Mishnaic and Medieval Hebrew);
(2) Bible study (Biblical Hebrew);
(3) Talmud study (Aramaic with Biblical, Mishnaic and Medieval Hebrew);
(4) reading and speaking Modern Hebrew.

As part of the linguistic landscape, Hebrew was given visual expression at the school in a multitude of ways. Hebrew words were seen on bulletin boards in classrooms and hallways, and Hebrew lettering was personalized and individualized through the garments and jewelry that the students wore to class on a daily basis; boys wore hand-made skullcaps (called in Hebrew *kippot*, or singular, *kippah*) with their Hebrew names embroidered on the rim and girls wore charm necklaces with their Hebrew names. Additionally, it was common to hear students reciting Hebrew prayers before and after meals, and during morning and afternoon prayer services. Finally, teachers and students freely interspersed Hebrew words commonly used in school, such as *chafsaka* [recess], *yeladim* [children] and *boker tov* [good morning] in their conversations.

How Hebrew was talked about and used at Rothberg offers insight into the complex role that the language had in constructing and validating a Jewish sense of self and community. To start, there was no monolithic Hebrew language ideology. Rather, a constellation of complementary and often contradictory beliefs existed in the discourse and practices at the school. The most explicitly stated, and therefore most recognizable one, was the notion that Jewish education was predicated on the learning of Hebrew. In other words, Hebrew was inextricably linked to the educative project of passing on Jewish rituals, values and beliefs. This was made abundantly clear in an interview in which, when describing the place of Hebrew within the overall curriculum, an administrator summarized her thoughts by saying, 'Hebrew is the DNA of Jewish education' (interview, 10 November 2004).

This comment articulates an ontological and symbiotic connection between language and a social process. Like DNA, Hebrew here is endowed with the 'hereditary' material that will enable its users to grow and reproduce, linking the language with the future survival of the Jewish people. As a powerful metaphor, it reveals an assumption that language is the building block of identification and continuity.

This ideology linking Hebrew with Jewish learning saturated the learning experience at Rothberg, as it filtered its way through the daily actions and words of the faculty and students. As an axiomatic belief, its visibility was often most apparent when the assumption was challenged or questioned. Hence, when a Hebrew teacher harshly reacted to the students' use of English in the class with the comment, 'Without [Hebrew], it is not a Jewish day school. We can all go home', she validated and reaffirmed the Hebrew-Jewish education bond (fieldnotes, 22 March 2005).

This validation was also made visible in one lively impromptu discussion during recess in which several of the students were discussing their school with the researcher.

Sharon:	So, how would you explain to someone who had never heard of your school, and didn't know that there was such a thing as a Jewish day school, what a Jewish day school is? ... What makes a day school different from public schools or other private schools?
Ira:	That's pretty simple. We do Jewish things here. You know, the holidays, prayer, reading Talmud, learning Hebrew, like, you know, all that Jewish stuff.
Phil:	Yeah. You know, it takes a long time to learn all that Jewish guilt. (Laughter).
Adam:	Really funny fart-face. No, but seriously, we have to learn how to be Jews here. It's not just about wearing a *kippah*. Why else do you think we spend so much time learning Hebrew? Do you think Brandeis [a New York City public high school] students spend that much time learning French? No. I don't think so. They are not trying to become French.
Sharon:	Interesting point, Adam. So, learning Hebrew is a really important part of your education?
Benji:	Absolutely.
Ira:	Yup.
Adam:	Uh-huh.
Phil:	(Nodding in agreement.)

Sharon:	But, let me ask you guys, do you think that there could be a day school without any Hebrew classes? I mean, could there be a day school without Hebrew?
Ira:	I don't understand what you mean. What, what, what do you mean?
Sharon:	I mean, what would you think if the teachers here decided to stop teaching Hebrew? Would you still be getting a good Jewish education?
Benji:	That makes no sense. Why would they stop teaching Hebrew? Do you know something that we don't know? 'Cause my parents will be pretty pissed. I mean ...
Sharon:	They're not going to stop, don't worry. You still have your test this afternoon. (Laughter.) I'm just talking hypothetically. You know, can there be a day school that doesn't teach Hebrew?
Adam:	No. Like, duh, of course not. It's like, what's the point?
Phil:	Yeah, like, if we don't learn it, who is going to?
Ira:	I still don't get the question. Are you saying that *you* don't think that we should learn Hebrew?
Sharon:	No, not at all. That's not what I mean.
Benji:	Oh good. Because I was really confused. I mean, I thought you said you were Jewish. (Transcript, fieldnotes, 19 April 2005)

While it is easy to be deceived by the jovial tone and humorous remarks, this short interchange reflects the indubitableness the students ascribe to the role of Hebrew in their experiences of becoming educated Jews. So strong was their association between Hebrew and Jewish education that their attempt to imagine their educational experience devoid of Hebrew was nonsensical, confusing and agitating. While for Benji the idea of a Hebrew-less day school stood at odds with his parents' expectations, for Ira and Phil, their reactions suggest an awareness that Jewish education emptied of its Hebrew component lacks purpose and denies them of their right as inheritors of the language. Most telling is perhaps the final comment, 'I thought you said you were Jewish', in which Benji insinuates to the researcher that the link is so strong that it is unfathomable to imagine a Jew even considering the idea of untethering Hebrew from its central place in Jewish education. Seen in this way, Hebrew learning and use is an authenticating marker, differentiating between insiders (Jews) and others (i.e. non-Jews).

The centrality of Hebrew education was also institutionalized through the Hebrew-only policies in the classroom. As mentioned earlier, teachers and students were expected to use Hebrew as the language of instruction and conversation in the Hebrew language classroom – a common practice throughout many day schools. Translating Hebrew text to English in the Hebrew classroom was discouraged, as underscored in school policy and in practice. However, this policy ran into difficulties because of teachers' Hebrew proficiency levels and wide variance in the students' Hebrew proficiency levels.

With regard to the teachers at the school, many were non-native Hebrew speakers and had themselves acquired the language as students in day schools, in synagogue supplementary programs (i.e. Hebrew school) or in immersion programs (i.e. *ulpan*) in Israel (JESNA, 2004). As a result of the Hebrew-only policy, teachers inadvertently made and taught syntactic, phonological, semantic and pragmatic errors. Rachel, an eighth-grade Hebrew teacher, acknowledged this problem by stating,

> I don't feel *that* totally equipped personally in my own knowledge and skill with the language – you know, a comprehensive understanding of the grammar etc., so sometimes I just feel a little, like, uncertain which is a little frustrating. Obviously as a teacher you want to, like, put it all forward and feel confident in that. That I would say is one my biggest frustrations. (Interview, 11 April 2005)

While language ideologies among teachers reaffirmed the importance of Hebrew in Jewish education, teachers expressed reservations and questioned the Hebrew-only policy. This dissonance was later articulated when the subject turned to Rachel using more English in her classroom.

> 'Cause I definitely notice a difference in the kids when I'm speaking Hebrew than when I am speaking in English ... I don't know if I am projecting but I think that it's relatively palpable in terms of their attentiveness, their comfort. So the question is, how much of that is a worthwhile sacrifice in the name of the Hebrew language? I think with these kids, for too many of them, it is too big of a sacrifice. I made that judgment call, I don't know if I'm right and I don't know if the school fully supports it. (Interview, 1 April 2010)

There were many other factors that contributed to a difficult language-learning environment. Given that students came from families spanning the spectrum of religious observation, their exposure and commitment to Hebrew varied widely. While some students frequently attended weekly synagogue services, and therefore had more opportunities to interact with liturgical Hebrew, others only attended synagogue for bar mitzvah celebrations and/or holidays. This same variability applied to their exposure to native Hebrew speakers and trips to Israel. While some students had opportunities to speak and listen to Modern Hebrew outside of the classroom, many did not. Likewise, while some students had started day school in kindergarten, other students came to Rothberg after several years in the public schools, and had therefore only recently begun studying Hebrew. Finally, while the learning of Hebrew is an age-old practice, it is only relatively recently that high-quality and professionally developed teaching materials and textbooks have become readily available for the American market. For many years, teachers were left on their own to develop and adapt materials that had been designed for immigrants learning Hebrew in Israel.

All of these factors – teachers' proficiency, student heterogeneity and lack of materials – none of which were unique to Rothberg, have contributed to a sense that Hebrew teaching in the US has been an unsuccessful endeavor. Put differently, the ideologically driven rhetoric has not always matched the anticipated results. This sentiment was underscored by Moshe, a Hebrew teacher and himself a day school graduate, who said:

> I mean, I have friends who after K–12 [Jewish] day school every year can still barely put a sentence together. How is that possible? (Laughter.) Where have you been? Like, what are we doing in these Hebrew classes? (Interview, 12 April 2005)

Yet despite the challenges of teaching and learning Hebrew in a practical sense, students and faculty remained firmly entrenched within a belief system that valorizes Hebrew on the one hand and rejects Jewish multilingualism on the other. They eagerly embraced an ideology identifying Hebrew – and not English – as one of the sole means through which they connected to other Jews in the US and in Israel, and strongly felt that, in a hypothetical situation, Hebrew would be the cohesive glue that could bind them to Jewish people around the world. This image of Hebrew as connector was instantiated in stories that circulated in the classroom. In one story, Hebrew helped one of the teachers find a place to spend the Sabbath when she was backpacking in Europe and happened to come across some Hebrew speakers.[6] Yet another highly circulated story came from their two-week study tour to Israel in which students reported feeling 'one with the Jewish people' when they were able to participate in a Hebrew-only ceremony honoring the death of fallen soldiers (fieldnotes, 20 May 2005). These stories quickly became part of the folklore of the classroom, and reinforced the trope of Hebrew as bridge across national, religious and ethnic differences.

The valorization of Hebrew also implied a constellation of beliefs regarding its authenticity as the language of the Jewish people, while overlooking the historical fact that diasporic Jewish communities have always been multilingual (Spolsky & Shohamy, 1999). Despite the pedagogical challenges of teaching and learning a language that is not widely known in American society and is not a language used for informal communication in the students' homes, students and teachers never swayed from their belief that Hebrew is an iconic and symbolic proxy of Jewishness, and a language divinely entrusted to them. Even for those students with limited proficiency, their linguistic heritage was reflected in expressions of pride, identity and ownership. Hence, in response to a discussion about the use of Hebrew in prayer, Rebecca, a student placed in the lowest level of Hebrew class, stated, 'Hebrew is the language of the Jews. [God] listens to English when someone is praying who doesn't know Hebrew, but when you use Hebrew, God knows you're trying harder. He is really listening' (transcript, fieldnotes, 7 March 2005). In fact, the perceived difficulty of learning Hebrew was used to support this ideology. That the students could speak, write and read a language with a different orthography, phonetic system and grammar affirmed their sense of belonging to the Jewish people, succinctly summed up in the following comment by Seth: 'It's a language you love to know, but hate to learn' (fieldnotes, 10 February 2005).

Paradoxically, though, feelings of authenticity and legitimacy did not necessarily presuppose a need or desire to use Hebrew or excel in it. Hence, when opportunities arose to speak Hebrew with native speakers in the school or in Israel, students often opted to use English, and all but one student admitted that they rarely sought out opportunities to use Hebrew outside of the classroom. Additionally, students expressed doubts regarding how well they actually needed to know Modern Hebrew since they had no plans to move to Israel or, in the words of one of the students, 'be in the CIA' (fieldnotes, 10 February 2005). Students even expressed some disappointment in the amount of time that was devoted to Hebrew at the expense of learning Spanish, an additional language taught at the school. These expressions of doubt and pragmatism reflect a subtle resistance to the hegemonic role of Hebrew in their education, as well as a rejection of Hebrew serving as the sole proxy of their Jewish identity.

Conclusion

This study offers insight into the complexity and challenges of teaching Hebrew to non-Orthodox Jewish American youth attending a Jewish day school in New York City. The case of Hebrew in Jewish education demands that we adopt an expansive and dynamic conceptualization of bilingualism, along with less rigid ideas about bilingual education, as proposed by García (2009a). This is a challenge, as several factors set Hebrew education apart from other community and public school bilingual education programs. As described previously, Hebrew is not the home language of the American Jews who attend the wide range of Jewish educational programs in which learning Hebrew is so essential; while Hebrew is present in most Jewish homes because of its religious role within Judaism, English is the spoken language. Revitalization of Hebrew to make it suitable for everyday use only occurred in the second half of the 19th century; thus, its usage as a home language is quite recent. As such, actual proficiency in Hebrew varies widely among US Jews, mitigated by such factors as degree of religious observance and extent of formal study of the language.

Also unique is that American Jews feel especially at home in the US, where there are almost as many Jews as those living in Israel.[7] Thus while Israel is considered the Jewish homeland, US Jews do not have the geographical ties to it as a country of origin like the ties held by other immigrant groups; instead, most Jews have been in the US for several generations and feel part of American society. Thus to fully capture Hebrew in US Jewish education, as cultivating a bilingualism that is both living and present and not solely concerned with transmitting language, it is necessary to move beyond heritage language education toward a model of bilingual education that encompasses cultural practices. Likewise, bilingual education, as reconceptualized in the ways proposed by García (2009a and Chapter 1), has the fluidity to account for the complexity of Hebrew.

For American Jewry, learning Hebrew is about more than just language acquisition, as the language equally symbolizes and marks culture and identity. What this study reveals is that, while the philosophical and religious basis for teaching the varieties of Hebrew is securely rooted in romantic and ideological beliefs about the connection between the language and its people – embodied in the metaphor of Hebrew as 'the DNA' of Jewish education – ideologies are not always enacted in predictable or expected ways. For instance, the Hebrew-only policy in the language classroom is not only a challenge to implement, but is contested by teachers and students alike. As for the students of Rothberg, it remains to be seen if the school's concentrated efforts to cultivate Jewish identity among young US Jews through day school education will prove effective over the long term. As non-Orthodox Jewish day schools strive to securely situate themselves within the broader landscape of American schooling, they will undoubtedly need to reflect on questions surrounding the teaching and learning of Hebrew: what varieties are taught (by whom) and for what purposes, and perhaps most importantly, how and why these linguistic objectives are part of the process of educating the next generation of believers.

Notes

(1) Supplementary Jewish education continues to be the dominant model of formal Jewish education in the US. The majority of students receiving a Jewish education in the US today are enrolled in programs that meet on weekends and/or late weekday afternoons. No single term covers the range of these programs, which are variously referred to as religious schools, Hebrew schools, congregational schools, and more recently, as 'complementary schools' – i.e. they complement the education offered in public or private schools. Approximately 230,000 students study at the 2000–2100 supplementary schools located throughout the US. Because of its large Jewish population, New York has approximately 201 schools educating 28,000 students. One of the central goals of supplementary education is to teach Hebrew reading for participation in religious services and for bar/bat mitzvah celebrations (Wertheimer, 2008).

(2) Concurrently, the National Jewish Population Study of 1991 showed that only 4.2 million of the estimated 5.5 million American Jews self-identified as such, while 1.1 million were born Jews but claimed no religion.

(3) These community schools across the US constitute far more than half of all non-Orthodox school enrollment, and they continue to demonstrate growth, both in the number of schools (98 in 2008–2009 as compared with 75 in 1998–1999) and in enrollment, which has grown by more than 40% over the past decade (Schick, 2009).

(4) While Yiddish remains a home language among many Orthodox Jews, the language has largely been lost among non-Orthodox US Jews, first as a result of the Holocaust, in which the vast majority of Jews killed were Yiddish speakers, and later in the 20th century as a result of assimilation and a focus on Hebrew revitalization and monolingualism in Israel.

(5) The name of the school and all research participants are pseudonyms.

(6) Sabbath or, in Hebrew, *Shabbat*, is the Jewish weekly day of rest, which begins on Friday at sunset and ends on Saturday at sunset.

(7) It is estimated that 42.5% of the world's Jewish population lives in Israel, with a Jewish population of 5,703,700, and that almost as many – 42.1% or 5,650,000 – live in the US (DellaPergola, 2010).

13 Becoming Yiddish Speakers in New York: Burgeoning Communities of Bilingual Children[1]

Rakhmiel Peltz and Hannah Kliger

Introduction

In 2000, 22,407 Yiddish speakers over the age of five were recorded in Brooklyn Community District 1, which includes the Williamsburg area. This figure represents a 34% increase since 1990. In Brooklyn District 12, which includes the Boro Park area, there were 32,889 Yiddish speakers over the age of five, a 30% increase since 1990. Yiddish speakers are the largest linguistic minority in District 12.[2] While the high birth rate of Jews in those neighborhoods accounts in part for the vitality of Yiddish, increased involvement in Yiddish–English bilingual education is also of significance. This engagement is occurring not only in Brooklyn, but also in diverse locations in Rockland County, New York; Jerusalem and Bnei Brak, Israel; Antwerp, Belgium; and London, UK. Such localized growth in different locations across the globe is occurring in religiously observant communities of descendants of Holocaust survivors.

Although the first initiatives involving New York City Yiddish schools in the early 20th century represented an ideological commitment of educators and parents in the Diaspora to the language and culture of the 'old country' in Eastern Europe, contemporary efforts at bilingual Yiddish education in New York Hasidic schools since the Holocaust are a product of diasporic plural networks. Not only is the extinguished 'old country' no longer a source of cultural innovations and memories, but the new networks exhibit multiple motivations in their advocacy for Yiddish.

We will investigate the strategies employed for teaching children Yiddish today in New York City and the connections to earlier initiatives in bilingual Yiddish–English education. We argue that instruction in Yiddish has primarily always aimed not at the development of linguistic skills for language maintenance, but at supporting Jewish identity and membership in the Jewish group within American society. Such an overarching goal has been shared by both the religious and secular sectors of the American-Jewish community that remain connected to Yiddish and committed to its instruction. Furthermore, we will demonstrate that the current efforts at Yiddish instruction of New York City children are almost entirely within the Hasidic, religious sector that derives from Holocaust survivors and their descendants. Moreover, the success of teaching Yiddish at school parallels the degree of involvement with Yiddish communication by the family at home. In fact, we will demonstrate a 'network of collaboration', in which strategies of bilingual community education overlap. The choices of parents at home relate directly to the ideological positions of leaders in the community, which in turn interdigitate with policies and practices of administrators, teachers and students in the ethnic schools.

The Sociolinguistics of Yiddish

Yiddish is the language associated with Ashkenazic Jews who settled in Germanic lands in about the ninth century. By the 13th century, Jews started to move eastward, settling in Poland, Ukraine, Belorussia, the Baltic lands, Hungary and Romania. By the 18th century, a majority of the Ashkenazic Jews were living in East Central Europe. Further emigration that occurred in the largest numbers at the end of the 19th and beginning of the 20th centuries brought Yiddish from Eastern Europe to the Western hemisphere, Palestine (later the state of Israel), Western Europe, South Africa and Australia. The heartland of Yiddish in Eastern Europe was destroyed by the Nazis during World War II. Yiddish still exists in the 21st century, mostly in the lands to which Ashkenazic Jews emigrated at the end of the 19th century.

Yiddish evolved as a linguistic and cultural system resulting from the fusion of elements modified from several stock languages. The main components of Yiddish are Germanic, Semitic (derived from Hebrew and Aramaic) and Slavic (mostly derived from Belorussian, Czech, Polish and Ukrainian). Within traditional European society, Yiddish functioned as a vernacular in a diglossic relationship with *loshn koydesh* (the sacred tongue), Hebrew. Yiddish was the language of conversation in the family and community, as well as the language in which the sacred texts were studied, while Hebrew was the language of prayer and the language in which the Bible was read. The Aramaic of the Talmud, studied, discussed and analyzed by Ashkenazi scholars, adds another language to the equation. Such functional distribution is common to the language make-up of Jewish communities the world over. Analogous Jewish vernaculars arose throughout Jewish history in different parts of the globe. In addition, there is more complexity in the language repertoire of Jews since they also use the language of the dominant local culture and that spoken by their non-Jewish neighbors.

When Yiddish and other Jewish vernaculars are written, they use the same alphabet as Hebrew. The Yiddish alphabet deviates from Hebrew slightly when it comes to consonant sounds and more so in terms of vowel representations, enlisting new letter contributions together with diacritical marks.

Yiddish has been the main vernacular of Jewish immigrants to the US throughout American-Jewish history. Although Sephardic[3] Jews formed a sizable proportion of the immigrants in the early colonial period, by the 1700s most Jews were Yiddish speakers. Only toward the middle of the 19th century did German-speaking Jews, who had recently experienced language shift from Yiddish to German, arrive in the US. Since the first boats with masses of Yiddish-speaking Jews from Russia arrived by 1882, we can see that Yiddish was indeed the main spoken language of the Jewish immigrants, religious and secular, except for relatively short periods in American history. However, by the end of the 20th century, very few Yiddish-speaking immigrants were still alive, and those who remained were mostly the last of the Holocaust survivors and older immigrants from the former Soviet Union. Most Yiddish speakers at the present time are descendants of Hasidic[4] immigrants who arrived after the Holocaust; secular Yiddish speakers are hardly present in the contemporary Jewish population in the US.

Teaching Yiddish in New York City

There are few research reports on current efforts involved in teaching Yiddish. Literature on teaching Yiddish in New York is found largely in older studies of the supplemental Jewish secular schools in the US: we have little information about Yiddish instruction in religious schools, although the latter may have been the more common venue for Yiddish instruction. The secular schools, however, demonstrated greater commitment to both Yiddish language maintenance and curriculum. The secular schools started in 1910 in the city, peaked in about 1930, and experienced a steep decline in the 1960s (Freidenreich, 2010; Kliger & Peltz, 1990). In an early review of Jewish education in New York City, Dushkin (1918), reporting on the centrality of Yiddish language in these schools, noted with surprise that, in some of these secular schools, even the Bible was taught in Yiddish translation. Yiddish was the language of instruction, school management and all exchanges between teachers and pupils, as well as principals and parents. Even later in the century, when Yiddish was heard far less frequently on the streets of New York, one educator would clearly state that the Yiddish school taught more Yiddish than the Hebrew school taught Hebrew (Mark, 1947: 38). However, the relationship between home and ethnic mother tongue school changed dramatically from generation to generation, especially after the cessation of mass immigration of Yiddish-speaking Jews as a result of federal legislation curtailing immigration in 1924, irrevocably changing the status of Yiddish. By 1955, the third generation constituted the parent body of secular school pupils, suggesting in one school that Yiddish be spoken at parents' meetings in order to help parents learn the language and thereby enable it to be heard at home.[5]

We do not yet have a careful examination of Yiddish instruction in religious educational settings. For example, we would like to understand the situation in the independent schools known as Talmud Torahs, the afternoon and Sunday schools that arose in the 1920s and often taught Yiddish, in addition to Hebrew, the Bible, the prayer book and the Jewish holidays. During earlier years when much of Jewish education was in the hands of individual rabbis and teachers, almost no documentation is available about instruction in Yiddish literacy. By the World War II years, the main locus of Jewish ethnic and religious education moved into schools housed in and affiliated with Orthodox synagogues in New York City. Although English was the main language of instruction in these schools and facility in reading the prayer book in Hebrew was the curricular focus, we have little information about the possibility that Yiddish appeared in these institutions either as a language of instruction for translating Hebrew and Aramaic texts, or as a subject in and of itself.

The larger goal in all of these ethnic and religious educational efforts was for the children to gain knowledge of the culture and religion of the Jews in order for them to remain active participants within the family, local group and the Jewish people throughout the world. The other Jewish language taught in the various Jewish schools, including many of the Jewish secular schools, was Hebrew. Hebrew, much more commonly taught than Yiddish, was taught as the language of the Bible and prayer book, and the spoken language in the state of Israel, as well as the language of secular literature.[6]

During most of the 20th century, most Jewish day schools represented traditional Orthodoxy. In the traditional Orthodox yeshiva day schools, Yiddish was taught to young children, and as the children grew older, specifically the boys, Yiddish was used to translate the Bible and to discuss the Talmud. Explication of the texts was reserved for Yiddish, the Jewish vernacular, not Hebrew, the holy tongue. Yeshiva day schools were full-day schools for pupils who did not attend public school. They were usually administered by more strictly observant Orthodox authorities than the neighborhood synagogue schools. In most of these schools, Hebrew as the spoken language of the state of Israel was not emphasized. In 1960, 47 out of 87 yeshivas in New York City taught Yiddish. Of these Yiddish-teaching yeshivas, 35 were in Brooklyn. In fact, Brooklyn contained more than half of the Jewish day schools in the US at the time that taught Yiddish (Poll, 1981: 214–216).

Turning to the better-documented efforts at Yiddish instruction within the supplementary Jewish secular schools in New York City, in 1935, 6800 pupils attended these schools, representing 9.3% of all children in schools supported by the Jewish community (Mark, 1948). By 1951, however, only 4% of the Jewish school population in Greater New York was enrolled in these schools, according to a survey of the Jewish Education Committee (Ruffman, 1957). Teachers were trained for these Yiddish schools in New York's *Yidisher lerer-seminar* [Jewish Teachers' Seminary and Peoples' University] from 1918 to 1977 (Shteynboym, 1978–1979). However, the number of students in attendance does not tell the whole story. Students in the Yiddish afternoon schools scored higher in examinations on Jewish history, Jewish holidays and Hebrew than did students in the synagogue-affiliated Hebrew afternoon schools, the largely Orthodox, predominant locus for urban Jewish education. Only students from the Orthodox yeshiva full-day schools performed better overall than those in the Yiddish schools. Furthermore, the success of the Yiddish secular schools was also indicated in the data wherein the graduates of the Yiddish schools expressed the most positive opinions of all students about their Jewish education. As the number of years spent in the school increased, the child's enjoyment of the school program was shown to grow (Ruffman, 1957).

Throughout the years, the contribution of the secular Yiddish school to curriculum development in American-Jewish education far outweighed the proportional enrollment represented by these schools. The two history-changing occurrences for the Jewish people in the 20th century were the Holocaust and the establishment of the state of Israel. Whereas American-Jewish schools did not generally teach children about the Holocaust until the 1960s, the Yiddish schools had been informing their students from the onset about the Nazi government. In addition, even the non-Zionist Yiddish schools were 10 years ahead of most Jewish schools in teaching about the development of Jewish life in Palestine (Roskies, 1975: 18). Thus, the Yiddish schools were trail-blazers in informing students of essential issues in Jewish group identity formation in the 20th century. Instruction in the ethnic mother tongue cannot be appreciated solely in terms of proficiency in speaking, reading and writing, and thus in communicating directly with the different immigration generations. Yiddish instruction goes hand-in-hand with the teaching of age-old history and contemporary Jewish culture, but even more so with inculcating the framework for the building of personal and group identification.

Teaching Yiddish in the Contemporary Secular Jewish School

Few studies examine Yiddish teaching in contemporary times. Kadar (1996), however, has provided us with an ethnographic study that she conducted in a suburban New York City secular and ethnic Sunday school in 1995. Her goal was to study how the teaching of Yiddish language functions to transmit Jewish identity. She chose a contemporary school of the Workmen's Circle, a Jewish fraternal organization based in New York City that has helped to sponsor Yiddish schools for almost 100 years. One of the main current goals of these schools is to foster love of the Yiddish language.[7] Because of limited class time (45 minutes a week were relegated to Yiddish language instruction), outdated learning materials and little or no reinforcement at home or in the community, Kadar discounted the possibility of the attainment of understanding, speaking, reading or writing Yiddish in this school setting (Kadar, 1996: 3).

In addition to the limited class time for formal language instruction, the school provides other occasional opportunities for the children to learn Yiddish vocabulary associated with Jewish holidays, Jewish ethical values, Jewish literature and history. At the time of this study, Kadar (1996: 33) reported that, other than the few secular ethnic supplemental Jewish schools, only the secular Jewish day school, the Kinneret School in the Riverdale section of the Bronx, taught Yiddish (one hour each week to all students above the third grade, while Hebrew was taught for three hours each week).[8] The school she studied was founded 40 years earlier, convening then three days a week, but in 1980 it became a Sunday school meeting for three hours. In addition, the graduating class meets on Wednesday evenings to prepare for the graduation ceremony that serves in place of the bar- and bat-mitzvah.[9] The school also meets once a month on Friday nights to celebrate the ushering in of the Sabbath (*oyneg shabes*). The children attend the school for five years, starting at ages 5–7. Three instructors teach subject areas, Jewish history, Yiddish and Hebrew, in addition to a fourth who also serves as staff director. Two teachers teach Yiddish. At the time of the study, 30 students attended the school, which convened in a Conservative synagogue. Families were attracted to the school for several reasons: its secular ideology, the alternative it provided to synagogue membership, its position as a haven for intermarried couples, and because tuition was less expensive than in most Jewish schools (Kadar, 1996: 32, 33, 39–44).

Kadar's research techniques included participant observation in classes and a holiday celebration, a questionnaire to parents, and informal individual and group interviews with teachers, parents and graduates. She took part in a class of twelve 8- to 10-year-olds as they learned how to use specific words and phrases in conversational contexts while sitting in a circle. For example, an object was passed and they would learn to say 'a sheynem dank' [thank you] and 'nito far vos' [you're welcome/don't mention it]. The children also learned through conversation the words for 'fork', 'knife' and 'plate'. Already knowing the diminutive suffix for nouns, 'ele', one student, not knowing the noun in Yiddish for spoon, said, 'spoonele'. As soon as the class learned the word gopl for fork, they immediately used 'gopele' for 'small fork'. The children all addressed one another by their Yiddish names and, while learning food terms, sang the song Bulbes [potatoes]. This class was not taught by a trained teacher, but rather by a native Yiddish speaker who worked professionally as a psychotherapist.

Although students were involved in much conversation during class, they could not sustain a conversation in Yiddish, but mixed English in with their Yiddish words. Kadar also studied how the younger children learned Yiddish through art projects, songs and movement. However, she underscored that the main achievement of the school is to teach the children that Jewish values are to be associated with Yiddish words, and thus to connect their identity to being part of the Jewish people. They collect donations for charities and connect this with the positive value and requirement of tsdoke [charity]. In another class, the children are told a story in English, but they use the Yiddish phrase, epes fun gornisht [something from nothing], and through using the Yiddish words learn the value of making do with little and of valuing things that do not cost money. During the Purim holiday celebration, the children learn Yiddish terms that are used during Purim (Kadar, 1996: 58–60, 64–67, 70).

Overall, the school serves as a Jewish cultural forum for the families. In this case study, both the parents and the educators agree that Yiddish serves to help ensure that the children will identify as Jews and see themselves as communal partners, planning for a world that will need the values that Yiddish embodies. Kadar (1996: 74) notes that the Jewish cultural competency attained by the students exceeds that of their parents. Handing out a questionnaire to 24 families, she found that the median age of school parents was 43, 58% had had some Jewish education and 42% none, 63% responded that the secular philosophy was important to them, only 29% answered that the Yiddish program was a significant attraction, but 67% recognized the connection between the teaching of Yiddish language and the cultural values that they wished to transmit. However, 100% of the parents surveyed were convinced that the school transmits Jewish values. The Yiddish teachers interviewed felt frustrated that the families did not reinforce Yiddish language learning. In the group interviews, Kadar repeatedly heard the words 'home', 'heymish' [homey] and 'coming home' used to describe attachment to the school. Kadar identified the school mainly as a Jewish cultural center. In summary, cultural concerns were paramount, language mastery was minimal, and Yiddish was seldom used at home (Kadar, 1996: 81, 100, 101, 106,109; cf. Kliger & Peltz, 1990).

Teaching Hasidic Day School Girls Yiddish

After World War II, various subgroups of Hasidic Holocaust survivors built up an intense Jewish communal life in specific Brooklyn neighborhoods. The birthrate in these families is high today, and the contemporary Hasidic Jewish day schools in these neighborhoods constitute the largest and most serious effort expended on teaching children Yiddish in New York City.

A recently published book, based on ethnographic fieldwork during 1997–1999, concentrates on the education of girls of the Bobov[10] Hasidic subgroup in schools and at home in Boro Park, Brooklyn (Fader, 2009). Largely focusing on gender concerns in relation to identity formation and communication, Fader, a non-religiously observant woman, was not allowed to study the preschool for boys after her initial visits (Fader, 2009: 20). Therefore, the information here that is gleaned in relation to Yiddish education in schools, as well as in the family, relates to her observations of and reflections on young girls only. She monitored the classroom activities in kindergarten and first grade. In kindergarten, the girls learn the Hebrew and Yiddish alphabets[11] in preparation for reading instruction in the two languages, which occurs during the morning hours of the first grade. In the first grade, Bobov girls additionally study Yiddish grammar, spelling and vocabulary, whereas in the afternoon hours another teacher teaches them secular subjects in English. Fader (2009: 23) claims that it is at this stage of development that Yiddish fluency decreases for these girls.

As in the study of the secular Yiddish school, here, too, Yiddish education is closely linked to the teaching of Jewish values. As the Yiddish words are taught they are used to reinforce religious themes. When learning the word *klayd* 'dress', the teacher stresses to these little girls not to be materialistic and to be satisfied with only one Sabbath dress, like in the old days. Kindergarten girls are taught not to give in to the *yaytser hure* 'evil inclination'. Girls who misbehave have to sit in the corner on the time-out bench, called in Yiddish a *tshive-benkl* [chair of repentance]. Moreover, proper behavior at home spills over into the values taught in school, where the mother wants to extend her influence. For example, the mother of a two-year-old boy sent a *mitsve-tsetl* [good deed note] to school that described how the little boy went early that morning with his father and he *'davned azoy shayn'* [prayed so beautifully], whereupon the teacher rewarded the boy. Thus, language learning and acquisition of the Yiddish lexicon are paired with Jewish moral and religious development. In fact, the school has adopted a curriculum written in English to teach respectful behavior and proceeded to translate all the materials into Yiddish (Fader, 2009: 23, 34, 42, 47, 52, 129–130).

Based on studying the Bobov girls at school and at home with their mothers, Fader described the usage norm of Yiddish mixed with English words and English mixed with Yiddish words. She reported that recently the school's administrators attempted to institute a policy of increased use of Yiddish in school, especially unmixed with English. The teachers could not comply, however, complaining that the mixed form is how they normally express themselves in Yiddish, and that it reflects the language they used with their own mothers. This applied to using the word 'steps' instead of *trep* and using 'peach' for the word in Yiddish for that color. In writing such forms, the first-grade teacher transcribed the English word into Yiddish orthography and placed it in quotation marks. Whereas Yiddish educators of previous generations may have called for purism in the classroom, we see that both parents and teachers today are more tolerant of heteroglossic tendencies.

Besides the mixed form of Yiddish, Fader also observed that, in the first grade, Bobov girls gradually stopped speaking Yiddish and began speaking English, albeit mixed with Yiddish words, as their everyday language. She noted that some of the mothers are not fluent in Yiddish and do not demand that the girls speak Yiddish at home. Moreover, even the teachers who are fluent in Yiddish speak English among themselves at recess. For the girls, Yiddish has taken on the symbolic meaning of extreme religiosity because of its greater usage among Hasidic subgroups, viewed as being religiously more stringent. In the high school, the principal called a teachers' meeting to increase support of, and respect for, Yiddish. One of the high school girls had reacted to the performance of a play in Yiddish by the girls as, 'so nebby' [so unfashionable, unpopular] (Fader, 2009: 89, 108–110, 118–119, 121–123).

However, limited fluency and use by parents seem to have a negative impact on the linguistic skills attained in school.

Vaysman (2010) analyzes further the creative outlet provided by Hasidic schoolgirls' dramatic musical performances in 2007 and 2008. Everything is in Yiddish except for a few Hebrew numbers and, unlike Fader, Vaysman does not mention English words mixed into the Yiddish, but underscores Yiddish performance as a vehicle for impressing Jewish values on the girls. The first performance involves songs and skits written by one of the school principals for the graduation of the pre-first-grade school year of 6-year-old Satmar[12] girls in the Williamsburg neighborhood of Brooklyn. Satmar is known for its strictness of religious observance and adherence to Yiddish. The production stressed the necessity to respect one's mother, as well as the responsibility of Jewish mothers to maintain religious observance within the protective environment of the Jewish home. The performance of older high school girls in the next more elaborate production, which was put together by both students and faculty, taught the importance of faith in the Almighty if one must venture outside the Jewish community. The third play had an elaborate plot accompanied by music and dance performed by high school girls in the same Bobov community as described by Fader. The play focused on a contemporary friendship, as well as the return to religious observance by an immigrant Russian Jewish girl whose grandmother had sacrificed herself to remain observant in the Soviet environment that was hostile to Jews. Here Yiddish performance conveys complex struggles and challenges of contemporary relationships, issues of faith and ultimate religious redemption. This is a far cry from the simpler lessons of a safe role in the home promised to little girls. These excursions into performance analysis pointedly show that the medium of Yiddish, not English, provides the context for the crucial moral education.

These new plays demonstrate that the contemporary school is not using Yiddish to present the old classics. Rather, the educators are inventing discursive tools for teaching the changing norms of a contemporary, ethnoreligious community that is far from the immigrant community that built the first Yiddish schools in New York City a century ago.

Hasidic Infants and Toddlers Learn Yiddish in a Head Start Preschool

The Yeled Ve Yalda Early Childhood Center has been serving the Hasidic communities of Brooklyn since 1980.[13] Barrière (2010b) documents the work of establishing an assessment tool for language acquisition by the fast growing number of Yiddish-learning preschoolers. A total of 1080 children between birth and five years of age with Yiddish as their home language are provided with educational programs. This may represent the largest bilingual Yiddish preschool institution in the world. The children are served at four sites in the Williamsburg neighborhood and 10 sites in Boro Park, representing the following Hasidic subgroups: Belz, Bobov, Chabad, Ger and Satmar, as well as Northeastern (Lithuanian) Yiddish-speaking communities. The Board of Directors of the agency comes entirely from the Jewish community, and most of the management team is Jewish. The Policy Council includes Jewish family representatives, as well as non-Jews from the non-Jewish sites. As a Head Start center, in preschool classes of children between three and five in which a majority of the class comes from Yiddish-speaking homes, federal regulations require that at least one teaching professional speak Yiddish. Regulations require that the preschool children are involved in language and literacy activities in both Yiddish and English. Most of the Yiddish-speaking teachers have master's degrees and were themselves educated in bilingual schools. In teaching, they are encouraged to use Yiddish in all activities, from computers to cooking.

In establishing a background questionnaire for parents, Barrière and her team were sensitive to the entering child's gender, birth order and number of siblings, the specific dialect(s) of Yiddish spoken at home, as well as the parent speaking the dialect (Barrière, 2010b). Looking at a sample of 92 children between the ages of 14 and 38 months, the vast majority were exposed to Yiddish at least 75% of the time; Yiddish was the language used in a majority of cases among siblings; most mothers used a combination of Yiddish and English; and 67% of the children were exposed to the same dialects from both parents.

From the parent data, Barrière (2010b) was able to glean important findings related to Yiddish acquisition of young children. Looking at vocabulary development, for instance, children exposed to 100% to 75% Yiddish at home exhibit the same acquisition pattern according to chronological age and number of words produced, whereas children who are equally exposed to both languages demonstrate much slower development, and children exposed to 10% Yiddish show even slower progress in vocabulary. Yet, children exposed to both languages equally and who produce half the number of words of the more dominant Yiddish bilinguals have similar morphosyntactic development of features such as noun plurals and subject–verb agreement and can use these features productively (Barrière, 2010b). This is the first study of Yiddish acquisition in Hasidic Yiddish-speaking children. As the research project grows, professional staff will study Yiddish–English bilingual performance directly through observation of the children in the day care centers and preschools in order to correlate the findings with Yiddish usage at home.

Conclusions

From the beginning of the history of teaching Yiddish in secular Jewish schools in New York City a century ago, through the latest examples of contemporary Hasidim teaching their children in day schools, none of the projects sought a bilingualism that would give the children linguistic proficiency solely. All instructional school programs used Yiddish language instruction as a pathway for transmitting ethnocultural or religious conventions. In addition, we noted a dedication to teaching ethical and nationalistic values that these subgroups identified to be of core significance to their Jewish future in America.

In all the cases we discussed, the success of achieved bilingualism was dependent on the commitment to Yiddish usage in the family. A school program cannot stand alone. The secular schools themselves were originally neighborhood-based throughout the city, and the Yiddish-speaking home and neighborhood reinforced the lessons in school. Moves to the suburbs and decreased use of Yiddish within the family made the mastery of Yiddish more difficult to achieve, as we analyzed in the contemporary ethnography of the secular Jewish school. In the compact Hasidic population centers of Brooklyn, on the contrary, Yiddish is taught and maintained with varying success and accompanying percentages of bilingual usage, based on the support of school efforts within the home and neighborhood.

In his review of the Yiddish-related activities of secular and ultra-Orthodox Yiddish speakers in New York, Fishman (2001: 90) estimated the latter Yiddish-speakers at 300,000 and the former at 3000. The disappearance of the secular speakers contrasts with the situation of 100 years ago when the secularists were able to establish more than 100 neighborhood Yiddish schools in New York in a matter of a few years. Their children and grandchildren, however, did not produce a positive record of Yiddish language maintenance. Fishman (1982) exhorted the secularists to do as the Orthodox did if they wished to maintain intergenerational continuity of Yiddish and to reverse and resist language shift – to speak Yiddish within the household, to live close together with other members of the Yiddish-speaking community, to speak the language with neighbors, and to support neighborhood Yiddish-speaking institutions, such as schools, retail businesses and religious institutions.

The demographic data in the Brooklyn districts revealed not only language maintenance, but also an extremely high fertility rate. The Hasidic communities that we discussed derive largely from Holocaust survivors who came to the US in the late 1940s. We hope that researchers focused on the acquisition and maintenance of Yiddish–English bilingualism will analyze with a more nuanced eye the transmission of Yiddish, starting from the Holocaust survivors to their children, grandchildren and subsequent generations, at a time when the members of all these generations are still alive. It is hard to believe that a language and culture that were struck such an enormous blow by the genocidal acts of the Nazis more than 66 years ago are making such a remarkable comeback because of the high reproductive rate of these survivor communities and their capacity for maintaining their language, culture and religion at home, in school and in their intimate secondary institutions.

Our analysis of contemporary schools that teach Yiddish as an ethnic mother tongue has highlighted that these efforts are enmeshed with language-based activities and interactions at home, as well as with evolving ideological goals and strategies for a thriving future, both for the specific Jewish sub-group and community and for the Jewish people the world over.

Notes

(1) We dedicate this chapter to the memory of Dr Naomi Prawer Kadar (1949–2010), a child of Holocaust survivors, who appreciated through her research and life in general that the values of Yiddish education are closely linked to all aspects of the continuity of the Jewish people and humanity.

(2) Report of the New York City Department of City Planning (Barrière, 2010b: 170–171).

(3) Those deriving from Spain and Portugal (in contrast to Ashkenazim, who originated in Germany).

(4) Hasidism is a diverse popular religious movement of Jewish mysticism that arose in southeastern Poland in the 1750s and thrives until this day.

(5) Report of a parents' meeting at a suburban New York Yiddish school in Mt Vernon, Westchester County: Pedagogishe konferentsn fun di Sholem Aleykhem-shuln in 1954 un 1955 [Pedagogical conferences of the Sholem Aleichem schools in 1954 and 1955] (1972): 146.

(6) For Hebrew instruction in New York City, see Avni and Menken, this volume, and Schiff (1997/2002).

(7) This is the second listed principle in the Guidelines and Syllabus for the Shuln of the Workmen's Circle/Arbeter Ring of 1994 (Kadar, 1996: 31).

(8) Yiddish had been taught for the same allotted time as Hebrew in earlier years (Kadar, 1996: 33).

(9) Bar- and bat-mitzvah are the ritual ceremonies of traditional religiously observant, Jewish children at age 13 for boys and 12 or 13 for girls.

(10) Bobov (Yiddish town name) is the town in Poland where the original Hasidic subgroup developed.

(11) The consonants are similar, but there are several additional vowel representations in Yiddish.

(12) Satmar (Yiddish town name) is the Hungarian town of origin of these Hasidim.

(13) Yeled Ve Yaldaare, Hebrew words for 'boy and girl'.

Part 3

Community-Public School Alliances for Bilingualism

14 A Case Study of Bilingual Policy and Practices at the Cypress Hills Community School

Laura Ascenzi-Moreno and Nelson Flores

Introduction

Latinos in New York City have a long history of activism for high-quality bilingual education programs in public schools. However, the 1974 ASPIRA Consent Decree, an agreement made between a Puerto Rican-based organization and the New York City Department of Education (NYCDOE) regarding services to Puerto Rican students, betrayed the sentiments of most of this community activism. The decree allowed for the implementation of transitional bilingual programs, which limited bilingual instruction to students scoring below a certain threshold on an English language proficiency exam and restricted their time in bilingual programs to three years (Del Valle, S., 1998). Despite this setback, segments of the Latino community continue the struggle for quality bilingual education programs.

One such program is the Cypress Hills Community School, a pre-K–8 two-way immersion public school located in Brooklyn, New York. For over a decade, Cypress Hills Community School has been at the forefront of quality bilingual education, sustaining a tradition of community activism that once characterized the 1960s and 1970s. Community members have played a critical role in shaping the vision of the school, both as founding members and as active participants. As such, the school is an example of bilingual community education practices that are seldom found within schools. In fact, this activist tradition in which the school was founded has continued until today and upholds a changing and integrated notion of bilingualism that incorporates the languaging practices of the student body.

This chapter explores how a broad vision for community-based, high-quality bilingual education is developed and enacted in practice. We argue that the Cypress Hills case demonstrates that the realization of programmatic goals goes beyond language policy and practices. Rather, in order to develop these types of programs, strong and dynamic components at the school level, such as the governance structure and community and student participation, must be in place. It is important to note that this chapter places particular emphasis on students' perspectives in order to highlight the dynamic relationship between language practices and student input, an often overlooked, but essential, ingredient in the development of bilingual education programs.

Spanish Language Speakers in the US

The US has always been a multilingual nation and Spanish has been present since before its inception. In fact, the first permanent European settlers in what would later become the US were Spaniards attempting to expand their colonial empire. In addition, there were many Spanish speakers who became US citizens through the Louisiana Purchase in 1803 and through the annexation of large parts of Mexico as part of the Treaty of Guadalupe Hidalgo. This relationship with Spanish speakers took on an international dimension following the independence movements of Latin America and the creation of the Monroe Doctrine. The relationship between Spanish-speaking populations inside and outside of the US has always been a tumultuous one, yet many Spanish-speakers have made the US their home.

In 2008, 15.4% of the US population identified as Latino (US Census Bureau, 2008a).[1] This is a diverse and heterogeneous population in terms of nationality, language use and geographic location within the US. For one, this category includes members of all Spanish-speaking Latin American countries, with the top three nationalities being Mexican (64%), Puerto Rican (9%) and Cuban (3.4%). In terms of language use, not all people who identify as Latino speak Spanish. Yet the 2008 American Community Survey shows that about 76% of self-identified Latinos report using Spanish, and about 70% of these Spanish users report speaking English either very well or well. In short, the majority of self-identified Latinos in the US also self-identify as bilingual users of English and Spanish.

Table 14.1 Largest population and largest growth of Latinos by state (2006)

Rank	Largest Hispanic/Latino population	Largest growth in Hispanic/ Latino population
1	California	Arkansas
2	Texas	Georgia
3	Florida	South Carolina
4	New York	Tennessee
5	Illinois	North Carolina

Source: US Census Bureau (2006).

The Latino population is dispersed geographically throughout the US. Table 14.1 shows the states with the largest Latino populations, as well as the states that have experienced the most growth in this population since the last census data were collected. As can be seen, none of the states with the largest Latino populations have also experienced the greatest growth, indicating that Latinos have begun settling in new areas.

Spanish Speakers in New York State

New York State historically has had a large Latino population, although it has not experienced the growth that states in the South have experienced in recent years. According to the most recent census data, New York State has a total Latino population that is comparable to the national average (15.1%). However, the distribution by country of origin differs from national data. According to the US Census Bureau's 2008 American Community Survey, the largest groups are Puerto Ricans (36.6%), followed by Dominicans (15.9%) and Mexicans (9.1%). While Puerto Ricans continue to be the largest group in New York State, Dominicans and Mexicans have experienced tremendous growth in recent years.

Reported language use indicates that the New York State Latino population, like the national population, is for the most part bilingual. According to the 2008 American Community Survey, only about 18% of self-identified Latinos report speaking English only and approximately 70% of those who report speaking Spanish also report speaking English very well or well. Thus the majority of Latinos in New York State seem to use both Spanish and English in their daily lives.

In summary, the Latino population nationally and in New York is a bilingual population. This is no doubt partially a product of the grassroots activism around bilingual education that has been prevalent in the Latino community since the 1960s. While the ASPIRA Consent Decree in New York City marked a departure from the bilingual vision of this grassroots movement and reframed the debate from one concerning Latino education to one concerning students who did not speak English, Latino community activists have continued to mobilize to implement their vision of bilingual programs that truly support biliteracy and biculturalism for Latino students.

Forms of Bilingual Education for New York City Students

The following is a succinct review of the types of bilingual education programs available to emergent bilinguals, termed English language learners, and the percentages of these students who attend them in New York City. The three main types of programs through which students who are classified as English language learners receive language support are: English as a second language (ESL), transitional bilingual education (TBE) and dual language education (DL). The majority of students, or 70.7%, receive English language support through ESL. ESL is a monolingual model of education whereby a teacher works with a group of students, either by 'pulling out' students to a separate classroom or by 'pushing into' a classroom to provide English language instruction. ESL instruction mainly employs English as the vehicle for instruction.

Transitional bilingual education accounts for 19.3% of instruction for emergent bilinguals. The goal of TBE programs is to 'transition' students from their home language to English. Students who speak the same language are grouped into classes where the home language is used for instruction for a period of time, usually until they are deemed English proficient in accordance with the annual state proficiency exam.

Lastly, 3.7% of English language learners are in DL programs. The term 'dual language' is used widely by the NYCDOE to describe a broad range of bilingual program models that promote biliteracy. However, these program models may differ in a number of variables, including student composition, language allocation, parent participation and pedagogical focus. In this chapter, the term DL will be used when referring to NYCDOE programs. When referring to Cypress Hills Community School, the term 'two-way immersion' will be used, specifying that, in this DL bilingual program, emergent bilinguals and English speakers are grouped together to learn both language and content in two languages and through this interaction create new fluid ethnolinguistic identities that transcend traditional conceptions of bilingualism (García & Kleifgen, 2010).

Although DL programs account for less than 4% of the instruction that emergent bilinguals receive, this figure has increased since 2001 (Holloway, 2001). By 2009, the overall percentage of emergent bilinguals in DL programs had increased from 2.3% in 2001 to 3.7% of the emergent bilingual population in New York City. The increase in DL schools is a positive move in that, among the three programs described above, it is the one that is most likely to prepare students for an increasingly globalized world through the fostering of bilingualism in education.

However, it is important to examine under what conditions, and by whom, these programs have developed and how effectively they serve the communities in which they operate. Torres-Guzmán *et al.* (2005) caution that a gap between program labeling and implementation may exist. Many self-designated DL programs in reality fall far from programmatic goals. In taking into account the recent expansion of DL programs, it is important to consider the effect of an *external* push, or one originating from beyond the community, such as from the district, on the success of the program. This is in sharp contrast to the *internal* push, from community members, that served as the impetus for the creation of the Cypress Hills Community School, to which we now turn.

Cypress Hills Community School and its Context

Cypress Hills Community School is a pre-K–8, Spanish–English, two-way immersion school located in Cypress Hills, Brooklyn. The community of Cypress Hills is located in northeast Brooklyn. According to the 2000 Census, 42,341 people resided in Cypress Hills. Of its residents, 63% identified as Latino, 21% as Black, 6% as Asian, 5% as White and 5% as other races. At that time, 41% were immigrants. Their origins include the Dominican Republic, Ecuador, Mexico, Guyana, Honduras and other Central and South American countries. Cypress Hills is a linguistically diverse community; according to the 2000 Census, 65% of Cypress Hills residents age 5 and older speak a foreign language at home (E. Blank, Cypress Hills community demographics, personal communication, 6 August 2010). For the most part, residents are low-income, with a median annual income of US$32,241, or 74% of the City's median annual income. They also have low educational attainment levels. Forty-seven percent of area residents aged 25 and older do not have high school diplomas and 22% of adults have less than a ninth-grade education (Blank, personal communication, 2010).

The school population differs slightly from that of the community. Compared with the demographics of the neighborhood, there is a larger population of Latinos and fewer of the other ethnic groups. During the

2009–2010 school year, the demographic breakdown of its 270 students was: 84.7% Latino, 11.7% Black, 1.5% Asian, 0.7% white and 0.4% American Indian. Of the total student population, 48.54% of students were classified as 'English language learners'. According to the Comprehensive Educational Plan School Demographics and Accountability Snapshot from 2009–2010, the poverty rate was 88.4% (NYCDOE, 2010a).

Cypress Hills Community School: Origins and Language Model

Cypress Hills Community School was started in 1997 by parents and community members organized by the Cypress Hills Local Development Organization. Under its auspices, parents increasingly organized around issues of overcrowding and bilingualism. Parents perceived that existing neighborhood schools did not value their children's bilingualism. Rather, it was construed as a disadvantage. Therefore, the initial vision that framed the development of the school was forged by parents. Parents wanted a school that valued the continued development of student bilingualism. These goals are in line with those of the activists of the 1960s and 1970s who pushed for high quality bilingual education.

According to the school's 2008 Comprehensive Educational Plan, a document created by a team of parents, teachers and administrators to specify annual school goals, the school's vision is, 'for all students to become fully bilingual and bicultural, to be deeply concerned about themselves and each other, their community, their environment and the world'. Furthermore, language is not only seen as a tool for communication, but also as a means to access higher levels of academic success, social awareness and self-growth. The following excerpt from the 2008 Comprehensive Educational Plan attests to these principles:

> We believe that language is a tool for learning, not merely a subject to be learned as in foreign language classes. Therefore, it should serve as a mechanism for thinking about everything in life, including math and science, and allow for high levels of metacognition, reflection, analyses and presentations. It is in this context that we believe, greatly, in the benefit of ever increasing one's abilities in one's native language. (Cypress Hills Community School, 2008: 5)

This mission has guided, and continues to guide, the development of the Cypress Hills Community School. However, the core mission does not stand alone. Rather, other key components of the school are in place in order to ensure the program achieves its goals. These are the community-governance model, parent participation and student input.

The community-governance model at Cypress Hills was developed as an alternative to traditional school leadership. One distinguishing factor of this governance model is its co-directorship. In addition to a principal, the school is run by a parent co-director who has equal status with the principal. In addition, school policy is in part crafted and approved through a Governance Council, a body of parents, community members, teachers and administrators. These fundamental components of the alternative governance model have set a precedent for making the development of leadership skills of parents and teachers a priority across the school. Through this model, decision-making throughout the years has been marked by the combined experience and knowledge of administrators, parents and teachers.

An integral part of the school community, parents have been a driving force behind strengthening the school's two-way immersion program. For example, in 2004, the district selected the school to implement the Reading First program, a scripted curriculum and federal initiative that was to be imposed on the school. Parents were vocal opponents of the implementation of this new curriculum, because it would override the teacher-developed curriculum at the school, which tightly integrated content and language and built on the home language practices of the students. The advocacy of parents was the most powerful factor that dissuaded district officials from mandating the ill-fitting program at the school. Parents went into a meeting with district officials to defend the language-specific curriculum that was developed at the school, knowing that it had been attuned to their children's needs within a two-way immersion program. Ms V,[2] the Parent Co-Director, summarized the quality of parent advocacy this way:

Programs come and go ... but the school was created by parents who had ownership of the dual language program. They believed in the ideas and found value in the teacher-made curriculum, which they knew addressed the needs of their children and the community, rather than bringing in prescribed curriculum that had no attachment to the community. There were deep roots in what they believed in and they backed the curriculum designed at the school. (Interview, 20 May 2010)

This anecdote demonstrates how parents have been instrumental at key points in the development of the two-way immersion program. Parents, faculty and students, as leadership groups, have different roles in shaping the language model at the school, but maintain a common focus through their interaction in committees and other participatory spaces.

Ms L, the Principal Co-Director, describes the school's approach to policy as one of responsiveness and growth among school members. She states:

> One thing that we do well is continuous listening. The school isn't a 'fixed program'. We always see ourselves in development. I think we've been successful because we grow with the community and the students we serve. Our growth is defined by working together and developing understanding among everyone in valuing what we do. It becomes a rich experience for everyone and everyone is invested in making sure this project succeeds. (Interview, 20 May 2010)

One example of how school policy demonstrates responsiveness and growth is reflected by the history of the school's language allocation policy. A 50–50 language allocation model – meaning equal instructional time in both languages – has been in place at the school since its inception. Yet, how it has been implemented reflects how the school has taken account of changes in instructional priorities based on student development. At first, the two-way immersion program was a one-day English/one-day Spanish program and served only the elementary school. It was also a side-by-side model, in which students traveled from a Spanish classroom to an English classroom. This first model was in part adopted because of external pressure – it was the most prominent model existent in New York City in the late 1990s and therefore better assured acceptance by the district.

However, this structure morphed as teachers struggled with the best way to educate students as they developed their bilingualism. One of the first changes was to switch to 'self-contained' classrooms, in which one teacher instructs in both languages. The reason behind this shift was to enable teachers to have a better sense of students' simultaneous co-development of the two languages. In addition, teachers began to explore the idea of longer blocks of language immersion – opting for alternating weeks between languages (i.e. one week in English, one week in Spanish). This change reflects a continued commitment to 50–50 language allocation, but demonstrates changes to the program, given the needs of students and teachers, in particular the need to immerse students for longer periods of time and for teachers to understand students' growth in two languages. This shift reflects a break-away from the blind adoption of language models sponsored by the Department of Education, to the creation of models that allow students' natural languaging practices to develop organically. Further, some content teachers in the upper grades have begun to break away from the complete separation of the two languages in favor of *translanguaging*, a process of using dynamic and flexible bilingual practices to help students with meaning-making in the content areas (García, 2009a). We explore this development further in our discussion of student voices below.

This section demonstrates that, throughout the history of the Cypress Hills Community School, different members of the school community – parents, teachers and students – have taken on different roles. Initially parents defined the political importance of the program. After the school was established, teachers defined and re-defined the pedagogical characteristics of the program. Currently the program is explicitly opening up to student voices. This is an important shift because it signals a move towards incorporating students into the development of language policy rather than having language policy 'interpreted' by their teachers and parents for them. We now turn to student voices, to understand how the fluid ethnolinguistic identities that students develop at Cypress Hills can lead to the further refinement of language policies and practices at the school.

Bilingual Student Voices

Eighth-grade students were targeted for focus groups in May 2010. We focused on students in this grade because many had been in the school since the early grades, were on the cusp of leaving for middle school, and thus were reflecting on their education within the dual language program. Students were asked to describe their experiences of bilingualism and learning in and out of school.

Overall, students described bilingualism as a *dynamic process* that involves changes in both knowledge of language, shifts in meta-cognitive awareness, as well as changes in identity. In the following quote, Sandy reflects on how being bilingual is undergirded by a self-awareness of what 'understanding' means:

I think what makes me bilingual is knowing that I can support myself in a conversation, also understanding and knowing what I'm saying is a big part. Because you can know a lot of words, know how to say a sentence, but if you have no idea *what* you are saying ... being bilingual has to do with *understanding* both languages. (Focus group, 19 May 2010)

This quote provides an example of a student who has negotiated her emerging bilingualism through the creation of shifting identities that refuse to coalesce into the unchanging, autonomous individual assumed by much of the research on bilingualism (Norton, 1995). Malcolm, an African-American student who has been at the school since kindergarten, provides an example of how his emergent bilingualism leads to a shifting cultural identity. He says, 'I think I'm Latino because I hang out with 90% Latino people and they, like, changed who I am' (focus group, 19 May 2010). In short, Malcolm's emergent bilingualism allowed him to create a fluid ethnolinguistic identity that in many ways transcends the static conceptions of identity that are assumed by many school programs. Furthermore, Sandy continues by stating that being bilingual opens up doors to interacting with a greater number and diversity of people. When asked whether she thinks knowing Spanish is important she says, 'Spanish is an important asset because in life you are going to meet a lot of different types of people and you want to be able to communicate with them, relate to them and I think Spanish allows you to do that' (focus group, 19 May 2010).

Bilingualism is being redefined by students based on their experience of it at the school. For them, it encompasses both 'understanding' the languages and having a sense of *how language is used* in various contexts. It means being able to interact and learn in more than one language. For these students, language use and exposure to others in that language, in fact, changes who you are. In short, rather than language expressing a pre-existing identity that is already there, the linguistic performances that organically emerge from the language policy of the school are part of the construction of students' dynamic identities (Pennycook, 2004).

However, according to students, becoming bilingual is far from easy. It takes time, consistency and effort. The following quote by Malcolm exemplifies how a commitment to the program on the part of families and students is fundamental:

> What's helped me the most to learn Spanish was being in this school for so many years because I've been in this school for 9 years. At first, when I was younger, I refused to speak Spanish and then as I got older, I started processing ... because if I only came here for one year, I'd probably only know how to say, *'hola'* [hello]. (Focus group, 19 May 2010)

One of the reasons why it takes time is that students are not merely learning a second language, but rather simultaneously learning through two languages. This often requires that students use their strengths in one language to support learning in the other language. Aracelly speaks of both the benefits and the difficulty of moving between languages. She states:

> Para mí, es éste, *difficult*, porque hay que entender las cosas en dos idiomas y a veces no entiendes una cosa y tienes que ir a verlo en otro idioma.

[For me it's, well, *difficult*, because you have to understand things in two languages and you have to go look at the other language]. (Focus group, 19 May 2010)

In addition, students speak about clearly understanding and above all, valuing, bilingualism in their lives and their society. Students speak about how being bilingual allows one to communicate with others. In essence it offers them ways to become citizens of the world. Susana states, with respect to English, 'It's important to learn English because we are in the United States and English is the native language and no matter how many immigrants and how international the United States has become, still there is a necessity to know English, but not just here, but around the world too' (focus group, 19 May 2010). Susana's statement reveals an astute understanding of the importance of English as a cross-national language.

Yet, this acknowledgment of the importance of English is not seen as a reason to eliminate efforts at developing bilingual identities. On the contrary, Spanish is also viewed by students as powerful. Two of the most frequent reasons they gave included the presence of Latinos in this country – 'there's a lot of Hispanic influence in this country' – and the benefit of being bilingual for jobs (focus group, 19 May 2010). Emilia notes, 'If you want to be a teacher and if you work here, for example, you would have to know Spanish because it's a bilingual school and a bilingual program' (focus group, 19 May 2010).

These comments demonstrate that students do not see lives in English or Spanish as separate, but rather as complementary. The following quote demonstrates how one student, Malcolm, views bilingualism as providing access to a broader academic field. In speaking about doing research, he states, being able to communicate in two languages enhances his ability to develop a more accurate picture of a given community:

Say you want to do a survey and I want to use everyone in East New York, I just don't want to use people who speak English like Black people or something, I want to use Latino people ... that would mess up my data if I just use Black people because I want different perspectives for my surveys, so that is why Spanish is important. (Focus group, 19 May 2010)

How then does the school support students' dynamic experience of bilingualism? Students interviewed had strong opinions about the way in which the two-way immersion program model was implemented. They identified two basic ways in which language policy was instituted in classrooms. One method was defined by a strict adherence to conducting all classroom com-munication in one language. This method was defined by the students as 'Ms S's method'. In the other method identified, 'Mr D's method', students were permitted, if not encouraged, to use their entire language repertoire to make meaning of the content being covered, and they moved between English and Spanish depending on their level of understanding – a process García (2009a) refers to as translanguaging.

Students were divided about which method was best. In fact, many thought *both* approaches contributed to their learning. One student, Sandy, clearly had a preference for Ms S's method, saying:

> Ms. S, in our language intervention, she puts us out of our comfort zone to push us to do better, but some teachers just make it with whatever we are most comfortable with … Ms. S, she puts pressure on the students to do it [read, write and speak in Spanish] and it's more motivating, it's more challenging, so it puts you to the test, to see how much you are willing to do better. (Focus group, 19 May 2010)

Other students, however, saw the benefit of permitting the use of both lan-guages. Emilia stated, 'If it's an English day, but there are some people who understand Spanish better, you would want those people who understand Spanish better to get the Spanish textbooks and read along with us' (Focus group, 19 May 2010).

It is important to note that these two particular methodologies that the students identified with teachers are linked to the content areas and lan-guage goals. When the students referred to 'Ms S's method', they spoke about the techniques that she used during a course entitled 'language intervention'. The purpose of this class was to enhance students' language development in a given language. Alternatively, 'Mr D's method' referred to the techniques that the middle school social studies teacher used. This distinction is impor-tant in that it points to dynamic language policies that are responsive to the needs of students in different areas of instruction. When language is the content, such as in the ESL or Spanish as a Second Language class, classroom language use is restricted to the focal language. Whereas, when academic content is being taught, the language that students use can switch back and forth according to student needs. In other words, students are actively engaged in the co-construction of the language policies in their classrooms with their teachers, marking a shift from top-down static bilingual educa-tion models to thinking in terms of bilingualism in education that emerges from meaningful interaction of emergent bilinguals and their teachers (García *et al.*, 2011).

Conclusion

Torres-Guzmán *et al.* (2005: 471) write, 'no matter what label is given to an educational program and no matter how a program is held up as a panacea, much of its potential will be centered in the implementation process'. The advocates of the 1960s and 1970s envisioned bilingual programs as fundamental to the development of pluralistic schools within diverse communities. The original goals of bilingual programs embodied a much greater vision than simply language instruction.

The case of the Cypress Hills Community School illustrates ways in which these goals have unfolded. Parents have spearheaded the goals of the program while teachers have worked on the day-to-day implementation of a language allocation policy. However, both of these efforts have been made in collaboration with students.

As exemplified by the student voices, students view their bilingualism as a tool for understanding themselves better and as a means to engage in the wider community. Furthermore, they identify eclectic methods through which this can be done – both through strict separation of languages and through translanguaging practices. In fact, one way in which the Cypress Hills Community School has achieved the goals of bilingualism and biculturalism is by not focusing solely on language acquisition and language objectives, but rather by undertaking the development of the two-way immersion program as a 'humanistic project'.

In essence, language is inseparable from the people who use it. Accordingly, the implementation of the two-way immersion program at Cypress Hills has been rooted within the school community. Through the student voices highlighted here it becomes clear that the school has been able to foster bilingual lives in students, in addition to contributing to their linguistic proficiency in both languages.

Notes

(1) While the US Census uses the term Hispanic, we use the term Latino here because we are particularly interested in the vast majority of Spanish-speaking people in the US who come from Latin America, and not the population of Spain, since the former group includes the population of students served by bilingual programs in New York City.
(2) Pseudonyms are used throughout this chapter.

15 Building Bilingual Communities: New York's French Bilingual Revolution

Jane F. Ross and Fabrice Jaumont

Introduction

September 2011 marked the opening of two new French bilingual public elementary schools in New York City, as well as the addition of grade levels in already existing programs in four public elementary schools and one charter elementary school featuring a French immersion curriculum. Several parent groups and school principals already plan to expand these programs into Middle School. This is a considerable accomplishment amidst the widespread decline in the availability of foreign language instruction in elementary and middle schools nationwide, especially in schools serving lower socioeconomic status families, and in view of the often highly political attacks on bilingual education opportunities in public schools. As Rhodes and Pufahl (2010) confirmed in a recent survey, the overall picture of foreign language instruction in the US is worse than it was in the 1990s. Moreover, the gap in the availability of foreign language instruction has widened between rich and poor; a large number of elementary and middle school students in rural or lower socioeconomic status schools do not receive any instruction in languages other than English. Importantly, collaborations between multiple partners of different socioeconomic, racial and ethnic backgrounds, from government agencies to parent organizations, have motivated this transformation in the French–English bilingual education landscape in New York, a transformation that we argue is a virtual 'French revolution' in the schools. This 'revolution' serves as an example of the ways in which diverse ethnolinguistic communities can work together to re-conceptualize bilingual educational opportunities that clearly extend beyond prior models of immersion, transitional bilingualism or heritage language support. Serving recent immigrants from African, Caribbean and European countries, along with American children, these programs embody the concept of community bilingual education as formulated by García, Zakharia and Otcu (Chapter 1).

This chapter focuses specifically on the growth of French–English bilingual programs in New York City. The chapter is organized in three parts: an overview of French language communities in the US and the world, which helps provide a larger context for the case of New York City; a description of the broader context of French bilingual programs in the US; and a case study of New York City's French bilingual revolution, specifically the growth of French–English bilingual programs in New York City since 2002. The principle already well established by Fishman (1976) and others, that bilingual education is good for all, has resonated particularly well in the context of New York City's French-speaking communities, where parents from diverse backgrounds and ethnic communities have become builders of bilingual education opportunities for their children. These include European and Canadian expatriates in Manhattan and West Brooklyn, West Africans in Harlem and the Bronx, Haitians in East Queens and East Brooklyn, and North Africans in West Queens. We argue that it is above all this diversity in national origins, race and socioeconomic status that makes the French case unique. Furthermore, the benefits of having diverse partners and networks engaged in such dynamic processes have reinforced the sustainability and appropriateness of bilingual programming. This complex diaspora has helped to build bilingual community education opportunities in New York City that have reached beyond existing 'heritage language education' and 'bilingual' or 'dual language' models, creating a broad, extended global linguistic community.

French Language Communities in the US and the World

The presence of significant French-speaking communities in the US is not surprising. French is the third most common language other than English spoken in the US after Spanish and Chinese, and it is widely present both in traditionally French-speaking areas, such as Louisiana and Maine, and in urban settings with increasingly significant French-speaking immigration (Valdman, 2010).

Together, the six New England states, northern New York state and southern Louisiana constitute the historical stronghold of the French language in the US. Louisiana from its early history was a French colony, and Acadian or other French Canadian settlements in New England and upstate New York date back to the 18th century.[1] While these historically French regions account for only about a quarter of US users of French at home, they are interesting because they have preserved indigenous vernacular varieties of the language, and so add to the complex multinational ethnolinguistic communities that are together referred to as 'Francophonie'.

Determining the exact numbers of French speakers in the US is a complex task because so many are also speakers of additional languages, including Haitian Creole, Wolof, Bambara and Arabic, as well as English. The 2009 American Community Survey (US Census Bureau, 2009) reports that 1,305,503 people speak French at home in the US, and 86,220 in New York. The figures for French Creole spoken at home are 659,053 in the US, and 106,020 in New York. Haitian expert Flore Zéphir (2004) estimates that approximately 20% of Haitians residing in the US also speak French fluently.

Today major concentrations of French speakers are located in the New York City area, southern Florida and southern California. In California persons who declare the use of French at home are mostly French expatriates or relatively recent immigrants from Francophone countries such as Senegal, Mali or the Ivory Coast (Lindenfeld, 2000). Most of the speakers of French in southern Florida are probably bilingual members of the Haitian diaspora who are also speakers of Haitian Creole. One can also encounter 'oies blanches' [snow birds], or retired individuals from Québec who spend the winter months in Florida. In New York, scholars such as Zéphir (2004) and Peckham (2011) suggest that there are about 200,000 Haitian and Haitian American inhabitants in Brooklyn, where there is an *alliance des émigrés haïtiens* (Peckham, 2011). These scholars estimate the total Haitian population of New York City to be over 400,000, taking into consideration the large number of undocumented residents.

The Consulate of France reports about 70,000 French expatriates living in New York and the Québec Government Office reports nearly 100,000 Québecois immigrants. New York residents with family connections to various parts of the Francophone world include French speakers from Canada, Haiti, Senegal, Mali, Togo, the Ivory Coast, Guinea Cameroon, the Democratic Republic of Congo, Morocco, Algeria, Tunisia, Lebanon, Belgium, Switzerland and Luxembourg. New York's French speakers almost certainly number slightly more than 1 million (Globe-Gate Project, 2011).

Given the widespread presence of French as a global language, there is also every expectation that the numbers of speakers in the US will continue to grow. There are an estimated 220 million French speakers worldwide, including 72 million partial French speakers, whose native language is not French, but who use it on a regular basis, particularly in the 32 countries where French is an official national language and where French may be the official language of instruction in schools (Organisation Internationale de la Francophonie, 2011).

The Organisation Internationale de la Francophonie (OIF) comprises 75 states (including 19 observers) across the five continents, representing a total of over 870 million people and over one-third of the United Nations member states.[2] French speakers are also overwhelmingly young, and often highly mobile. In most of the 75 member countries of the OIF, 60% of the population is under 30 years old. Additionally, access to education in French is widely available internationally, thanks to a network of an estimated 900,000 French teachers worldwide. In all there are 96.2 million French speakers in the OIF member countries. With 18.9% of world exports and 19% of world imports, French-speaking countries account for 19% of world trade in goods.

Access to French–English Bilingual Schools

While affluent French expatriates in an urban center such as New York have generally been served by private French schools offering bilingual curricula, the recent waves of immigration from West Africa as well as from Haiti have had little access to such private schools. These recent immigrants represent a significantly increased Francophone presence in New York and other urban centers, including Miami and Boston, although much of this growth remains largely hidden in official statistics. Combined with a significant demand from French expatriate families for access to bilingual public elementary and middle school programs, these newer French-speaking communities have helped to mobilize support for bilingual school programs in French and English, programs that are essential to the long-term survival of these French-speaking communities.

The framework offered by Ruiz (1988), establishes three language orientations that have applications in the context of French-speaking communities in the US. The modernist view of language-as-a-problem opened opportunities for transitional bilingual programs, which have in turn set the precedent for some French heritage language courses, particularly in high schools serving new immigrants. Many of these students either have no access to French as a foreign language classes in their schools or, in cases where such foreign language instruction is available, cannot adequately be served because their oral or written proficiency in French is so different from that of their primarily English-speaking classmates. While not offering a fully bilingual program, the French heritage language classes have sought to provide important linguistic and cultural support to encourage students to maintain sometimes fragile home bilingualism. These classes have often been the outcome of successful collaborations among multiple community partners, including the schools, private foundations, the French government and local community associations.

The second of Ruiz's orientations, that language is a right, plays an interesting dual role for families with French nationality living in the US. The French government itself promotes and protects access to French language education for French citizens living outside the boundaries of France through an extensive network of over 450 state-supported or affiliated schools internationally, as well as financial support for other distance learning programs for French families. In New York City, and elsewhere in the US, this French governmental support has provided significant resources for French families who exercise their right to access such programs by negotiating with local public school authorities to support French language instruction in public primary and middle schools.

Finally, Ruiz's characterization of language diversity as a resource helps to describe the multiple ways in which families, including many non-French speakers, have come to support the creation of bilingual French–English educational opportunities for their children.

Overview of French Bilingual Programs in the US

There are many types of bilingual education programs around the world (García, 2009a). Among the many methods of bilingual education in the US, the approach called immersion uses the additional language initially in part or in full (Cummins & Swain, 1986). In the US, immersion programs are often adapted so that students are doubly immersed in the child's home language and another language. Often these programs are known as 'double immersion'. When the groups consist of both English speakers and speakers of the other language, these programs are often referred to as 'two-way immersion', 'two-way bilingual education' or 'dual language bilingual education'. In this chapter we will refer to these programs as dual-language bilingual education.

The authors have identified more than 130 institutions in 27 states and 80 cities that offer instruction in both French and English in public schools.

These include French immersion bilingual programs for non-French speakers and dual-language bilingual education programs for both Francophones and Anglophones. Both of these programs are offered in public and charter schools. Additionally, there are 50 bilingual programs in private schools that serve mainly expatriate families, but also include local families who can pay the often high tuition and fees. Finally, there are other forms of home language support for Francophone students, including French Heritage Language programs for Francophone students in public schools and community-based organizations.

Public institutions provide the vast majority of dual-language bilingual education and immersion bilingual education programs, suggesting that French bilingual education is not reserved only for families who can afford private school tuition. While most students in these programs are native speakers of English, the presence of French and Francophone immigrant communities is helping to make an even stronger case for expanding these bilingual programs. Almost one-third of these schools, which follow rigorous academic standards and language requirements, are directly affiliated with the French Ministry of Education, receiving various forms of financial and curricular support, including, in some cases, extensive scholarship aid for French citizens, accreditation and teachers from the French public civil service. These institutions are part of a network of 470 schools outside of France that often require students to meet all requirements of the French public school system, as well as the requirements of local state education systems.

Our survey, conducted in 2008, indicates large disparities in French–English bilingual education programs in the US. For example, the numbers of teachers involved varies between 1 and 42 teachers in any one school. Similarly, the number of students per school engaged in French–English bilingual education ranges from 65 to 770, supported by budgets between US$0 and $30,000. In addition, a variety of methodological approaches are used across programs. Overall, our survey shows that French–English bilingual programs are offered in 38 school districts in the US. That includes approximately 130 public schools, and involves 15,000 students and 600 teachers. Another 50 private schools offer a French–English bilingual program accredited by France, serving 15,000 students.

Most French–English bilingual programs in New York City are of the dual-language bilingual education type. According to the New York City Department of Education (NYCDOE), dual language programs foster bilingualism, biliteracy, enhanced awareness of linguistic and cultural diversity, and high levels of academic achievement through instruction in both languages. Most French–English dual-language programs are located in neighborhood public schools, although many are charter, magnet or private schools. These programs generally start in kindergarten or the first grade and extend for at least five years, and many continue into middle school and high school. In 2007 there were two French dual-language bilingual education programs at the elementary level and one at the middle school level in New York City. By 2011 there were six at the elementary level, one in middle school and one elementary program in a charter school. In addition to producing excellent speakers of French, they provide an alternative for French-speaking families who have immigrated to US urban centers, whether temporarily, such as in the case of French expatriates, or more permanently, such as for immigrants or refugees from North and West Africa and Haiti, who through bilingual education also learn English. For such populations, bilingual education delivers a tool for integration into American society, and also a means to maintain their connection to French, an official language of their respective countries of origin.

In smaller urban areas, the creation of French–English bilingual programs has been more traditionally the fruit of collaboration between 'parents who had background in the French language and wanted their children to be exposed to another language', as one program coordinator in Eugene, Oregon communicated by email in our 2008 survey. It was also in the interests of this school's board, which responded to parent demand for foreign languages and succeeded thanks to the determination of one particular administrator.

In smaller towns, the presence of French–English bilingual programs is not explained by the presence of Francophone families per se. It is at times connected to issues of cultural heritage, as is the case of Louisiana, which created the Council for the Development of French in Louisiana (CODOFIL) through Act 409 in 1968. The stated purpose of the CODOFIL was 'to do any and all things necessary to accomplish the development, utilization, and preservation of the French language as found in Louisiana for the cultural, economic and touristic benefit of the state' (CODOFIL, http://www.codofil.org/english). In other cases, interest in French bilingualism is connected to student achievement. For example, in towns such as Milton, Massachusetts and Edina, Minnesota, French–English bilingual programs are offered to high socioeconomic and primarily homogeneous communities, with many students scoring highly on tests and attending some of the highest rated universities in the US. Thus the purposes and impetus behind French–English bilingual programming varies greatly across the country, much like the content, form, size and related budgets.

New York's French Bilingual Programs and the Role of Parent Organizations

In the New York Metropolitan area, French-speaking expatriate families traditionally could choose from among the City's four private bilingual schools: Lycée Français of New York; United Nations International School, which offers a bilingual French section along with other language sections; the French-American School of New York; and Lyceum Kennedy. Through these schools, families seek to offer their children the possibility of achieving fluency in French and eventually completing the French Baccalaureate diploma at the end of high school, while also achieving a high level of academic proficiency in English.

However, in the late 1990s the New York area experienced an influx of young French families who could neither afford to live in Manhattan nor pay these schools' expensive tuition. At the same time, areas of New York City, such as Brooklyn's Carroll Gardens, West Harlem and the South Bronx, witnessed a significant and steady increase in their French-speaking populations, including not only French nationals, but also Haitians and West Africans, who hoped to maintain their children's French language skills while also helping them to adapt to their new English-speaking environment. As these families began to explore possibilities for establishing French programs in their neighborhood public schools, a growing synergy emerged between multiple partners – French, Francophone and Francophile. The French Embassy, various US foundations, the NYC Department of Education's Office of English Language Learners, as well as parent associations such as *Education Française à New York* (EFNY), have collaborated to develop French–English bilingual programs in the City's public schools, or within community-based organizations.

Parent associations have been of critical importance in promoting French–English bilingual programs and generating the larger community and governmental support necessary to sustain innovative programs in both private and public schools. The International School of Brooklyn provides an illustrative example of the significant role of parents in such processes. Responding to grassroots organizing by 10 French expatriate families in the Prospect Heights neighborhood of Brooklyn, the school first offered immersion playgroups in Park Slope, Cobble Hill and Brooklyn Heights while laying the foundation for the preschool opening. In September 2005, it launched a private preschool program with 16 students in its inaugural class. It now serves 200 families, including not only those from French-speaking homes, but also families from Spanish-speaking homes and those from English-speaking homes who are interested in learning either French or Spanish.

Soon after, EFNY was formed in 2005, through the initiative of French expatriates. Their goal was to share the French language with their children and to offer financially feasible options for educating their children in French. They began by offering after-school classes in neighborhood public schools under the supervision of volunteers. These programs benefited from funding from the French government, which maintains an Agency for French Education Overseas (*Agence pour l'Enseignement Français à l'Etranger*). The Agency coordinates over 461 schools outside of France, including 50 in the US. It offers special grants to support classes in French as a Mother Tongue (*Français Langue Maternelle*) where no French schools are otherwise available for French citizens living abroad. Classroom space for these programs has been offered at no cost by public schools, which then benefit from the expanded after-school offerings that often include non-EFNY parents. These factors (the organization of EFNY parents and volunteers, free classroom space, French as a Mother Tongue funds) allow the after-school program to keep their operational costs relatively low.[3]

Seeking to expand beyond the after-school option and offer a full bilingual French program for their children, the EFNY parents began exploring options for opening dual-language bilingual programs within some of the public elementary and middle schools. These parents were opposed to private education, both because of the high costs (tuition is around US$25,000 per year) and especially because they had a strong commitment to public education and a belief that public schools should serve the needs of the community. Seeking a public option, the EFNY organizers approached public school principals in targeted neighborhoods and also sought financial assistance through the French Embassy and French Ministry of Education.

In 2008 a group of parents associated with EFNY formed a separate organization called Friends of New York French-American Bilingual and Multicultural Education with the goal of establishing a K–12 bilingual French–English charter school. Under New York State regulations, the proposal required that organizers demonstrate strong community support. As a result, the group sought additional support from the other French language communities, some of whom had already been in touch with the French bilingual dual-language and heritage language initiatives.

At public hearings the organizers presented over 155 signatures of parents with children eligible for enrollment to satisfy its target enrollment. The proposed school also received 26 letters of support from community leaders, foundations and community organizations.[4] Additionally, letters were provided from faculty at New York University, Columbia University and the City University of New York. The NYCDOE sent a letter and posted the notice on its website, notifying the public and independent schools of the proposed application. A successful public hearing was held on 12 February 2009. The result was the creation of the New York French-American Charter School (NYFACS), which is described below.

Current French Bilingual Initiatives in New York's Public School System

In September 2007, three schools introduced the first public French dual-language bilingual program in New York City history: an elementary school in Brooklyn, one in Manhattan, and a middle school in the Bronx. The programs were developed not only to serve the French families who had initiated the EFNY project, but also to meet the needs of a growing number of diverse Francophone immigrant children who are emergent bilinguals, better known as English language learners. In the four years since those pioneer programs were created, three more schools have introduced French dual-language programs at the elementary level, and at least three more anticipate opening their doors over the next four years. These programs in French and English are geared toward Francophone, Anglophone and French–English bilingual students, as well as students who speak little or no English. Each individual school assures its own enrollment.[5]

In November 2004, representatives from the French Embassy, various foundations and New York University met in order to plan a project to serve recent Francophone immigrants within public high schools in New York. The French Heritage Language Program was the result of this plan, aimed at offering linguistic and cultural enrichment while also facilitating English language acquisition by students of Francophone origin studying in New York public schools. The program's main objective is to promote bilingualism by helping students maintain or develop linguistic proficiency in French and keep a connection to their respective cultures and identities, while increasing their opportunities for success in their new environment.[6]

Manhattan International High School, a school that specifically serves only new immigrants who are English language learners, was the first to launch the French Heritage Language Program initially as an after-school option in the fall of 2005. Some of the students of Manhattan International High School are refugees from African countries, such as the Democratic Republic of Congo, Guinea and the Ivory Coast, whose education has been interrupted by war. These students strive to acquire basic literacy skills in their home languages as well as in French, which according to high school staff will facilitate improvement of their English.

In the spring of 2005, a series of encounters with students and staff from the high school shed light on the importance of a French program for students. Many students felt like they were 'losing' their French or having trouble acquiring higher linguistic skills that would allow them to succeed in a French-speaking environment; many expressed their desire to return to their home country in the future; all hoped to pursue their studies after high school (meeting transcript, 10 April 2005). French proficiency could be a major asset for students who wish to continue their studies in Québec, France or their French-speaking homelands, such as Senegal, Mali or Haiti. The school was aware that, in order for students to succeed in learning English, they also needed to master their home language, such as Creole, Bambara, Wolof, Kikongo, Lingala or French.

The New York French American Charter School (NYFACS) was officially approved in September 2009 and opened its doors in central Harlem one year later. It follows a double immersion program, offering a bilingual and multicultural curriculum. The school served 150 students in grades K–2 during the first year of instruction. It plans to grow to 300 students in grades K–5 in year five, and eventually serve students through grade 12. NYFACS serves a diverse group of students with various home languages in a manner reflective of Community School District 5: 20% French; 40% English; 10% Spanish; and 30% from bilingual homes, including French, English, Haitian Creole, Wolof, Bambara and other West African languages.

The mission of the NYFACS is to develop global citizens who are well prepared to assume leadership in a multicultural society. The school seeks to blend the rigorous standards of learning that are characteristic of the French educational system with American approaches that value individuality and critical thinking. From grades K to 3, instruction is 75–80% in French (French reading and writing, science, social studies, art, music) and 20–25% in English (English reading and writing, mathematics, English as a second language, French as a second language, as needed). The goal is to reach 50% instructional time in French (French literature and composition, science, history and geography, art, music) and 50% in English (English literature and composition, mathematics, social studies, physical education, English/French as a second language, as needed) in the middle school. Thus the combined efforts of multiple partners have helped to achieve a significant range of opportunities for French bilingualism in New York, opportunities that represent educational spaces which go beyond simple maintenance of a home language or heritage language, as some bilingual programs propose, or the acquisition of fluency in a second language, as suggested by many immersion programs.

The dynamic multiethnic communities that have come together in creating these programs have also reinforced English language learning, producing impressive results when considering the high scores reached by these schools' third-grade students in the standardized state tests. Although confidential, the data that the authors were able to retrieve showed that children who were registered in these French dual-language programs from the kindergarten year scored above 80% in both the third-grade New York State English Language Arts and the Mathematics tests – a score two to three times higher than those of monolingual children in similar New York city schools.

Challenges for French Bilingual Initiatives

As French–English bilingual programs in New York have grown, several major challenges have arisen. One challenge has been the difficulty of recruiting highly effective French bilingual teachers, in part because of difficulties finding bilingual candidates with the required certification and expertise, or obtaining visas and certification for native French teachers who could work in these schools. At present, most teaching candidates are from the US.

In 2012 Hunter College's School of Education added a French track to its bilingual education programs. Based in New York City, Hunter College has offered the Masters in Bilingual Education for Spanish-speaking teacher-candidates since 1983, as well as a bilingual extension for those who already hold New York State teacher certification. In an effort to extend its expertise to French-speaking teacher-candidates, Hunter College started offering two French-specific bilingual education courses starting in January 2012. Teachers who successfully complete the French track of the Masters in Childhood or Early Childhood Bilingual Education are eligible to apply for teaching positions in New York City's French dual-language programs. Upon graduation, students are recommended for certification in Early Childhood (birth to grade 2) or Childhood Education (grades 1–6), in addition to the Bilingual Extension in French. Furthermore, teachers who have initial or professional certification in Early Childhood Education or Childhood Education, and want to teach in bilingual programs, may apply for the Advanced Certificate in Bilingual Extension. Such developments are likely to contribute positively to teacher recruitment concerns.

There is also an acute need for appropriate educational materials to support French–English biliteracy, especially books adapted to the levels of student proficiencies as well as mathematics and science textbooks. A further challenge is posed by the need to improve academic outcomes for Francophone English language learners. Ongoing professional development opportunities, including collaboration among schools that offer French–English bilingual programs, would be particularly beneficial in eliminating unnecessary duplication of efforts and inefficiencies. Institutions express a strong desire to train their teachers in specific techniques of bilingual education, but lack the necessary funds.

In addition, it has become apparent that a data tracking system designed to track student progress in two languages would significantly improve identification of individual student strengths and weaknesses, allow for more effective targeted differentiated instruction, and provide for multiple analysis platforms to track teacher effectiveness and student progress. Preliminary teacher data analysis and collaboration in existing French programs have already yielded encouraging results for English language learners on a small scale. For example, 100% of second-grade students who entered the French–English bilingual program at PS 58 in Brooklyn in 2007–2008 are performing at or above grade level in French, according to the Teachers College Independent Reading March benchmark (PS 58 internal survey).

Finally, there is strength in numbers. As more grades are added each year and more schools are offering these programs in New York City and in the greater New York area, the critical mass of learners and teachers in the field should receive closer attention from school authorities, editors and researchers alike.

Conclusion

In order to succeed, French–English bilingual programs in New York require a solid tri-partite partnership – strong commitment from the schools' leadership, very qualified and dedicated teachers, and ceaseless involvement from the parents at all levels. Schools hosting these programs also benefit from the diversity of the population they serve and the diversity of the teaching staff, able to incorporate linguistic and cultural differences into their pedagogy. French-speaking parents from diverse backgrounds and ethnic communities have become builders of bilingual education opportunities for their children as well as the children of non-French speakers. In so doing French-speaking communities are strengthening the linguistic bonds that unite them and reinforcing the sustainability and appropriateness of bilingual programming. Simultaneously, the model of early language acquisition through immersion is offering new possibilities for non-French-speaking families who seek to embrace the learning and mastery of an international language. This model is also rich in cognitive advancement and beneficial to the brain's executive control functions, as neuroscience researchers have come to consensus about.

Thus from the collaboration of various governmental and nongovernmental partners has emerged a rich landscape of French–English bilingual programs and opportunities for certification in New York. This is the French bilingual revolution that has been achieved through the willingness of different communities to work together – the fruit of multiple partners from local, national and international organizations, private foundations, parent groups and the flexibility of the Department of Education.

Notes

(1) For example, historian Malcolm Comeaux (1978) suggests that four unique Cajun subcultures have developed according to where Acadians live in Louisiana. In an essay, 'Louisiana's Acadians: the environmental impact', Comeaux says that there are 'four distinct environments in south Louisiana, and through time Cajuns learned to inhabit and exploit each'. He identifies those environments as (1) the levee lands along the Mississippi River, Bayou Lafourche and Bayou Teche, (2) the prairies of southwest Louisiana, (3) swamplands such as the Atchafalaya Basin and (4) coastal marshes.

(2) OIF members include: (1) 56 Member States and Governments – Albania, Principality of Andorra, Armenia, Kingdom of Belgium, French Community of Belgium, Benin, Bulgaria, Burkina Faso, Burundi, Cambodia, Cameroon, Canada, Canada-New-Brunswick, Canada-Quebec, Cape Verde, Central African Republic, Chad, Comoros, Congo, Cyprus, Democratic Republic of the Congo, Djibouti, Dominica, Egypt, Equatorial Guinea, France, Gabon, Ghana, Greece, Guinea, Guinea-Bissau, Haiti, Ivory Coast, Laos, Lebanon, Luxembourg, Republic of Macedonia, Madagascar, Mali, Morocco, Mauritius, Mauritania, Moldova, Monaco, Niger, Romania, Rwanda, Saint Lucia, São Tomé and Principe, Senegal, Seychelles, Switzerland, Togo, Tunisia, Vanuatu, Vietnam; and (2) 19 Observers – Austria, Bosnia-Herzegovina, Croatia, Czech Republic, Dominican Republic, Georgia, Hungary, Latvia, Lithuania, Montenegro, Mozambique, Poland, Serbia, Slovakia, Slovenia, Thailand, Ukraine, United Arab Emirates.

(3) There are currently eight locations for the after-school programs: Middle School at LAB (Manhattan), MS 51 (Brooklyn), PS 234 (Tribeca), PS 41 (Greenwich Village), PS 58 (Brooklyn-Carroll Gardens), PS 59 (Midtown East), PS 363 (East Village), PS 84 (Upper West Side). These after-school programs serve about 250 students, the majority of whom are French citizens or of French-speaking origins.

(4) Such as Congressman Charles Rangel – 15th Congressional District; Robert Jackson – 7th City Council District; Mr W. Franc Perry, Chairman of Community Board 10; the *Organisation International de La Francophonie*; the Embassy of France to the US; the Delegate General for the Québec Government House; French Education in New York; the Senegalese Association in America; the Association des Frères Ivoiriens en Amérique; the Association of Togolese in the USA; the United Malian Women Association; the Malian Association of New York; the Harlem Business Alliance; the Calyon Credit Agricole; the TCW Group, Inc.; the Consulate and the Mexican Culture Without Borders, and others.

(5) When this chapter was written, New York's French dual-language programs were serving close to 800 students. By the time these programs reach full capactiy (to grade 5) they will serve 1300 students each year. The public schools with

dual-language and bilingual programs are PS 58 (Caroll Gardens, Brooklyn), PS 73 (Bronx), PS 84 (Upper West Side), PS 151 in Woodside (Queens), PS 133 (Park Slope, Brooklyn), PS 110 (Greenpoint, Brooklyn) and the New York French-American Charter School (Harlem).

(6) The Program currently serves 300 students in six different international high schools (Bronx International HS, International Community HS in the Bronx, Brooklyn International HS, International HS at Lafayette in Brooklyn, International HS at Prospect Heights in Brooklyn, International HS at Union Square, and three different community centers: Malian Cultural Center (Bronx), Bethanie SDA Church (Brooklyn) and Eben-Ezer SDA Church (Brooklyn).

16 Trilingualism of the Haitian Diaspora in New York City: Current and Future Challenges

Isabelle Barrière and Marie-Michelle Monéreau-Merry

Introduction

Significant numbers of Haitians have been migrating to the US since 1957 for economic and political reasons. The immigrants who came after François Duvalier took power in 1957 included political rivals and socioeconomic elites, who were followed by middle-class populations (Joseph, 2002). After Duvalier's son took over in 1971, substantial numbers of working-class Haitians arrived in the US. The earthquake that devastated Haiti on 12 January 2010, which triggered an upsurge in immigration (Wasem, 2010), has given rise to a questioning of the divisions between social classes both in Haiti and in the Haitian diaspora (Lahens, 2010). All layers of Haitian society were affected, and the majority of families of Haitian descent in the diaspora have lost relatives and/or friends.

The earthquake affected the most populated area of the country, including the capital. Although there are still debates about exact figures, an estimated 3 million people (that is more than a third of the total population) were affected (CBS News, 2010). In addition to the casualties, infrastructure, including schools and the university, were also badly affected by the earthquake, and many schools have yet to be re-opened. One consequence of the earthquake is that the international community, through its rescue, relief and reconstruction work, learned that Haitian Creole is the main or only language of the majority of Haitians. This fostered international initiatives to make Haitian Creole language resources freely accessible (Barrière, 2010a).

This chapter describes the linguistic and educational situation of the Haitian diaspora in New York City (NYC). In both NYC and Haiti, French has increasing support despite the fact that Haitian Creole is spoken by the majority of Haitians and contributes, along with Vodou culture, to a distinctive sense of national and cultural identity. We argue that the debates about language(s) to be used for instruction in schools in Haiti play an important role in how the languages of the Haitian diaspora are used and taught in NYC. The chapter describes the complex efforts of the NYC Haitian community to educate their children through the use of different linguistic resources, and the meanings attached to each of the three languages negotiated by Haitians in the US – Haitian Creole, French and English. However, before we turn to New York, it is important to describe the sociolinguistic and educational landscape of Haiti.

Sociolinguistic and Educational Landscape of Haiti

Presently Haiti has two official languages, French and Haitian Creole. Haitian Creole is the most widely spoken creole in the world, with 12 million speakers. Outside of Haiti, it is spoken in the Bahamas, Cuba, the Dominican Republic, France, Canada and the US, where Haitian-speaking immigrants number 546,000. US-born Americans of Haitian ancestry number 310,000 (2008 figure, Camarota, 2010).

Haitian Creole is the language of the majority of the population of Haiti. Haitians themselves refer to it as either 'Haitian Creole' or 'Creole', and the US census includes it under the category of 'French Creole'. Although the authors favor Haitian (see Barrière, 2010a, for explanations), in this chapter, the term Haitian Creole is used.

Haitian Creole emerged in the 17th and 18th centuries from the contact of French and African languages. To a much lesser extent, the development of Haitian Creole was influenced by the language of the Taynos, the original inhabitants of the island, the Native American language Arawak (sometimes called Carib), from which the name Haiti is derived (Étienne, 1974/2009; DeGraff, 2007). The African populations who were enslaved and brought to Haiti in the 15th century came from various African geographical areas and spoke West African Kwa languages and Central African Bantu languages

(DeGraff, 2007), including Ewe(gbe) (spoken in Ghana and Togo) and Fon(gbe) (used in Benin and Togo).

French and Haitian Creole are not mutually intelligible; although the Haitian Creole lexicon contains a substantial proportion of words borrowed from French, the syntaxes of the two languages greatly differ (see DeGraff, 2007). Similarly, although both French and Haitian Creole use the Roman alphabet, their orthographic systems are very different.

Early descriptions of the sociolinguistic situation of Haiti characterized it as diglossic; that is, two varieties of a language, or two languages, are used in complementary distribution, one in formal contexts and formally learned and the other in informal contexts (Ferguson, 1959; Fishman, 1972a). The accuracy of this characterization of the linguistic situation has been challenged (Dejean, 1993; Étienne, 1974/2009; DeGraff, 2005, 2009, 2010a, 2010b). Although French, a colonial legacy and a spoil of war (*'butin de guerre'*; e.g. Saint-Fort, 2010), co-exists with Haitian Creole at a societal level, it is only spoken by 10% of the population (DeGraff, 2009). In contrast, all Haitians speak Haitian Creole. Haiti therefore includes a (largely rural) population with low socioeconomic status made up of a majority of monolingual speakers of Haitian Creole and a (largely urban) population of higher socioeconomic status who use both Haitian Creole and French (Joseph, 1983).

French, the colonial language, was declared official in 1918. Almost 70 years later, in 1987, Haitian Creole was made a co-official language. Despite their legal equality in the constitution, Haitian Creole and French have not enjoyed the same social status. This has seriously impacted the education of Haitians in Haiti and in the US.

Until 1987, French was used as the only medium of instruction. As a consequence, an official orthography of Haitian Creole was not established until the 1980s, and Haitian Creole only began to be taught in Haitian schools in 1987.

French benefits from an annual budget of US$2 billion, which includes US$1.5 billion collected by French-speaking private schools from Haitian parents, US$250 million from the Haitian Ministry of Education and roughly US$3 million from the International Organization of Francophonie (Joseph, 2011). As argued by Joseph (2011), the disparity between the investment in French, which is only spoken by 10% of the population and understood by 15%, and that in Haitian Creole is not in line with the message conveyed by the constitutional recognition of French and Haitian Creole as co-existing official languages. According to both DeGraff (2009) and Joseph (2011), initiatives focused on French hinder the development of Haiti; they do not enable monolingual speakers of Haitian Creole to participate in national democratic debates (DeGraff, 2010a).

Drastic progress has been made in literacy rates in the past 60 years. Whereas among the population aged 85 and older, slightly fewer than 40% of urban residents and fewer than 15% of rural residents are literate, the rate of literacy among 15- to 19-year-olds has reached about 75% in rural areas and almost 95% in urban areas (IHSI, 2009). These increases have been interpreted as resulting from education policies that favor the use of Haitian Creole as a medium of instruction (Mather, 2010).

With the need to rebuild the education system and infrastructure destroyed by the earthquake, the debate on the language(s) that should be used for instruction has been revived (DeGraff, 2010a, 2010b). A recent petition in favor of Haitian Creole as one of the media of instruction, developed by Dejean (2010), argues that the use of Haitian Creole, not French, will lead to the democratization of education in Haiti. It has been endorsed by Haitians in Haiti and in the diaspora, including linguists (e.g. Michel DeGraff) and education specialists (e.g. Fabienne Doucet), and by international experts in the fields of education and linguistics (e.g. Noam Chomsky).

The fact that Haitian Creole orthography was developed relatively recently and has only been taught to the youngest generations has had an impact on the literacy of Haitian immigrants to the US. Substantial numbers of Haitian immigrants arrived with poor literacy skills, and others have learned to read and write in French, rather than in Haitian Creole. In contrast, more recent immigrants, especially those who attend public schools, tend to have literacy skills in Haitian Creole.

The important role that religion plays in the intergenerational transmission of Haitian culture and languages in the diaspora is better understood in light of its status in Haiti. Both Haitian Creole and Vodou contribute to a distinct Haitian identity and are historically tied to the events that mark the birth of the first Black Independent Republic, a source of pride among Haitians. They can both be thought to constitute creative, symbolic and 'organized responses to oppression' (Bellegarde-Smith, 2006: 105). They have both shared a common fate in that they have benefitted little from logistic support (i.e. both infrastructure and financial) either in Haiti or in the diaspora, compared with the church (vs Vodou) and French (vs Haitian Creole). In this context, it is not surprising that the increase in the status of Haitian Creole in the 1980s was paralleled by a growing recognition of the positive contribution of Vodou to the Haitian way of life.

Both the strong tie between Vodou and anti-colonialism, and Western conceptualizations of Vodou have contributed to its demonization. Vodou is present in medicine (more than 90% of Haitians have no access to Western medicine and therefore consult Vodou healers), literature, music and the visual arts (Guetjens, 2012). Bellegarde-Smith (2006:103) has said: 'As with Judaism in Israel and Shinto in Japan, Vodou helped define the Haitian nationality and ethos'.

The Haitian Diaspora in the US

Demographic profile

According to Camarota (2010), more than 800,000 people in the US are of Haitian ancestry, including those US-born and foreign-born. The census figures regarding language use are more difficult to interpret for three related reasons. The census lists the two official languages of Haiti in an ambiguous way: French (including Patois, Cajun) and French Creole. The latter category includes several languages that have emerged partly as the result of contact with French, not only Haitian Creole. Secondly, given that the term 'patois' is used to refer to different French and English 'creoles' (Lewis, 2009), it is not clear which of the two census options monolingual Haitian Creole speakers would select, especially given the long history of negative attributes associated with Haitian Creole. Thirdly, for those who are fluent in Haitian Creole and French, the census does not provide the option of selecting more than one language.

According to the 2009 American Community Survey 2008 figures, 1,332,633 US residents declared that they use French (including Patois, Cajun), and 646,109 declared that they speak French Creole. French and French Creoles are among the top 10 languages other than English spoken by students aged 5–17 that are labeled as having 'Limited English Proficiency', following Spanish, Chinese and Vietnamese (Migration Policy Institute, 2010). With respect to the Haitian population above the age of five, 81% speak a language other than English at home, which is 60% more than the national average (Buchanan et al., 2010).

Two thirds of the more than 800,000 people with Haitian ancestry in the US reside in two states: almost half in Florida (376,000), where Haitian Creole is the second most commonly spoken language after Spanish, and about 20% in New York (191,000; Buchanan et al., 2010).

Present educational issues and achievement of Haitians

In addition to negative misconceptions of Haitians as an uneducated and disease-ridden population, Haitian students also confront misperceptions about their linguistic skills. Many Haitians do not speak English when they enter the US education system, and they are assumed to systematically speak French. Additionally, Haitian Creole-speaking professionals are not typically available within the school system. Furthermore, the American and Haitian school systems differ and students' placement is further complicated by the fact that students often do not have their Haitian school records (Rennalls, 2006). As a consequence of all these factors, Haitians end up in inappropriate classes, placed either in special education classes or in classes too advanced for them. Haitian students are also confronted with the racism that other black communities experience in the American education system (Rennalls, 2006).

The children of Haitian migrants who move to low socioeconomic status neighborhoods often come into contact with African-American and other Caribbean communities. As a result, they tend to become not only multilingual, but multidialectal, that is, adding African-American English and/or West Indian English varieties to their linguistic repertoire (Joseph, 2002). Second-generation Haitian immigrants tend to develop one of three possible identities: a Black American identity, a Haitian or Haitian (Black) American identity, or an immigrant identity (Waters, 1996). According to Stepick (1992), Haitians that adopt the behaviors of African-Americans of low socioeconomic status may become members of a subculture that rejects the positive values of education. In contrast, more affluent Haitians who live in middle-class neighborhoods fare better. They are less likely to be confronted by anti-black racism, and thus the development of their Haitian identity is less hindered.

Haitians in New York

Demographic and sociolinguistic profile

New York City is home to more than 180,000 residents of Haitian ancestry (Center for the Study of Brooklyn, 2010). Lower- and middle-class Haitians tend to reside in Brooklyn (86,637 Haitians), with more than 50% residing in the Eastern/Flatbush area, while most middle- and upper-class Haitians and their descendants live in Queens and some in Manhattan (42,064 Haitians). In Queens, 30% of Haitians earn incomes below the poverty line, whereas more than 50% of Brooklyn Haitian residents fall below the poverty line.

Only 20% of Brooklyn Haitians have a bachelor's degree, compared with 27.9% for the population of the borough as a whole. The discrepancy is smaller in Queens, where 26.9% of Haitian residents have a college degree compared with the borough average of 28.1%. Not surprisingly, the average income of Haitians in Queens tends to be higher than that of Haitians in Brooklyn, but compared with the average incomes in their boroughs, Haitian residents in both boroughs fare well.

No Haitian enclave can be identified in NYC (Rivers, 2011). Yet, the vibrancy of Haitian languages and cultures in New York is felt in town halls (such as in Flushing, Queens), museums (such as the Brooklyn Museum of Arts), restaurants, schools and Haitian newspaper offices. Various bookshops specifically serve the Haitian population by selling literary, historical and linguistic publications written in Haitian Creole, French and English, and children's books that reflect the languages and culture of Haiti. In most of these contexts, the languages used include a combination of Haitian Creole, French and English.

The Haitian church and language

The Christian church is a resource within the Haitian community. Numerous Haitian churches exist in both Queens and Brooklyn. Besides religious services, the church provides information about legal residency, citizenship and employment opportunities. Haitian churches tend to have French or English names, and most of them use a combination of languages during the service and/or have services in different languages. The selection of the languages of the service is often the result of heated discussions (Buchanan, 1979).

Currently, Haitian churches in Crown Heights Brooklyn, such as the Seventh Day Adventist church known as Hebron, conduct services in three languages. There is a youth choir, which is generally composed of children who were born in Haiti. In addition, US-born American Haitians participate in the choir. Singing in the youth choir provides a context for learning to read Haitian Creole, as well as French. Children listen to songs in Haitian Creole and French, and transcribe the words. Members of the congregation who are proficient in writing Haitian Creole and/or French correct their spelling and model the correct pronunciation of words during choir practice sessions. The youth primarily express themselves in English, with lexical borrowing from Haitian Creole.

Although the use of Haitian Creole and French in the church support the transmission of the languages and literacy of these two languages to a certain extent, there is much variation with respect to the academic and literacy skills in both Haitian Creole and French that US-born Haitians reach in adulthood since, as we will see below, there are few opportunities for them to develop literacy in Haitian Creole.

Although Vodou is practiced in NYC, it does not benefit from a visible infrastructure. Vodou gatherings occur through word of mouth and rituals are usually conducted in Haitian Creole.

Educational Programs for Haitians in NYC

Fueled by the declaration of Haitian Creole as a co-official language in Haiti and its introduction into the educational system, a number of public bilingual English–Haitian Creole programs were started in New York City in the 1980s. In Brooklyn alone, there were five elementary schools, three intermediate schools and eight high schools that had bilingual English–Haitian Creole programs for immigrant Haitian students who were emergent bilinguals (see Cerat, 2011). Teacher education programs for bilingual Haitian teachers were developed in which Haitian teachers, who had never had the opportunity to learn to read or write Haitian Creole in Haiti, were first taught to read and write Haitian Creole.

Today, however, only one elementary school (PS 189), one intermediate school and one high school, all in Brooklyn, offer bilingual English and Haitian Creole programs for Haitian immigrant students (Cerat, 2011), and the education of Haitian students is not limited to Haitian Creole only, but includes French. In addition, although an assistance center to provide support for Haitian newcomers (HABETAC) has been in operation since 1993, it is scheduled to close as of this writing. As we will see below, the organized efforts of the Haitian community today are also organized around French/English, the community having left most of the efforts on behalf of solely Haitian Creole to Brooklyn grassroots groups such as Flanbwayan, Kongo and Gran Chimen (Cerat, 2011). We first turn to briefly describing the efforts on behalf of Haitian Creole of the Haitian assistance center, as well as the elementary school program at PS 189, before we describe other efforts on behalf of the other language of Haitian identity – French – in L'École bilingue and other French programs.

HABETAC

In 1993, the New York State Education Department and the Bilingual Education program of The City College of New York worked together to establish the Haitian Bilingual/ESL Technical Assistance Center (HABETAC) at City College, later located at Brooklyn College. HABETAC provides technical assistance to school districts with Haitian emergent bilinguals, while increasing the status of Haitian Creole in NYC. For instance, every year, HABETAC organizes the Haitian Creole Spelling Bee for students in grades 3–8. Conferences on the education of Haitian students are also held.

The Bilingual Center, PS 189, Brooklyn

The Bilingual Center, PS 189, in Brooklyn uses Haitian Creole, French and Spanish in instruction. Alongside English, these three languages are reflected in signs on the school premises. Recently, a 'dual' bilingual English–Haitian Creole program that enrolls dominant Haitian Creole and English speakers was started in the school. The program begins at the kindergarten level and extends until the eighth grade. Teaching is done in two languages, and homework is given in both English and Haitian Creole. During the initial stages of English or Haitian Creole acquisition, students are allowed to use both languages in written assignments. However, over time, students are strongly encouraged to separate their two languages in preparation for the English Language assessments. The students are also presented with the option of studying other languages such as French and Spanish.

L'École Bilingue (also known as the The Hebron Seventh Day Adventist Bilingual School)

L'École Bilingue – founded by an educator and pastor of Haitian descent – is a parochial school affiliated with the Adventist Church. The mission of the school is to maintain and develop the French language among children of Haitian descent in a religious and academically rigorous context. Sixty percent of the student body is of Haitian descent, with the remaining portion being from the Caribbean diaspora. All the students study the French language as a daily subject. Haitian Creole is not implemented in the school curriculum. When asked about the absence of Haitian Creole as a subject, the French teacher, of Haitian descent, indicated that for historical reasons parents want their children to acquire the French language. However, with the recent elevation of Haitian Creole in Haiti, the teachers felt that Haitian Creole should be used in the curriculum in the future. In the words of a teacher, 'We are Haitian and we must preserve our culture'.

Haitian culture is emphasized to the students. This is especially evident during Flag Day on 18 May. The students in this school learn and re-enact the events that led to the Haitian Revolution, which is a source of pride among Haitians. The systematic teaching of French to all students is supported by the general school budget.

French programs in New York public schools

In 2007, the French Embassy launched an initiative, 'French Goes Public', that established French teaching programs in US public schools, including some in NYC (Jaumont, 2008; Ross & Jaumont, Chapter 15). Haitian community leaders have been involved in the development and implementation of these programs. Haitian students make up 29% of these French programs across NYC (Jaumont, 2010, personal communication) and they constitute the majority of students in Brooklyn. Haitians make up half of the 120 students enrolled in the French Heritage Language Program, which consists of after-school and during-school French language lessons. Two-hundred and fifty Haitians are enrolled in the High School Equivalency program taught in French. Étienne (1974/2009) believes that this initiative of the French government has had a positive impact on the Haitian diaspora.

Learning Haitian Creole in NYC

Given that there is a lack of education professionals and speech language pathologists who possess the linguistic skills required to respond to the needs of Haitian students, classes in Haitian Creole for adults are very important. In response to this need, Brooklyn College has been offering Haitian Creole classes – an initiative that a growing number of universities have followed since the earthquake. Courses targeted to students of Haitian ancestry who already know some Haitian Creole have been developed. Joseph (2008) has documented the positive effects of these courses on both the linguistic and literacy skills of the students, as well as on their sense of identity.

In the aftermath of the earthquake in Haiti, the need for speakers of Haitian Creole has become more obvious and has given rise to a number of initiatives. For instance, the Alliance Française in New York ran a Haitian Creole course in 2010. At the national level, free language resources have been made available. Carnegie Mellon University has been sponsoring the compilation of a corpus of Haitian Creole for translation purposes (http://www.speech.cs.cmu.edu/haitian/). Although the project is not complete, the international community is now more aware that not all Haitians speak French, and that Haitian Creole is the language spoken by the majority of Haitians.

Although all these initiatives are important, they may not be sufficient to ensure the transmission of Haitian Creole to second- and third-generation students. Unless Haitian Creole is given an important role in the education of the Haitian diaspora, Haitians will remain illiterate in what is their main home language. To ensure the trilingualism that all Haitians in the US need, more educational efforts are needed.

In a recent article, Étienne (2010) criticizes French institutions in NYC for their lack of recognition and support of the Francophonie of Haitians in the diaspora. Yet, as we have seen both in Haiti and in NYC, the teaching of, and in, French receives much more support than that in Haitian Creole. Étienne seems to assume that all Haitians in NYC have a French-speaking legacy and/or should aspire to be competent in French, which is not the case for all Haitians.

The challenge that the Haitian community in the US is facing regarding the transmission of their linguistic heritage lies in trying to foster the development of three languages in a US education system that is designed for English monolinguals and that does not value bilingualism and multilingualism. The complexities of Haitian language use and the goal of trilingualism evade all US educational circles.

Conclusion

Strategic language and literacy planning for Haitians require more accurate information on the use of different languages at home. A first step in this direction would be to label Haitian Creole for what it is in the US Census, instead of it being included under the category of French Creole or French (including Patois and Cajun). Secondly the Haitian population is multilingual and this fact needs to be reflected in the options that can be selected in the Census.

In order to improve the education of Haitian children, educators must become aware of two now well-documented facts: (a) the status of Haitian Creole as a distinct language and a key ingredient in the expression of Haitian identity; and (b) the diverse linguistic profiles of students of Haitian ancestry, acknowledging both their linguistic competence and their linguistic desires, as well as their complex linguistic heritage. This heritage includes the use of both Haitian Creole and French, and varies at an individual level. The Haitians' relations to both Haitian Creole and French constitute strengths in a context in which, at an international, national and regional level, more linguistically skilled professionals are needed to respond to the needs of both Haitian Creole-speaking and French-speaking students. However, these strengths can only positively contribute to the professional, cultural and linguistic landscape of the US if the needs of Haitian students are addressed.

Addressing these needs requires the recognition that currently there is more support for French than for Haitian Creole. As suggested by Joseph (2011), for Haiti, the skills of Haitian community leaders who were involved in the implementation of Francophonie could be used for the implementation of successful educational policies to foster academic literacy skills in Haitian Creole. This in turn would enhance the rich, multifaceted and complex linguistic legacy of the Haitian diaspora and ensure that children of Haitian descent are equipped to succeed in a global and multilingual world.

Acknowledgments

The two authors thank Professor Jude Piquant of Brooklyn College and Bathe Faustin for sharing their experience with Haitian Creole-speaking students and their insights into Haitian Creole. The first author also wishes to thank the students Ericka Bouckard, Schifra François, Yarnelle Lafleur and Esther Saint Jean for sharing their insights; Prince Guetjens for his insights into Haitian Creole and Haitian culture and his feedback on this article; and Prince Guetjens and fellow Haitian and Vodou artists for enriching her life.

17 Russian Bilingual Education across Public, Private and Community Spheres

Tatyana Kleyn and Beth Vayshenker

Introduction

Russian speakers[1] make up a diaspora that stretches from Russia to the Baltic Republics, across Central Asian nations to Israel, Canada and the US. Although the status of Russian has been heavily influenced by political factors, such as the breakup of the Soviet Union in 1991, the language has remained prominent on a global scale. Russian speakers living in the US, and in New York City (NYC) in particular, are diverse in their ethnicities, immigration experiences and religions. Nevertheless, within the US the Russian language has the possibility to bring together many groups that are currently separated by borders, beliefs and backgrounds.

Russian bilingual programs in NYC are characterized by their diversity across people and program models. The participants range from immigrants to US-born students, from those born in Russia to those from former Soviet Republics that no longer have Russian as the official language, from those with familial ties to the Russian language and culture to those who come from different ethnic and linguistic groups and hold an interest in the Russian language and its culture(s). The diversity of the programs, where the focus goes beyond languages and cultures to academic content, demonstrates the combined goals of many Russian bilingual programs: cultural and linguistic development and connectivity alongside deepened content knowledge in areas long associated with Russian traditions, such as mathematics and the arts.

Both programs described here support the bilingual practices of American ethnolinguistic communities who use Russian for a variety of purposes and reasons as part of their linguistic repertoires. The American students in these programs exemplify diversity in many forms. Yet, they all participate in bilingual programs that are created or supported by the community. These programs allow children to not only learn and use Russian (alongside English), but also to engage in performative aspects of the language and its associated cultures. These programs offer students increased opportunities for their futures, including economic, social and cultural benefits that are now required for a globalizing world and as part of the plural networks of the Russian-speaking diaspora.

Within this chapter we provide a background of the evolution of the Russian language, as well as the immigration history of Russian speakers to the US. Then we review the academic achievement of Russian-speaking immigrant and US-born students in NYC schools. Finally, we look closely at two different bilingual programs, a private community Saturday school and a public one-way bilingual immersion program, to show the varied opportunities for the inclusion of home (and additional) languages and cultures in the education of students from predominantly Russian-speaking backgrounds. We now turn to the historical and present-day aspects that have impacted the Russian language and its speakers across countries and continents.

The Russian Language and the Script

The Russian language falls under the umbrella of Indo-European languages and draws on proto-Slavic roots. Many modern-day Russian components emerged from Old Church Slavonic, a language mainly found in sacred biblical texts. Two Greek brothers, St Cyril and St Methodius, were instrumental in developing the first known Slavic alphabet, called Cyrillic, in the late ninth century. Their impetus was to translate the Bible in order to preach Christianity to communities in Slavic regions (Hingley, 2003). By the 10th century three streams of Slavic developed: West Slavic, South Slavic and East Slavic. The latter is what we have come to know as Russian. Peter the Great, the Tsar most recognized for his drive to westernize the Russian Empire, initiated its orthography reform in the early 18th century (Millar, 2004). This movement eliminated characters rendered unnecessary for the language's utility. The result was the Cyrillic alphabet, a system used in Russian and other Slavic and non-Slavic languages such as Bosnian, Macedonian, Moldovan, Tajik and Ukrainian.

Locating Russian and its Contact Languages

Even prior to the onset of Communism, Russia's leadership russified surrounding nations, imposing the Russian language and culture on those in the Russian Empire. As a result of the creation of the Union of Soviet Socialist Republics (USSR) in 1922, the Russian language had the opportunity to come into contact with other languages spanning from the Baltic to the Central Asian republics. The former Soviet republics include present-day Armenia, Azerbaijan, Belarus, Estonia, Georgia, Kazakhstan, Kyrgyzstan, Latvia, Lithuania, Moldova, Russia, Tajikistan, Turkmenistan, Ukraine and Uzbekistan. People in each former Soviet republic spoke different languages; therefore, Russian was spoken alongside the languages originally associated with the region. With the introduction of Communism in these republics, the Russian language made its way willingly, and often forcefully, into many formal domains of life, such as government, education and business.

The Soviet government strongly advocated for Russian to trump the languages of the republics by mandating its usage. These efforts extended to schools. For example, schools in present-day Ukraine were obligated to identify Russian language textbooks as 'native language' textbooks, whereas those in written in Ukrainian were referred to as 'Ukrainian language' textbooks, demonstrating the government's push to russify its Soviet republics (Bilinsky, 1981). A clear effort was made to distinguish and position the Russian language as official and even indigenous to the region.

Although Russian was considered the official language during the Soviet era, the languages of these republics remained spoken at the personal or informal level, thereby creating plurilingual contexts for their bilingual speakers. Since the fall of the USSR in 1991, Russian has remained a thriving language in many of the former Soviet republics, as a residual effect of the 69-year Soviet presence. In addition, waves of immigration enabled Russian to interact with Hebrew and Yiddish in Israel, German in Germany, and English in the US and Canada.

History of Russian-speaking Immigrants to the US

The volatile relationship between Russia and the US during the era of the Russia Empire and the period leading up to and including the Cold War drove different waves of immigration to the 'land of gold', as many Russian speakers refer to the US. Several waves of immigration to the US occurred, starting in the late 19th century. The first major influx of immigrants, totaling over 3 million, arrived on US soil seeking religious tolerance and better economic opportunities. This wave was prompted by increased Jewish persecution in Russia in the form of systemized pogroms, which gained momentum after the assassination of Tsar Alexander II in 1881. The Jews were used as a scapegoat for the death of this popular and progressive Tsar. Restrictions imposed on Jews in Russia included quotas limiting Jewish entry to high schools and universities and limited mobility to the outskirts of the Russian Empire, restricting residence to the area known as the Pale of Settlement. There was general looting perpetrated by ethnic Russians, and a government apathetic to these discriminatory policies (Hingley, 2003).

Once the tsarist regime had been fully ousted by the Bolsheviks in 1917, the new Soviet government implemented restrictions on emigration, making it nearly impossible to leave the Former Soviet Union (FSU). Tensions between the Soviet and US governments brought immigration to an all time low, marking the second wave, with 6000 persons emigrating from the FSU between 1920 and 1969 (US Department of Homeland Security, 2009). The passage of the Refugee Relief Act in 1953 once again opened US borders for 'escapees from communist domination' (FAIR, 2008). However, it was not until the early 1970s that the US saw a spike in immigration from the FSU. Demonstrations by Jewish protesters demanding visas to leave for Israel and the US and international pressure on the Soviet government resulted in increased immigration. This marked the third wave of immigration, from 1970 to 1990, which brought 61,000 Soviet citizens to the US, quadruple the numbers from 1920 to 1969.

As evidenced by the surge in immigration during the 1990s, the political situation in the FSU eroded and Communism collapsed in 1991. The former Soviet republics reclaimed their sovereignty and the doors of immigration reopened. The fourth wave, post dissolution of the Soviet Union, saw numbers that continued to rise each decade: 433,000 immigrants between 1990 and 2000 and 562,000 between 2000 and 2009 (US Department of Homeland Security, 2009). More recently, with improved US–Russian relations, greater numbers of Russian speakers have begun to migrate to the US for economic purposes, marking the second highest percentage change in immigration rates noted for this timeframe, behind only Vietnam (US Census Bureau, 2010).

US Demographics and Present Settlements

There are 881,723 Russian-speakers across the US (US Census Bureau, 2009). They tend to reside in large cities, as urban living is also the norm for many Russian-speaking immigrants, who come from cities such as Kiev, Tashkent and Moscow. The four cosmopolitan areas with the highest numbers of Russian-speakers in 2007 were New York City (30%),

Los Angeles (6.3%), Chicago (4.6%) and San Francisco (3.7%) (US Census Bureau, 2010).

Russian-speaking immigrants comprise a religiously, ethnically and racially diverse group, emigrating from 14 different countries. As such, cultures and traditions vary widely across this immigrant group, with some countries holding Eastern European values and others resembling a blend of Eastern European, Asian and Middle Eastern traditions. Their proficiency and connectivity to the Russian language also vary owing to the status of the language in their home country, its presence or absence in schools and the nation's political position in relation to Russia. Therefore, one can no longer identify a Russian 'speech community' within the US and beyond. Instead, speakers form 'diasporic plural networks' with areas of convergence and divergence across languages, cultures and geographic regions. Nevertheless, the Russian language serves as a bridge that connects people throughout their nations of origin and in the US. When it comes to their English development, 50% of Russian-speakers in the US and 63% residing in NYC feel that they 'speak English less than very well' (US Census Bureau, 2009). Clearly, Russian speakers in the US are at different places in their bilingualism.

Demographics and New York Communities

New York State is home to over one-quarter of all Russian-speakers in the US, which makes it the largest Russian-speaking population across the 50 states. In 2009 the state was home to 202,225 speakers of Russian (US Census Bureau, 2009). New York City's five boroughs account for 90% of the Russian-speaking population in the state.

In 2008, the Russian language was the third most commonly spoken language other than English in the NYC region, following Spanish and Chinese. The largest concentration of Russian speakers in the US is found in Brooklyn. A total of 63% of the city's Russian speakers reside in Brooklyn, 20% are in Queens and the remaining 17% are scattered among the remaining three boroughs of Manhattan, Bronx and Staten Island (US Census Bureau, 2008c). According to the Jewish Community Study of New York, there are 202,000[2] Russian-speaking Jews living within the city's five boroughs (Ukeles & Miller, 2004).

Educational Achievement in Schools

The literature on Russian-speaking students in US schools and their academic achievement is sparse. Possible reasons for the invisibility of this group may be that Russian-speaking students have traditionally fared well in schools, and as a result, have not garnered specific attention in the research. Many Russian-speaking immigrants arrive in the US with strong formal schooling backgrounds, especially in the areas of maths and science, and some exposure to the English language. Second, most are white and middle class. Finally, because of the group's diversity, it is difficult to study Russian speakers. Nevertheless, within the NYC school system there has been some attention on this student population.

In 2009/2010, Russian speakers made up 1.9% of students labeled 'English language learners' (ELL) in NYC schools. They are the seventh largest ethnolinguistic emergent bilingual group in the city (Infante, 2010). This is a decrease from the previous decade, when Russian-speaking emergent bilinguals comprised 12.5% of the whole emergent bilingual population, and were the fourth largest ethnolinguistic group in NYC schools (Stiefel et al., 2003). The reasons for this decrease are twofold. First, the more recent multilingual immigrants from former Soviet republics may not identify Russian as their primary language owing to the reclaiming and repositioning of other languages in their home countries. Second, the US, NYC included, has seen a rise in immigration from other regions of the world, specifically Latin America and Southeast Asia (Camarota, 2007).

In 2008, 34% of Russian-speaking emergent bilinguals at the fourth-grade level met the NY State ELA exam (English Language Arts) standards, compared with 61.5% of English-proficient students who took the test. Russian-speaking emergent bilingual fourth-graders were placed eighth, after those who spoke Polish, Korean, Chinese, French, Punjabi, Bengali, and Urdu. At the eighth-grade level, 13% of Russian-speaking emergent bilinguals met the NYS ELA standard, outscored only by Korean and Polish emergent bilinguals. In 2008 77% of Russian-speaking fourth-graders and 59% of eighth-graders met the state maths exam standards. These results place Russian emergent bilinguals in the top half of standardized achievement for NYC students labeled English language learners (NYCDOE, 2009a).

When we consider the achievement of Russian-speaking bilingual students who are deemed 'English proficient' by the NYC schools (and are not labeled English language learners), they also do well on standardized tests. Overall, these bilingual students score 0.675 standard deviations above English (only) speakers on English reading assessments and 0.856 standard deviations above English speakers on standardized assessments in maths (Stiefel et al., 2003). Therefore, Russian-speaking bilingual students tend to do well academically when compared with others. The reasons may stem from high levels of formal education of their parents. Furthermore, students may also be attending the enrichment community programs we describe in the next section that not only provide them with support in home language practices, but also deepen their academic content learning. Finally, students who are immigrants or the children of immigrants who willingly came to the country may do better in schools owing to a heightened awareness of the educational and economic opportunities available to them in the US in contrast to their family's country of origin (Ogbu & Simons, 1998).

NYC Russian Bilingual Programs

While many children of Russian-speaking families acclimate to US schools where the primary language of instruction is English, there are alternatives in maintaining, developing and extending their children's bilingualism. New York City Russian bilingual programs exist in both the public and private sectors.

At the private level, NYC is home to cultural centers that offer Russian language classes in addition to programs in the arts for children and adults; private schools that offer after-school and Saturday-school Russian language and cultural enrichment programs; and bilingual summer camps that allow children to use the Russian language through activities that integrate the arts and academic content. These programs, started by families and organizations, create opportunities for children to have consistent exposure to the Russian language and culture, aspects that are often absent in their formal schooling. They are sustained through tuition funds that allow them to secure space, hire educators and advertise to the larger Russian-speaking community. Private and community-based programs are more difficult to quantify, as no database exists to track the wide range of programs available in NYC. An Internet search reveals that these programs are mostly found in the boroughs of Brooklyn and Manhattan, with fewer than five programs geared toward students at the Pre-K–12 school grade group.

Within the public schools there are only two Russian language programs at the elementary level, one that is designed for students who are deemed gifted and talented, and another for Russian-speaking and non-Russian-speaking students to learn together in a two-way bilingual immersion program. Most Russian-speaking emergent bilingual students are placed in English as a Second Language programs. These sparse bilingual offerings within the public schools speak to the devaluing of the education of students in languages other than English and the subsequent push for communities to create their own programs where languages are viewed as an asset for all American children.

The sections that follow provide a descriptive overview of two Russian bilingual programs in NYC. The first is a privately run Saturday program that offers instruction in the Russian language, but goes beyond just language to incorporate academics and the arts. The second case is that of a public school two-way bilingual immersion program that became the focal point of a heated debate around its existence in a multicultural and multilingual neighborhood. While the programs differ in many ways, they share the ethnolinguistic group's desire to make Russian language education a central aspect of their children's education.

Saturdays of learning Russian language, culture and academic enrichment

SchoolPlus is located in Manhattan, a borough that does not have a large percentage of Russian speakers and in a neighborhood that is not densely populated by Russians. Nevertheless, the school creates its own language and learning community with its students and their families, who predominantly come from Russian-speaking backgrounds. They come together on Saturdays during the academic year to take part in a range of courses in Russian, as well as in different content areas and the arts. The school, which has been in existence for seven years, rents classroom space from a private university. It is part of a larger organization of similar educational sites that began in order to allow families to provide their children with the opportunity to develop their Russian language and cultural connections, while also supporting academic enrichment.

The diversity of the student body is reflective of the school's Russian focus, as well as the multiculturalism prevalent in NYC. Some students are immigrants or children of Russian-speaking immigrants, while others are products of inter-ethnic marriages and have one parent who speaks Russian. Approximately one-quarter of these families are of Jewish descent, which is reflective of the larger Russian Jewish population in NYC and the US, who fled from former Soviet republics as political refugees. The majority of students, who range from 3 to 12 years of age, come from families with Russian-speaking backgrounds. Some students grew up bilingually while others have been exposed to Russian in their homes, but over time have grown to speak only English. The latter group may approach the Saturday classes with resistance and even resentment towards their parents for 'forcing' them to spend their time learning Russian, while others have already moved through the defiance and/or shame of speaking a language other than English and have come to embrace their home language and are willing or even happy to have the chance to become bilingual.

Students of non-Russian speaking backgrounds come to the school for a variety of reasons. One Japanese-American student had a Russian-speaking nanny as a young child and was in the program to continue his language learning. An African-American student played the violin, and as a result of the musical heritage associated with the Russian culture, wanted to take this a step further and study the language. The school positions the Russian language as a resource for students from all backgrounds (Ruiz, 1988), and as an asset for their futures.

The Saturday program is set up to provide a wide range of courses as options for its students. The school offers leveled Russian classes to those who are native speakers, as well as students learning it as an additional language. Beyond the Russian classes, students may also take classes in English, maths, physics, chess, theater and art. Some of these classes are offered in Russian, but others are taught through English. The rationale behind offering such courses is to expose students to areas for which the culture associated with Russian has traditionally been known. As such, the foundation of numeracy, in-depth mathematical knowledge and love of the discipline take center stage at the school, side by side with the Russian language.

The Russian drama classes allow students to participate in staged performances of modern Russian writers and poets as well as world-famous authors whose works are translated into Russian. During the winter of 2010, the drama class put on a well-attended and received performance of 'Кошкин дом' ['The Cat's House'], a tale by Pavel Shumil. Chess is a sport that has been dominated by Russian players and has become closely connected with Russian culture. The school boasts a champion Russian chess player who teaches beginner and advanced classes. The FSU is also known for its strong background in the areas of maths and physics. This is evidenced by the many FSU-educated immigrant engineers and scientists in the US. Both of these classes are instructed in English by teachers who have Russian-speaking backgrounds, most of whom hail from the FSU. They may use different methods of instruction and thereby go beyond the Russian language to bridge its cultural strengths and pedagogical traditions. The program provides students with a space to become bilingual as they perform their bicultural identities through the various opportunities.

SchoolPlus is a hub for Russian language learning, cultural connectivity and academic development. The vision of the school, as elaborated by the director, is for students to love learning, especially when it comes to their bilingual abilities and in academic areas such as maths and science. The school fills a gap in terms of language offerings, pedagogy and cultural ties that are missing from the education of many Russian-speaking children and those who want to learn more about Russian language and culture. As evidenced by the program's name, the educational center both enhances and enriches the education that children receive in their formal K–8 schools.

A community's fight for a public school's Russian bilingual education program

Aside from the community Russian programs available across the boroughs of NYC, a small number of public schools also offer Russian bilingual education programs to their students. A two-way or dual-language bilingual education program was started in a heavily populated Russian-speaking community with family backing, regional and central office support and an interest by the school's then-principal and staff (J. Fraga, personal communication, 16 June 2010). This program was the first Russian program of its kind in its region. It began as a side-by-side model with an English and Russian component teacher at the kindergarten level, and has since grown by one grade level each year. Although the program was intended for both Russian- and English-speaking students (as well as those from other language groups), almost all of the students came from Russian-speaking families. As such, the program began to resemble a one-way bilingual immersion program. Year by year the program began to gain momentum as the only such program in the City. Russian-speaking families began to move into the surrounding neighborhood to be able to offer their children a bilingual education through their home language as well as English.

Following three years of implementation and the retirement of the program's founding principal, the school's new administration announced plans to shut down the program because of budget and space issues, as well as low student achievement, insufficient interest and enrollment. Ironically, this announcement came only two years after the US government rolled out its National Security Language Initiative. Russian was listed among the 'critical languages' under this plan 'to expand US foreign language education beginning in kindergarten and continuing throughout formal schooling and into the workforce with new programs and resources' (US Department of Education, n.d.: 1).

This announcement launched a battle, pitting the school's newly formed administration and parents of different ethnolinguisitic groups against Russian-speaking families, Russian activist groups and larger immigration advocacy organizations, such as the New York Immigration Coalition, Advocates for Children and the New York State Association of Bilingual Education. Although the school had a large Russian-speaking student body, it was also diverse, with students of Chinese, Spanish and Arabic speaking populations, among others. Although the root causes of the proposed shut-down by the administration were programmatic in nature, the debate became racially and ethnically contentious in ways never originally intended. Some parents whose home languages were not offered in the school's programming for their children began to feel resentment around the perceived catering to the white Russian-speaking students and their families. In addition to linguistic and racial differences, some of the students in the Russian program were also Jewish. Anti-Semitism might also have been a factor in the attempt to close down the Russian bilingual program. Taken together, the negative sentiments that were developing toward the Russian-speaking families, coupled with the administration's stance, stirred tensions along racial and ethnolinguistic lines and subsequently threatened to shut down the Russian bilingual program, the only one of its kind in all of NYC.

In an effort to save the program, the Russian-speaking parents took it upon themselves to investigate the achievement of students in the program, as well as parental interest and enrollment, the areas of concern raised by the administration. They uncovered that students were scoring well on standardized measures, to the extent that they outperformed emergent bilinguals who were not in dual language bilingual programs, as well as English-speaking students in general education programs (A. Benjamin-Gomez, personal communication, 10 May 2011). Furthermore, it was found that the number of applications for the program was sufficient for it to continue and receive funding (M. Kalenkevitch, personal communication, 2 January 2011). As the conflict waged on, petitions were circulated on both sides of the issue among NYC media outlets.

One of the key advocates of the school, a member of the Metropolitan Russian-American Parent Association, wrote the following in a letter that was disseminated across educational and immigration-related listserves:

Regardless of the orientation outcome, we all Russians, Asians, Latinos and others live in the same neighborhood and our children go into the same school. The hate that is growing right now is going to stay in our neighborhood and in our school. This is dangerous. This has to be stopped before it turns into something tragic. (Email communication, 12 June 2009)

The New York Immigration Coalition, a prominent advocacy group for immigrant rights in the City, also took to the internet via list-serves to take a stance in favor of continuing the school's bilingual program from the perspective of supporting the rights of all immigrant groups:

Despite the cultural and linguistic differences that may exist between different communities, immigrant parents, regardless of their countries of origin, share a lot in common … Russian immigrant parents fought to establish this program, because they determined that it would help their children learn English, while maintaining their native language.

We as members of other immigrant communities stand with them in support of this program. Our communities have absolutely nothing to gain from closing the only Russian dual language program, a program that is designed to help immigrant students learn English and succeed in school. We hope that members of all of the school's vibrant and diverse communities will also stand with the Russian parents and their allies as they fight to keep this important program open. (Email communication, 15 June 2009)

Following many contentious meetings, letters and media attention, the program was ultimately allowed to continue. It was deemed that there would be enough students entering at the kindergarten level to keep it running and growing one grade level per year. This outcome demonstrates the importance of the community and its role as advocates in public education, as it highlights the need to provide many and varied ways for students to become bilingual in different educational settings. Furthermore, it positions families as central figures in the language programming decisions of schools, as opposed to the more common method of implementing external (and often monolingual) mandates for bilingual American children.

The Accept–Reject Spectrum of Russian Bilingual Education in Private–Public Spheres

The diaspora of Russian speakers across the globe is vast. NYC brings together this diverse group and provides a range of spaces for emergent bilingual students to use and develop their Russian language in both private and public educational settings. While the Russian bilingual education programs across public and private spheres intersect in terms of their values and goals, rooted in their desire to make the language a relevant part of children's education and future, they also diverge in their degree of acceptance. In private schools, such as the one discussed here, the programs tend to be embraced by a diverse group of students and their families, who have all chosen the school and as a result have laid a strong foundation of support for the program to exist and thrive. Within public education settings, there can be more of a competitive nature for language programming, especially in areas with significant racial, ethnic and linguistic diversity. Therefore, the creation of public programs requires intra- and inter- group conversations to develop language programming that is equitable and considers larger issues of demographics, systemic availability and inclusion of different stakeholders.

The importance of a combination of private and public Russian bilingual education offerings is essential to meeting the logistical, geographical, economic, linguistic and academic needs and desires of the diverse students and families these programs serve. The cases described here offer lessons for educational planning for emergent bilingual programs across ethnolinguistic groups. First, while it is important to develop students' bilingual practices, it is also important to make positive connections to cultural aspects associated with the related language(s). Educators can seek out pedagogical approaches that have been successful in other countries and languages. Therefore, looking at bilingual programs through the languages of instruction alone is a rather narrow lens that can fail to take in the richness of an ethnolinguistic community.

The number of Russian-speaking children in NYC far exceeds the number of students who have the opportunities to use the language in schools. As a result, Russian-speaking bilinguals may find their home language and culture absent from formal schooling. For students to have access to a culturally and linguistically relevant education we must rely on the combination and partnership of public schools, private programs and community support, be it geographically founded or created by common beliefs, to come together to ensure that bilingual students are not only bilingual in their homes, but also in their schools and communities.

Notes

(1) Within this chapter we use the term Russian speakers, as opposed to Russians, because it more accurately reflects the diversity of a population that originates from and inhabits the nations across the Former Soviet Union, as well as other regions of the world.

(2) There are discrepancies in the reporting of the number of Russian speakers in New York, particularly among Jewish households, as evidenced in the statistics from American Community Survey (US Census Bureau, 2009) and the Jewish Community Study of New York (Ukeles & Miller, 2004).

18 Mandarin–English Bilingual Education in New York City: A Case Study of Supplementary Education in the Chinese Community

Wen-Tsui Pat Lo

Introduction

It is well known that many Asians value education above personal pleasure and would make drastic sacrifices in order to achieve academic success. Becoming proficient in English, of course, is the pre-requisite of achieving academic success in American society. At the same time, spoken by over a billion people in the world and over a half a million people in New York City, Mandarin Chinese is emerging as one of the most sought after languages to learn in the 21st century. As more students learn Chinese as a foreign language in the US, Chinese heritage language learners, as well as recent Chinese immigrant students, have sensed a growing need for the use of Mandarin Chinese language and have organized community support to maintain this language while working hard to master content area learning in English. This chapter provides a brief overview of the Mandarin language and Chinese immigrants in the US, with a particular focus on education-related issues.

The Chinese community has a long-established culture of enrolling children in cram schools and complementary test prep programs. Their approach is to drill and practice until a task is done correctly. However, many after-school and weekend programs organized by the Chinese community, who use public schools as their program sites, have adopted some of the teaching approaches of their host schools. In doing so, they attempt to strike a balance between methods of rote learning and encouraging creative thinking, supported by individual attention to learning. Through strong channels of communication, after-school program teachers provide pertinent information for and about the students they share with the regular day school teachers. At times, many of these not-for-profit organizations also play an import role in supporting immigrant children by attending to their social and psychological needs and by working as mediators, or communicators, between public schools and the families of their students.

A case study of PS 20 in Queens demonstrates the ways in which New York City's self-reliant Chinese community supports Chinese students to become bilingual Americans through diverse educational programming in collaboration with one public school. Drawing on the teachers' and students' linguistic repertoires, a dynamic approach to bilingual community education supports the learning of emergent bilinguals in this Chinese-speaking community.

The Mandarin language

Mandarin Chinese, recognized as an official language in China, Taiwan and Singapore, is the first language of approximately 885,000,000 people worldwide, making Mandarin speakers the largest first-language group. The number of Mandarin Chinese speakers exceeds the combined total of Spanish, English and Bengali first-language speakers (Lewis, 2009). Chinese who speak other 'dialects' such as Shanghainese, Cantonese and Fukienese[1] are mostly bilingual and learn Mandarin as an additional language.

The basic sentence structure of Chinese follows the subject–verb–object order. It has no morphological changes. For example, there are no subject–verb tense agreements or singular and plural distinctions. Time is indicated by adverbial phrases while the form of the verb stays unchanged.

A unique feature of the spoken language, which presents a great challenge to many language learners, is its tonal system – the same sound with different tones bears different meanings. A simple sound 'yi' has over 100 corresponding characters, with four different tones in Mandarin Chinese. Speakers of other Chinese dialects may also have difficulty pronouncing the four tones correctly, as they are affected by the tones in their own dialects, making context extremely important in oral language comprehension. For example, some dialects, such as Cantonese and Shanghainese, have more than four tones.

The Chinese written language is character-based. Unlike other early pictograph-based writing systems, which eventually developed a phonetic alphabet to represent the sounds of their spoken languages, Chinese is the only major writing system that has continued its pictographic-based development without interruption. However, not all Chinese characters are impressionistic depictions of concrete objects. Many Chinese characters have incorporated meanings and sound, as well as visual images, into a coherent whole.

Chinese characters have also been used in countries neighboring China. Names in Korea and Japan can still be written in 'Hanja' and 'Kanji', both meaning 'Han' (Chinese) characters. Both languages, especially Korean, have borrowed much vocabulary from the Chinese (Omniglot, 1998). Before local writing systems were developed, ancient Korean literature and documents were recorded in Chinese characters (see Chapter 5).

Modern written Chinese is depicted in two forms: simplified characters, which are common in Mainland China and Singapore, and traditional characters, which are common in Taiwan and Hong Kong. Although both forms can be observed in Chinese ethnic neighborhoods in the US, most of the street signs and store signs are in traditional characters. No matter which form they use, Chinese-speaking students in the US have at least one more challenge: the character-based language does not offer the use of cognate strategies, as observed with students from Roman alphabet language backgrounds who are learning English or developing related languages. While Spanish-speaking students can make an easy transfer from 'tradicional' in Spanish to 'tradition' in English, Chinese students have to memorize the meaning of the English word and must often rely on a dictionary.

The People's Republic of China created the Roman alphabet-based Pinyin system in the 1950s as an auxiliary tool to help people pronounce each character. Today, Pinyin is widely used to assist with early literacy development and learning Chinese as a foreign language. However, the Chinese sound represented by the Roman alphabet letter may differ from the sound that the same letter represents in English. For example, the Chinese sound 'ts' is represented by the Roman alphabet letter 'c' in Pinyin.

Understanding the striking differences between the Chinese and the English languages, one can imagine the challenges that face Chinese immigrant students when trying to adjust to American society and to excel academically. Yet, Chinese immigrant students as a group outperform students from other ethnic groups. How do they do it? Before we present a case study to exemplify how the New York City Chinese community makes extra efforts to adapt to the mainstream culture while keeping its own identity, one must have an understanding of the history of Chinese immigration to the US and some of the educational issues particular to the Chinese community.

History of Chinese immigration to the US

Chinese immigration to the US started in the mid 19th century when immigrants worked as laborers, receiving little pay for their work. Despite the contributions they made in building railroads and mining, the Chinese suffered racial discrimination and were referred to as the 'yellow peril'. In 1882, The US Congress passed the Chinese Exclusion Act, which prohibited immigration from China for the following 10 years. This law, which was extended in 1892, was the only US law to prevent immigration and naturalization on the basis of race (Chin, 1998). Other laws passed thereafter not only excluded new immigrants, but also denied citizenship and prevented Chinese from marrying Caucasians or owning land (Chin, 1996).

Owing to historical hostility and discrimination, earlier Chinese immigrants mostly settled in 'Chinatown' areas, taking low-paying jobs and establishing their own grocery, laundry and restaurant businesses. These immigrants mostly spoke Cantonese or Toisanese (Taishanese). Many of their children, despite the hurdles they had to overcome, have successfully become part of mainstream American society.

The current wave of Chinese immigration started with the passing of the Immigration and Nationality Act of 1965, which raised the quota of Asian immigrants.[2] In the 1970s, immigrants primarily from Taiwan and Hong Kong began to settle in the US. With the passage of the 1979 Refugee Act, overseas Chinese who fled Vietnam, Cambodia and Laos arrived as refugees to find a new home in the US, thus making the Chinese community even more diverse in languages and origins.

In the 1980s, the origins of the wave of Chinese immigrants extended beyond Taiwan, Hong Kong and major cities in China to the coastal towns and villages of the Fujian and Zhejiang provinces. This relatively new group of immigrants, who came to America in pursuit of a better life, changed the composition of some neighborhoods and formed new Chinatowns. Some entered the US illegally, paying a great deal of money to smugglers (or 'snake heads' in Chinese) and working long hours to pay back the smuggler debt and to send money home. In some cases, their children who were born in the US were sent back to China to save childcare expenses. Upon returning to the US and entering school, these children are identified as English language learners and face social and language adjustment issues.

In 2009 there were 3,204,379 people of Chinese ancestry in the US, 3,106,005 of whom claimed their ancestry as Chinese, whereas 98,374 claimed to be Taiwanese (US Census Bureau, 2009). The Chinese are the largest Asian ethnic group. About half of the immigrants from China have settled primarily in two states – California (1,197,709 total in 2009) and New York (562,094 total in 2009; US Census Bureau, 2009). Surprisingly, Wyoming and Nebraska have seen a rapid increase in the Chinese immigrant population in recent years. Metropolitan areas with large Chinese-American populations include Los Angeles, San Francisco, San Diego, Houston, Dallas, New York, Philadelphia, Chicago, Washington, DC and Boston (Ameredia, 2008).

Chinese-Americans are a very diverse group. They arrived in the US at different times and from different areas and they speak different dialects. Sometimes communication between the subgroups of Chinese immigrants is difficult, affected by differences in language and political ideologies.

However, Asians are perceived to be the model minority (Le, 2011b). Despite a history of adversity and hardship, Asian-Americans have a higher college degree attainment rate and greater median family income than whites, blacks, Latinos and Native Americans. Chinese-Americans, who comprise the largest ethnic group of Asian-Americans, are considered leaders in this model minority image (Le, 2011a). However, this seemingly successful group does not represent all Chinese-Americans. Many, especially new arrivals, struggle to make ends meet.

Present educational issues

The Chinese regard education as the primary way to change their lives for the better. The national system of high-stakes examinations has been the traditional mechanism for success and advancement in China since the seventh century. Therefore, Chinese parents and students are very familiar with high-stakes examinations that emphasize national standards and results-driven learning. As such, they seldom spend time questioning why students are tested so often or whether the tests really reflect student learning. Instead, they invest their energy and money in preparing their children to meet the examination challenge. Test preparation programs or 'cram schools' are very common in the Chinese community. Parents are willing to make sacrifices to provide their children with additional opportunities for academic learning.

The portrayal of a model minority, discussed previously, also applies to students. In New York City, Asian students have the highest graduation rate at 80.1% and the lowest dropout rate at 5.9%, outperforming other ethnicities (NYCDOE, 2010b). The 2009 school enrollment data indicate that, in the highly competitive specialized high schools, Asians comprise approximately 60% of the student population (e.g. Stuyvesant High School, 67.3%; Bronx High School of Science, 61.4%; and Brooklyn Technical High School, 57.4%). Furthermore, Suárez-Orozco *et al.*'s (2008) five-year longitudinal study found that, among five groups of immigrant students from China, the Dominican Republic, Central America, Haiti and Mexico, Chinese students were the only group whose grade-point average did not decline over the five-year period.

Research indicates, however, that the characteristics of Chinese culture that facilitate this high educational achievement come at a price. For example, Gielen and Lei (2010) reported maladaptive psychosocial consequences, such as adolescents (especially girls) exhibiting high rates of depression and anxiety, low levels of self-esteem, excessive self-criticism and feelings of guilt. Furthermore, not all Chinese-American students are academically well prepared. Qiu and Zhao (2009) point out that Asian-American students' academic achievement is the result of conscious choice, not genetic determination, and their academic excellence tends to mask their psychological problems. They recommend treating each student as an individual, understanding that Asian-American students do not excel in all areas, and acknowledging, identifying and addressing the psychological problems that may arise from the pressure to excel.

This is particularly true in the case of recent immigrant students. Educators need to make a conscious effort to treat each student individually. Chinese immigrant students have diverse needs; some have a better command of English and prior knowledge of academic content. They need support to connect their new learning to their existing knowledge. Others are just starting to learn English, while some may not have been exposed to the content knowledge that they are now required to master. In some cases, students start schooling late or have missed school for a few years and are playing 'catch up'.

Recently-arrived older adolescent immigrant students, in particular, exhibit difficulties learning English and the demanding content area material at the same time. Some students are 'persuaded' to leave the regular school and to participate in the General Educational Development (GED) program after reaching 18 years of age. However, without Chinese bilingual support in the GED program, these students rarely complete the GED preparation program because they must take the tests in English.[3]

The educational experiences of Chinese students are further impacted by encounters with bias and discrimination. Chinese students are often victims of bullying by non-Chinese students. There have been reports of serious tensions and confrontations both inside and outside of schools. The National Education Association (2005) reported that Asian-American and Pacific

Islander students are 'the targets of both overt and subtle forms of racism'. Notably, the unjust treatment of Chinese students in Brooklyn's former Lafayette High School (Gootman, 2004) and the assault on Chinese students in Philadelphia (Thompson, 2010) resulted in a ruling by the Justice Department that requires school districts to devise and implement plans to prevent such occurrences. While extreme bias incidents like those at Lafayette High School and the Philadelphia School District have ceased, an anti-Asian-American bias lingers and needs to be addressed.

The Language in New York City and its Educational Programs

Demographics and New York communities

In New York City, 313,812 reported speaking Chinese at home in 2000 (US Census Bureau, 2000) and that figure has been estimated to have risen to nearly half a million in 2010 (New York City Department of City Planning, 2011). The Borough of Queens has the largest Chinese population. New York City Department of Education data indicate that emergent bilinguals, those classified as English language learners (ELLs) from Chinese speaking backgrounds, comprise 11.4% (17,068) of the total ELL population and are the second largest language group (NYCDOE, 2009b). The Chinese-speaking emergent bilinguals are concentrated in Manhattan's Chinatown, Brooklyn's Sunset Park and Queens' Flushing areas, where neighborhoods are established as 'Chinatowns'. There are more Chinese-speaking recent immigrant students residing in Brooklyn (NYCDOE, 2009b).

Manhattan Chinatown, the poorest of the three Chinese ethnic neighborhoods, started out as an area where Cantonese was the dominant language in the early days of immigration. However, with the influx of recent immigrants from other parts of China, many dialects, such as Shanghainese, Fukienese and Wenzhouese, are now also spoken. Mandarin Chinese, as the official language in China and second language to many Chinese immigrants, has become prevalent and has gained popularity as the common language for communication. All of the schools in this neighborhood have Chinese bilingual staff members and have some form of bilingual education to provide language and academic assistance to newly arrived immigrants.

Brooklyn's Chinatown is the newest and the fastest growing Chinese neighborhood in New York City. The population shift within the past 10 years challenges educators to meet the needs of recent immigrant students from China. For example, PS 105, located on 59th Street, just two blocks away from the busy Eighth Avenue, now has the largest population of Chinese recent immigrants, with over 800 Chinese ELLs requiring English as a second language (ESL)/bilingual services. Neighboring schools also have large Chinese populations and require appropriately licensed Chinese bilingual staff, especially those speaking various dialects, to meet the needs of their students and families.

Schools in Flushing serve a more diverse population, including Koreans and Indo-Paks, as well as Latinos, African-Americans and Caucasians. PS 20 and JHS 189 are in the heart of Flushing and both have a high population of Chinese students. Recognizing the changing demographics of the Chinese student population, many schools have started to add Chinese bilingual programs and staff members who speak Mandarin.

Educational programs

While many public schools work hard to serve their Chinese speaking emergent bilinguals, the number of Chinese transitional bilingual programs (TBE) has decreased at the high school level. The decrease is due to the creation of small high schools that have reduced the pool of students necessary to form bilingual classes in these schools. There are currently 32 schools, including elementary, middle and high schools, that offer Chinese TBE programs. On the other hand, five elementary and one high school offer dual language programs in Mandarin Chinese and American English (NYCDOE, 2010c), with the purpose of serving recent immigrant students and heritage language learners, as well as students from other language backgrounds.

Chinese as a foreign language programs have also been on the increase nationwide in response to international recognition of the emerging economic and political power of China, despite the decrease of other foreign language programs (Rhodes & Pufahl, 2010). During the 2010–2011 school year, 63 public and charter schools and 25 private schools were reported to have a Chinese language program in New York City (ALBETAC, 2010).

In addition to the public and private day programs, there are more than 60 Chinese language programs in New York City offered during the time that schools are not in session. Although there is no official count, it is estimated that these programs serve over 13,000 students with 1100 teachers. All these programs and schools provide Chinese language and culture instruction with the goal of nurturing young Chinese-Americans to become bicultural and biliterate. Some receive the support of free textbooks and professional development from the governments of Taiwan or the People's Republic of China.

In addition to Chinese language programs, there are many independent not-for-profit and for-profit after-school and weekend programs that reinforce and extend the instruction received during the school day, such as ESL instruction, test preparation, academic acceleration and enrichment. Some programs include recreational and cultural activities, such as Chinese dance and Kung-fu. After-school programs that lease space from public schools often serve to complement and supplement services offered during the school day.

The majority of after-school and weekend programs are self-sustaining through nominal tuition fees. A handful of these programs are subsidized by New York City government. Some of them run after-school centers and summer programs, providing a combination of Chinese language and academic enrichment for students. Although only some of these program teachers are New York State certified, program directors make every effort to ensure alignment and cohesion with the public school curriculum and standards.

With these features in mind, the following case study of PS 20 in Flushing will be presented to show how a public school collaborates with different community-based organizations in serving their shared Chinese bilingual student populations through after-school and weekend programs. Classroom observations will be used to illustrate how teachers in the various programs housed at the school address their students' learning needs by making use of their multiple linguistic resources. The case suggests that a dynamic approach to bilingual community education supports the various learning needs of emergent bilinguals in this Chinese-speaking community.

PS 20 in Flushing: A Case Study of After-school and Weekend Programs in a Bilingual Community

Located in the heart of Flushing, Queens, PS 20 has a diverse student population. Although the school offers after-school programs with its Title I and Title III funds,[4] these programs are limited in scope and do not fulfill the range of learning supports needed by PS 20's bilingual community. However, the school's convenient location has attracted several not-for-profit organizations that house their learning support programs there.

Of the 1460 students that comprise PS 20's total population, 65% are East and South Asian, mostly of Chinese language backgrounds. Of the total population, 40% receive ESL service and of these 70% are Chinese (NYCDOE, 2010d). A Mandarin bilingual program is provided at the kindergarten level. Newly arrived Chinese immigrant students in other grades receive Chinese language support in content area learning from ESL and classroom teachers who speak Mandarin. Beyond the regular school hours, there are five academic enrichment after-school programs and two weekend programs operated by not-for-profit organizations.

Principal Victoria Hart of PS 20[5] welcomes these programs to 'build the sense of support to the community' (interview, 6 January 2011). She considers the providers part of the PS 20 family, although she admits that sharing space can sometimes be challenging. In order to maintain on-going communication, she convenes bimonthly meetings with the directors of the support programs to discuss administrative and educational issues. On parent–teacher conference afternoons and evenings, teachers from these programs volunteer to work as translators; sometimes they also provide additional information about the children they help after school (interview with Hart, 6 January 2011). Thus, through a joint commitment, the support programs and the housing school actively collaborate to support their shared students.

Description of after-school and weekend programs

Five academic after-school programs co-exist and use more than 30 classrooms throughout the three-story public school building. Together, they serve 550 students from grades 1 to 6 from 3:30 to 6:00 pm daily. Most of these students are from the housing school, PS 20. Some are from neighboring schools. About 90% of these children are of Chinese background. The Chinese American Planning Council (CPC) is the largest program and has the longest history of serving children at PS 20. Other programs include Huanyu School, Weibo Organization, Little Sweet Geniuses and PEACE Academy. The CPC program receives funding from the New York City Department of Youth and Community Development for its 200 identified low-income-family children and it charges a minimal fee for another 40 children. The other four programs are managed by not-for-profit community-based organizations. Parents pay about US$200–250 monthly to enroll their children in the program.

It is worth noting that the directors of these programs are experienced educators. Ms Lois Chin Lee (Director of the CPC) is a trained reading specialist and has worked with students for 40 years as a teacher and an administrator. Ms Sumin Liu (Huanyu School) was a teacher, a curriculum coordinator and a principal in an academically high performing elementary school in Zhengzhou, China. Ms Jianbo Wei (Weibo Organization) is recognized as an outstanding early childhood program teacher in China. These experienced leaders may use different approaches in their programs, but they share the same vision of helping Chinese immigrant students succeed in school and contribute to American society in the future.

Academics are the focus of all five programs. In addition to homework help, the programs offer structured teaching and learning. Supplementary readings are aligned with the New York City curriculum; mini-lessons are designed to help students with targeted language skills; cultural projects help students learn about American culture while supporting their home cultures. Instruction in these after-school programs is mostly conducted in English; however, the Chinese-speaking bilingual staff uses both languages to get the message across. Further, while memorization and drills continue to be valued, students are encouraged to express their opinions and ideas.

CPC's after-school program at PS 20 started in 1987 and currently serves 240 students in grades 1–5. Each of its 12 classes has two teachers and at least one volunteer from a local high school or college. Ms Lee proudly explains her philosophy of education as adopting the 'whole child' approach. As such, the CPC program incorporates music and arts, a sports component and social skills development. Other activities include civics education and community service during the summer (interview with Lee, 20 December 2010). Having been recognized for its uniqueness in collaborating with the public school and successfully managing the after-school and summer programs, CPC at PS 20 received the prestigious 'Effective School Award' in 2001 from the Council of Supervisors and Administrators (CSA; New York City principals and supervisors union) and was featured in the February *CSA News* (Silverstein, 2011).

With a heavy emphasis on academics, the other programs proudly report the learning progress of their students. Ms Liu (Huanyu School) specifically conducted an informal study in 2009 and found that students who attended the after-school program scored significantly higher on the Huanyu summer school placement test in reading than those who did not (personal communication, 2010).

Many Chinese parents believe that bringing up their children to be bilingual will not only help maintain their cultural heritage, but will also increase opportunities for their children's future employment. Although the number is increasing, Chinese language programs are still not common in public schools. On Saturdays, Huanyu and Weibo are open for Chinese language learning. In the Saturday program, schools use totally different sets of books that focus on Chinese language arts. The program teachers may or may not be English-proficient, but they bring with them a wealth of knowledge and experience. For example, Ms Zuo, the Program Coordinator of Weibo, is among several staff members who have graduated from prestigious Chinese teacher education universities and have taught for many years in China. A few teachers are also studying to become New York State certified teachers.

A general concern shared by all of the after-school and weekend programs is the need for psychological and social guidance and support for children and their families. Culturally, many Chinese parents place complete trust in schools, leaving the responsibility for academic education to teachers. Most parents of the after-school program students also work long hours and may not be proficient in English. Therefore, they rely on the bilingual staff in the after-school program to help them resolve educational and sometimes life issues. The bilingual staff invests time talking to parents about how to work with schools. According to CPC Director Lee, 'It is important that a parent comes to school knowing how his or her child's name is spelled in English and what grade the child goes to. We are here only to teach them how to do it; we do not do it for them because they need to learn' (interview, 20 December 2010).

In some cases, both parents work out of state and children are entrusted to friends and relatives. Sometimes, the children do not get to see their parents for weeks. In other cases, new immigrant students who were born in the US, but were sent back to China for childcare, rejoin their parents several years later. They need to get to know their parents while trying to make sense of their new environment. The emotional stress experienced by children sometimes leads to violent or withdrawn behaviors. With the support and care of the after-school programs, children's behaviors have improved.

After-school program classroom snapshots

The following snapshots, drawn from classroom observations of the various programs on two different occasions, help paint a picture of how teachers address their students' learning needs and how the dynamic interactions draw on students' linguistic repertoires. In this way, these language interactions appear to serve various purposes, including attention-seeking, negotiating meaning and inclusion.

Ms Augustus, a teacher in the CPC program, was conducting a Read Aloud activity in English in her kindergarten class.
She reviewed five spelling words that the children had learned and wrote the numbers 1 to 5 on the board as the children called out the numbers: 'One, Two . . .'. Then a Chinese boy called out: 'Tres, Cuatro, Cinco'. Ms. Augustus looked at the boy and wondered out loud: 'Where did you learn that Spanish?' The class laughed and they continued to count in English. (Fieldnotes, 20 December 2010)

In this lesson, a boy draws on his linguistic repertoire to call out numbers in Spanish during a counting activity, making connections between the languages he is learning beyond the after-school program. He appears to use this strategy in order to gain attention from the teacher and the class. At the same time, this vignette illustrates that the student appears to be aware that such linguistic interactions are viewed favorably in a space where languages are respected.

Meanwhile, in another class, Ms Zhao sat next to a new immigrant first-grade student to help him with his homework. She asked him questions in both Chinese and English. Other non-Chinese speaking staff members also support Chinese students by learning a few phrases in Chinese. For example, Ms Abbasi, who speaks Urdu, Hindi, Punjabi, Bengali and Farsi, is now able to give simple commands in Chinese: 'boyaojianghua' [no talking], she says to the children jokingly as she reviews their homework (fieldnotes, 20 December 2010). In this way, teachers assist students to negotiate meaning by drawing on their linguistic resources and paying respect to their home languages.

In a third class consisting of second- and third-grade students (Weibo School), a student, Jimmy,[6] appeared to participate enthusiastically in an English grammar lesson presented by his teacher, Mr Dan Barrish (fieldnotes, 20 December 2010). Jimmy spoke fluent English, but according to his teacher, he would 'make many mistakes in grammar' (personal communication, 20 December 2010). Hence, the mini-lesson of the day was on regular and irregular past tense.

During the break, Jimmy joined a group of five boys sharing a comic book (in English) based on Japanese 'Bakugan' characters. Although all of the boys spoke Chinese, they switched back and forth from English to Chinese and from Chinese to English. When a non-Chinese-speaking boy, Danny, joined in their conversation, the boys spoke in English to include him (fieldnotes, 20 December 2010).

These classroom vignettes suggest that the language use in the after-school programs is dynamic with speakers of Chinese and English in different places along a continuum. Students and adults alike use language to communicate for various purposes. The common understanding is that language is used to 'make sense' of the things around them. For the purposes of the after-school program, both Chinese and English are used to help students excel academically. Therefore, there are no rules dictating that only a specific language should be used at a particular time. Instead, the bilingual children and staff use all available means to make connections to each other and to support learning. Such 'sense-making' strategies have been described by García (2009a) as 'translanguaging' practices.

Conclusion

Instead of looking at language learning in a linear way, scholars have viewed bilingualism, which can be recursive and simultaneous, as dynamic (García, 2009a). This case study suggests that bilingual educators in the Chinese community of New York are no different. By drawing on their own linguistic repertoire and that of their students, and by creating spaces for dynamic bilingualism, they support students in their academic learning and social development. Dynamic bilingual models suggest that, in a multicultural and multilingual environment, it is common to observe multiple languages being used in order to make sense of surroundings. In contrast, 'English only' policies do not draw upon all of the linguistic skills of 'emergent bilinguals' (García & Kleifgen, 2010) and cannot effectively assess the learning of these children.

In the process of becoming proficient bilinguals, these children can sometimes be misunderstood as having learning disabilities (Klingner *et al.,* 2008). In order to help students learn better and exhibit what they know, educators need to draw on students' full repertoire of language skills. Even though standardized testing is mostly conducted in English, students who are in the process of learning should be allowed and encouraged to express themselves and demonstrate their learning in multiple ways, including using various forms of art as well as using their home language practices.

Several findings can be drawn from the study of after-school and weekend programs in the Chinese community. First, the high regard for education and testing focuses attention on results-driven academic preparation, even in the after-school childcare programs. By enrolling their children in the academically focused Chinese after-school and weekend programs, parents who work long hours not only solve their childcare problem, but also provide additional opportunities to help their children achieve academic success.

Second, the Chinese community demonstrates a high level of self-reliance through supplementary educational support. Instead of depending on the public school system, the not-for-profit programs and the test prep 'cram schools' (which can generate great profits) are flourishing in the Asian community as a manifestation of this self-reliance practice.

Third, except for the Chinese language programs, whose purpose is to help students build Mandarin language proficiency, other weekend or after-school programs are mostly conducted in English. Bilingual educators provide translation and clarification to help children make sense of their learning. This practice has been claimed to be effective in helping recent immigrant children achieve academic success in the after-school programs.

Furthermore, although many Chinese children enter school not speaking English or sometimes having low literacy skills in Chinese, their parents are willing to make 'necessary sacrifices' such as personal pleasure and family time to invest in their children's education. As a result, the children may start at about the same preparedness level as their peers from other language backgrounds, but because of the extra hours of study and the discipline of hard work, they excel over time. The case study of PS 20 focused on children in grades 1–5, but the same observation may be made for older children, as demonstrated by Suárez-Orozco *et al.* (2008).

Finally, the narrow focus on academic achievement by parents some-times leads to the neglect of the social and emotional needs of their children. This can create maladjustment, rebellion and depression, particularly for adolescents. Thus, educators must be sensitive to individual students' social and emotional needs and address these alongside academic needs, as demon-strated by the programs highlighted in this case study.

Much is still needed in bridging the gap that exists in educational and parental approaches and expectations within and between Chinese and American cultures. The practice at PS 20 exemplifies how after-school and weekend programs can provide an additional venue to enhance students' academic learning and to bridge the communication gap between schools and parents, while respecting Chinese traditional values and a culture of trust in education.

Nevertheless, while the self-reliant educational support practice of the Chinese community is greatly appreciated, schools need to continue explor-ing ways to support emergent bilingual students. Schools need to strategize how to best support academic learning for these students, which should include providing native language support. They also need to address the psychological and social adjustment issues for parents and students. As schools implement these educational practices, they will be able to provide a better learning environment for all children.

Notes

(1) While considered as dialects by most Chinese, they are linguistically different and considered as separate languages by many linguists. However, because they share the same writing system (simplified or traditional format), they share most of the vocabulary.

(2) For the purpose of this paper, the term 'Asia' and 'Asian' throughout is used to refer to the region and peoples of East and Southeast Asia.

(3) The GED is offered in Spanish, French and Braille as an alternative to English, but not in Chinese.

(4) Title I monies are federal funds for economically disadvantaged students. Title III monies are federal funds for immigrant students and English language students. Both are used to support academic achievement.

(5) I have received permission to use the principal's name.

(6) The names of all students have been changed for the purposes of confidentiality.

Part 4

Bilingual Resources for a Global Future: Recommendations

19 Beyond Community: Networks of Bilingual Community Support for Languages other than English in New York City

Maureen T. Matarese

Introduction

A community's ability to support and maintain its cultural and/or ethnic language has been a formal subject of study for nearly 50 years. Early work in this area, spearheaded by Fishman (1966), explored the maintenance of indigenous, colonial and immigrant languages in the US. From these studies emerged a field of inquiry, encompassing numerous studies of language maintenance across the US (Fishman *et al.*, 1985) and in New York City (García, 1997/2002). This chapter examines one such study engaging a cross-institutional research team to investigate various forms of community-initiated and community-funded institutional support for languages other than English (LOTEs) in New York City. These institutions – educational, religious, community centers and media – often evolved out of, and were financially supported by, local language communities. However, frequently these community institutions also partnered with city, state and/or national, and even international, agencies. The data emerging from this study provides important insights into community-initiated LOTE-supporting institutions, discussed in this chapter. However, these constitute an incomplete portrait of community language maintenance in New York.

After examining and presenting the data, this chapter argues for a shift in the epistemology and methodology of language maintenance and the sociology of language research. I offer here a re-conceptualization of this research using a post-structural lens through which community language support can be viewed, in order to elicit findings that capture the complexity of language use and maintenance in the 21st century. After presenting descriptive statistical analyses of community-based institutional language support, I offer a spatial, post-structural paradigm for understanding community language maintenance that intersects with what García, Zakharia and Otcu (Chapter 1) call 'diasporic plural networks'. The chapter argues that, while existing paradigms for language maintenance research have generated useful insights, the research community should consider alternative methodologies that are able to capture language maintenance in its complexity.

Language Maintenance Research

Joshua A. Fishman's substantial research has convincingly shown that 'language loyalty' prompts communities to support their languages and cultures, often through institutional means (Fishman, 1966: 21). A community's language maintenance efforts may be driven by threats to the mother tongue. Bilingual community education, in particular, may primarily be a response to a sense of threatened language identities, whether the threat is overt or implicit.

Fishman's work has prompted countless other studies. Some of this research has examined the development, use and impact of one particular type of institution on language maintenance. For example, religious institutional support for LOTEs has been widely examined. In one such study, Woods (2004) showed how the use of Latvian language in a Latvian Lutheran church in Australia helps the community maintain ties to their Latvian culture. Radio stations have also been found to provide language maintenance, such as in studies of Native American communities (Browne, 1996; Peterson, 1997). In addition, a substantial body of research examines the effects of schooling on language maintenance (e.g. Hornberger, 1988), exploring minority language maintenance, development or loss according to the type of schooling. On a broader scale, García (1997/2002) conducted a large-scale analysis of how LOTEs were used in New York City, in an effort to describe the rich multilingualism of New York City (NYC). Many of these studies follow Fishman's original methodological paradigm, utilizing broad statistical analysis, as well as supplementary qualitative interviews and observation.

Historical Developments in Sociolinguistics and the Post-structural Turn

Sociolinguistics has undergone several theoretical shifts since the field was initiated in the 1960s, but it began by paying attention to structural characteristics of groups and their relationship to language use (Fishman, 1972b). Labov's (1966) research, along with other variationist sociolinguistics that followed, is a prime example of this structural approach, which currently persists alongside newer theoretical directions in sociolinguistics (Duranti, 2003).

The study of sociolinguistics has been influenced by critical theory, attending to structural power asymmetries, hierarchy and hegemony. For example, variationist research describing African-American English seeks to establish social justice (Baugh, 1999; Labov, 1972; Labov & Waletzky, 1967). Fishman's sociology of language research (Fishman, 1972a, 1972b; Fishman *et al.*, 1985), while not professedly informed by critical theory, advocated for linguistic social justice, equity and language maintenance to support cultural identity. From more qualitative linguistic traditions, Canagarajah (1999) and Phillipson's (1992) work on linguistic imperialism established critiques of World English, and Pennycook (2001) developed a broader critical framework for applied linguistics as a field. Whereas many utilized critical theory to highlight power asymmetries between and among language groups, Fairclough (1992) developed a critically focused discourse analytical methodology that tailored analysis toward connecting discourse with critiques of social and political contexts.

However, while structural and critical theories have been embraced, post-structuralism has received a less than warm welcome among sociolinguists. Research on language and gender (Eckert & McConnell-Ginet, 1999; Hall & Livia, 1997) and language and identity (Holland *et al.*, 1998), for example, has taken a post-structural turn. However, few sociolinguists invoke this framework. Post-structuralism is often connected with postmodernism, and is therefore thought to reject grand narratives and critique modernity. In its weak form, however, post-structuralism has been critiqued as merely re-conceptualizing empirical categories, noting the complexity, variability and overlap that make those structural categories less useful. While admittedly post-structuralism runs the risk of reducing structural categories into meaningless fragments, the former paradigms (structuralism, whether critical or not) lend themselves to essentializing, rendering individuals and groups of people to ill-fitting categories. As Coupland (2001: 18) argues, 'sociolinguistics' tolerance of independent variables such as sex, class or age readily essentializes people into these groupings'.

Bilingual research has considered some post-structural alternatives. Hornberger's (1988) continua of biliteracy established an interconnected framework for understanding bilingualism vis-à-vis one's exposure to language; the social contexts that shape that exposure; language and literacy influences; and formal and informal education. Thus Hornberger's framework emphasizes the intersecting planes of influence on a bilingual learner. In a related vein, García's (2009a) work on translanguaging establishes a post-structural framework that expands the notion of bilingualism itself, highlighting its hybridity and challenging its assumed dichotomous-ness. She suggests that:

> bilingualism is not simply linear but *dynamic*, drawing from the different contexts in which it develops and functions. More than ever, categories such as first language (L1) and second language (L2), base and guest languages, host and borrowing languages, are not in any way useful, because the world's globalization is increasingly calling on people to interact with others in ways that defy traditional categories. In the linguistic complexity of the twenty-first century, bilingualism involves a much more dynamic cycle where language practices are multiple and ever adjusting to the multilingual multimodal terrain of the communicative act. (García, 2009a: 53)

Her theory of 'dynamic bilingualism' dismisses the duality of bilingualism as a structural category, suggesting rather that what constitutes 'bilingualism' is heteroglossic, evolving and polymorphic.

Fishman (2002: 350–351) alluded to such an approach when he reflected on multilingualism in NYC:

> Whenever I note the Chinese and Spanish options on my neighborhood bank's ATM machine, I think how lucky I am to be living in a once Jewish, but now vibrantly Irish, neighborhood of a city that enables and encourages all of its citizens to opt for their own ethnic identities if and whenever they are of a mind to do so. In such a city, the link to language is latent for some, halting to others and blatant for yet others, but it is always there. A post-structural sociology of urban life, one that more fully recognizes the importance of diverse human motives, goals, efforts, and interests, including among them the reluctance to being submerged in the non-descript mainstream ... is now beginning to emerge. Perhaps such a post-structural sociology of America's cities, and of New York in particular, will not trivialize the very linkages and options which cities in general, and New York in particular, invigorate.

This chapter takes the view that globalization is rendering the rigid categories of past research less useful, and therefore seeks to describe what a post-structural sociolinguistics approach to the study of language support might look like. In so doing, I first describe the findings from a 2004/2005 study that examined institutional support of LOTEs in New York City (Matarese & Raña, 2004). I then consider research methodologies that could enhance this area of research and conclude by reflecting on the future of institutional language maintenance research.

A LOTE Study in NYC

The goal of the 2004/2005 study reported here was to examine institutions that arose from, and were at least partially financially supported by, language communities in New York City and that used LOTEs. A language was considered to have 'support' if its language community had institutions of the kind identified in Table 19.1. The study included New York City LOTE-supporting institutions that were primarily independently funded *and* that were initiated by LOTE-speaking communities. In this chapter, I refer to such institutions as 'community-funded'. Thus, public institutions, or institutions that were primarily funded by the US government, and businesses related to language learning or foreign language classes, were excluded

Table 19.1 Criteria for inclusion of institutions

Institutional category	Criteria for inclusion
Educational institutions	Primary function is educational, teaches LOTE(s)
Religious institutions	Primary function is liturgical, uses LOTE(s) in liturgical or vernacular contexts
Community organizations/centers	Community centers and non-governmental organizations that utilize LOTE(s) in center/ organization functions and/or services
Televised media	Use LOTE(s) in programming that New Yorkers watch, regardless of point of origin
Radio media	Use LOTE(s) in programming that New Yorkers listen to, regardless of point of origin
Print/electronic press	Use LOTE(s) in press that New Yorkers regularly read and buy, limited to US publication origin

from the research. Like those that came before, this chapter distances itself from terms like 'heritage language', which connote languages of the past, and instead focuses on 'living' language institutions created and maintained by a vibrant and dynamic network of community speakers.

The research team used telephone directories, internet research and in-person observations to identify community-funded educational institutions, religious institutions, community organizations or centers, televised and radio media, and print and electronic press that supported LOTEs. Phone calls were made when necessary to confirm the source of financial support and to get any additional information. Each researcher entered data into a uniform Access database developed by the author that included: unique identifiers for each institution token; a set of 'general' codes (institution type code, name of institution, etc.); contact information; historical information; particulars on language use; information regarding the specific use of the LOTE; and funding. The individual access databases were then compiled into a master Access database for analytical purposes.

The study yielded institutional community support for 72 LOTEs in New York City, although only 30 of these languages were found to have four or more supporting institutions. These are presented in Figure 19.1, to show the number of institutions for each language in 2004/2005. While not an exhaustive list, a total of 1730 institutions were identified by the research team.

As illustrated by Figure 19.1, of the total number of institutions identified, Spanish and Hebrew appear to have the most institutions, each with

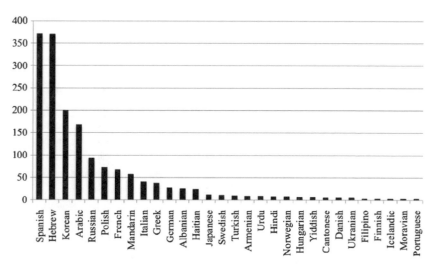

Figure 19.1 Number of community-funded institutions identified per LOTE, 2004/2005

21% of the total. They are followed by Korean (12%), Arabic (10%), Russian (5%), Polish (4%), French (4%) and Chinese (3%). These figures, however, tell a different story when we consider institutional support in light of the overall number of LOTE-speakers in New York City. Figure 19.2 depicts the number of community-funded LOTE-supporting institutions per 5000 speakers. Only the top 11 languages, those languages with more than 25 institutions, are included in the figure.

As represented in Figure 19.2, there is approximately one community-funded Spanish-supporting institution for every 5000 Spanish speakers,[1] and less than one institution per 5000 Chinese speakers. Thus, it would appear that the largest language communities in New York City – Spanish and Chinese – have the least community-funded institutional support. According to US Census data, between 2000 and 2010 the Hispanic/Latino population grew by 43% and 'the Asian population grew faster than any other major race group between 2000 and 2010', also growing by 43% (Humes *et al.*, 2011: 4). Such growth may explain the relatively low level of support for Spanish and Chinese in proportion to the size of the language community.

French, Italian and Russian have between 2 and 3.5 institutions per 5000 speakers. In recent years, the African Francophone communities in

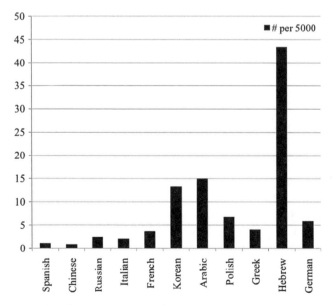

Figure 19.2 Number of community-funded institutions identified per 5000 LOTE speakers, 2004/2005

NYC have, with their numbers, supported the institutional vitality of French in NYC (see Ross & Jaumont, Chapter 15), and the language continues to carry the prestige of French culture. Italian is also well represented institutionally in NYC, particularly through the many local and regional sports clubs. Spoken mostly by Jewish émigrés, Russian in NYC is supported by a strong network of institutional support (see Kleyn & Vayshenker, Chapter 17). In addition, the Russian Orthodox Church offers Russian some support.

There are approximately four community-funded Greek-supporting institutions per 5000 speakers. The Greek Orthodox Church has supported a strong network of churches, but also of Greek day schools, as well as supplementary schools (see Hantzopoulos, Chapter 8). Thus, it is not surprising that Greeks have more institutional support proportionally. In addition, however, the Greek population is declining; thus, the long-established institutions show the dwindling population more support.

German and Polish have just over five institutions per 5000 speakers. These language groups have long-established roots in New York City. German is primarily supported by community centers, including film societies, sports clubs and language learning societies. Polish has equally distributed support, with 24 churches, 18 community centers or organizations and 11 schools. The Polish Catholic community provides substantial support to that language and most schools are attached to churches, although there are also many community centers supporting language through the arts.

Korean and Arabic have between 13 and 15 institutions per 5000 speakers. In the case of Korean, this has to do with the strong network of Korean community churches (see Chung, Chapter 5). Arabic is also supported, mainly by mosques and Islamic schools and centers (see Zakharia & Menchaca Bishop, Chapter 11). Such cases, again, illustrate the strong role of religion in language support and maintenance (Fishman, 1966).

Speakers of Hebrew have the highest proportion of community-funded LOTE supporting institutions – nearly 43 institutions per 5000 speakers. Thus, Hebrew is the language most supported in NYC. This has to do with Hebrew's double role as a classical liturgical language, as well as being the revitalized language of Israel that marks Jewishness. This means that synagogues support the use and study of Hebrew to read the Torah. The role of Hebrew as a revitalized modern language in Israel also spurs the study of modern Hebrew among Jews in the US. Finally, the long history of Jewish resistance to anti-Semitism and the Holocaust in particular means that institutional group support has been the very fabric of Jewish life in the US, and especially in NYC, where 12% of the population is Jewish (Berger, 2003; see Avni & Menken, Chapter 12).

Different Types of Community-funded LOTE-supporting Institutions

Educational institutional support for LOTEs

According to NYC Department of Education data from 2010, 66% of English language learners (ELLs) are Spanish-speaking and 12.8% of ELLs are Chinese-speaking. Thus there are five times as many Spanish speaking emergent bilinguals as there are Chinese, corresponding to city-wide data on numbers of speakers for the top two languages (Infante, 2010). Bengali speakers make up 3.3%, Arabic speakers 2.8%, Haitian Creole speakers 2.2% and Urdu speakers 2.0% of ELLs. The other top language groups all comprise less than 2% (Russian, French, Albanian, Korean, Punjabi and Polish; Infante, 2010).

The research team of the 2004/2005 study was asked to identify community-funded schools that support LOTEs, that is, educational institutions who teach LOTEs that have been initiated by the language community and that are supported primarily through independent funds. Figure 19.3 describes the number of such schools identified per LOTE group.

Some languages appear to be disproportionally well supported, whereas others are not supported at all. For example, although in 2005 there were 1,808,878 Spanish-speakers in the city, only 24 schools were identified that

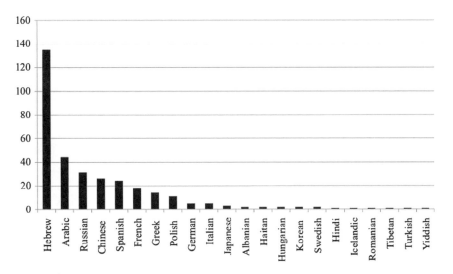

Figure 19.3 Number of community-funded educational institutions identified per LOTE, 2004/2005

were in whole or in part community-funded. In contrast, Hebrew, which had 42,721 speakers in NYC in 2005, had five and a half times as many community-funded schools ($n = 135$).

This portrait of community-funded educational institutional support, however, is not representative of the total LOTE support provided by educational institutions in New York City. To demonstrate how schools support LOTEs in the city more broadly, the contrastive chart in Figure 19.4 presents the number of identified community-funded educational institutions in conjunction with government-funded (public) schools where LOTEs were used in instruction. Government-funded schools are further divided into (1) transitional bilingual programs that offer instruction in LOTEs until students become proficient in English and (2) so-called 'dual language' bilingual schools, where LOTEs are used regardless of students' proficiency.

As illustrated in Figure 19.4, while Hebrew and Arabic received far more community-funded educational support, Spanish received the most language support when government-funded schools are also considered. Arabic also has more government-funded transitional bilingual education support (totaling two) than Hebrew, which has none. This is because Arabic speakers are more likely to be immigrants and therefore receive government-funded

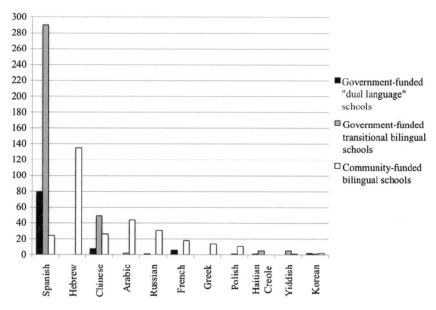

Figure 19.4 Number of government-funded and community-funded educational institutions per LOTE, 2004/2005

support for programs that engage Arabic to assist students in 'transitioning' to the English language. In contrast, Hebrew language learners in New York are largely English speakers (see Avni & Menken, Chapter 12). Hebrew educational institutions are supported primarily by private means, which is not surprising given the language's use in religious contexts.

Languages of recent immigrants were more likely to receive government funding for bilingual schools. The largest LOTE-speaking groups in the city (Spanish and Chinese) overall have the greatest government-funded bilingual education support, mostly for transitional programs. Because they are the languages of recent immigrants, often poor, the communities have not poured resources into institutions that support their languages and cultures. This is especially so in the case of Spanish-speakers, and it might have consequences for the future prospects of Spanish in NYC.

Religious institutional support for LOTEs

Whether the language is directly tied to religious practices and liturgy (like Arabic, Hebrew, Greek, and formerly Latin) or utilized as a local variety in services (as in the use of Spanish in the Catholic mass or Pentecostal church service), language and religion can be closely linked and in either case speak to issues of faith, identity and community (Woods, 2004). The research team identified a wide variety of LOTE-supporting religious institutions, the results of which are illustrated in Figure 19.5.

Of the four LOTE groups with the highest number of identified religious institutions, two are liturgical languages and two are not. Liturgical

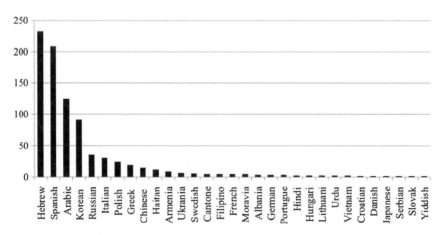

Figure 19.5 Number of religious institutions identified per LOTE, 2004/2005

languages, or languages specifically used for religious services and ceremonies, include Hebrew and Classical or Qur'anic Arabic. Hebrew has the greatest number of religious institutional supports ($n = 232$; 27% of identified institutions), which is fitting given its status as a liturgical language tied primarily to religious practices in the Jewish faith (Schiff, 1997/2002). Arabic, also a language with liturgical ties, has 124 supporting religious institutions (15%) to enable Muslims, whether from the Arabic-speaking community or not, to read the Qur'an and engage the teachings of the mosque.

The research of Woods (2004) describes a variety of non-liturgical languages used in religious services, facilitating the maintenance of cultural and linguistic identity. In this data set, the Spanish language has significant support from religious institutions (25% of the total), primarily situated in Roman Catholic and Pentecostal religious communities where liturgical services are offered in Spanish. This has to do with the large number of Spanish-speakers in New York and their need for religious services in a language that is meaningful to them. The same can be said for the use of Korean, a non-liturgical language used by the religious community in Korean Christian churches (see Chung, Chapter 5).

Community centers and organizational support for LOTEs

Community centers and non-profit organizations often lend support to a LOTE, either by simply offering services (health, welfare, educational, etc.) through that language or by offering the community a space to come together for activities, cultural and otherwise (often in that LOTE). The data for centers and organizations identified by the research team is given in Figure 19.6.

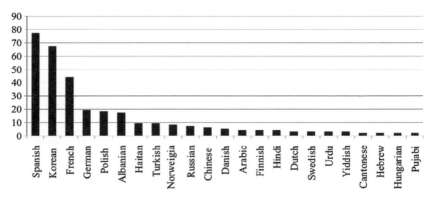

Figure 19.6 Number of community organizations identified per LOTE, 2004/2005

According to the data collected, Spanish, Korean and French had 23, 20 and 13% of the total number of community organizations, respectively. Hebrew, which had the highest numbers of community-funded educational and religious institutional support, had substantially fewer community center and non-profit support, perhaps because religious institutional spaces (synagogue, temple, etc.) provide opportunities for community gathering, although further research would be required in order to consider the reason for relatively fewer community centers and organizations.

European languages with smaller language communities in New York City (e.g. French, Polish and German) are very well represented, although language groups with larger language communities like Russian and Chinese have fewer institutions. Proportionally speaking, the Korean community has the most identified community institutions per 20,000 speakers – almost 18, while Spanish and Chinese both have less than one institution per 20,000 speakers.

There were only four Arabic community institutions identified that specifically dealt with Arab community issues and did not provide other services like religious prayer and schooling. The issue of categorical overlap is addressed further in the Discussion section; however, it should be noted that investigations of the Arabic institutions, in particular, highlighted significant overlap, such that many religious institutions were either called 'centers' or additionally served as community centers, offering counseling and financial assistance. Many of these religious institutions calling themselves 'centers' also included elementary, K–12 and/or Qur'anic-teaching weekend schools. Thus, while there were only four official community organizations, if all Arabic centers were counted, there were more than 100. The issue of institutional overlap and methodological approaches to avoid such confusion with the designation of categories will be elaborated upon in the Discussion.

Media support for LOTEs

Of the four institutional types, the research team identified comparatively few media institutions supporting LOTEs (including print, television and radio). According to the data collected, Spanish enjoys the most support, although primarily through televised programming. Korean, Russian and Polish have substantial support through printed material (see data in Figure 19.7).

It should be noted that only printed media from the US was considered and only AM/FM radio stations were included. More print sources were identified than radio or television sources, with the exception of Spanish.

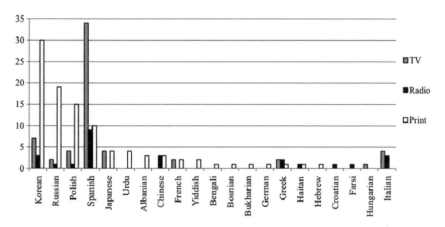

Figure 19.7 Number of media institutions per LOTE, 2004/2005

US-based cable television supports the fewest LOTEs, with the exception of Spanish language television and radio, a finding also identified by Fishman *et al.* (1985). Notably, Fishman *et al.* (1985: 65) found that the periodical press supported LOTEs the least, which they suggest is a result of 'weak' 'literacy traditions ... among American ethnolinguistic minorities'. Their finding contrasts with this study in which there were many LOTE-supporting printed presses, particularly if we include available online presses.

Technological developments bringing media from across the world, including satellite television, web-streaming television, digital/internet-radio stations and online newspapers, were not included owing to logistical constraints. However, it is clear now that excluding digital media presents challenges and potential inaccuracies to the data presented. Satellite television, providing access to television in LOTEs, has grown, and while radio stations in LOTEs are not plentiful, online radio stations are. For Arabic alone, over 38 online radio stations were located, almost all in Arabic or minimally with Arabic music, from the US and Canada. Moreover, one website lists 23 nations with large Arab populations, each of which have streaming radio and television stations; some countries have multiple stations, and Europe has several stations that also cater, at least in part, to Arabic-speaking people (Arabic radio stations, 2011). Likewise, the number of newspapers that are available online far outweighs the number available in print. As García (2009a) suggests, globalization has prompted us to consider new approaches to social interaction. We must consider the institutional spaces that we visit from the comfort of our living rooms and the many ways in which the web contributes to language maintenance.

In summary

The 2004/2005 study identifies several important trends in institutional support for LOTEs in New York City. First, it appears that Hebrew institutional support is greater than any other. This has to do with its liturgical role, as well its position as the language of a religious minority that has developed its own system of support. Although Spanish is spoken by many in New York City, it has little community-funded institutional support.

The following section addresses one major challenge that impacted data analysis: the problem of categories and the subsequent need for more and varied information. I then turn to proposing a methodological approach that could address this issue.

The Problem of 'Categories'

As suggested by post-structural thought, the sorting of institutions into 'categories' is theoretically problematic. However, it is not only in theory that these categories resist generalization. Institutions across the data set were noted as having secondary or tertiary functions: a church, mosque or synagogue with a school attached; a religious institution that does not conduct liturgy but rather is a religious organization; or a parochial school that serves dual functions. Because such a crossover was clear, especially between educational and religious institutions, a Pearson correlation was conducted. Results suggested that educational and religious institutions were highly correlated and were found to be significant at the 0.01 level. Fishman *et al.* (1985) had similar results, which he suggests indicate the potential for educational and religious institutions inhabiting the same geographic space – institutions that fit more than one category.

There are several examples of other complicated overlappings across institutional type. For example, there are many religious institutions that also include gathering/community center spaces, as well as schools. This was especially so in the case of the Arabic data. One particular Arabic center, despite having an organization-like name, has a school that serves pre-Kindergarteners to high school. The center also provides congregational prayer and assists with funerals and marriages, thus having a religious capacity. How might this institution be categorized? What is its primary function? These questions can be asked of many institutions in this study, which may have multiple designations.

Another issue with categories had to do with the meaning of community-funded institutions. Many organizations had multiple sources of funding or resource support, including US and non-US government funding, as well as private funds. For example, French language programming is supported by multiple sources of funding and partnerships (see Ross & Jaumont, Chapter 15), and Hindi teaching at the Hindu Temple Society is supported by Canadian government curricular resources (see Ghaffar-Kucher & Mahajan, Chapter 4). Thus the issue of support networks further confounds categories.

The field of knowledge management, a sub-field within technology research, has addressed this issue by designating items with 'tags', multiple keywords that are linked to characterizations, descriptions and other objects. Tagging is used on popular websites like Facebook when, for example, a picture is tagged to include the five friends in the photo. Tagging is primarily used in knowledge management and knowledge management research (Grudin, 2006), but could be used in the analysis of institutions. That is, rather than categorizing each institution according to type, which essentializes it, each institution could be tagged with a series of individual attributes (e.g. education K–12, religious services, community supper night, counseling and support services, Spanish languages classes for adults, funding sources). Institutions, therefore, would be represented as they are: hybrid community organizations with multiple, fluid, dynamic roles. Tagging, however, only solves one part of the categorization issue, the other part of which concerns how one interprets and presents the data once all institutions have been tagged.

Human Geography: The Future of Sociology of Language Research?

As applied linguist Rampton (2006) suggests, the divisions and lines separating language groups from one another are blurred and ever-changing. Human geography research, and specifically geographic information systems (GIS) research, however, could easily be used for future sociology of language research studies. Human geography has increasingly moved toward an interest in spatial relationships across a geographic spectrum (Flowerdew, 2004). Research issues dealing with location potentially fall under geography's jurisdiction (Longley et al., 2005: 4) and can examine local issues surrounding health care, transportation, driving, or 'the global diffusion of the 2003 ... SARS epidemic'. Longley et al. (2005) suggest that geographic, spatial analyses can be used for a variety of social science research questions. GIS could provide this study with a map of New York City, on which are pinpointed thousands of institutions. Each institution is given a tag or series of tags that denote the attribute(s) of that institution. GIS analysis of such data could take a variety of directions. Fishman (2002: 351) argued that perhaps 'a post-structural sociology of America's cities, and of New York in particular, will not trivialize the very linkages and options which cities in general, and New York in particular, invigorate', and perhaps GIS could better situate and describe these 'options'.

The final challenge would be to define the 'linkages' between institutions. Latour's (1999: 5) actor-network theory (ANT) may provide a means of better understanding the linkages between LOTE-supporting institutions. ANT organizes society around networks, or 'associations', rather than through geographically tied spaces, shifting from 'static and topological properties to dynamic and ontological ones'. ANT 'allows us to think of a global entity – a highly connected one – which remains nevertheless continuously local' (p. 4). An 'actor' network suggests that some actant (motivator, not necessarily human) facilitates movement across the network. In bilingual contexts different actants (e.g. speakers of LOTEs, bureaucrats, administrators, policy documents, translated paperwork, community events, school lesson plans, religious services and media) prompt and facilitate support for LOTEs, creating a dynamic network. As such, with a GIS map that identifies our coded LOTE-supporting institutions, we could, then ask ourselves, what do we want to know about the connections between these institutions? We could follow several case studies and chart their connections with these different institutions, and we could examine the extent to which language community institutions cluster around community neighborhoods. We could follow only those institutions that have strong connections between religious tags, educational tags and shared membership between the two. Actor network theory, which strives to highlight the dynamism within a complex network, could also help us consider how to map the connections to online and other globalized resources that support LOTEs every day.

Globalization inherently suggests increasing interconnectivity, forging linkages that do not only exist in trade. A post-structural approach to mapping language resources in the 21st century would shed further light onto the data presented in this chapter. Associations between institutions in New York City reveal complex *language community networks*, webs of support for speakers of LOTEs. These networks do not stop at the geographic boundaries of the five boroughs. Rather, these associations extend outward – across oceans and through cyberspace. The next steps for this type of research, therefore, should involve tagging institutions according to their practices, as well as tracing institutional associations both within and across geographic boundaries – capturing the varied, ever-changing web that characterizes the dynamism of language community networks.

Acknowledgment

This study was jointly designed by Joshua Fishman, Ofelia García and Ricardo Otheguy. It was supported by Multilingual Apple research teams at Teachers College, Columbia University and at the City University of New York (CUNY) Graduate Center. I coordinated the team of graduate student researchers who gathered data for this study, particularly at Teachers College. Rocio Raña was the co-research coordinator at the CUNY Graduate Center. The data would not have been collected without the hard work of those research teams.

Note

(1) Data for numbers of language speakers in New York City comes from the US Census Bureau (2005).

20 American Multilingualism for a Global Future: Recommendations for Parents, Educators and Policy-makers

Ofelia García

A lot has been said about bilingual community education in the preceding pages. Here we limit ourselves to making a few key recommendations to parents, educators and policy-makers. Because parents are often the educators in bilingual community education efforts and they are most often in charge, those recommendations are directed to them, as well as to the teachers. However, the recommendations for the US public school sector are directed first to educators and then to policy-makers, since unfortunately parents have so little to say about those efforts. Our overall recommendation is then this – that policy-makers, educators, parents and communities have to be able to collaborate and trust each other if we are going to raise a generation of bilingual Americans.

For Parents and Educators in Bilingual Community Education Efforts

- *Understand that these are American children for whom English is an important language.*
  - ○ Use the children's English productively, to construct their bilingual proficiency.

- o   Translanguage to ensure that children are making sense of the lesson.
- o   Allow children to translanguage to build proficiencies, make sense of what is going on, and perform new language practices.
- *View American children's bilingualism as dynamic, a result of English and LOTEs in contact.*
  - o   Understand that American children's proficiency in the LOTE will not be the same as that of children in other sociolinguistic contexts.
  - o   Understand that children will not be able to completely separate practices in one language from those in the other.
  - o   Remember that your goal is not to produce a 'balanced' bilingual child. Bilingual children are not two monolinguals in one.
  - o   Do not expect just to 'add' a language. Bilingualism is not about 'adding' separately, but about integrating and performing dynamically.
  - o   Recognize that for these children there are no 'first' or 'second' languages. There are simply different language practices, which interact dynamically. What you are doing is helping them develop their language practices by adding new practices and extending their linguistic repertoires.
  - o   Be familiar with the extent of the children's total linguistic repertoire, including all language practices not recognized in the particular bilingual community setting.
- *Understand that these are American children, living in the US. Thus, they have strong American identities.*
  - o   For American children to learn other language practices, they must have a high degree of 'investment' (Norton, 1995). Introduce additional language practices as a way for children to invest in their American identity, extending it further, and not as a 'foreign' identity linked to another place and time.
  - o   Build children's multiple identities, and not just the one associated with a 'heritage' culture.
  - o   Instill pride in their identity as bilingual plural Americans, and not just in a 'heritage' culture.
  - o   Extend children's understandings of the world and of global interconnections and opportunities.
- *Understand the diasporic plural networks of US society.*
  - o   Do not assume that children that attend these programs are the same or that the group is homogeneous. Ask the children about their backgrounds, national-origin, histories of migration, home language practices, cultural practices and values.

- ○ Recognize the language and other forms of diversity within communities. Refer to this often and ask children to share their different language practices within this diversity.
- ○ Have children share their differences with each other. Build connections across differences.
- ○ Learn about scaffolding and individualizing instruction (aka, differentiation), so that children with different linguistic practices can be included in the lessons.
- *Make connections to the children's other contexts, including their other teachers and educational settings.*
  - ○ Ask children about the totality of their educational experiences.
  - ○ Know what children know in English, in the language being taught, as well as in other languages. Review their other academic texts in language arts, as well as subject matter.
  - ○ If possible, visit some of the other educational settings in which students learn. Become familiar with some of their teachers, and let them know about the importance of the bilingual community education efforts you are involved with.
  - ○ Ask the other teachers to encourage and appreciate the students' LOTEs and cultural practices within the community. This will help children take their community education more seriously.
- *Make connections to others who will facilitate your efforts, but do not let others control.*
  - ○ It is possible to accept funds, help and support from US federal and local funds, foreign funds, as well as funds of groups and members of the ethnolinguistic community in the US. However, it is important that all understand *'your'* goals as community participants, and that it is you who control the education of your children.
  - ○ Observe lessons and pedagogies in different educational contexts, including those in US public schools, other bilingual community education efforts, and foreign education systems. Become familiar with different pedagogical practices and traditions. Do not adopt any of them wholesale, but take features of each to construct appropriate pedagogical practices for American children who also need to appreciate different educational traditions and purposes.
- *Understand your role as much more than an educator or representative of 'a' language and culture, but as a guide to difference and an ambassador of tolerance in the US.*
  - ○ Use the community's language resources to ensure that children understand the different varieties of the language in the community,

and the differences that exist with the standard being taught in the program.

o Send the children into the community to do language activities that will enable them to understand differences.

o Bring community members of different social classes, ages, genders, backgrounds to the school to make children aware of differences.

o Use the differences observed to build tolerance towards others and other groups.

o Focus on the heterogeneity of the community, rather than on its homogeneity.

o Review the history of the group, not as told by nation-states, but as understood within a broader global experience.

o Review also the history of the group in the US, including issues of discrimination, racism and linguicism, but also opportunities and successes.

For Educators in US Public Schools

- *Recognize the importance of these bilingual community education efforts.*
  o Invite students to share their experiences in these other educational settings. Ask them to share what they know as a result, what they have learned, what skills and resources they now possess.
  o Ask students to bring in material that they have prepared in the other educational setting, in other languages. Display them on bulletin boards, alongside work done in public schools.
  o Allow children to write in languages other than English, and display that writing also in classrooms.
  o Ask parents involved in bilingual community education efforts to share the resources that exist in the community. Share this information with other parents so that they may use these opportunities.
  o Invite students who attend these bilingual community education efforts to perform in your school in different languages, and represent various cultural and historical events.
- *Build a network of community educators in your neighborhood.*
  o Invite these other educators to your professional development activities, and share pedagogical practices.
  o Invite them to visit your school and your classrooms.
  o Share instructional material with them.
- *Promote bilingualism/multilingualism in your school and recognize the multiple identities of teachers and students.*

o   Label classroom spaces with all the languages represented in your school.
o   Sing songs in many languages. Encourage students' performances in other languages.
o   Discuss historical events in world history and contextualize some of these events by involving children and parents in the discussion, and in some performances.
o   Make all students aware of the languages of the community. Take a tour of the neighborhood. Take photographs of signs in different languages, people in different dress, food from different contexts. Listen to people speak in public places. Record some of these conversations.
o   Invite parents to tell a story in a language other than English. Have them record the stories you tell in English in different languages, and make those recordings available to students.
o   Compare and contrast languages other than English with English whenever possible. Use students who speak these languages to offer points of comparison.
o   Allow students to consult material on the internet written in other languages, as well as books, to complete projects. Have students share the different sources.
o   Have students who speak languages other than English explore newspaper articles about certain events in those languages. Compare the ways in which stories are constructed in those languages with those written in English.

For Policy-makers in US Public Schools

•   *Develop an official way of recognizing the efforts of American children in these schools.*
o   Give official credit for language learning in these educational spaces.
o   Establish a system of 'language passports', such as the one developed by the European Union, so that children are recognized for their language and cultural experiences beyond those in English in the US, and those in mainstream schools. Involve children's parents in providing the information and enter these educational experiences into a language record, which will accompany the children as they progress through the grades. These language records will then be shared with the children's teachers.

- *Collaborate with bilingual community education efforts as equal partners.*
    - ○ Become informed of the many resources that bilingual community education offers. Learn about these efforts and understand how they contribute to the holistic education of the children in the public schools.
    - ○ Prominently display on the local educational agency's web page the resources available, as well as a discussion of the advantages of attending these bilingual community education programs.
    - ○ Disseminate information about these programs in schools, and encourage parents to have their children participate.
    - ○ Encourage educators to find out more about these educational programs and become involved in assisting them, whenever possible.
    - ○ Share professional development opportunities with educators in these community programs.

These are but some of the recommendations that may move these bilingual community education efforts into the future. Without the close collaboration of mainstream US public schools, these efforts will remain marginal, and will continue to have the effect of further minoritizing bilingual US communities. The American educational establishment must recognize the potential of these bilingual community education efforts to make American children competitive and efficient in a global world. Only then will these efforts go beyond their position as 'heritage' programs, and move into the 'global' stature that bilingualism must hold in the US.

References

Ahmed, F. (1986) *Turks in America: The Ottoman Turk's Immigrant Experience*. Greenwich, CT: Columbia International Press.

ALBETAC (2010) New York City Chinese language programs 2010–2011. Asian Languages Bilingual ESL Technical Assistance Center – Online document: http://steinhardt. nyu.edu/scmsAdmin/media/users/dtk234/2011_JAN/2010_NYC_Chinese_Program. pdf

Alliance for the Advancement of Heritage Languages (2011) Heritage language programs database project – Online document: http://www.cal.org/heritage/profiles/index. html

Ameredia (2008) Chinese American demographics (Census 2000). Ameredia – Online document: http://www.ameredia.com/resources/demographics/chinese.html

American Community Survey (2007) Place of birth for the foreign-born population. US Census Bureau – Online document: http://www.nyc.gov/html/dcp/pdf/census/ acs_pob_07.pdf

Arab American Institute (AAI) (*ca* 2010a) Quick facts about Arab Americans – Online document: http://aai.3cdn.net/63c6ecf052bdccc48f_afm6ii3a7.pdf

Arab American Institute (AAI) (*ca* 2010b) Demographics – Online document: http:// www.aaiusa.org/pages/demographics/

Arabic Radio Stations (2011) Online document: http://arabic-media.com/radiotv.htm

Avni, S. (2008) Educating for continuity: An ethnography of multilingual language practices in Jewish day school education. PhD thesis, New York University.

Bailey, B. (2007) Heteroglossia and boundaries. In M. Heller (ed.) *Bilingualism: A Social Approach* (pp. 257–274). New York: Palgrave.

Baker, C. (2006) *Foundations of Bilingual Education and Bilingualism* (4th edn). Clevedon: Multilingual Matters.

Barrière, I. (2010a) L'Haïtianophonie aux Etats-Unis. *Haïti Liberté* 4 (3), 18–19.

Barrière, I. (2010b) The vitality of Yiddish among Hasidic infants and toddlers in a low SES preschool in Brooklyn. In W. Moskovich (ed.) *Yiddish – A Jewish National Language at 100. Jews and Slavs* (Vol. 22; pp. 170–196). Jerusalem/Kyiv: Hebrew University of Jerusalem and National University of Kyiv.

Bartlett, L. and García, O. (2011) *Additive Schooling in Subtractive Times: Bilingual Education and Dominican Immigrant Youth in the Heights*. Nashville, TN: Vanderbilt University Press.

Baugh, J. (1999) *Out of the Mouths of Slaves*. Austin, TX: University of Texas Press.

Bayoumi, M. (2008) *How does it Feel to be a Problem?: Being Young and Arab in America*. New York: The Penguin Press.

Bellegarde-Smith, P. (2006) Resisting freedom: Cultural factors in democracy – the case for Haiti. In C. Michel and P. Bellegarde-Smith (eds) *Vodou in Haitian Life and Culture: Invisible Powers* (pp. 101–115). Gordonsville, VA: Palgrave Macmillan.

Benson, K. and Kayal, P.M. (eds) (2002) *A Community of Many Worlds: Arab-Americans in New York City*. New York: Museum of the City of New York/Syracuse University Press.

Berger, J. (2003, 16 June) City milestone: Number of Jews is below million. *New York Times* – Online document: http://www.nytimes.com/2003/06/16/nyregion/city-milestone-number-of-jews-is-below-million.html?pagewanted=all&src=pm

Bilinsky, Y. (1981) Expanding the use of Russian or russification?: Some critical thoughts on Russian as a lingua franca and the 'language of friendship and cooperation of the peoples of the USSR'. *The Russian Review* 40 (3), 317–332.

Blackledge, A. and Creese, A. (2010) *Multilingualism: A Critical Perspective*. London: Continuum.

Blommaert, J. (2010) *The Sociolinguistics of Globalization*. Cambridge: Cambridge University Press.

Borjian, M. and Borjian, H. (2011) Plights of Persian in the modernization era. In J. Fishman and O. García (eds) *Handbook of Language and Ethnic Identity: The Success–Failure Continuum in Language and Ethnic Identity Efforts* (Vol. 2; pp. 254–267). New York: Oxford University Press.

Bourdieu, P. (1991) *Language and Symbolic Power*. Cambridge, MA: Harvard University Press.

Bozorgmehr, M. (2007) Iran. In M.C. Waters and R. Ueda with H. Marrow (eds) *The New Americans: A Guide to Immigration since 1965* (pp. 469–478). Cambridge, MA: Harvard University Press.

Bozorgmehr, M. and Sabagh, G. (1988) High status immigrants: A statistical profile of Iranians in the US. *Iranian Studies* 21 (3/4), 5–36.

Brinton, D., Kagan, O. and Bauhaus, S. (eds) (2007) *Heritage Language Education: A New Field Emerging*. London: Routledge.

Brooklyn Amity School (BAS) (2011) Home page – Online document: http://www.amityschool.org/

Browne, D. (1996) *Electronic Medial and Indigenous Peoples: A Voice of Our own?* Ames, IA: Iowa University Press.

Bruner, J. (1996) *The Culture of Education*. Cambridge, MA: Harvard University Press.

Buchanan, A.B., Albert, N. and Beaulieu, D. (2010) The population with Haitian ancestry in the United States: 2009. American Community Surveys Briefs US Department of Commerce – Online document: http://www.census.gov/prod/2010pubs/acsbr09-18.pdf

Buchanan, S.H. (1979) Language and identity: Haitians in NYC. *International Migration Review* 13 (2), 298–313.

Calder, T. (2008) Power point presentation: 補習校における母語支援 －プリンストン日本語学校の実践から (Japanese only) – Online document: http://www.slidefinder.net/2/2008calder/23357071

Camarota, S.A. (2007) Immigrants in the United States, 2007: A profile of America's foreign born population. Center for Immigration Studies – Online document: http://www.cis.org/articles/2007/back1007.pdf

Camarota, S.A. (2010) Fact sheets on Haitian immigrants in the United States – Online document: http://www.cis.org/HaitianImmigrantFactSheet

Canagarajah, S. (1999) *Resisting Linguistic Imperialism in English Teaching*. Oxford: Oxford University Press.

Castellanos, D. (1983) *The Best of Two Worlds. Bilingual–Bicultural Education in the U.S.* Trenton, NJ: New Jersey State Department of Education.

CBS News (2011) Haiti raises quake death toll on anniversary – Online document: http://www.cbc.ca/news/world/story/2011/01/12/haiti-anniversary-memorials.html

Center for the Study of Brooklyn (2010) Haitian demographic information produced for the Brooklyn Community Foundation and United Way of NYC – Online document: http://www.studybrooklyn.org

Cerat, L. (2011) *Myths and Realities: A History of Haitian Creole Language Programs in New York City.* Unpublished manuscript.

Chhaya Community Development Corporation (Chhaya-CDC) (2001) South Asians in NYC – Online document: http://www.chhayacdc.org/ourissues_sasians.html

Chin, G.J. (1996) The civil rights revolution comes to immigration law: A new look at the Immigration and Nationality Act of 1965. *North Carolina Law Review, 75,* 273–345.

Chin, G.J. (1998) Segregation's last stronghold: Race discrimination and the Constitutional Law of Immigration. *UCLA Law Review* 46, 1–74.

Cho, G. (2000) The role of heritage language in social interactions and relationships: Reflections from a language minority group. *Bilingual Research Journal* 24 (4), 369–384.

Chomsky, W. (1957) *Hebrew: The Eternal Language.* Philadelphia, PA: The Jewish Publication Society of America.

City of New York Department of Education (2011) The 2010–11 Demographics of New York City's English language learners – Online document: http://schools.nyc.gov/NR/rdonlyres/3A4AEC4C-14BD-49C4-B2E6-8EDF5D873BE4/108227/DemoRpt0722.pdf

Çolak, Y. (2004) Language policy and official ideology in early republican Turkey. *Middle Eastern Studies* 40 (6), 67–91.

Collier, S. (2006) 'And ain't I a woman?' Senegalese women immigrants, language use, acquisition, and cultural maintenance in an African hair-braiding shop. In J. Magubane, J.P. Hutchinson and D.A. Worman (eds) *Selected Proceedings of the 35th Annual Conference on African Linguistics* (pp. 66–75). Somerville, MA: Cascadilla.

Comeaux, M. (1978) Louisiana's Acadians: The environmental impact. In G.R. Conrad (ed.) *The Cajuns: Essays on Their History and Culture* (pp. 145–157). Lafayette, LA: Center for Louisiana Studies.

Commission on Jewish Education in North America (1991) *A Time to Act (Et la'asot).* Lanham, MD: Mandel Associated Foundations, JCC Association and JESNA in collaboration with CJF.

Compton, C. (2001) Heritage language communities and schools: Challenges and recommendations. In J.K. Peyton, D.A. Ranard and S. McGinnis (eds) *Heritage Languages in America: Preserving a National Resource* (pp. 145–165). McHenry, IL: Center for Applied Linguistics and Delta Systems.

Constantakos, C. and Spiradakis, J. (1997) Greek in New York. In O. García and J. Fishman (eds) *The Multilingual Apple: Languages in New York City* (pp. 143–166). New York: Mouton de Gruyter.

Constantinou, S.T. (2002) Profiles of Greek Americans. In K. Berry and M. Henderson (eds) *Geographical Identities in America: Race, Place, and Space* (pp. 92–115). Reno, NV: University of Nevada Press.

Consulate-General of Japan in Los Angeles (n.d.) The Japanese American community in transition – Online document: http://www.la.us.emb-japan.go.jp/e_web/e_m06_26.htm

Cordero-Guzmán, H. and Quiroz-Becerra, V. (2005) Mexican Hometown Associations (HTA) in New York. Unpublished manuscript, New York City University. Online

document: http://www.wilsoncenter.org/publication/mexican-hometown-
associations-hta-new-york
Corson, D. (1999) Community-based education for indigenous cultures. In S. May (ed.)
    Indigenous Community-Based Education (pp. 8–19). New York: Multilingual Matters.
Coupland, N. (2001) Sociolinguistic theory and social theory. In N. Coupland, S. Sarangi and
    C. Candin (eds) *Sociolinguistics and Social Theory* (pp. 1–26). Essex: Pearson Education.
Crawford, J. (1992) *Language Loyalties: A Sourcebook on the Official English Controversy.*
    Chicago, IL: University of Chicago Press.
Crawford, J. (2004) *Educating English Learners: Language Diversity in the Classroom* (5th edn).
    (Formerly *Bilingual Education: History, Politics, Theory and Practice.*) Los Angeles, CA:
    Bilingual Educational Services.
Creese, A. and Blackledge, A. (2010) Translanguaging in the bilingual classroom: A peda-
    gogy for learning and teaching? *Modern Language Journal* 94 (1), 103–115.
Creese, A., Baraç, T., Bhatt, A., Blackledge, A., Hamid, S., Li Wei, Lytra, V., Martin, P.,
    Wu, C. and Yağcioğlu-Ali, D. (2008) Investigating multilingualism in complementary
    schools in four communities. Final Report for the ESCR for Project no.
    RES-000-23-1180.
Cristillo, L.A. (2008) Religiosity, education and civic belonging: Muslim youth in New York
    City public schools: Preliminary findings of a citywide opinion survey of Muslim high
    school students. Unpublished manuscript, Teachers College, Columbia University.
Cristillo, L.A. and Minnite, L.C. (2002) The changing Arab New York community. In K.
    Benson and P.M. Kayal (eds) *A Community of Many Worlds: Arab-Americans in New York
    City* (pp. 124–139). New York: Museum of the City of New York/Syracuse University
    Press.
Cummins, J. (1979) Linguistic interdependence and the educational development of bilin-
    gual children. *Review of Educational Research* 49, 222–251.
Cummins, J. (1983) *Heritage Language Education: A Literature Review.* Toronto: Ontario
    Institute for Studies in Education.
Cummins, J. (2007) Rethinking monolingual instructional strategies in multilingual
    classrooms. *The Canadian Journal of Applied Linguistics*, 10 (2), 221–240.
Cummins, J. and Danesi, M. (1990) *Heritage Languages: The Development and Denial of
    Canada's Linguistic Resources.* Toronto: Our Schools/Our Selves Educational
    Foundation, Garamond Press.
Cummins, J. and Swain, M. (1986) *Bilingualism in Education: Aspects of Theory, Research and
    Practice.* London: Longman.
Cypress Hills Community School (2008) Comprehensive education plan – Online docu-
    ment: http://schools.nyc.gov/documents/oaosi/cep/2008-09/cep_K089.pdf
Das, S.K. (1991) *A History of Indian Literature, 1800–1910: Western Impact, Indian Response.*
    New Delhi: Sahitya Akademi.
DeGraff, M. (2005) Linguists' most dangerous myth: the fallacy of Creole exceptional-
    ism. *Language in Society* 34 (4), 533–591.
DeGraff, M. (2007) Haitian Creole. In J. Holm and P. Patrick (eds) *Comparative Creole
    Syntax: Parallel Outlines of 18 Creole Grammars* (pp. 101–126). Westminster Creolistics
    Series, 7. London: Battlebridge.
DeGraff, M. (2009) Creole exceptionalism and the (mis)education of the Creole speaker.
    In J.A. Kleifgen and G. Bond (eds) *The Languages of Africa and the Diaspora: Educating
    for Language Awareness* (pp. 124–144). Bristol: Multilingual Matters.
DeGraff, M. (2010a) Language barrier: Creole is the language of Haiti and the education
    system needs to reflect that. *Boston Globe* – Online document: http://www.boston.

com/bostonglobe/editorial_opinion/oped/articles/2010/06/16/language_barrier_in_
haiti/

DeGraff, M. (2010b) Baryè lang an Ayiti: Kreyòl se lang peyi a; se pou sa fòk lekòl fèt an
Kreyòl. *Le Nouvelliste*, August – Online document: http://www.lenouvelliste.com/
article4.php?newsid=82891

Dejan, Y. (1993) An overview of the language situation in Haiti. *International Journal of the
Sociology of Language* 102, 73–83.

Dejean, Y. (2010) Are we going to use the sand of Haiti to rebuild our schools? Are we
going to use Creole, the only language known by all Haitians, as the language of
instruction? Rebati. *Ayiti Cheri. The Haitian Experience* (23 June 2010) – Online document: http://ayiticheri.com/rebati/

Del Valle, J. (2000) Monoglossic policies for a heteroglossic culture: Misinterpreted multilingualism in modern Galicia. *Language and Communication* 20, 105–132.

Del Valle, S. (1998) Bilingual education for Puerto Ricans in New York City: From hope
to compromise. *Harvard Educational Review* 68 (2), 193–217.

Del Valle, S. (2003) *Language Rights and the Law in the United States*. Clevedon: Multiligual
Matters.

Della Pergola, S. (2010) World Jewish population 2010, North American Jewish data bank.
Storrs, CT: Mandell L. Berman Institute – Online document: http://www.jewishda
tabank.org/PopulationStatistics.asp

Demakopoulos, S. (1989/2000) *Do You Speak Greek?* New York: Seaburn Press.

Deumert, A., Inder, B. and Maitra, P. (2005) *Language, Informal Networks and Social
Protection: Evidence from a Sample of Migrants in Cape Town, South Africa*. London:
Sage.

DiNapoli, M.A.H. (2002) The Syrian–Lebanese community of South Ferry from its ori-
gins to 1977. In K. Benson and P.M. Kayal (eds) *A Community of Many Worlds: Arab-
Americans in New York City* (pp. 11–27). New York: Museum of the City of New York/
Syracuse University Press.

Diner, H. (2006) *The Jews of the United States, 1654–2000*. Berkeley, CA: University of
California Press.

Doğançay-Aktuna, S. (1993) Turkish language reform in a language planning framework: Its impact on language use of Turkish Cypriot high school students. Paper
presented at the Annual Meeting of the American Association of Applied
Linguistics.

Doğançay-Aktuna, S. (1998) The spread of English in Turkey and its current sociolinguistic profile. *Journal of Multilingual and Multicultural Development* 19 (1), 24–39.

Dragoumis, M. (2006) Demotic versus Katharevousa. *The Athens News* – Online document: http://www.athensnews.gr/old_issue/13205/15253

Duranti, A. (2003) Language as culture in US anthropology. *Current Anthropology* 44 (3),
323–347.

Dushkin, A.M. (1918) *Jewish Education in New York City*. New York: Bureau of Jewish
Education.

Eckert, P. and McConnell-Ginet, S. (1999) New generalizations and explanations in language and gender research. *Language in Society* 28 (2), 185–202.

Edwards, J. (1994) *Multilingualism*. London: Routledge.

Elkin, J. (2002) The burgeoning day school world: What lies ahead. *Contact* 4 (2), 3–5.

Elliott, A. (2008, 28 April) Critics cost Muslim educator her dream school. *New York Times* –
Online document: http://www.nytimes.com/2008/04/28/nyregion/28school.
html?fta=y&pagewanted=all

Engel, S. (1997) The guy who went up the steep nicken: The emergence of storytelling during the first three years. *Zero to Three: National Center for Infants, Toddlers, and Families* 17 (3), 1–9.
Epstein, N. (1977) *Language, Ethnicity and the Schools: Policy Alternatives for Bilingual–Bicultural Education.* Washington, DC: The Georgetown Univesity Institute for Educational Leadership.
Estable, A. (1986) Immigrant women: From the outside looking in. *Breaking the Silence* 10 (1), 32–33.
Étienne, G. (1974, 2009) *Le Créole, une langue* ... Posthumous edition of annotated 1974 PhD Dissertation, Le Créole du Nord d'Haïti: Étude des niveaux de structure, Strasbourg University, France. Montreal: Edition du Marais.
Étienne, A. (2010) *La francophonie à l'haïtienne en mileu américanophone* – Online document: http://eprints.aidenligne-francais-universite.auf.org/441/1/Francophonie_haitienne.pdf
Fader, A. (2009) *Mitzvah Girls: Bringing up the Next Generation of Hasidic Jews in Brooklyn.* Princeton, NJ: Princeton University Press.
FAIR (Federation for American Immigration Reform) (2008) History of US immigration laws – Online document: http://www.fairus.org/site/PageNavigator/facts/research_us_laws/
Fairclough, N. (1992) *Discourse and Social Change.* London: Polity Press.
Ferguson, C.A. (1959) Diglossia. *Word* 15, 325–340.
Fishman, J.A. (1966) *Language Loyalty in the United States. The Maintenance and Perpetuation of non-English Mother Tongues by American Ethnic and Religious Groups.* The Hague: Mouton.
Fishman, J.A. (1971) The impact of nationalism on language planning. In J. Rubin and B. Jernudd (eds) *Can Language be Planned?* (pp. 3–20). Honolulu, HI: University Press of Hawaii.
Fishman, J.A. (1972a) Bilingualism with and without diglossia and diglossia with and without bilingualism. *Social Issues* 23 (2), 26–38.
Fishman, J.A. (1972b) *The Sociology of Language: An Interdisciplinary Social Science Approach to Language in Society.* Rowley, MA: Newbury House.
Fishman, J.A. (1976) *Bilingual Education: An International Sociological Perspective.* Rowley, MA: Newbury House.
Fishman, J.A. (1980a) Ethnic community mother tongue schools in the USA: Dynamics and distributions. *International Migration Review* 14, 235–247.
Fishman, J.A. (1980b) Ethnocultural dimensions in the acquisition and retention of biliteracy. *Basic Writing* 3, 48–61.
Fishman, J.A. (1980c) Minority language maintenance and the ethnic mother tongue school. *Modern Language Journal* 64, 167–172.
Fishman, J.A. (1982) Yidish, modernizatsye un re-etnifikatsye: An emeser un faktndiker tsugang tsu der itstiker problematik [Yiddish, modernization and re-ethnification: A true and factual approach to the current problem]. *Afn shvel* 248, 1–6.
Fishman, J.A. (1985a) *The Rise and Fall of the Ethnic Revival.* Berlin: Mouton de Gruyter.
Fishman, J.A. (1985b) The sociology of Jewish languages from a general sociolinguistic point of view. In J. Fishman (ed.) *Readings in the Sociology of Jewish Languages* (pp. 3–21). Leiden: Brill.
Fishman, J.A. (1991) *Reversing Language Shift: Theoretical and Empirical Foundations of Assistance to Threatened Languages.* Clevedon: Multilingual Matters.
Fishman, J.A. (2001) A decade in the life of a two-in-one language: Yiddish in New York City (secular and ultra-Orthodox). In J.A. Fishman (ed.) *Can Threatened Languages be Saved?* (pp. 74–100). Clevedon: Multilingual Matters.

Fishman, J.A. (2002) Do ethnics have culture? And what's so special about New York anyway? In O. García and J.A. Fishman (eds) *The Multilingual Apple: Languages in New York City* (pp. 341–351). New York: Mouton de Gruyter.

Fishman, J.A. and Nahirny, V. (1966) The ethnic group school and mother tongue maintenance. In J.A. Fishman et al., *Language Loyalty in the United States* (pp. 92–126). The Hague: Mouton.

Fishman, J.A., Nahirny, V., Hoffman, J. and Hayden, R. (1966) *Language Loyalty in the United States: The Maintenance and Perpetuation of non-English Mother Tongues by American Ethnic and Religious Groups*. The Hague: Mouton.

Fishman, J.A., Gertner, M.H., Lowy, E.G. and Milán, W.G. (1985) *Ethnicity in Action: The Community Resources of Ethnic Language in the United States*. Binghamton, NY: Bilingual Press.

Flowerdew, R. (2004) Peter Haggett. In P. Hubbard, R. Kitchin and G. Valentine (eds) *Key Thinkers on Space and Place* (pp. 155–159). Thousand Oaks, CA: Sage.

Foreign Language Enrollments in K–12 Public Schools: Are Students Prepared for a Global Society? (2010) Alexandria, VA: American Council on the Teaching of Foreign Languages.

Freidenreich, F.P. (2010) *Passionate Pioneers: The Story of Yiddish Secular Education in North America, 1910–1960*. Teaneck, NJ: Holmes and Meier.

Furman, N., Goldberg, D. and Lusin, N. (2007) *Enrollments in Languages other than English in United States Institutions of Higher Education, Fall 2006*. New York: Modern Language Association.

Furman, N., Goldberg, D. and Lusin, N. (2010) Enrollments in languages other than English in United States institutions of higher education, Fall 2009. New York: The Modern Language Association of America – Online document: http://www.mla.org/pdf/2009_enrollment_survey.pdf

Gal, S. and Irvine, J. (1995) The boundaries of languages and disciplines: How ideologies construct difference. *Social Research* 62 (4), 967–1001.

Gal, S. and Woolard, K. (2001) *Languages and Publics*. Manchester: St Jerome Press.

Gambhir, S. (2001) Truly less commonly taught languages and heritage language learners in the United States. In J.K. Peyton, D. Ranard and S. McGinnis (eds) *Heritage Languages in America: Preserving a National Resource* (pp. 207–228). McHenry, IL/Washington, DC: Delta Systems and Center for Applied Linguistics.

Gándara, P. and Contreras, F. (2009) *The Latino Education Crisis: The Consequences of Failed Social Policies*. Cambridge, MA: Harvard University Press.

Gándara, P. and Hopkins, M. (eds) (2010) *Forbidden Language: English Learners and Restrictive Language Policies*. New York: Teachers College Press.

García, O. (1997/2002) New York's multilingualism: World languages and their role in a U.S. city. In O. García and J.A. Fishman (eds) *The Multilingual Apple: Languages in New York City* (pp. 3–50). Berlin: Mouton.

García, O. (2005) Positioning heritage languages in the United States. *Modern Language Journal* 89 (4), 601–605.

García, O. (2009a) *Bilingual Education in the 21st Century: A Global Perspective*. Malden, MA: Wiley/Blackwell.

García, O. (2009b) Livin' and teachin' la lengua loca: Glocalizing US Spanish ideologies and practices. In R. Salaberry (ed.) *Language Allegiances and Bilingualism in the United States* (pp. 151–171). Bristol: Multilingual Matters.

García, O. (2010) Bilingualism in education in the multilingual apple: The future of the past. *Journal of Multilingual Education Research* 1, 13–34.

García, O. (2011a) Educating New York's bilingual children: Constructing a future from the past. *International Journal of Bilingual Education and Bilingualism* 14 (2), 133–153.

García, O. (with Makar, C., Starcevic, M. and Terry, A.) (2011b) Translanguaging of Latino kindergarteners. In K. Potowski and J. Rothman (eds) *Bilingual Youth: Spanish in English Speaking Societies* (pp. 33–55). Amsterdam: John Benjamins.

García, O. (2011c) From language garden to sustainable languaging: Bilingual education in a global world. *Perspective. A Publication of the National Association for Bilingual Education* September/October, 5–10.

García, O. (forthcoming) Dual or dynamic bilingual education? Empowering bilingual communities. In R. Rubdy and L. Alsagoff (eds) *The Global–Local Interface. Language Choice and Hybridity*. Bristol: Multilingual Matters, in press.

García, O. and Fishman, J.A. (1997/2002) *The Multilingual Apple: Languages in New York City*. Berlin: Mouton de Gruyter.

García, O. and Otheguy, R. (1997) No sólo de estándar vive el aula: Lo que nos enseñó la educación bilingüe sobre el español de Nueva York [The classroom doesn't live through standard alone: What bilingual education taught us about Spanish in New York]. In M.C. Colombi and F.X. Alarcon (eds) *La enseñanza del español a hispanohablantes: Praxis y teoría [Teaching Spanish to Spanish Speakers: Praxis and Theory]* (pp. 156–174). Boston, MA: Houghton Mifflin.

García, O. and Kleifgen, J. (2010) *Educating Emergent Bilinguals: Policies, Programs and Practices for English Language Learners*. New York: Teachers College Press.

García, O., López, D. and Makar, C. (2010) Language and identity in Latin America. In J.A. Fishman and O. García (eds) *Handbook of Language and Ethnic Identity* (pp. 353–373). Oxford: Oxford University Press.

García, O., Flores, N. and Chu, H. (2011) Extending bilingualism in US secondary education: New variations. *International Multilingual Research Journal* 5 (1), 1–18.

Gee, J.P. (1999/2005) *An Introduction to Discourse Analysis: Theory and Method*. London: Routledge.

Genishi, C. and Dyson, A.H. (2009) *Children, Language, and Literacy: Diverse Learners in Diverse Times*. New York: Teachers College Press.

Georgakas, D. (2004–2005) The now and future Greek America: Strategies for survival. *Journal of Modern Hellenism* Winter, 21–22.

Gibson, G. (1988) *Accommodation without Assimilation: Sikh Immigrants in an American High School*. Ithaca, NY: Cornell University Press.

Gielen, U.P. and Lei, T. (2010) Dragon seed: Chinese immigrant youths in New York City. *New York Academy of Science Conference*, New York.

Glinert, L. (1991) The 'Back to the Future' syndrome in language planning: The case of modern Hebrew. In D.F. Marshall (ed.) *Language Planning: Focusschrift in Honor of Joshua A. Fishman* (pp. 215–243). Philadelphia, PA: John Benjamins.

Globe-Gate Project (2011) University of Tennessee–Martin – Online document: http://globegate.utm.edu

González, N., Moll, L.C. and Amanti, C. (2005) *Funds of Knowledge: Theorizing Practices in Households, Communities, and Classrooms*. Mahwah, NJ: Lawrence Erlbaum.

Gootman, E. (2004, 2 June) City to help curb harassment of Asian students at high school. *The New York Times* – Online document: http://www.nytimes.com/2004/06/02/nyregion/city-to-help-curb-harassment-of-asian-students-at-high-school.html?scp=3&sq=lafayette%20high%20school&st=cse

Gordon, R.G. Jr (ed.) (2005) Ethnologue: Languages of the world (15th edn). Dallas, TX: SIL International – Online document: http://www.ethnologue.com/

Goren, A. (1970) *New York Jews and the Quest for Community: The Kehillah Experiment, 1908–1922*. New York: Columbia University Press.

Greek Census (2001) United Nations Economic Commission for Europe – Online document: http://www/unece.org/stats/census/2000/Welcome.html

Greek Orthodox Archdiocese of America (2011) School directory – Online document: www.goarch.org/archdiocese/departments/education/schooldirectory

Grudin, J. (2006) Enterprise knowledge management and emerging technologies. *Proceedings of the 39th Hawaii International Conference on Systems Sciences. HICSS'06* 3: 57a.

Guetjens, P. (2011) La scission de 1950: La mise en échec de la peinture populaire haïtienne au Centre d'Art Haïtien (1945–1950), Unpublished manuscript.

Gutiérrez, K. (2008) Developing a sociocritical literacy in the third space. *Reading Research Quarterly* 43(2), 148–164.

Hall, K. and Livia, A. (1997) *Queerly Phrased: Language, Gender, and Sexuality*. New York: Oxford University Press.

Hall, S. (1990) Cultural identity and diaspora. In J. Rutherford (ed.) *Identity: Community, Culture, Difference* (pp. 222–237). London: Lawrence and Wishart.

Hantzopoulos, M. (2005) English only?: Greek language as currency in Queens, New York City. In Z. Zakharia and T. Arnstein (eds) *Languages, Communities, and Education* (pp. 3–8). New York: Society of International Education at Teachers College.

Harris, R. (2009) *After Epistemology*. Gamlingay: Brightpen.

Harshav, B. (2007) *The Polyphony of Jewish Culture*. Palo Alto, CA: Stanford University Press.

Hayhoe, R. (1979) Written language reform and the modernization of the curriculum: A comparative study of China, Japan, and Turkey. *Canadian and International Education* 8 (2), 14–33.

Hayhoe, R. (1998) Language in comparative education: Three strands. *Hong Kong Journal of Applied Linguistics* 3 (2), 1–16.

Hellenic Education Network Abroad (2011) Greek schools USA – Online document: http://www.greekeducation.net/greekschoolsusa.htm

Heller, M. (2006) *Linguistic Minorities and Modernity: A Sociolinguistic Ethnography*. London: Continuum.

Herder, J.G. (1986/1772) Essay on the origin of language. In *On the Origin of Language: Jean-Jacques Rousseau and Johann Gottfried Herder* (pp. 87–166) (J.H. Moran and A. Gode, trans.). Chicago, IL: University of Chicago Press.

Hingley, R. (2003) *Russia, A Concise History* (revised and updated edn). London: Thames and Hudson.

Holland, D., Lachicotte, W., Skinner, D. and Cain, C. (1998) *Identity and Agency in Cultural Worlds*. Cambridge, MA: Harvard University Press.

Holloway, L. (2001, 24 January) One language one day, a second one the next. *New York Times* – Online document: http://www.nytimes.com/2001/01/24/nyregion/one-language-one-day-a-second-one-the-next.html

Hornberger, N. (1988) *Bilingual Education and Language Maintenance*. Dordrecht: Foris.

Horowitz, B. (1999) Jewishness in New York: Exception or the rule? In S.M. Cohen and G. Horencyzk (eds) *National Variations in Jewish Identity* (pp. 223–240). Albany, NY: State University of New York Press.

Horrocks, G. (1997) *Greek: A History of the Language and its Speakers*. Boston, MA: Addison-Wesley – Online document: http://www.aafny.org/cic/briefs/newyorkbrief.pdf

Humes, K., Jones, N. and Ramirez, R. (2011) Overview of race and Hispanic origin: 2010. United States Census Bureau – Online document: www.census.gov/prod/cen2010/briefs/c2010br-02.pdf

Hurh, W.M. and Kim, K.C. (1984) *Korean Immigrants in America: A Structural Analysis of Ethnic Confinement and Adhesive Adaptation.* Rutherford, NJ: Fairleigh Dickinson University Press.

Hutton, C. (2010) Mother tongues as intellectual property and the conceptualization of human linguistic diversity. *Language Sciences* 32 (6), 638–647.

Ihm, H.B., Hong, K.P. and Chang, S.I. (2001) *Korean Grammar for International Learners.* Seoul: Yonsei University Press.

IHSI (Institut Haïtien de Statistique et d'Informatique) (2009) Grandes leçons tirées du 4ème Recensement Général de la Population et de l'Habitat – Online document: http://www.ihsi.ht/pdf/projection/GDESLECONSRAP_D'ANALYS_VERFINAL_21-08-2009.pdf

Imam, S.R. (2005) English as a global language and the question of nation-building education in Bangladesh. *Comparative Education* 41 (4), 471–486.

Infante, A. (2010) *English Language Learners (ELLs) in New York City.* New York: Office of ELLs, Department of Education.

Internet World Stats (2011) Internet world users by language: Top 10 languages – Online document: http://www.internetworldstats.com/stats7.htm

Irvine, J. (2009) Stance in a colonial encounter: How Mr. Taylor lost his footing. In A. Jaffe (ed.) *Stance: Sociolinguistic Perspectives* (pp. 53–71). Oxford: Oxford University Press.

Jamal, A. and Naber, N. (eds) (2008) *Race and Arab Americans Before and After 9/11: From Invisible Citizens to Visible Subjects.* Syracuse, NY: Syracuse University Press.

Jaumont, F. (2008) French–English programs in New York City's public schools: Back to school for 2008–2009 – Online document: http://www.adfeusa.org/documents/French%20Programs%20in%20NYC%202008-09.pdf

Jeon, M. (2008) Korean heritage language maintenance and language ideology. *Heritage Language Journal* 6 (2), 54–70.

JESNA (Jewish Education Service of North America) (2004, Spring) *Agenda: Jewish Education: Educator Recruitment and Retention,* 17 – Online document: http://www.jesna.org/document-manager/cat_view/41-jesna-publications/45-agenda-jewish-education

Jo, H.-Y. (2001) Heritage' language learning and ethnic identity: Korean-Americans' struggle with language authorities. *Language, Culture and Curriculum* 14 (1), 26–41.

Jones, J.S. (2010) Bangladeshi Americans – Online document: http://www.everyculture.com/multi/A-Br/Bangladeshi-Americans.html

Joseph, C.M.B. (2002) Haitian Creole in New York. In O. García and J.A. Fishman (eds) *Multilingual Apple: Languages in New York City* (pp. 281–299). New York: Mouton de Gruyter.

Joseph, P.G. (2011) Haiti et la Francophonie. *Haiti Liberté* 4 (32), 7–18.

Joseph, Y. (1983) L'identification des codes linguistiques chez l'enfant haïtien. In L.D. Carrington (ed.) *Studies in Caribbean Languages* (pp. 245–251). St Augustine, Trinidad: Society for Caribbean Linguistics.

Joseph, Y. (2008) An Apran Kreyòl: Haitian Creole in the college classroom and beyond. MA thesis, The Graduate Center, CUNY.

Kadar, N. (1996) Yiddish in the secular Jewish school today: An ethnographic study. MA thesis, Columbia University.

Kang, J. (n.d.) Punjabi migration to the United States: A story of great tenacity – Online document: http://sikhfoundation.org/PunjabiMigration_JSKang.html

Katouzian, H. (1981) *The Political Economy of Modern Iran*. New York: New York University Press.

Kaya, İ. (2003) Shifting Turkish American identity formations in the United States. PhD thesis, The Florida State University.

Kaya, İ. (2004) Turkish-American immigration history and identity formations. *Journal of Muslim Minority Affairs* 24 (2), 295–308.

Kayyali, R.A. (2006) *The Arab Americans*. Westport, CT: Greenwood Press.

Kenner, C. (2004) *Becoming Biliterate: Young Children Learning Different Writing Systems*. Stoke-on-Trent: Trentham.

Kim, B-L. (1988) Language situation of Korean-Americans. In S.L. McKay and S.-L.C. Wong (eds) *Language Diversity: Problem or Resource? A Social and Educational Perspective on Language Minorities in the United States*. New York: Newbury House.

King, C.R. (1994) *One Language, Two Scripts: The Hindi Movement in Nineteenth Century North India*. Bombay: Oxford University Press.

Kliger, H. and Peltz, R. (1990) The secular Yiddish school in the United States in socio-historical perspective: Language school or culture school? *Linguistics and Education* 2, 1–19.

Klingner, J.K., Joover, J. and Baca, L. (2008) *Why do English Language Learners Struggle with Reading? Distinguishing Language Acquisition from Learning Disabilities*. Thousand Oaks, CA: Corwin Press.

Kloss, H. (1977) *The American Bilingual Tradition*. Rowley, MA: Newbury House.

Kolsky, E. (1998) Less successful than the next: South Asian taxi drivers in New York City. *SAGAR: South Asian Graduate Research Journal* 5 (1) – Online document: http://www.modelminority.com/joomla/index.php?option=com_content&view=article&id=328:less-successful-than-the-next-south-asian-taxi-drivers-&catid=47:society&Itemid=56

Kornfilt, J. (1997) *Turkish*. London: Routledge.

Koshy, S. (n.d.) Historicizing racial identity and minority status for South Asian Americans. Asian Pacific American Collective History Project. University of California, Los Angeles – Online document: http://www.sscnet.ucla.edu/history/faculty/henryyu/APACHP/teacher/research/koshy.htm

Kouritzin, S. (2000) Immigrant mothers redefine access to ESL classes: Contradiction and ambivalence. *Journal of Multilingual and Multicultural Development* 21 (2), 14–32.

Kroskrity, P.V. (2000) Regimenting languages: Language ideological perspectives. In P.V. Kroskrity (ed.) *Regimes of Language: Ideologies, Polities, and Identities* (pp. 1–34). Santa Fe, NM and Oxford: School of American Research Press.

Kurtz-Costes, B. and Pungello, E.P. (2000) Acculturation and immigrant children: Implications for educators. *Social Education* 64 (2), 121–125.

Labov, W. (1966) *The Social Stratification of English in New York City*. Washington, DC: Center for Applied Linguistics. (2nd edn, 2006, Cambridge: Cambridge University Press.)

Labov, W. (1972) *Language in the Inner City*. Philadelphia, PA: University of Pennsylvania Press.

Labov, W. and Waletzky, J. (1967) Narrative analysis. In J. Helm (ed.) *Essays on the Verbal and Visual Arts* (pp. 12–44). Seattle, WA: University of Washington Press.

Lahens, Y. (2010) *Failles*. Paris: Sabine Wespieser.

Latour, B. (1999) *Pandora's Hope: Essays on the Reality of Science Studies*. Cambridge, MA: Harvard University Press.

La Unión (2010) *Nowhere to Turn: A Report on the Reality of Mexican-American Students in New York City's Public Schools*. Brooklyn, NY: La Unión Press.

Lave, J. and Wenger, E. (1991) *Situated Learning: Legitimate Peripheral Participation*. Cambridge: Cambridge University Press.

Le, C.N. (2011a) Population statistics and demographics. Asian Nation – Online document: http://www.asian-nation.org/population.shtml

Le, C.N. (2011b) The model minority image. Asian Nation – Online document: http://www.asian-nation.org/model-minority.shtml

Lee, J.S. (2002) The Korean language in America: The role of cultural identity in heritage language learning. *Language, Culture and Curriculum* 15 (2), 117–133.

Lee, J.S. and Kim, H.-Y. (2007) Heritage language learners' attitudes, motivations, and instructional needs: The case of postsecondary Korean language learners. In K. Kondo-Brown and J.D. Brown (eds) *Teaching Chinese, Japanese, and Korean Heritage Language Students: Curriculum Needs, Materials, and Assessment*. New York: Routledge.

Lewis, G. (2002) *The Turkish Language Reform: A Catastrophic Success*. New York: Oxford University Press.

Lewis, P.M. (ed.) (2009) Ethnologue: Languages of the world (16th edn). Dallas, TX: SIL International – Online document: http://ethnologue.com

Lindenfeld, J. (2000) *The French in the United States: An Ethnographic Study*. Westport, CT: Bergin and Garvey.

Logan, J.R., Zhang, W. and Alba, R.D. (2002) Immigrant enclaves and ethnic communities in New York. *American Sociological Review* 67 (2), 299–322.

Longley, P., Goodchild, M., Maguire, D. and Rhind, D. (2005) *Geographic information Systems and Science*. Chichester: Wiley.

López, D. (1996) Language: Diversity and assimilation. In R. Waldinger and M. Bozorgmehr (eds) *Ethnic Los Angeles* (pp. 139–163). New York: Russell Sage Foundation.

Lorenz, J.H. and Wertime, J.T. (1980) Iranians. In S. Thernstrom (ed.), *Harvard Encyclopedia of American Ethnic Groups* (pp. 521–524). Cambridge, MA: Harvard University Press.

Luo, S.H. and Wiseman, R.L. (2000) Ethnic language maintenance among Chinese immigrant children in the United States. *International Journal of Intercultural Relations* 24 (3), 307–324.

Ly, P. (2005, 9 January) A wrenching choice. *Washington Post* A09.

Maira, S.M. (2002) *Desis in the House*. Philadelphia, PA: Temple University Press.

Makoni, S.B. (2011) Sociolinguistics, colonial and postcolonial: An integrationist perspective. *Language Sciences,* 33 (4), 680–688.

Makoni, S. and Pennycook, A. (2007) *Disinventing and Reconstituting Languages*. Clevedon: Multilingual Matters.

Mann, G.S. (2008) The teaching of Punjabi in American universities: Present situation and future prospects. International Conference on the Teaching of Punjabi. Unpublished manuscript, Punjabi University.

Mark, Y. (1947) Changes in the Yiddish school. *Jewish Education* 19, 31–38.

Mark, Y. (1948) Draysik yor yidishe shul in Amerike 1918–1948 [Thirty years of Yiddish schools in America]. *Gedank un lebn* 5, 1–41.

Massey, D.S., Durand, J. and Malone, N.J. (2002) *Beyond Smoke and Mirrors: Mexican Immigration in an Era of Economic Integration*. New York: Russell Sage Foundation.

Matarese, M. and Raña, R. (2004) Multilingual ecology of New York. Conference presentation. New York: Research Institute for the Study of Language in Urban Society (RISLUS) Forum.

Mather, P.A. (2010) Discussion: Re: Medium of instruction for Creole languages. *The LINGUIST Discussion List*, Vol. 21-3762 – Online document: http://permalink.gmane.org/gmane.science.linguistics.linguist-list/28190

Menken, K. and García, O. (eds) (2010) *Negotiating Language Policies in Schools: Educators as Policymakers*. New York: Routledge.

Migration Policy Institute (2010) ELL Information Center fact sheet series, 3 – Online document: http://www.migrationinformation.org/ellinfo/FactSheet_ELL3.pdf

Millar, J.R. (ed.) (2004) *Encyclopedia of Russian History*. Farmington, MI: Thomson Gale.

Min, P.G. (2000) Korean-Americans' language use. In S.L. McKay and S.-L.C. Wong (eds) *New Immigrants in the United States: Readings for Second Language Educators*. Cambridge: Cambridge University Press.

Min, P.G. and Kim, D.Y. (2005) Intergenerational transmission of religion and culture: Korean protestants in the US. *Sociology of Religion*, 66 (3), 263–282.

Mintz, A. (1993) Introduction. In A. Mintz (ed.) *Hebrew in America* (pp. 13–26). Detroit, MI: Wayne State University Press.

Modern Greek Studies Association (2011) – Online document: http://www.mgsa.org

Monger, R. and Barr, M. (2010) *Nonimmigrant Admissions to the US: 2009*. Department of Homeland Security.

Morrow, N. (1997) Language and identity: Women's autobiographies of the American immigrant experience. *Language and Communication* 17 (3), 177–185.

Mossayeb, S. and Shirazi, R. (2006) Education and immigration: The case of the Iranian-American community. *Current Issues in Comparative Education* 9 (1), 30–44.

Motashari, A. (2003) Factsheet on the Iranian-American Community. Iranian Studies Group Research Series, October 2003 – Online document: http://www.isgmit.org/

Myhill, J. (2004) *Language in Jewish Society: Towards a New Understanding*. Clevedon: Multilingual Matters.

Naber, N. (2008) Introduction: Arab Americans and US racial formations. In A. Jamal and N. Naber (eds) *Race and Arab Americans Before and After 9/11: From Invisible Citizens to Visible Subjects* (pp. 1–45). Syracuse, NY: Syracuse University Press.

Naff, A. (2002) New York: The mother colony. In K. Benson and P.M. Kayal (eds) *A Community of Many Worlds: Arab Americans in New York City* (pp. 3–10). New York: The Museum of the City of New York/Syracuse University Press.

Nagaoka, Y. (1998) A descriptive study of Japanese biliterate students in the United States: Bilingualism, language-minority education, and teachers' role. PhD thesis, University of Massachusetts Amherst.

Nahir, M. (1977) The five aspects of language planning. *Language Problems and Language Planning* 1 (2), 107–122.

Najam, A. (2007) *Portrait of a Giving Community: Philanthropy by the Pakistani-American Diaspora*. Cambridge, MA: Asia Center Global Equity Initiative, Harvard University.

Nakane, C. (1972) *Japanese Society*. Berkeley, CA: University of California Press.

National Education Association (2005) *A Report on the Status of Asian Americans and Pacific Islanders in Education: Beyond the 'Model Minority' Stereotype*. Washington, DC: National Education Association.

New York City Department of City Planning (2010) New York City profile – Online document: http://www.nyc.gov/html/dcp/html/lucds/cdstart.shtml

New York City Department of City Planning (2011) New York City and boroughs, 2009 American Community Survey. NYC Department of City Planning – Online document: http://www.nyc.gov/html/dcp/pdf/census/nyc_boros_09_asians.pdf

Norton, B. (1995) Social identity, investment, and language learning. *TESOL Quarterly* 29 (1), 9–31.

NYCDOE (New York City Department of Education) (2007, Summer) New York City's English language learners: Demographics and performance. Office of English Language Learners – Online document: http://schools.nycenet.edu/offices/teach learn/ell/DemoPerformanceFINAL_10_17.pdf

NYCDOE (New York City Department of Education) (2009a) Diverse learners on the road to success: The performance of New York City's English language learners. Office of English Language Learners – Online document: http://schools.nyc.gov/NR/rdonlyres/3B377E6B-5E22-4E63-A4DA-2B7FD14E5D62/57000/ELLPerformanceRep ort2009.pdf

NYCDOE (New York City Department of Education) (2009b) *The 2008–09 Demographics of New York City's English Language Learners*. NYC Department of Education.

NYCDOE (New York City Department of Education) (2010a) CEP school demographics and accountability 2009–10 – Online document: http://schools.nyc.gov/documents/oaosi/cepdata/2009–10/cepdata_K089.pdf

NYCDOE (New York City Department of Education) (2010b) Graduation and dropout reports: Cohorts of 2001 through 2005 (Classes of 2005 through 2009). NYC Department of Education – Online document: http://schools.nyc.gov/Accountability/data/GraduationDropoutReports/default.htm

NYCDOE (New York City Department of Education) (2010c) New York City transitional bilingual education (TBE) programs. NYC Department of Education – Online document: http://schools.nyc.gov/NR/rdonlyres/90EC9B10-88FF-4A06-98BC-23CC495032C9/83634/TBESPRING2010_FINAL.pdf

NYCDOE (New York City Department of Education) (2010d) PS 20 School comprehensive educational plan 2009–2010. New York City Department of Education – Online document: http://schools.nyc.gov/documents/oaosi/cep/2009-10/cep_Q020.pdf

NYCDOE (New York City Department of Education) (2011) The 2010–2011 demographics of New York City's English language learners – Online document: http://schools.nyc.gov/NR/rdonlyres/3A4AEC4C-14BD-49C4-B2E6-8EDF5D873BE4/108227/Demo Rpt0722.pdf

NYSED (New York State Department of Education) (2004) Learning standards for native language arts: Building the bridge – Online document: http://www.p12.nysed.gov/biling/resource/NLA.html

NYSED (New York State Department of Education) (2010) Accountability reports – Online document: http://www.p12.nysed.gov/accountability/reports.html

Obeng, S.G. (2008) Language maintenance among Akan-Ghanaian immigrants living in the United States. In T. Falola, N. Afolabi and A. Adesanya (eds) *Migrations and Creative Expressions in Africa and Africa Diaspora* (pp. 179–217). Durham, NC: Carolina Academic Press.

Ogbu, J., and Simons, H.D. (1998) Voluntary and involuntary minorities: A cultural–ecological theory of school performance with some implications for education. *Anthropology and Education Quarterly* 29 (2), 158–188.

Omniglot (1998) Korean. Omniglot: Writing systems and languages of the world – Online document: http://www.omniglot.com/writing/korean.htm

Orfalea, G. (2006) *The Arab Americans: A History*. Northampton, MA: Olive Branch Press.

Organisation Internationale de la Francophonie (IOF) (2011) – Online document: http://www.francophonie.org

Otcu, B. (2009) Language maintenance and cultural identity construction in a Turkish Saturday school in New York City. Ed.D. thesis, Teachers College Columbia University.

Otcu, B. (2010a) *Language Maintenance and Cultural Identity Construction: An Ethnography of Discourses in a Complementary School in the US.* Saarbrücken: VDM Müller.

Otcu, B. (2010b) Heritage language maintenance and cultural identity formation: The case of a Turkish Saturday school in New York City. *Heritage Language Journal* 7 (2), 112–137.

Otheguy, R. (2003) Las piedras nerudianas se tiran al norte: Meditaciones lingüísticas sobre Nueva York. *Insula* July–August, 679–680.

Otheguy, R. and Otto, R. (1980) The myth of static maintenance in bilingual education. *The Modern Language Journal* 64 (3), 350–356.

Otheguy, R. and Zentella, A.C. (2011) *Spanish in New York: Language Contact, Dialect Leveling and Structural Continuity.* Oxford: Oxford University Press.

Owusu, T.Y. (1998) The role of Ghanaian immigrant associations in Toronto, Canada. *International Migration Review* 34 (4), 1155–1181.

Park, E. (2006) Grandparents, grandchildren, and heritage language use in Korean. In K. Kindo-Brown (ed.) *Heritage Language Development: Focus on East Asian Immigrants.* Philadelphia, PA: John Benjamins.

Partnership for Excellence in Jewish Education (2007) *10 Years of Believing in Jewish Day School Education.* Boston, MA: Partnership in Excellence in Jewish Education.

Peckham, B. (2011) New York needs French – Online document: http://www.utm.edu/staff/globeg/nyadvocat.html

Pedagogishe konferentsn fun di Sholem Aleykhem shuln in 1954 un 1955 [Pedagogical conferences of the Sholem Aleichem schools in 1954 and 1955] (1972) In Sh. Gutman (ed.) *Der derekh fun Sholem Aleykhem Folk Institut: A historisher iberblik [The Path of the Sholem Aleichem Folk Institute: An Historical Review]* (pp. 139–148). New York: Sholem Aleichem Folk Institute.

Penny, R.J. (1991) *A History of the Spanish Language.* Cambridge: Cambridge University Press.

Pennycook, A. (2000) English, politics, ideology: From colonial celebration to postcolonial performativity. In T. Ricento (ed.) *Ideology, Politics and Language Policies: Focus on English* (pp. 107–119). Amsterdam: John Benjamins.

Pennycook, A. (2001) *Critical Applied Linguistics: A Critical Introduction.* Mahwah, NJ: Erlbaum Associates.

Pennycook, A. (2003) Global Englishes, rip slyme, and performativity. *Journal of Sociolinguistics* 7 (4), 513–533.

Pennycook, A. (2004) Performativity and language studies. *Critical Inquiry in Language Studies* 1 (1), 1–19.

Pennycook, A. (2010) *Language as Local Practice.* London: Routledge.

Perry, D.L. (1997) Rural ideologies and urban imaginings: Wolof immigrants in New York City. *Africa Today* 44 (2), 229–260.

Peterson, L.C. (1997) Tuning in to Navajo: The role of radio in native language maintenance. In J. Reyhner (eds) *Teaching Indigenous Languages* (pp. 214–221). Flagstaff, AZ: Northern Arizona University Press.

Peyton, J.K., Ranard, D.A. and Mc Ginnis, S. (eds) (2001) *Heritage Languages in America: Preserving a National Resource.* McHenry, IL: Center for Applied Linguistics and Delta Systems.

Phillipson, R. (1992) *Linguistic Imperialism.* Oxford: Oxford University Press.

Phinney, J., Romero, I., Nava, M. and Huang, D. (2001) The role of language, parents and peers in ethnic identity among adolescents in immigrant families. *Journal of Youth and Adolescence* 30, 135–153.

Pioneer Academy of Science (PAS) (2011) Home page – Online document: http://www. pioneeracademy.org/

Poll, S. (1981) The role of Yiddish in American ultra-Orthodox and Hasidic communities. In J.A. Fishman (ed.) *Never Say Die!: A Thousand Years of Yiddish in Jewish Life and Letters* (pp. 197–218). The Hague: Mouton.

Portes, A. and Hao, L. (1998) *E pluribus unum*: Bilingualism and loss of language in the second generation. *Sociology of Education* 71, 269–294.

Portes, A. and Rumbaut, R.G. (2001) *Legacies: The Story of the Immigrant Second Generation.* Berkeley, CA: University of California Press.

Qin, D.B. (2006) 'Our child doesn't talk to us anymore': Alienation in immigrant Chinese families. *Anthropology and Education Quarterly* 37 (2), 162–179.

Qiu, W. and Zhao, Y. (2009) How good are the Asians? Refuting four myths about Asian-American Academic achievement. Phi Delta Kappa International – Online document: http://www.pdkmembers.org/members_online/publications/Archive/pdf/k0901zha.pdf

Ramírez, A.Y.F. (2003) Dismay and disappointment: Parental involvement of Latino immigrant parents. *The Urban Review* 35 (2), 93–110.

Rampton, B. (1995) *Crossing: Language and Ethnicity among Adolescents.* London: Sage.

Rampton, B. (2006) *Language in Late Modernity. Interaction in an Urban School.* Cambridge: Cambridge University Press.

Reagan, T. (1996) *Non-Western Educational Traditions: Alternative Approaches to Educational Thought and Practice.* Mahwah, NJ: Lawrence Erlbaum.

Rennalls, P.A. (2006) Black middle school students' perceptions of success and their influence on academic performance. PhD thesis, Florida International University.

Rhodes, N. C. and Pufahl, I. (2010) *Foreign Language Teaching in U.S. Schools: Results of a National Survey.* Center for Applied Linguistics, Washington, DC – Online document: http://www.cal.org/projects/Exec%20Summary_111009.pdf

Rivera-Sánchez, L.G. (2002) Belongings and identities: Migrants between the Mixteca and New York. Unpublished manuscript, New York.

Rivers, N. (2011) The search for Haiti Town: A comparative study of the Haitian communities in Miami and NYC. *Brooklyn College Undergraduate Research Journal,* 2 – Online document: http://www.brooklyn.cuny.edu/pub/departments/bcurj/pdf/RiversNatali.pdf

Romaine, S. (1994) *Language in Society: An Introduction to Sociolinguistics.* Oxford: Oxford University Press.

Roskies, D.K. (1975) *Teaching the Holocaust to Children: A Review and Bibliography.* Jersey City, NJ: Ktav Publishing House.

Rouchdy, A. (ed.) (1992) *The Arabic Language in America.* Detroit, MI: Wayne State University Press.

Ruffman, L.L. (ed.) (1957) *Survey of Jewish Education in Greater New York 1951–1952: Findings and Recommendations.* New York: Jewish Education Committee.

Ruiz, R. (1988) Orientations in language planning. In S. McKay and S.L. Wong (eds) *Language Diversity: Problem or Resource?* (pp. 3–25). New York: Newbury House.

Saint-Fort, H. (2010) Le mythe de la langue française: Butin de guerre des ex-colonisés francophones? *Potomitan: site de promotion des cultures et des langues créoles* – Online document: http://www.potomitan.info/ayiti/langue3.php

Sassen, S. (1991) *The Global City: New York, London, Tokyo.* Princeton, NJ: Princeton University Press.

Sawaie, M. and Fishman, J.A. (1985) Arabic-language maintenance efforts in the United States. *Journal of Ethnic Studies* 13 (2), 33–49.

Schick, M. (2000) Jewish day schools. In D. Ravitch and J. Viteritti (eds) *City Schools: Lessons from New York* (pp. 269–290). Baltimore, MD: The Johns Hopkins University Press.

Schick, M. (2009) *A Census of Jewish Day Schools in the United States 2008–2009.* New York: Avi Chai.

Schiff, A. (1997/2002) Hebrew in New York. In O. García and J.A. Fishman (eds) *The Multilingual Apple: Languages in New York City* (pp. 203–227). Berlin: Mouton de Gruyter.

Schiller, N.G., Basch, L. and Blanc, C.S. (1995) From immigrant to transmigrant: Theorizing transnational migration. *Anthropological Quarterly* 68 (1), 48–63.

Sharon-Krespin, R. (2009) Fethullah Gülen's grand ambition: Turkey's Islamist danger. *Middle East Quarterly* 16 (1), 55–66.

Shin, S.J. (2005) *Developing in Two Languages: Korean Children in America.* Clevedon: Multilingual Matters.

Shin, S.J. (2006) High-stakes testing and heritage language maintenance. In K. Kondo-Brown (ed.) *Heritage Language Development: Focus on East Asian immigrants* (pp. 127–144). Amsterdam: John Benjamins.

Shinge, M. (2008) The National Security Language Initiative and the teaching of Hindi. *Language, Culture, and Curriculum* 21 (3), 269–279.

Shirazi, R. and Nazemian, V. (2005) Iranians and the Persian speaking community in New York: A socio-linguistic survey. Conference paper presented at the 2nd Annual Conference on the Iranian Diaspora at College Park, MD.

Shohamy, E. (1999) Language and identity of Jews in Israel and in the diaspora. In D. Zisenwine and D. Schers (eds) *Present and Future: Jewish Culture, Identity and Language.* Tel Aviv: Tel Aviv University.

Shteynboym, Y. (1978–1979) *Di geshikhte fun Yidishn lerer-seminar un folks-universitet in Nyu-york 1918–1968* [The History of the Jewish Teachers' Seminary and Peoples' University in New York 1918–1968]. Jerusalem.

Silverstein, A. (2011, February) At PS 20, the Principal, APs and teachers work with after-school. *CSA News,* 8–9.

Sinclair, J.M. and Coulthard, M. (1975) *Towards an Analysis of Discourse: The Language of Teachers and Pupil.* London: Oxford University Press.

Skutnabb-Kangas, T. (1981) *Bilingualism or Not: The Education of Minorities.* Bristol: Multilingual Matters.

Smith, R.C. (2006) *Mexican New York: Transnational Lives of New Immigrants.* Berkeley, CA: University of California Press.

Sohn, H-M. (2001) *The Korean Language.* Cambridge University Press.

South Asian Americans Leading Together (SAALT) (n.d.) Demographic characteristics of South Asians in the United States: Emphasis on poverty, gender, language ability, and immigration status – Online document: http://www.saalt.org/attachments/1/Demographic%20Characteristics%20of%20SA%20in%20US.pdf

Spolsky, B. (2000) Language motivation revisited. *Applied Linguistics* 21 (2), 157–169.

Spolsky, B. and Shohamy, E. (1999) *The Languages of Israel: Policy, Ideology, and Practice.* Clevedon: Multilingual Matters.

St Demetrios Astoria School (2010) Cathedral – Online document: http://www.saint demetriosastoria.com/

Stalikas, A. and Gavaki, E. (1995) The importance of ethnic identity: Self-esteem and academic achievement of second-generation Greeks in secondary school. *The Canadian Journal of School Psychology* 11 (1), 1–9.

Stepick, A. III (1992) The refugees nobody wants: Haitains in Miami. In G.J. Grenier and A. Stepick III (eds) *Immigration, Ethnicity and Social Change* (pp. 57–82) Gainesville, FL: University of Florida.

Stiefel, L., Schwartz, A.E. and Conger, D. (2003) *Language Proficiency and Home Languages of Students in New York City Elementary and Middle Schools*. Urban Education Project.

Stoller, P. (2002) *Money has no Smell: The Africanization of New York City*. Chicago, IL: University of Chicago Press.

Suárez-Orozco, C., Suárez-Orozco, M. and Todorova, I. (2008) *Learning a New Land: Immigrant Students in American Society*. Cambridge, MA: Harvard University Press.

Sung, B.L. (1985) Bicultural conflicts in Chinese immigrant children. *Journal of Comparative Family Studies* 16, 255–269.

Sung, J.S. (2003) The history of the activities and roles of educational groups including Korean schools. In *100 Years of Korean Immigration to New York*. Seoul: The Memorial Commission for 100 Years of Korean Immigration to the US. [In Korean.]

Taylan, E.E. (ed.) (2002) *The Verb in Turkish*. Philadelphia, PA: John Benjamins.

Teague, D. (2009) *Intifada NYC* [documentary]. New York: Brooklyn Vitagraph Company.

Thompson, K. (2010) Justice reaches pact with Philadelphia schools in '09 attacks on Asian American Students. *The Washington Post* – Online document: http://www.washingtonpost.com/wp-dyn/content/article/2010/12/15/AR2010121506380.html

Torres-Guzmán, M., Kleyn, T., Morales-Rodríguez, S. and Han, A. (2005) Self-designated dual-language programs: Is there a gap between labeling and implementation? *Bilingual Research Journal* 29 (2), 453–474.

Tse, L. (2001a) *Why Don't they Learn English? Separating Fact from Fallacy in the US Language Debate*. New York: Teachers College Press.

Tse, L. (2001b) Resisting and reversing language shift: Heritage-language resilience among US native biliterates. *Harvard Educational Review* 71, 676–708.

Turkish Connection (1996–2007) Turkish radio, TV, and newspapers – Online document: http://www.turkishconnection.com/media.htm

Turkish Olympiad (2011) Home page – Online document: http://turkisholympiad.com/

Ukeles, J. and Miller, R. (2004) Jewish community study of New York: 2002. UJA Federation of New York – Online document: http://www.ujafedny.org/jewish-community-study-2002/

US Census (2000) Census 2000 Brief. Language use and English-speaking ability – Online document: http://www.census.gov/prod/2003pubs/c2kbr-29.pdf

US Census Bureau (2000) Census Profile: New York City's Bangladeshi American population – Online document: http://www.aafny.org/cic/briefs/bangladeshi.pdf

US Census Bureau (2005) 2005 American Community Survey US Census Bureau – Online document: http://factfinder.census.gov/servlet/DatasetMainPageServlet?_program=ACS&_submen

US Census Bureau (2006) Hispanics in the US – Online document: http://www.census.gov/population/www/socdemo/hispanic/files/Internet_Hispanic_in_US_2006.pdf

US Census Bureau, American Factfinder (2006–2008). 2006–2008 American community survey 3-year estimates. Retrieved from: http://factfinder2.census.gov/faces/nav/jsf/pages/index.xhtml

US Census Bureau (2007a) Bangladeshi American population estimates – Online document: http://factfinder.census.gov/servlet/IPTable?_bm=y&-geo_id=01000US&-qr_name=ACS_2007_1YR_G00_S02018&-qr_name=ACS_2007_1YR_G00_S0201PR&-qr_name=ACS_2007_1YR_G00_S0201T&-qr_name=ACS_2007_1YR_G00_S0201TPR&-ds_name=ACS_2007_1YR_G00_&-reg=ACS_2007_1YR_G00_S0201:033;ACS_2007_1YR_G00_S0201PR:033;ACS_2007_1YR_G00_S0201T:033;ACS_2007_1YR_G00_S0201TPR:033&-_lang=en&-redoLog=false&-format=

US Census Bureau (2007b) American Community Survey (2007) Place of birth for the foreign-born population – Online document: http://www.nyc.gov/html/dcp/pdf/census/acs_pob_07.pdf

US Census Bureau (2007–2009) American Community Survey 3-year estimates – Online document: http://factfinder.census.gov

US Census Bureau (2008a) American Community Survey summary tables – Online document: http://factfinder.census.gov

US Census Bureau (2008b) American Community Survey 'People reporting ancestry' – Online document: http://www.census.gov/compendia/statab/2011/tables/11s0052.xls

US Census Bureau (2008c) Language spoken at home by ability to speak English for the population 5 Years and Over, New York City and Boroughs, 2008 American Community Survey – Online document: http://home2.nyc.gov/html/dcp/pdf/census/nyc_boros_06_07_08_language.pdf

US Census Bureau (2009) 2009 American Community Survey. Washington, DC – Online document: http://www.census.gov

US Census Bureau (2010) Language use in the United States: 2007 – Online document: http://www.census.gov/prod/2010pubs/acs-12.pdf

US Decennial Census (1980, 1990, 2000) Washington, DC: Government Printing Office.

US Department of Education (2008) Enhancing foreign language proficiency in the United States: Preliminary results of the National Security Language Initiative – Online document: http://www.ed.gov/about/inits/ed/competitiveness/nsli/about.html

US Department of Education (n.d.) National Security Language Initiative – Online document: http://www.aplu.org/NetCommunity/Document.Doc?id=50

US Department of Homeland Security (2009) Persons obtaining legal permanent resident status: Fiscal years 1820 to 2009 – Online document: http://www.dhs.gov/files/statistics/publications/LPR09.shtm

US Equal Employment Opportunity Commission (2010) *Debbie Almontaser v. New York City Department of Education and New Visions for Public Schools.*

Valdés, G. (2000) *Spanish for Native Speakers: AATSP Professional Development Series Handbook for Teachers K–16*, Vol. 1. New York: Harcourt College.

Valdés, G. (2001) Heritage language students: Profiles and possibilities. In J.K. Peyton, D.A. Ranard and S. McGinnis (eds) *Heritage Languages in America: Preserving a National Resource* (pp. 37–77). McHenry, IL: Center for Applied Linguistics and Delta Systems.

Valdés, G. (2006) Toward an ecological vision of languages for all: The place of heritage languages. In A.L. Heining-Boynton (ed.) *2005–2015: Realizing our Vision of Languages for All* (pp. 135–151). Upper Saddle River, NJ: Pearson/Prentice Hall.

Valdés, G., Lozano, A. and García-Moya, R. (1980) *Teaching Spanish to the Hispanic Bilingual: Issues, Aims and Methods.* New York: Teachers College Press.

Valdman, A. (ed.) (2005) *Le français en Amérique du Nord: Etat présent.* Québec: Les Presses de l'Université Laval.

Valdman, A. (2010) French in the USA. In K. Potowski (ed.) *Language Diversity in the United States* (pp. 110–127). Cambridge: Cambridge University Press.

Van Dyck, K. (2006, 25 May) Gringlish and how languages interact. Interview with Vivienne Nilan. *Kathimerini English Edition, Herald Tribune,* 6.

Vásquez, V.M. (2004) *Negotiating Critical Literacies with Young Children.* Mahwah, NJ: Lawrence Erlbaum.

Vaysman, E.B. (2010) Contemporary Yiddish-language productions at Hasidic girls' schools and camps. In W. Moskovich (ed.) *Yiddish – A Jewish National Language at 100. Jews and Slavs* (Vol. 22; pp. 197–204). Jerusalem/Kyiv: Hebrew University of Jerusalem and National University of Kyiv.

Wang, S.C. and Green, N. (2001) Heritage language students in the K–12 education system. In J.K. Peyton, D.A. Ranard and S. McGinnis (eds) *Heritage Languages in America: Preserving a National Resource* (pp. 167–196). McHenry, IL: Center for Applied Linguistics and Delta Systems.

Warsi, M.J. (2003) Heritage language teaching: Issues regarding Hindi–Urdu in the United States. *South Asian Language Review* 13 (1–2), 137–145.

Wasem, R.E. (2010) US immigration policy on Haitian migrants. Congressional Research Service. Report for Congress – Online document: http://www.congressionalre searchreports.com/report/2010/01/15/us-immigration-policy-haitian-migrants

Waters, M.C. (1996) Ethnic and racial identities of second generation Black immigrants in New York City. In A. Portes (ed.) *A New Second Generation* (pp. 65–87). New York: Russell Sage Foundation.

Wenger, B. (2007) *The Jewish Americans: Three Centuries of Jewish Voices in America.* New York: Doubleday.

Wertheimer, J. (1999) Jewish education in the United States: Recent trends and issues. *American Jewish Yearbook* 99, 3–115.

Wertheimer, J. (2008) *A Census of Jewish Supplementary Schools, 2006–2007.* New York: Avi Chai.

Wiley, T. (1996) *Literacy and Language Diversity in the United States.* McHenry, IL and Washington, DC: Delta Systems and Center for Applied Linguistics.

Williams, C. (1996) Secondary education: Teaching in the bilingual situation. In C. Williams, G. Lewis and C. Baker (eds) *The Language Policy: Taking Stock.* Llangefni: CAI.

Woods, A. (2004) *Medium or Message? Language and Faith in Ethnic Churches.* Clevedon: Multilingual Matters.

Zakharia, Z. (2006) Language belief and community in a women's Arabic literacy class in New York. Unpublished manuscript presented at the 50th Annual Conference of the Comparative and International Education Society, Honolulu, HI.

Zeleza, P. (2003) Introduction. In P. Zeleza (ed.) *The Study of Africa: Disciplinary and Interdisciplinary Encounters* (Vol. 1; pp. 1–35). Dakar: Codestria.

Zentella, A.C. (2001) Spanish in New York. In O. García and J. Fishman (eds) *The Multilingual Apple: Languages in New York City* (pp. 167–202). Berlin: Mouton de Gruyter.

Zéphir F. (2004) *The Haitian Americans.* Westport, CT: Greenwood Press.

Index